CW00518795

Company Law
and the
Human Rights Act 1998

Alan J Dignam BA PhD

Lecturer in Law,
Queen Mary & Westfield College, University of London

David Allen BSc LLB FRICS MCI Arb

Barrister,
7 Kings Bench Walk, Temple

Butterworths
London Edinburgh Dublin
2000

United Kingdom	Butterworths, a Division of Reed Elsevier (UK) Ltd, Halsbury House, 35 Chancery Lane, LONDON WC2A 1EL and 4 Hill Street, EDINBURGH EH2 3JZ
Australia	Butterworths, a Division of Reed International Books Australia Pty Ltd, CHATSWOOD, New South Wales
Canada	Butterworths Canada Ltd, MARKHAM, Ontario
Hong Kong	Butterworths Asia (Hong Kong), HONG KONG
India	Butterworths India, NEW DELHI
Ireland	Butterworth (Ireland) Ltd, DUBLIN
Malaysia	Malayan Law Journal Sdn Bhd, KUALA LUMPUR
New Zealand	Butterworths of New Zealand Ltd, WELLINGTON
Singapore	Butterworths Asia, SINGAPORE
South Africa	Butterworths Publishers (Pty) Ltd, DURBAN
USA	Lexis Law Publishing, CHARLOTTESVILLE, Virginia

A CIP Catalogue record for this book is available from the British Library.

ISBN 0 406 93030 9

Printed by Hobbs the Printers Ltd, Totton, Hampshire

Visit Butterworths LEXIS *direct* at: http://www.butterworths.com

Foreword

The Right Honourable Lord Hoffmann

Lord Denning once compared the introduction of European Community law to an incoming tide, flowing up the estuaries and rivers of England. In the early years of our membership of the Community, few lawyers paid any attention to European law. It had an immediate impact upon some specialist areas, such as competition law and intellectual property, but the general run of practitioners were untroubled by the distant gathering of the waters. Gradually, over the past 25 years, it has become clear that few parts of our law are likely to be unaffected.

The coming into force of the Human Rights Act 1998, however, is more like a sudden inundation. On 2 October 2000 the whole of our common and statute law, past and to come, was made subject to an overlay of legal principles contained in the European Convention on Human Rights. And this time, practitioners were made fully aware of the impending flood. Of course there will be many parts of the law which the Act will leave unaffected. Some areas, such as public law and criminal procedure, are obviously in the front line. But all lawyers, whatever their expertise, will need some guidance on whether they are likely to be able to keep their feet dry.

The primary object of this book is to give such help to company lawyers. The authors have the necessary academic and practical knowledge of the subject to be able to identify the points on which practitioners may need guidance or at least reassurance. The method is to give, in the first part of the book, a general overview of the Human Rights Act 1998 in general and then, in the second, to deal in more detail with its potential impact upon aspects of company law. In a market which offers many works on human rights, this book should enable company lawyers to find what they need within a single volume.

Leonard Hoffmann

Preface

Books are somewhat like icebergs when it comes to research and writing. On the surface appear the authors (and sometimes the occasional penguin) but below the surface, invisible to the naked eye, lies the vast contribution made by others to the work in question. This book is no different in that it could not have been completed without the enormous selfless contributions made by others. Our thanks go to the Department of Law at Queen Mary & Westfield College, University of London, for providing general support, time and funding for this book. Special thanks go to Dr Paul Mitchell and Kenneth Armstrong who gave up their valuable time to answer questions and read draft chapters despite their own busy schedules and looming deadlines. Thanks go to Bob Burns, the law librarian at Queen Mary, whose humour and invaluable research support made the task in hand less onerous. We are particularly grateful to Professor Brian Cheffins, Dr David Tomkin and Stephen Braviner who provided insightful comments on early drafts of the book, and to Rabinder Singh for trying. Thanks also to Marina Milner and Nick Hadaway whose interest and assistance was much appreciated. We owe an enormous debt of gratitude to Stephanie Knauth, without whose tireless and exceptional research none of this would have been possible. We are grateful to the Rt Hon Lord Hoffmann both for writing the Foreword and for his additional support and good humour in the face of unreasonable demands. We would also like to thank the staff at Butterworths for their hard work in producing the final product on schedule. Finally, we would like to thank those closest to us, Liz, Lorraine, Imogen and Thomas, who have suffered most over the past year.

The law is as stated at the end of July 2000. Unless indicated otherwise the opinions expressed and any errors or omissions are ours.[1]

Alan J Dignam
David Allen
July 2000

1   Any comments or queries generally would be gratefully received at a.dignam@qmw.ac.uk

Contents

Part one

Human rights and the Human Rights Act 1998

Chapter one

A brief history of human rights   3

Chapter two

The European Convention on Human Rights   15

Contents

Contents

Contents

Part two

Companies and the Human Rights Act 1998

Chapter seven

Companies and the HRA   149

Chapter eight

Companies and victim status   173

Chapter nine

Corporations and fair trial   193

Contents

Contents

Contents

Contents

Table of statutes

Page numbers in **bold** indicate that the Act is quoted in part of in full.

Table of statutes

Table of European legislation

Page numbers in **bold** indicate that the legislation is quoted in part of in full.

Table of European legislation

Table of cases

A

Table of cases

C

Table of cases

Table of cases

Table of cases

J

K

L

Table of cases

M

N

O

Table of cases

P

Q

R

Table of cases

Table of cases

S

Table of cases

Table of cases

Table of cases

xxxix

Table of cases

Decisions of the European Court of Justice are listed below numerically.
These decisions are also included in the preceding alphabetical list.

Introduction

The Human Rights Act 1998 ('HRA') has a profound effect on the English legal system. The Act gives further effect to most of the rights and freedoms guaranteed under the European Convention on Human Rights ('ECHR'). Four decades of case law emanating from the European Court of Human Rights ('ECtHR') have entered English law and jurisprudence at a stroke. Indeed, it was the recognition by the Home Office of the profound effect of the Act which delayed its commencement for two years.[1] Although this book considers the general impact of the HRA on the English legal system, it is ultimately concerned with the effect of the Act on corporations and company law. While the ECHR contains the word 'human' in its title, and companies are clearly not 'human',[2] the Strasbourg court has always allowed companies to enjoy guaranteed rights under the ECHR, provided they could obtain *locus standi* by establishing themselves as 'victims of an unlawful act' within the meaning of ECHR Article 34. This they could do for some rights and freedoms but not others. For example Article 12 which guarantees a right to 'men and women' to marry, or by implication, Article 3 prohibiting torture, will not be applicable to artificial entities. However, other articles such as Articles 6 (Right to a fair trial), 8 (Right to Privacy), 10 (Freedom of expression), and Article 1 of Protocol 1 (Right to Property) have all been held by the ECtHR to be applicable to companies and/ or their officers. As with the ECHR, any legal or natural person similarly has standing for the purposes of the HRA where they can show they are a victim of a rights violation. It is on the ECtHR's treatment of the corporation and the implications of this for English law that we focus in this book.

1   The delay to commencement was explained by the Home Office as being necessary because of the need for a 'very extensive programme' *(sic)* of judicial education to take place; and Whitehall to consider the impact of the legislation: see David Panick QC, 'Justice denied on the Human Rights Act', *The Times*, Thursday 20 May 1999.
2   A human being is defined by the *Oxford English Dictionary* as 'a person; a man, a woman, a child; a member of the species *Homo Sapiens*'.

Introduction

By using the corporation as the focus of this book we have attempted to straddle the traditional public/private law divide that exists within the English legal system. In general private lawyers have had little to do with public law concepts. The HRA changed this overnight, as rights and their associated interpretative techniques now pervade all areas of law. It is because of this that we have aimed the book primarily at private lawyers who will now have to utilise rights based arguments in the private law sphere. In particular two types of private lawyers are addressed. First, those who have traditionally had little to do with public law concepts and need guidance as to the application of the HRA both generally and specifically its impact on companies; and second, private lawyers who have some knowledge of the HRA but need to know about specific impacts on their area of law ie the effect of Article 8 (privacy) on freedom of expression for media companies, Article 6 (fair trial) on the corporate veil, the Department of Trade and Industry and insolvency practitioners, or the responsibilities of privatised utilities under the HRA. In order to serve these constituencies the book is divided into two sections. The first 'Human Rights and the Human Rights Act 1998' provides a comprehensive guide to the ECHR and the operation of the ECHR rights in English law through the Human Rights Act 1998. The second part of the book 'Companies and the Human Rights Act 1998' provides a thematic approach to the HRA's impact on companies by looking at specific areas of corporate behaviour where a rights based system impacts.

Part one

Human rights and the Human Rights Act 1998

Chapter one

A brief history of human rights

Like many other things devised by man, laws are subject to a process of development – continuous and evolutionary most of the time, and only on rare occasions discontinuous and revolutionary. Such processes tend to follow certain consistent sequences, and to exhibit some typical phases. It is therefore difficult to make much sense of any set of laws at any given time, let alone to understand them fully, without some knowledge of the processes by which they have developed. Probably more than for any other discipline, history is an essential component of the study of law.[1]

While the ultimate objective of the first part of this book is to introduce the reader to the Human Rights Act 1998 (HRA), as Sieghart suggests above, the history of how the HRA came to be enacted is essential for a proper understanding of its potential impact. The HRA's origins lie in the document it incorporates (at least partially) into domestic law, the European Convention on Human Rights (ECHR), and it is the origins of that document on which we focus in this chapter. The ECHR is of relatively recent vintage and forms part of a progressive recognition of international human rights over the course of the 20th century. However the origins of those developments in the 20th century and of our present understanding of human rights lie in the more distant past. The importance of the origins of the ECHR goes beyond providing a background understanding of that document. The proper working of the interpretative methods of the European Court of Human Rights

1   Sieghart, P 'The International Law of Human Rights' (1983) Clarendon, p 3.

(ECtHR) cannot be properly understood and applied without understanding core human rights concepts such as the rule of law. It is on providing that understanding that we focus in this chapter.

Sovereign power

Prior to the 17th century the sovereign was theoretically free to do as he wished to his subjects. The reality of sovereign power was however somewhat different: certain compromises had to be made in order to maintain power, as King John realised in 1215 when signing the Magna Carta Liberatum. The Magna Carta while not by a long way a universal bill of rights was an open recognition by the sovereign of the rights of certain powerful interests ie the barons and the church. While the sovereign within a state could technically exercise complete control over individual subjects, in reality that ability was restricted by the need to placate powerful subjects and the ability or willingness of subjects to accept control. As the Magna Carta states in Article 61:

> [s]ince We have granted all these things for God, for the better ordering of our kingdom, and to allay the discord that has arisen between us and our barons, and since we desire that they shall be enjoyed in their entirety, with lasting strength, forever, we give and grant the barons the following security:
> (1) The barons shall elect twenty-five of their number to keep, and cause to be observed with all their might, the peace and liberties granted and confirmed to them by this charter.

Ultimately if a sovereign's exercise of power lost the support of his subjects or a powerful part of his subjects he could be overthrown. In terms of the exercise of power through laws, the concept of a *just* sovereignty developed because it was necessary to maintain the legitimacy of sovereign power.

Justice however is a nebulous concept which has differing meanings depending on the society measuring the concept. Aspects of culture, religion, history and race impact on whether something is *just*. In Western Europe in the Middle Ages the sovereigns' laws were measured against Christian concepts of divine law.[2] Should the dictate of the sovereign ignore or be contrary to canon lawyers' interpretation of divine law, the dictate itself was unjust.[3] This meant that the legitimacy of sovereign power could be questioned and the act of rebellion itself legitimised because of a claim to a higher divine dictate over which secular law held no sway '[f]or the law-giver is thought of not so much as an arbitrary law-maker as rather a specially strong and clear revealer of the True and the Good. God is the only law-giver in the fullest sense of term.'[4]

2   The same measure was applied by Jewish, Islamic and ancient Greek societies. See Lauterpacht, H *International Law and Human Rights* (1968), pp 80-83.
3   See the work of St Thomas Aquinus, *Summa Theologica* Lib II, pt II. Although in finding that the citizen obeying an unjust law is 'relatively good' by being 'amenable to the regime' Aquinas was careful not to encourage rebellion. 1a 2ae Q 92 art 1.
4   Fritz, Kern, *Kingship and Law in the Middle Ages* (1939) Basil Blackwell, p 157.

Rebellion however is a dangerous business and one must be sure of the grounds upon which the rebellious act is based. While the legitimacy of divine law retained its primacy over the course of the 15th, 16th, and 17th centuries the Renaissance and the Reformation meant that it was no longer unquestioned as a legitimate basis for rebellion. The 18th and 19th centuries with the progression through the Enlightenment and into the revolution in industry and science, advanced the move away from divine standards. Other sources for measuring whether laws were *just* or not had to be found. These sources were found in the work of political philosophers such as Hobbes, Burke, Locke, Hume, Bentham, Mill, Spinosa, Montesquieu, Kant, Rousseau and Marx.

It was in revolution that the search for new political philosophies found its voice. The English revolution of 1688 was followed by the enactment of a Bill of Rights in 1689. The rebellion of the American colonies against the British crown was followed by the Declaration of Independence in 1776 invoking the principle of self-determination and the Federal Bill of Rights in 1791.[5] The French revolutionaries followed the same pattern in the *declaration des droits de l'homme et du citoyen* 1791.[6] In each case the revolutionaries sought a dual purpose in enshrining these documents. First the documents attempted to strike at the previous regime by setting out the behaviour that had led to revolution. This provided a justification for the rebellious act. For example the English Bill of Rights in 1689 states 'the late King James the Second, by the assistance of divers evil counsellors, judges and ministers employed by him, did endeavour to subvert and extirpate the Protestant religion and the laws and liberties of this kingdom.' In the French declaration of 1789 the same pattern is evident. As it states:

> [t]he representatives of the French people, organized as a National Assembly, *believing that the ignorance, neglect, or contempt of the rights of man are the sole cause of public calamities and of the corruption of governments,* have determined to set forth in a solemn declaration the natural, unalienable, and sacred rights of man, in order that this declaration, being constantly before all the members of the Social body, shall remind them continually of their rights and duties; in order that the acts of the legislative power, as well as those of the executive power, may be compared at any moment with the objects and purposes of all political institutions and may thus be more respected, and, lastly, in order that the grievances of the citizens, based hereafter upon simple and incontestable principles, shall tend to the maintenance of the constitution and redound to the happiness of all.

Second and most importantly the documents contained a catalogue of rights, which could be used as standards against which future dictates of a sovereign power could be judged. However the basis of those values was still unclear as at times divine authority was claimed and at others authority emanated from the people.[7]

5   Malanczuk, Peter, *Akehurst's Modern Introduction to International Law* (7th edn, 1997) Routledge, p 14.
6   The declaration was first proclaimed on 26 August 1789. It then became the first part of the French Constitution, promulgated on 3 September 1791.
7   Plamenatz, John *Man and Society; Political and Social Theories from Machiavelli to Marx Volume I- from the Middleages to Locke* (2nd edn, 1992) Longman, pp 233-288.

It is in the American and French texts that we find the core concepts of modern human rights. Those concepts are: the *principle of universal inherence*, by which every human being has rights by virtue of their humanity alone; the *principle of inalienability* whereby no human being can have those rights removed or voluntarily remove those rights; and the *rule of law* whereby conflicts of rights are to be resolved by constant, independent and impartial application of just laws and procedures.[8]

The American and French revolutionaries used the form of a written constitution to enshrine these principles. As such they represented law of the highest order floating above and beyond the reach of the state power and restricting negatively the areas in which the state could legitimately operate. By the beginning of the 19th century political theory had gone beyond the negative application of rights and developed concepts of positive rights or affirmative rights whereby the state was not just negatively constrained by enshrined rights but had positive obligations to act against injustice and inequality.[9] By the beginning of the 20'h century a philosophy of rights had arisen. However while those rights could govern the relationship between the individual and their state no such concept of rights existed between nation states.

The rise of the nation state

While political philosophers between the 17th and early 20th century were alive to the need for values to protect the rights of individuals within their respective societies, in the realm of international law only states mattered.[10] Relationships in the international arena were conducted between individual states who governed a particular geographical location and exercised power over those located within that particular geographic sphere.[11] Relations between states were not governed by the norms found within particular societies. There were no laws or common political institutions to govern behaviour between states, any agreements that arose between states either bilaterally or multilaterally represented only tacit agreements for the benefit of each state.[12] No police could patrol the agreements or judges adjudicate them.[13] If the benefit of a particular agreement ceased to flow to a particular state it could withdraw. The only mechanism of enforcement left to the other state to the agreement was to demand reparations, impose sanctions if it

---

8   See in particular the preamble to the French declaration above.
9   The rise of these ideas parallels the development of socialism as a political theory and can see in the Constitutions of Russia in 1918, Mexico in 1917 and Germany in 1919. See Steiner, Henry and Alston, Philip, *International Human Rights in Context* (1996) Clarendon Press, p 189.
10   See Cobban, Alfred, *The Nation State and National Self-Determination* (1969) London.
11   See p 5, n 5 (Malanzuk).
12   Jones, J W 'The 'pure' theory of International Law' (1935) 16 *British Yearbook of International Law* p 5.
13   See Shaw, Malcolm N *International Law* (4th edn, 1997) Cambridge University Press, p 18.

had the capacity and, in the last resort to go to war.[14] In this period it is war or the threat of war that is the defining feature of international relations.[15]

In no sense was there an international community. Such rules of international behaviour as there were, over conduct at sea, diplomatic representation and recognition of national sovereignty, were agreed for the individual benefit of each state and not in any sense to further interests which went beyond the sum total of each state's individual interest. Should a state violate an agreement it was a matter purely between the violator and the victim. As Cassese described it:

> [t]he international community was truly a juxtaposition of subjects, each concerned only with its own well-being and its freedom of manoeuvre, each pursuing only its own economic, political and military interests, each bent more on consolidating and if possible expanding its power and authority than on protecting any general interests.[16]

While states could legitimately react to each other with regard to matters in the international sphere each sovereign state had complete freedom to do as it wished within its own territory. This broke down into two concepts a) personal sovereignty; which constituted the state's exclusive rights to deal with its citizens; and b) territorial sovereignty; which constituted the state's right to do as it wished to its territory. This meant that the treatment of each state's citizens within its own state was of no concern to any other state and had no place in international law. However, the treatment of each state's nationals outside their own territorial boundaries was a matter that had always been a concern of international law.[17] Over time the treatment of a state's nationals abroad came to be regarded as an extension of the state's national sovereignty. Should a state fail to provide adequate protection for the life, liberty and property of a foreign national, this would be treated in international law as a breach of the personal sovereignty of the state from whence the foreign national came.

It is important to note that this concept did not give rise to individual rights in international law against a state. This had two significant consequences for the individual national travelling abroad. First should the state, whose sovereignty had been damaged by the acts of another state against its nationals abroad, decide to do nothing (as it might well do if it was opposing a powerful state) the individual national who had been aggrieved would have no cause of action. Second should an individual be denied, for example protection of their property, while operating in another state, that omission was considered a breach of their home state's national sovereignty for which the home state could claim compensation. If the home state chose to pursue that claim, the compensation belonged to the state and not to the individual. The compensation represented reparations for the damage to the state's personal sovereignty. The individual had no claim to the compensation awarded.

14 See p 6, n 13 (Shaw) p 24.
15 See Locke, J 'The Second Treatise of Government' ch 3: 'Of the State of War' (1690).
16 Cassese, A *Human Rights in a Changing World* (1990) Polity Press, p 13.
17 Guha, R 'Is the Law of Responsibility of States for Injuries to Aliens a Part of International Law?' (1961) 55 *American Journal of International Law* p 863.

The citizen of a state who travelled abroad did so under the protection of its home state and in many cases had greater protection outside their home state than within. The individual had become the beneficiary of international standards only as a side effect. The primary focus of protecting nationals' abroad was the interference with a nation's sovereignty.

While the primacy of national sovereignty was maintained throughout the 17th and 18th centuries, the 19th century began to see limited exceptions.[18] The idea of humanitarian intervention began to evolve, Gladstone in particular promoted a foreign policy based on this concept, in reaction to the massacre of 12,000 Bulgars by Ottoman troops in 1876.[19] As he stated at the time:

> our Government ... shall apply all its vigour to concur with the other States of Europe in obtaining the extinction of the Turkish executive power in Bulgaria ... Of all the objects of policy, in my conviction, humanity, rationally understood, and in due relation to justice, is the first and highest.[20]

Technically in international law this was no concern of Britain and a matter purely for the Ottoman Empire which had sovereignty over the Bulgarian people.

In the same period certain treaties were concluded which regulated conduct which was exclusively based on humanitarian grounds. The General Act of the Berlin Conference on Central Africa in 1885 and the Brussels Conference on the African Slave Trade in 1890 considered that slavery was forbidden under international law.[1] The Red Cross was founded as a private association under the laws of the canton of Geneva in 1863.[2] It placed itself at the forefront of the recognition of humanitarian issues in international law through treaties such as the Hague and Geneva Conventions on the conduct of war and treatment of prisoners of war.[3] Conventions were concluded in Berne in 1906 regulating night work by women

---

18   Fonteyne, J P, 'The Customary International Law Doctrine of Humanitarian Intervention' (1974) 4 *California Western International Law Journal* 203. See also p 6, n 13 (Shaw) p 201.

19   See Matthew, H C G *Gladstone – 1875-1898* (1995) Clarendon Press, p 31.

20   Gladstone 'The Bulgarian Horrors and the Question of the East' (1876) quoted in Eyck, Erich *Gladstone* (1938) Unwin, pp 257-258.

1   See Münch, F 'Berlin West Africa Conference 1884/1885' (1992) in Bernhardt, R *Encyclopedia of Public International Law* Vol I, pp 389-391 and p 5, n 5 (Malanczuk) pp 13 and 21.

2   See p 13, n 13 (Shaw) p 888. On the Red Cross generally see Hutchinson, John F, *Champions of Charity: War and the Rise of the Red Cross* (1996) Boulder, Westview and Forsythe; David P 'Human Rights and the Red Cross in Historical Perspective' *Human Rights Quarterly* (1997) 686-692.

3   The full titles of the Geneva Conventions of 1864 and 1906 were the Convention for the Amelioration of the Condition of the Wounded in Armies in the Field and the Convention for the Amelioration of the Wounded and Sick in Armies in the Field. These were accompanied by the three Hague Conventions of 1899 (mainly on the law of land and maritime warfare) and the thirteen Hague Conventions of 1907. For the full texts see *Texts of the Geneva Conventions of 1864 and 1906* in 129 Consolidated Treaty Series 361, 202 Consolidated Treaty Series 144 and 'Texts of the Hague Conventions' in: Roberts, A/ Guelff R (eds) *Documents on the Law of War* (2nd edn, 1989).

and the prohibition of white phosphorus in the making of matches.[4] In 1913 the Basle Conference passed four Conventions covering night work by women and young persons, maternity protection and the introducing a minimum working age in industry.[5] In 1919 the International Labour Organisation was formed to promote the protection of industrial workers.[6]

Other developments in international law during the 19th century were more sinister. In particular the work of the German Bluntschli[7] and the Italian Mancini[8] advocated the emphasis of international relations be placed on nations, groups who shared a common culture, language and usually race, rather than states. Mancini in particular argued that each sovereign state should legitimately contain only one nation. The formation of the Italian and German states as well as the recognition of nationalities in the reforming of boundaries of European states after the First World War was in some ways a recognition of these ideas.[9] However it was over the course of the two World Wars of the 20th century that the focus of international relations moved to recognise the role of the individual as well as the state.

The 20th century wars

It is often in extreme situations that ideas are forged and so it was through the shock of the two world wars of the 20th century that a human rights agenda arose in the international arena. Over the course of the First World War both Lenin and President Wilson began to advocate concepts of self-determination for the people of the world. While the rhetoric of both leaders was similar they were some way apart in terms of their interpretation of the extent of self-determination. Lenin was advocating independence for the colonial peoples and for a realignment of states along national lines ie a breakup of the German, Austro-Hungarian, Ottoman, French and British Empires.[10] Wilson however had a more cautious approach allowing for limited forms of self-determination within the existing colonial system.[11] With regard to

4   Follows, J W *Antecedents of the International Labour Organisation* (1951) Clarendon Press, p 161 and p 6, n 13 (Shaw) p 201.
5   Alcock, Anthony, *History of the International Labour Organisation* (1971) Macmillan Press, p 46.
6   See Betten, Lammy 'At its 75th Anniversary, the ILO Prepares Itself for an Active Future' (1994) 12 *Netherlands Quarterly on Human Rights* 425, p 6, n 13 (Shaw) p 24 and p 6, n 9 (Steiner/Alston) p 114.
7   Buntschili, J C, 'Jede Nation ist Berufen und Berechtigt, einen Staat zu Bilden' in *Allgemeine Staatslehre* (6th edn, 1866) Berlin p 107.
8   Mancini, P S, (1873) *Dritto Internazionale – Prelezioni con un Saggio su Machiavelli* (1873) Giuseppe Marghieri, Naples.
9   Cassese, Antonio, *Self-Determination of Peoples* (1995) Cambridge University Press, p 13.
10   Lenin, V I, 'The Socialist Revolution and the Right of Nations to Self-Determination' (1916) in Lenin, V I, *Selected Works* (1969) London, p 159.
11   See generally Knock,Thomas J, *To End All Wars - Woodrow Wilson and the Quest for a New World Order* (1992) Oxford University Press. For a more detailed consideration of Wilson's concept of self-determination see Pomerance, M, (1976) 'The United States and Self-Determination: Perspectives on the Wilsonian Conception' 70 *American Journal of International Law*, pp 1-27 and Hannum, H, 'Rethinking Self-Determination' (1993) 34 *Virginia Journal of International Law* p 1 at 3.

the nation issue he approached the problem the same way, in that he advocated that borders be reconsidered at the end of the war either to give people the option to choose a new state structure or to provide for new systems within the existing Empires. While self-determination did become a reality for some nations within the Austro-Hungarian and Ottoman Empires for most it was a disappointment.

The formation of the League of Nations after the First World War in 1919 marked a significant, if limited, development in international relations. Its significance was in the creation of a forum for an international community.[12] As Walters stated:

> [i]t [the League] was the first effective move towards the organisation of a world-wide political and social order, in which the common interests of humanity could be seen and served across the barriers of national tradition, racial difference, or geographical separation.[13]

Its limitations could be seen in the unwillingness of the Western powers to address issues that might threaten their national systems. Agreement could be achieved regarding self-determination for the nations of the defeated empires ie the German, Austro-Hungarian and Ottoman, because it strengthened the Western powers' positions. However the inclusion into the League of Nations Covenant of a quite limited provision recognising equality among individuals, an important human rights principle, was rejected by the Western powers.[14] A principle of equality was perceived by the Western powers as a threat to their colonial administrations and in the case of the US as threatening the existence of racial segregation in many US states. A declaration of equality of races at an international level would make the maintenance of inequality at a domestic level untenable and thus was unacceptable.[15]

By the 1930s the limitations of the League of Nations to provide any solution when the matter at hand concerned a Western power were becoming more obvious. In 1933 the question of Germany's treatment of the Jews came before the Council of the League of Nations.[16] During the ensuing debate on the treatment of minorities the Polish delegate set out minimum standards of rights that must accrue to each human being. The German delegate argued that German laws were being misconstrued by subordinate authorities and that those misconstructions would be corrected. The Council then merely invited Germany to end the violations.

The matter returned to the Council some months later when a report on the treatment of minorities was placed before the Council.[17] The French delegation

---

12   Hegarty, Helga and Leonard, Siobhan (1999) *Human Rights - An Agenda for the 21st Century* Cavendish Publishing, p 3.
13   Walters, F P, *A History of the League of Nations* (1965) Oxford University Press, p 1.
14   It was introduced by the Japanese delegates see Miller, D H *The Drafting of the Covenant* (1929) G P, Putnam's Sons, p 342.
15   On the opposition of the Western powers see Zimmerman, A, *The League of Nations and the Rule of Law 1918-1935* (1936) Macmillan, p 258.
16   See p 6, n 9 (Steiner/Alston) pp 114-115.
17   See p 7, n 16 (Cassese) pp 18-21 for a full description of these events.

made a proposal aimed at ending the discrimination against Jews in Germany. Illustrating the impotence of the League the German delegation defeated the proposal stating that they considered the treatment of the Jews a purely internal affair and describing the Jews as a special problem unlike other minority questions. Shortly after this vote Germany withdrew from the League of Nations over the disarmament issue further illustrating the League's ineffectiveness.[18]

The role of legal theory

In the early to mid 19th century, doctrines such as Utilitarianism and the ideas of Bentham in particular were influential within the legal process.[19] They grew up in reaction to values which where either divine or natural in origin. Progress in science and industry had created a society which valued objective proof, which neither divine nor natural values provided. This proof was found in concepts such as Utilitarianism. As Cotterrell put it, Bentham:

> had recognised the need for a coherent doctrine to guide the rational reform of law and to dispose of common law archaism and had found this in the principle of utility. Utility required that law making and legal institutions be designed to promote the greatest happiness of the greatest number of people. Utility would replace traditional, self-serving or subjective moral evaluations with a rational evaluation of the worth of particular practices, institutions and policies in terms of how far they served the common good, measured in terms of maximisation of satisfaction of the actual desires of the greatest possible number of the population.[20]

However from the mid 1860s onwards the work of Austin[1] with its Utilitarian roots[2] and its Positivist approach to the law became more significant.[3] As Davies and Holdcroft consider:

---

18   See p 10, n 13 (Walters) p 550.
19   See Bentham, J, *Of Laws in General* edited by H L A Hart (1970) University of London Athlone Press, and Bentham, J, *A Comment on the Commentaries and A Fragment on Government* edited by J H Burnes and H L A Hart (1977) University of London Athlone Press, London
20   Cotterrell, R, *The Politics of Jurisprudence* (1989) Butterworths, pp 55-56.
1   See Austin, J, 'The Province of Jurisprudence Determined' (1832) reprinted in *The Province of Jurisprudence Determined and the Uses of the Study of Jurisprudence* (1955) Wiedenfeld and Nicolson, London, pp 1-361, Austin, J, 'The Uses of the Study of Jurisprudence' (1863) reprinted in *The Province of Jurisprudence Determined and the Uses of the Study of Jurisprudence* (1955) Wiedenfeld and Nicolson, London, pp 363-393 and Austin, J, *Lectures on Jurisprudence or the Philosophy of Positive Thought* edited by R Campbell (1885) John Murray.
2   For a consideration of the relationship between Bentham and Austin's work see Morison, W L, *John Austin* (1982) Edward Arnold, pp 38-48.
3   While the work of Austin was influential on the practitioners at the time it was not until the publication of Dicey's *The Law of the Constitution* (1885) which expressed Austin's ideas in a more practical way that they really took off.

[P]ositivism stands against blurring the distinction between law as it is and law as it ought to be: it does not follow from the mere fact that a rule violates certain standards of morality that it is not a rule of law. An iniquitous, unjust law remains a valid law. Moral evaluation is to play no role in the description of what law or the legal system is.[4]

Positivism generally formed the interpretive framework within which the judiciary operated from the late 19th century until after the Second World War. In terms of the development of international human rights it had a detrimental effect. Concepts of justice when interpreting a nation's laws were irrelevant and combined with the traditional application of national sovereignty each state could pass laws mistreating its people or a part of them in the full knowledge that the international community could do nothing.

The atrocities committed by the Nazis before and during the Second World War damaged the Positivist position. Both the changing academic and judicial views after the war were reflective of the shared experiences of nations during the war years and the shock of the Nazi regime, which operated in a perfectly legal manner within a Positivist framework. By the 1960s the reaction to pure Positivism had begun to produce tangible change, the publication of Hart's *The Concept of Law*[5] saw the beginning of a softer Positivism and in response the rise of rights.[6] The same reaction is evident in the behaviour of the UK judiciary after the war. As Allen commented at the time:

> [t]here seems to be less reluctance than formerly in superior courts either to overrule previous, and sometimes old, precedence, or else to sterilise them by the semi-fictions of 'distinguishing' them on tenuous grounds of fact or law by recourse to the doctrine of incuria. With the help of a certain degree of 'judicial valour', new opportunities seem to be opening up of escaping from the bondage which carries 'consistency' or 'loyalty' to unprofitable extremes ...[7]

Patterson in his detailed work on judicial attitudes in this period also noted this reaction from the judiciary:

> [t]wo factors which seem to suggest that at least four Law Lords (Lords Reid, Radcliffe, Denning, and MacDermott) did not subscribe to the prevailing orthodoxy in interpreting the judicial role in 1957, were their preference for principles rather than precedence and their willingness on occasion to take account of the need to keep the common law in step with changing social conditions.[8]

---

4   Davies, H and Holdcroft, D, *Jurisprudence* (1991) Butterworths, p 4.
5   Hart, H L A, *The Concept of Law* (1961) Oxford University Press.
6   See the work of Ronald Dworkin first published in the mid-1960s reprinted in *Taking Rights Seriously* (1977) Duckworth.
7   Allen, C K , *Law in the Making* (1964) Clarendon, p 357.
8   Patterson, A, *The Law Lords* (1982) Macmillan, p 135.

The rise of international human rights

The Second World War had a dual effect. First it created an environment, because of the Nazi atrocities, within which human rights came to be valued generally. Second the actions of the German state were carried out in a perfectly legal manner without the ability of the international community to intervene. Traditional concepts of national sovereignty and legal theory such as Positivism had to be rethought in international law. A new system had to be devised in which the rights of individuals were central.

It was in the formation of the United Nations (UN) that voice was given to these concerns.[9] The UN Charter signed at San Francisco on 26 June 1945 placed human rights on the international agenda.[10] Though vague in form the UN Charter stated that among the organisation's purposes was 'promoting and encouraging respect for human rights and the fundamental freedoms for all'.[11] It further contained a pledge by UN members to take action to achieve 'universal respect for, and observance of, human rights and fundamental freedoms for all'.[12]

It was not until 1948 when the UN proclaimed the *Universal Declaration of Human Rights* (UDHR) that human rights became a proper focus for international relations.[13] The UDHR was both a reaction to the experiences of the Second World War and a reflection of fears for the future. Both Churchill and Roosevelt had expressed their desire to see certain protections in place after the war. On 6 January 1941 Roosevelt gave what became known as the 'four freedoms speech'. In clear unequivocal terms he looked forward to a post war new world order: '[i]n future days, which we seek to make secure, we look forward to a world founded upon four essential freedoms.'[14] Those freedoms he described as, freedom of speech and expression, freedom for every person to worship God in their own way, freedom from want and freedom from fear.[15]

However the immediate post war years were also characterised by concerns about the aggressive intentions of the USSR. It was in this development that Churchill found a focus for human rights. In his famous 'Iron Curtain' speech in 1946 Churchill asked the question:

> [w]hat then is the overall strategic concept which we should inscribe today? It is nothing less than the safety and welfare, the freedom and progress, of all the homes and families of all the men and women in all the lands. And

9   On the formation of the United Nations see Roberts, A and Kingsbury, B, *United Nations, Divided World* (2nd edn, 1993), Oxford University Press and p 6 n 13 (Shaw) p 825.
10 On the drafting of the Charter itself see Goodrich, L M, Hambro, E and Simons, A P, *Charter of the United Nations* (3rd edn, 1969), New York and Simma, B *The Charter of the United Nations* (1995) Oxford.
11 UN Charter Article 1 section (3).
12 UN Charter Articles 55 and 56.
13 See Brownlie, Ian, *Basic Documents on Human Rights* (3rd edn, 1998) Clarendon Press, p 21.
14 US Hearing Documents, 77th Session of Congress, 1st Session.
15 Zevin, B D, *Nothing to Fear - The Selected Addresses of Franklin Delano Roosevelt* (1947) Hodder and Stoughton, pp 258-264.

here I speak particularly of the myriad cottage or apartment homes where the wage-earner strives amid the accidents and difficulties of life to guard his wife and children from privation and bring the family up in the fear of the Lord, or upon ethical conceptions which often play their potent part. To give security to these countless homes, they must be shielded from the two giant marauders, war and tyranny'.[16]

A human rights agenda for the international community was seen by the US and Britain as essential to avoid the mistakes of the past but also to deal with the USSR.

As a result the debate on the UDHR broke evenly into two camps. On the one hand were the Western democracies plus satellites, who despite their imperial past and present were pushing for firm commitments to human rights on the international agenda. On the other hand were the Soviet Union and its satellites who were hostile to human rights. This was not just because Stalin ran the USSR as a dictatorship but was also because Marxist ideology precluded the focus on the individual. The USSR in 1948 had according to its dogma achieved the integration of the individual and the community and so individual rights were irrelevant. Social and economic rights were however not irrelevant to Marxist theory and it was on this point that the USSR did make a contribution to the UN debate on the UDHR.[17]

The debate progressed with the Western democracies advocating a system of rights based on the British, US and French traditions of civil and political rights and the USSR while primarily suspicious of the human rights agenda arguing for the inclusion of economic and social rights.[18] In the end the UDHR contains elements of both these concepts of rights. The natural law traditions of the West appear in the focus on the dignity of humans and the equality and inalienability of their rights.[19] Economic and social rights are represented in the recognition of the individual as part of society with a right to social security and a duty to the community.[20] On 10 December 1948 the declaration was adopted in Paris. Of the 56 member states of the UN at the time 48 voted for the declaration and 8 abstained (USSR, Byelorussia, Czechoslovakia, Poland, Ukraine, Yugoslavia, Saudi Arabia, and South Africa).[1] In the end it was a draw: both sides managed to get the other to accept ideologies alien to their national systems.

---

16   'The Sinews of Peace', Westminster College, Fulton Missouri, 5 March 1946 in Cannadine, David, *The Speeches of Winston Churchill* (1989) Penguin Books, p 296 this citation on p 297.

17   See Kolakowski, L, 'Marxism and Human Rights' in *Daedalus – Journal of the American Academy of Arts and Sciences* (1983) p 81 and Lukes, S, *Marxism and Morality* (1987) Oxford University Press, pp 61-99.

18   They also saw human rights as potentially a weapon to beat the Western colonial powers. See the contribution of the Soviet delegation at the General Assembly on 10 December 1948: 183 Plenary Meeting.

19   See UNDHR Article 1.

20   See UNDHR Articles 22-30.

1   On the vote and abstentions see p 13, n 13 (Brownlie) p 21.

Chapter two

The European Convention on Human Rights

Any preoccupation with ideas of what is right or wrong in conduct shows an arrested intellectual development.[1]

The European Convention on Human Rights (ECHR) was born out of the same events as the Universal Declaration on Human Rights (UDHR) and was heavily influenced by that document.[2] It is the product of the Council of Europe[3] an organisation formed in 1949 to further European political integration as a protection against the USSR and to ensure that the atrocities of the Second World War would never be repeated. As with the formation of the UN the Council of Europe placed human rights among its objectives.[4] As the Statute of the Council states, its aim is to seek greater unity through co-operation and concerted action on 'economic, social, cultural, scientific, legal and administrative matters and in the maintenance and further realisation of human rights and fundamental freedoms'.[5] Commitment to human rights in the Council document was, unlike the UN founding document, a condition of membership, breach of which could lead to suspension and withdrawal from the organisation.[6]

1   Oscar Wilde *Phrases and Philosophies for the Use of the Young* (1894).
2   On the drafting of the ECHR see p 13, n 13 (Brownlie) p 326.
3   The Council has at the time of writing 41 members made up of most of the Western, Central and Eastern European states.
4   On the formation of the Council generally see Robertson, A H, *The Council of Europe - Its Structure, Functions and Achievements* (2nd edn, 1961) Stevens and Sons.
5   87 UNTS 103; UKTS (1949), Cmd 7778.
6   Statute of the Council of Europe, Article 8.

In 1950 the Convention was signed by the contracting states and entered into force in 1953. It differs from the UDHR in that its focus is primarily upon civil and political rights rather than social and economic rights. While the presence of the USSR in the UN ensured the inclusion of social and economic rights in the UDHR no such imperative existed in the Council of Europe debate. It does, however, contain some Articles which are economic and social in orientation such as, Article 4 (freedom from forced labour), Article 8 (the right to respect for family life), and Article 11 (freedom of association). Specific economic and social rights were however added in March 1952 in the text of the First Protocol in the form of a right to property in Article 1 and the right to education in Article 2.[7]

The articles and protocols[8]

Article 1: State obligation to secure the rights and freedoms domestically.

Article 2: The right to life.

Article 3: Freedom from torture or inhuman or degrading treatment or punishment.

Article 4: Freedom from slavery, servitude or forced or compulsory labour.

Article 5: The right to liberty and security of the person.

Article 6: The right to a fair trial.

Article 7: Freedom from retroactive criminal offences and punishment.

Article 8: The right to respect for private and family life, home and correspondence.

Article 9: Freedom of religion.

Article 10: Freedom of expression.

Article 11: Freedom of assembly and association.

Article 12: The right to marry and to found a family.

Article 13: The right to an effective national remedy.

Article 14: Freedom from discrimination in respect of protected rights.

Article 15: Derogation in time of war or other public emergency.

Article 16: Restrictions on the political rights of aliens.

Article 17: Restrictions on activities subversive of Convention rights.

Article 18: Prohibition of the use of restrictions for an improper purpose.

First Protocol, Article 1: The right to property.

First Protocol, Article 2: The right to education.

---

7   See Robertson, A H, 'The European Convention on Human Rights: Recent Developments' (1951) BYIL 359.

8   The Articles and Protocols are examined in full in Chapter 4.

First Protocol, Article 3: The right to free election.

Fourth Protocol, Article 1: Freedom from imprisonment for non-fulfillment of a contractual obligation.

Fourth Protocol, Article 2: Freedom of movement within a state and the freedom to leave its territory.

Fourth Protocol, Article 3: The right of a national not to be expelled from and to enter a state's territory.

Fourth Protocol, Article 4: Freedom of aliens from collective expulsion.

Sixth Protocol: Freedom from the death penalty.

Seventh Protocol, Article 1: Freedom from expulsion of individual aliens.

Seventh Protocol, Article 2: The right to review in criminal cases.

Seventh Protocol, Article 3: The right to compensation for miscarriages of justice.

Seventh Protocol, Article 4: *Ne bis in idem* (Freedom from double jeopardy).

Seventh Protocol, Article 5: Equality of rights of spouses.

The operation of the Convention

The ECHR also differs from the UDHR in that it required the formation and maintenance of a system for the enforcement of obligations taken on by the contracting states. Three institutions were formed originally to carry out this task, the European Commission of Human Rights,[9] the European Court of Human Rights[10] (ECtHR) and the Committee of Ministers of the Council of Europe.

Originally the ECHR was primarily conceived as providing a forum for interstate disputes. If one state was mistreating its citizens a mechanism was available for other states to interfere through the ECHR.[11] It has not, however, operated in that manner as its primary focus has become the individual petition.[12] Thus our focus in this work will be the individual application rather than the procedure for interstate disputes.

Where the contracting state has accepted the right of individual petition[13] – as the UK did in 1966 – an individual applicant[14] can bring a complaint against a state for violations of rights contained in the ECHR. The ECHR has undergone some major operational changes in the past decade. Protocol 11 has completely overhauled the operation of the court. In doing so Protocol 11 has changed the numbering of the Articles. For the purposes of clarity and given that much of the case law of the

9   Formed in 1954.
10   Formed in 1959.
11   See Article 33 (formerly Article 24).
12   By 1996 only 11 interstate disputes had been brought.
13   See Article 34 (formerly Article 25).
14   This includes any person, non-governmental organisations and groups of individuals.

ECtHR was decided under the old system, we have set out below both the old and new procedures of the ECHR as they apply to individual applicants. In covering the old procedure, because the case law refers to the old Article numbers, we have referred to the Article numbers as they then were with a footnote to the new Article numbers if there is an equivalent under the new procedure.

Procedure of the old system

The role of the Commission

An individual applicant could lodge a complaint against a contracting state alleging he was the victim of a violation of a right contained in the ECHR. The Secretariat of the Commission would then request any further information it needed. This acted as a filter to weed out hopeless/frivolous applications. The complaint was then subject to scrutiny by the Commission to determine the admissibility of the complaint. In doing so the Commission applied Articles 26 and 27.[15] Article 26 set out two conditions: a) all domestic remedies must be exhausted and b) the case must come before the Commission within six months of a final decision at a domestic level. Article 27 compelled the Commission to reject any claim which was anonymous, substantially the same as another matter previously examined by the Commission or other international process, incompatible with the ECHR or manifestly ill founded.

If the Commission found that a claim was admissible it was required under Article 28 to draw up a report establishing the facts of the case. This process took the form of a judicial hearing with both sides represented by legal counsel. At the end of the fact finding process Article 28 (1) (b) compelled the Commission to see if a friendly settlement could be reached between the parties. If such a settlement could be reached the Commission then drew up a short report covering the facts and recording the solution reached. If a settlement was not reached the Commission drew up a detailed statement of the facts and an opinion as to whether a violation of the ECHR had occurred. It could also under Article 31 include such proposals for remedy as it saw fit. Once this process was complete the report was passed to the Committee of Ministers.

The Committee of Ministers

If the respondent state had accepted the compulsory jurisdiction of the Court, the Commission and/or any contracting party could, within three months of the passing of the Commission report to the Council of Ministers, bring the case before the Court for a final decision. If this did not happen the matter fell under Article 32 to the Committee of Ministers for adjudication. The Committee of Ministers was primarily a political organ made up of the Foreign Ministers of all the contracting states. They did however carry out a residual judicial function. When a case fell to the Committee for adjudication they decided as to a violation by voting on the matter. A two-thirds majority was needed to make a decision. In practice however either

---

15   Now the admissibility criteria are contained in Article 35.

the findings of the Commission were confirmed or the parties would reach a settlement before the Committee voted.

The real role of the Committee lay in the enforcement of decisions. In that sense it had responsibility for ensuring remedial action by a violating state when a decision had been made by either the Committee or the Court. When dealing with a Committee decision, under Article 32 (2) the Committee stated a timeframe within which the violating state must do whatever was necessary to correct the violation. It was however usual for the violating state to set out remedial action once the Commission had found against it. Where a decision of the ECtHR had been made the judgment was also passed to the Committee, who had responsibility for its execution.[16] The violating party would then be required to explain what action had been taken to give effect to the judgment of the Court. Should this remedial action prove to be insufficient there was little formal power available to the Committee to enforce its decision. There was however the ultimate threat in Article 8 of the Statute of the Council of Europe which provided for suspension and withdrawal from the Council of Europe should the contracting party disregard its commitment to human rights agreed to in Article 3 of the Statute of the Council of Europe. This indeed happened to Greece in 1969.

The European Court of Human rights

The original Convention in 1950 provided that only the Commission or a contracting state could pass a case to the Court. As a result when a contracting party was held to have violated a right in the ECHR it could effectively appeal the Commission decision to the Court. The same avenue of appeal was unavailable for individuals. This remained the case until 1990 when Protocol 9 was agreed in order to facilitate individual petitions to the Court. It came into effect in 1994 but only for those states that had ratified the Protocol. There existed two procedures for passing a case to the Court: a) the original procedure whereby only the Commission or those states who had not ratified Protocol 9 could place the matter before the Court; and b) The Protocol 9 procedure whereby if the contracting party had ratified Protocol 9 an individual could take a case to the Court. Protocol 9 created a procedure whereby an individual could place their case before a special panel of three judges who would decide if the case should go forward to the Court.[17] If the panel decided in the negative the case remained with the Committee of Ministers for final resolution.

When a case was referred to the Court by whatever procedure, Article 43 of the ECHR provided for a Chamber of nine judges. As the workload of the Court increased it became common for the Chamber to pass important cases to a plenary Court. In 1993 a provision was introduced to allow the use of Grand Chambers. If the matters in the case raised one or more serious questions regarding the interpretation of the ECHR the Chamber could pass it to a Grand Chamber of 19 judges. Also, if there was the possibility of conflict with a previous judgment of the Court the case had to go to a Grand Chamber. The plenary Court was therefore only used on rare occasions after 1993.

16   Article 54.
17   Article 48 (2).

ECHR OLD PROCEDURE

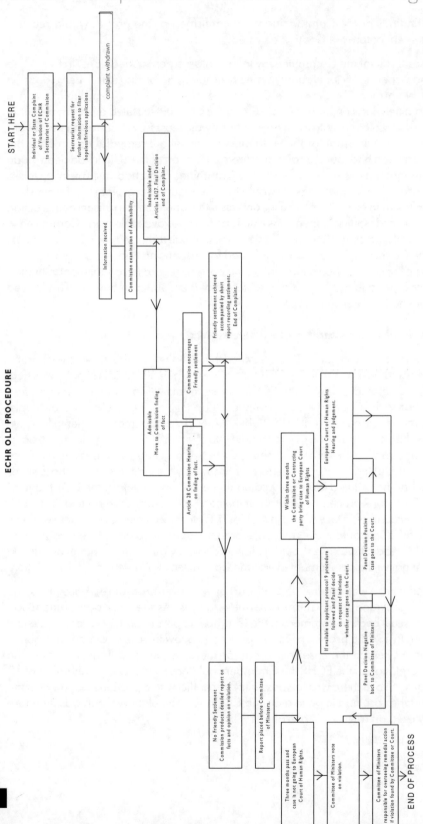

START HERE

Individual or State Complaint of Violation of ECHR to Secretariat of Commission

Secretariat request for further information to filter hopeless/frivolous applications

complaint withdrawn

Information received

Commission examination of Admissibility

Inadmissible under Articles 26/27. Final Decision end of Complaint.

Admissible Move to Commission finding of fact.

Article 28 Commission Hearing on finding of fact.

Commission encourages Friendly settlement

Friendly settlement achieved accompanied by short report recording settlement. End of Complaint.

No Friendly Settlement Commission produces detailed report on facts and opinion on violation.

Report placed before Committee of Ministers.

Within three months the Commission or Contracting party bring case to European Court of Human Rights

If available to applicant protocol 9 procedure followed and Panel decide on request of individual whether case goes to the Court.

European Court of Human Rights Hearing and Judgement.

Panel Decision Positive case goes to the Court.

Panel Decision Negative back to Committee of Ministers

Three months pass and case is not going to European Court of Human Rights.

Committee of Ministers vote on violation.

Committee of Ministers responsible for overseeing remedial action if violation found by Committee or Court.

END OF PROCESS

20

If the Court found that a violation of a right contained in the ECHR had occurred the Court could not order remedial action. It could however under Article 50 (now Article 41) of the ECHR give 'just satisfaction' to the victim. This normally consisted of the Court awarding damages and the victim's costs. The judgment would then be sent to the Committee of Ministers who were responsible for its enforcement.[18]

The Court, as the final avenue of appeal, had the last say as to the interpretation of the Convention. If the Court's findings differed from that of the Commissions the Court's interpretation prevailed. While there was no concept of binding precedent in that the Court and Commission were not bound to follow their previous decisions, the Commission had to follow the precedent set by the Court.[19] There are however many matters regarding the Convention that the Court has never considered, particularly regarding admissibility, and here the jurisprudence of the Commission is significant. Where there are Court decisions on admissibility they should be accorded great weight because of their rarity.[20]

The new European Court of Human Rights

Background

In the almost 50 years since the ECHR was opened for signature a number of significant changes have occurred. Eleven Protocols have been adopted broadly covering additions to the rights guaranteed in the Convention (ie Protocols 1, 4, 6, 7); while other changes have attempted to streamline the operation of the Court. The most important of these streamlining Protocols are Protocol 9 (which allows individual applicants to bring cases before the Court) and Protocol 11 (which permitted the restructuring of the Court itself). It is to Protocol 11 that we now turn in considering the operation of the new European Court of Human Rights.

The increasing workload of the Court during the 1980s and the addition of new contracting states after 1990 caused a huge backlog of cases within the ECHR system. In 1981 the Commission registered 404 applications; by 1993 it was registering 2,037, and by 1997 it was registering 4,750 with a backlog of some 12,000 unregistered files. The Court had seven cases referred to it in 1981; by 1993 that figure was 52 and in 1997 119.[1]

The operation of the system was at breaking point and it was eventually agreed by the Council members that the system should be overhauled. On 11 May 1994

---

18 See above on Committee of Ministers.
19 For where the Court has departed from its previous interpretation see *Huber v Switzerland (1990) A188*; on the operation of binding precedent in the Court see *Cossey v United Kingdom* (1990) 13 EHRR 622. See also Chapter 3.
20 See for example *Agrotexim v Greece* [1996] 21 EHRR where the court decided the admissibility of an action brought by shareholders for an act aimed at the company. See further Chapter 8.
1 Source: Council of Europe see http://www.echr.coe.int/eng/INFORMATION%20NOTES/infodoc%20revised%202.htm Subsequent developments.

Protocol 11 'restructuring the control machinery' was agreed and opened for signature. The aim of the Protocol was to simplify the structure through the creation of a single permanent Court. The Commission was to disappear and the Committee of Ministers to have its judicial function removed. The judicial function would be entirely held by the new Court.[2] After some four years during which the ratification process took place, and a further year for preparation, the new European Court of Human Rights came into operation on 1 November 1998. The Commission however had such a backlog of cases that it was allowed to continue until 31 October 1999 to clear the system.

The operation of the new Court

A permanent Court now exists replacing the old Commission, Court and Committee of Ministers in its adjudication function.[3] The new Court consists of a number of judges equal to that of the State parties to the Convention. All of the judges although appointed by the member states sit in their personal capacity.[4] The Court is divided into four sections. Each section is gender and geographic balanced and takes account of the differing legal traditions among the member states.[5] Within each section the structure is the same: the Court sits as either Committee, Chamber or a Grand Chamber.[6] The Committee, composed of three judges, forms the lower tier of the Court and exercises the filter function that the Commission had previously carried out with regard to individual applications. The Committee has the power to declare individual applications inadmissible.[7] The criteria for assessment remain the same as applied under the Commission.[8] The Chamber is made up of seven judges and forms the next tier of the Court.[9] Chambers can consider the admissibility of applications as well as the merits of the case.[10] The Grand Chamber made up of seventeen judges forms the final tier. The Grand Chamber decides on cases of exceptional importance, where there is an important Convention point at issue or where there is a potential conflict with a previous decision of the Court.[11] It can also consider requests for advisory opinions from the Committee of Ministers.[12]

2   On Protocol 11 see http://www.coe.fr/eng/legaltxt/155e.htm.
3   Article 19 ECHR as amended by Protovol 11.
4   Article 20 and 21, para 2. At the date of writing there are 41 judges.
5   See Rule 25, paras 1 and 2 Rules of Court of the European Court of Human Rights as in force at 1 November 1998. Note also that para 5 provides for the expansion beyond four sections to accommodate the future growth of the Council and Court. The Rules can be found at http://www.echr.coe.int/Rules%20of%20Court%20eng.html.
6   Article 27 p 1 ECHR; more specifically for the composition of the Committee see Rule 27, for the Chambers see Rule 26 and for the Grand Chamber Rule 24.
7   Article 28.
8   Except that the admissibility criteria are now contained in Article 35. See above text on the old procedure.
9   Article 27, para 1.
10   Article 29.
11   Article 31.
12   Article 47.

Applying under the new system

Individual applications can be lodged directly with the Court in Strasbourg by alleging a breach by a contracting state of one of the Convention rights.[13] The Registry of the new Court will communicate with the applicant and request further information where necessary. This forms an important part of the screening process similar to that previously carried out by the Secretariat of the Commission designed to get rid of ridiculous and/or hopeless applications.[14] After passing the Registry stage the application is assigned to a section of the Court and the President of the section designates a judge rapporteur.[15] The judge rapporteur conducts a preliminary examination of the case and decides whether it should be dealt with by a Committee or a Chamber. The case would only go to a Chamber directly if the judge rapporteur considers that it raises a matter of principle regarding the Convention or he concludes that the application cannot be declared inadmissible.[16]

A normal individual application will go to a Committee to be examined by three judges one of whom will be the judge rapporteur.[17] They will examine the case and declare it admissible or reject it; a negative decision is final.[18] Applications which are not declared inadmissible by Committee or which go directly to Chamber move to be considered there. It is the judge rapporteur who is responsible for the preparation of the file for the Chamber and to be the primary reference point for the parties.[19] The Chamber consisting of seven members determines both the admissibility and the merit of an application.[20] This is usually done as separate decisions but sometimes a single decision is given containing both.[1]

The first stage of the Chamber's deliberations with regard to admissibility are normally through written submissions.[2] The Chamber could, if it wished, decide to hold a full hearing on the admissibility issues at which point it would usually also consider the merits of the case.[3] The Chamber will decide on the admissibility issue by majority vote[4] and produce a judgment which contains reasons and is made public.[5] While at any point a friendly settlement could be reached, it is usually after the admissibility issue has been dealt with and allowed that the Chamber will provide facilities, through the intermediary of the Registrar, for negotiating a friendly settlement.[6]

13   Article 34.
14   On the operation of the registry see Article 25 ECHR and Chapter III – Rules 15 to 18 Rules of Court.
15   Rule 49, para 1.
16   Rule 49, para 2b.
17   Article 27, para 1 in conjunction with rule 27, para 1.
18   Article 28 and rule 53, para 3.
19   Rule 49.
20   Article 27, para 1 and Article 29, paras 1 and 2.
1   Article 29, para 3.
2   Rule 54.
3   Rule 54, para 4.
4   Rule 23, para 2 and Rule 56, para 1. If the decision is not unanimous then the Chamber must state the votes for and against.
5   Rule 56, para 1-2 and Article 40, para 2.
6   Article 38, paras 1b and 2, Rule 62, paras 1 and 2.

Once the admission of the application has been allowed by the Chamber it is usual to invite the submission of further evidence from both parties[7] and claims for 'just satisfaction' under Article 41 from the applicant.[8] The Chamber then moves to a full hearing on the merits of the application.[9] The procedure is adversarial and public.[10] In exceptional circumstances the Chamber may allow hearings in camera. All evidence filed with the Court Registrar is accessible to the public.[11] While it is possible for individual applicants to submit applications without legal representation,[12] once the application has been declared admissible and moves to a hearing, legal representation is required.[13] The Council of Europe has a legal aid scheme to cover applicants who have insufficient means.[14]

At any point in the procedure the Chamber may relinquish jurisdiction to the Grand Chamber should the application raise issues of Convention principle or if a conflict with previous case law is likely.[15] Should the Chamber intend to do this it issues a notice of intention to relinquish to the parties who have one month to provide any reasoned objections they may have.[16] Should one or both parties object to the relinquishment, the application remains with the Chamber and it proceeds as normal. If no objection is filed the matter goes to the Grand Chamber.

Following the consideration of the merits of the case and in the absence of a friendly settlement the Chamber will render judgment. Decisions of the Chamber on the merits of the case are taken by majority.[17] Each judge of the Chamber can append to the judgment a separate opinion either dissenting or concurring.[18] After judgment has been delivered any party may within three months request the case be referred to the Grand Chamber.[19] Any application to move to Grand Chamber is examined by a Grand Chamber panel of five judges. The move to the Grand Chamber will only be allowed if the application raises serious questions regarding the application or interpretation of the Convention or it raises an issue of general importance.[20]

A Chamber judgment is final after three months have passed and no Grand Chamber request has been received.[1] It can become final earlier, if the parties declare they have no intention of pursuing an application to Grand Chamber, or if a request to go to Grand Chamber was received, considered and rejected by a

7   Rule 59, para.1.
8   Rule 60.
9   Rule 59, para 2.
10   Article 40, para 1.
11   Article 40, para 2.
12   Rule 36, para 1.
13   Rule 36, para 3.
14   Rules 91–96.
15   Article 30, Rule 72, para 1.
16   Rule 72, para 2.
17   Rule 23, para 2.
18   Article 45, para 2 and Rule 74, para 2.
19   Article 43, para 1.
20   Article 43, para 2.
1   Article 42 and Article 44, para 2b.

panel of the Grand Chamber.[2] If a panel accepts that the Grand Chamber should hear the case, the Grand Chamber will consider the issue and produce a decision by majority, which is final.[3] All final decisions of the Court are definitive and binding in international law.[4] The responsibility of overseeing the execution of judgments lies, as it did under the old system, with the Committee of Ministers. The Committee must verify whether the state found in violation has taken adequate remedial action to comply with the judgment of the Court.[5]

As with the old system there is no concept of binding precedent in that Committees and Chambers of the Court are not bound to follow their previous decisions. However Grand Chamber Decisions are of greater authority than Chamber decisions and Chamber decisions are of greater weight than Committee decisions. Within that hierarchy unanimous decisions and large majority decisions carry greater weight than majority decisions. As the Convention is a dynamic document the age of a decision is crucial as the older it is the more likely the Court could depart from that position citing the 'living' interpretation of the ECHR.[6] As with the old system, matters of admissibility will most likely be dealt with at the Committee and Chamber stages. Therefore the case law on admissibility will mainly be found at the lower levels of the court. Should there be a decision of the Grand Chamber on an admissibility matter it will be of great importance given its rarity.

2   Article 42 and Article 44, paras 2a and 2c.
3   Article 43, para 3, Rule 23, para 2 and Article 44, para 1.
4   Article 46, para 1.
5   Article 46, para 2.
6   For where the Court has departed from its previous interpretation see *Huber v Switzerland (1990) A188* on the operation of binding precedent in the Court see *Cossey v United Kingdom* (1990) 13 EHRR 622. See also Chapter 3 on interpretation of the Convention as an evolving document.

ECHR NEW PROCEDURE

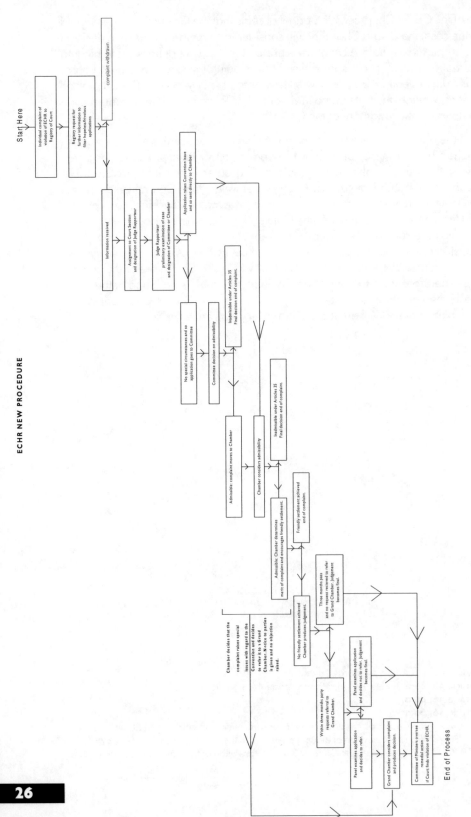

Chapter three

Interpreting the European Convention on Human Rights

When people are least sure, they are often most dogmatic.[1]

The rule of law

As described above the values contained in the ECHR have drawn heavily on Western ideas of civil and political rights. One of the core values found in Western texts is the 'rule of law'. The Statute of the Council of Europe and the preamble to the Convention both emphasise the importance of the 'rule of law'.[2] As such the European Court of Human Rights has repeatedly placed emphasis on the judicial role in ensuring the individual's protection from arbitrary interference by the authorities. In *Klass v Germany*[3] the Court considered:

> [t]he rule of law implies, inter alia, that an interference by the executive authorities with an individual's rights should be subject to an effective control which should normally be assured by the judiciary, at least in the last resort,

1   JK Galbraith *The Great Crash 1929* (1955).
2   See Appendix 2.
3   (1978) 2 EHRR 214.

judicial control offering the best guarantees of independence, impartiality and a proper procedure ...[4]

In particular Article 8 rights of privacy and Article 5 right to liberty have been areas of the Convention where the Court has stressed the importance of safeguards against arbitrary interference by the state.[5]

Allied to the Court's concept of the 'rule of law' is the interpretation of certain Articles of the ECHR. Articles 2, 5, 6-11 of the Convention specify a number of legal certainties with regard to the rights contained in the ECHR. For example Article 2 provides for 'conviction of a crime for which this penalty is *provided by law'*, Article 5 provides that '[n]o one shall be deprived of his liberty save in the following cases and in accordance with a procedure *prescribed by law'* and Article 6 provides that 'everyone charged with a criminal offence shall be presumed innocent until proved guilty *according to law'*. These individual rights and freedoms cannot be interfered with by the state unless there is a clear legal basis for doing so.

When interpreting what *law* means in the context of state interference with these rights, the Court has taken a broad approach. This concept of *law* covers both written and unwritten law and a measurement of how accessible the law is and how foreseeable the punishment.[6] The Court has also recognised that the state sometimes needs to confer wide discretion on its organs through a statute if those organs are to function effectively. On this basis imprecise wording in a statute will not necessarily mean that there is no legal basis for an act of the state.[7]

The Vienna Convention

The ECHR is an international treaty, which falls within the Vienna Convention on the Law of Treaties 1969.[8] The Vienna Convention in Articles 31-33 lays out the rules for the interpretation of international treaties.[9] The primary focus of interpretation is that a treaty be 'interpreted in good faith in accordance with the ordinary meaning to be given to the terms of the treaty in their context and in the light of its object and purpose'.[10] The European Court of Human Rights has followed the rules of the Vienna Convention when interpreting the ECHR.[11]

4   State interference with the judicial process will be contrary to the Court's view of the rule of law. See *Benthem v Netherlands* (1985) 8 EHRR 1 and *Van de Hurk v Netherlands* (1994) 18 EHRR 481.
5   With regard to Article 8 (privacy) and the Court's insistence on safeguards see *Kruslin v France* (1990) 12 EHRR 528, *Niemietz v Germany* (1992) 16 EHRR 97 and *Funke v France* (1993) 16 EHRR 297. With regard to Article 5 (liberty) see *Winterwerp v Netherlands* (1979) 2 EHRR 387, *Brogan v United Kingdom* (1988) 11 EHRR 117 and *Aksoy v Turkey* (1996) 23 EHRR 553.
6   See *Kruslin v France* (1990) 12 EHRR 528.
7   See *Kokkinakis v Greece* (1993) 17 EHRR 392 and *SW v United Kingdom* (1995) 21 EHRR 363.
8   See Brownlie, I, *Basic Documents in International Law* (4th edn, 1995), Oxford University Press, pp 388-425.
9   Ibid (Brownlie) pp 401-402.
10   Art 31 para1 Vienna Convention.
11   See *Golder v United Kingdom* (1975) 1 EHRR 524.

Over time the Court has placed great weight when interpreting the ECHR on fulfilling the 'object and purpose' of the ECHR. In the *Belgian Linguistics case*[12] and *Soering v United Kingdom*[13] the Court has considered that the general object and purpose to be achieved by the ECHR is both the protection of individual human rights and democratic ideals and values.[14] In the early years of the Court's jurisprudence it was unclear whether the Court would adopt a quite limited role in achieving these objects, giving the benefit of the doubt to contracting states,[15] or whether the ECHR would be treated as a European bill of rights which imposed objective criteria on contracting states as regards the legitimacy of their laws.[16] As the European Court of Human Rights stated in *Ireland v United Kingdom* when considering the special nature of the Convention:

> [u]nlike international treaties of the classic kind, the Convention comprises more than mere reciprocal engagements between contracting states. It creates, over and above a network of mutual, bilateral undertakings, objective obligations which, in the words of the Preamble, benefit from a 'collective enforcement'.[17]

It has been this latter objective view that has prevailed in the case law and has led to a focus on an evolutionary approach to the rights contained in the ECHR.[18]

The dynamic Convention

The ECHR has not been interpreted as a static document stuck in the mindset of the framers of the 1950s. It has been interpreted as a living-evolving document that should be interpreted in line with the general standards present in the contracting states at the time of interpretation. As Bernhardt states:

> [t]his 'dynamic' interpretation dispenses with consideration of the preparatory work and the intentions of the drafters of the treaty at least to the extent to which modern convictions and conditions have been substituted for those which existed in law and society at the time of the conclusion of the treaty.[19]

In *Tyrer v United Kingdom*[20] the Court considered whether corporal punishment in the Isle of Man was a degrading punishment in breach of Article 3 of the ECHR. The Court placed great weight on the evolutionary aspect of the Convention when stating:

12   (1968) 1 EHRR 252.
13   (1989) 11 EHRR 439.
14   Both these aims are found in the Convention itself. See above on the formation of the Council of Europe.
15   See for example the opinion of Judge Fitzmaurice in *Golder v United Kingdom* (1975) 1 EHRR 524.
16   See the Court's judgment in *Wemhoff v Germany* (1968) 1 EHRR 55 and the majority in *Golder*.
17   (1978) 2 EHRR 25.
18   In 1995, the Court referred to the Convention as a 'constitutional instrument of European public order (ordre public)' in *Loizidou v Turkey* (1995) 20 EHRR 99.
19   Bernhardt, R 'Thoughts on the interpretation of Human Rights Treaties' in Matscher, F and Petzold, H ed, *Protecting Human Rights: The European Dimension Studies in Honour of Gérard J Wiarda* (1988) Carl Heymanns Verlag KG, Koeln, pp 65-71 at p 69.
20   See *Tyrer v United Kingdom* (1978) 2 EHRR 1.

the Convention is a living instrument which as the Commission rightly stressed, must be interpreted in the light of present-day conditions. In the case now before it the Court cannot but be influenced by the developments and commonly accepted standards in the penal policy of the member states of the Council of Europe in this field.[1]

At what point the standards become general European standards remains elusive and a certain caution is evident in the Court's references to the evolutionary character of the ECHR. Should a single state be isolated in promoting a practice which impacts on human rights which is out of line with other European states, the Court is more likely to rely on the evolutionary character of the ECHR in finding a violation.[2] However, in order to establish a general standard it appears that more than a simple majority of states with similar standards is needed. In interpreting the legal relationship between a mother and her illegitimate child the Court considered:

at the time when the Convention of 4 November 1950 was drafted, it was regarded as permissible and normal in many European countries to draw a distinction in this area between the 'illegitimate' and the 'legitimate' family. However the Court recalls that this Convention must be interpreted in the light of present-day conditions … the Court cannot but be struck by the fact that the domestic law of the *great majority* of the member states of the Council of Europe has evolved and is continuing to evolve…[3]

The line between an evolutive interpretation of the Convention and judicial legislation is sometimes a fine one which the Court has at times been accused of over-stepping. For example in *Cruz Varas v Sweden*[4] the Swedish government had deported a Chilean national despite a request from the Commission under Rule 36 (now Rule 39) of the Rules of Procedure not to do so. Rule 36 allowed that the Commission could 'indicate to the parties any interim measure the adoption of which seems desirable in the interests of the parties or the proper conduct of the proceedings before it.' It fell to the Court to consider whether the Swedish government, by ignoring the Commission request, had breached its obligation in Article 25 (1) (now Article 34) not to interfere with the effective exercise of the right of petition. The Court found that the Convention did not contain any provision for interim measures and that Rule 36 was a purely internal rule of procedure invented by the Commission and as such had no power to bind contracting parties. However the Court found that the subsequent practice of the contracting states had amounted to almost total compliance with Rule 36 and that this could be interpreted as establishing the agreement of the contracting states to a new interpretation of Article 25 (1).[5]

1   *Tyrer v United Kingdom* (1978) 2 EHRR 1, see *also Dudgeon v United Kingdom* (1981) 4 EHRR 149, *Soering v United Kingdom* (1989) 11 EHRR 439, *B v France* (1987) *A-232-C* para 45-48.
2   See *Tyrer v United Kingdom* (1979) 2 EHRR 330.
3   *Marckx v Belgium* (1979) 2 EHRR 330, see also *Loizidou v Turkey* (1995) 20 EHRR 99 which emphasised that the evolutionary approach had to be preferred as the intentions of the framers represented only the intentions of a minority of the present Contracting states.
4   (1991) 14 EHRR 1.
5   For a critical evaluation of the evolutive interpretation see van Dijk, p and Van Hoof G J H, *Theory and Practice of the European Convention on Human Rights*, (3rd edn, 1998) Kluwer Law, The Hague, pp 77-80.

There are some limits to this form of evolutionary interpretation, as Harris et al point out:

> the Convention will not be interpreted to reflect change so as to introduce into it a right that was not intended to be included when the Convention was drafted. For this reason, Article 12, which guarantees the right to marry, could not be interpreted as including a right to divorce, even though such a right is generally recognised in Europe. In this way, a line is sought to be drawn between judicial interpretation, which is permissible, and judicial legislation, which is not.[6]

The evolutionary character of the ECHR has allowed it to interpret rights in accordance with general movements in European society on the assumption that this is a positive evolutionary process essential for the continued existence of a living European Bill of Rights. However the evolutionary character of the ECHR may be a double-edged sword which, with the entry of Central and Eastern European states to the Council of Europe who generally have lower standards with regard to human rights issues, may dilute the general standard the Court could call upon. In essence the ECHR could potentially de-evolve. The Committee of Ministers has been extremely concerned about this matter and has gone to great lengths to stress that the inclusion of the Central and Eastern European states must not be at the cost of lowering of norms and standards already established within the Council of Europe.[7] States wishing to be members must accept the pre-existing values without lowering any of the Council standards and therefore adjust their legal systems accordingly.[8]

Victim status

In order to apply to the Strasbourg court successfully an applicant must be a 'victim'. Article 34 of the Convention provides that the court can receive applications from 'any person, non-governmental organisation or group of individuals claiming to be a victim of a violation'. Article 34 does not go on to provide a definition of 'victim' status and so the Court has defined the concept. The Strasbourg case law provides that a victim is a person who is at risk of or is actually and directly affected by the act or omission by the state.[9] Relatives of individuals who have been directly affected can also fulfil victim status.[10] Professional associations, non-governmental associations and trade unions can all fulfil victim status as long as they can identify

6   Harris, D J, O'Boyle, M and Warbrick, C, *Law of the European Convention on Human Rights* (1995) Butterworths, p 8.
7   See Drzemczewski, Andrew, 'The Council of Europe's Co-Operation and Assistance Programmes with Central and Eastern European Countries in the Human Rights Field' *Human Rights Law Journal* (1993) pp 229-247.
8   See the Court's backing of this position in *Loizidou v Turkey* (1995) 20 EHRR 99. On the difficulties Russia has in meeting the standards see Bernhardt, Rudolf/ Trechsel, Stefan/ Weitzel, Albert/ Ermacora, Felix, 'Report on the conformity of the legal order of the Russian Federation with Council of Europe standards' (1994) *Human Rights Law Journal,* pp 249-287.
9   See *Marckx v Belgium* (1979) 2 EHRR 330.
10 See *McCann v United Kingdom* (1995) 21 EHRR 97.

a member or member directly affected and show evidence of their authority to act for them.[11] Companies are considered to fulfil victim status without having to show that a member has been affected by an act.[12] Although sometimes non-governmental organisations have been able to claim victim status themselves it has been on the basis of an assumption that the claim is brought on behalf of its members.[13] For example in *Christians Against Racism and Fascism v United Kingdom*[14] an association of religious groups was held to fulfil victim status after a march planed by the association was banned. However, in general, public interest groups cannot in themselves claim victim status unless they can show a member has been directly affected.[15] Pure public interest litigation does not exist at the Strasbourg level. This is very different than the position in domestic law.[16]

Autonomous meaning and real and effective interpretation

Terms that fall for interpretation to the ECtHR are given an autonomous meaning. That is the court does not necessarily accord the term the meaning the domestic authority has given to it. If domestic legislation describes a particular action as a civil offence it may be considered by the Strasbourg court to be criminal if it has the same effect as a criminal offence.[17] The Strasbourg court will also interpret rights so as to 'guarantee not rights that are theoretical or illusory but rights that are practical and effective'.[18] Therefore the right to fair trial includes not just the availability of a court system but effective access to it. This may in certain circumstances mean a right to legal aid.

The doctrine of a margin of appreciation and the principle of proportionality[19]

In interpreting the ECHR two interpretive tools loom large, the doctrine of a margin of appreciation and the principle of proportionality.[20] While the ECtHR starts with the presumption that the Convention Rights and Freedoms should be respected it does recognise occasions when restrictions on rights are allowable. In assessing when this is the case it uses the doctrine of a margin of appreciation and the principle of proportionality.

11 See *Confederation des Syndicats Medicaux Français v France* (1986) 47 DR 255.
12 See Chapter 8.
13 However see *Council of Civil Service Unions v United Kingdom* (1987) 50 DR 228 where a trade union was a victim.
14 (1980) 21 DR 138.
15 See *Klass v Germany* (1978) 2 EHRR 214.
16 Victim status under the ECHR is a narrower concept than 'standing' as it presently exists in RSC Order 53 for the purposes of judicial review. See Chapters 6 and 8.
17 See *Engel v Netherlands (No 2)* (1979-1980) 1 EHRR 706. See also Chapter 11.
18 *Airey v Ireland* (1979) 2 EHRR 305 at 314.
19 See Volume 19, No 1 of the *Human Rights Law Journal* of 30 April 1998 which is devoted exclusively to the Doctrine of the Margin of Appreciation.
20 See Van Dijk, p and van Hoof G J H, (1998) *Theory and Practice of the European Convention on Human Rights*, (3rd edn, 1998) Kluwer Law, The Hague 1998, pp 71-95.

The doctrine of the margin of appreciation is a literal translation from the French language version of the case law and would be perhaps better expressed in English as a doctrine of a margin of discretion. It derives from administrative law concepts prevalent in the German and French courts and is based on a respect for democracy, subsidiarity and a recognition of the limitations of the judicial role in complex policy formulations.[1] The doctrine of the margin of appreciation allows the contracting states a certain measure of discretion when operating in a manner which affects a Convention right.[2] The phrase was first coined in *Lawless v Ireland (No 3)* where the Court stated:

> having regard to the high responsibility that a government bears to its people to protect them against any threat to the life of the nation, it is evident that a certain discretion – a certain margin of appreciation – must be left to the government.[3]

The Court elaborated on the concept in *Buckley v United Kingdom* in stating that '[b]y reason of their direct and continuous contact with the vital forces of their countries, the national authorities are in principle better placed than an international court to evaluate local needs and conditions.'[4]

The Court uses the margin of appreciation doctrine, recognising a certain discretion available to the states when interfering with Convention rights but measuring and restricting its extent should the state go too far.[5] For example should the state wish to interfere with an individual's property, thus affecting a Convention right protected by Protocol 1, Article 1, it is allowed a certain amount of discretion by the Court to interfere with the right if it is in the public interest.[6] In *Handyside v United Kingdom*[7] the Court had to consider whether a restriction of the right to freedom of expression in Article 10 could be justified for the protection of morals. The Court, while heavily emphasising the Court's supervisory role as regard the extent of the margin of appreciation, deferred to the national authority's judgment as to the content of morals and the necessity of a measure to protect them.[8] The factors relevant to the Court's decision will be the nature of the Convention right,[9] the significance of

---

1   Yurow, 'The Margin of Appreciation Doctrine in the Dynamics of European Human Rights Jurisprudence' 3 Conn. JIL 111. This makes the German and French jurisprudence on state discretion of great value in determining how the margin will operate in domestic law. See Chapter 14 (research) for sources of French and German law.
2   For opposing views on the need for a margin see Mahoney, P 'Universality Versus Subsidiarity in the Strasbourg Case Law on Free Speech' (1997) *European Human Rights Law Review* p 364 and Lord Lester 'Universality Versus Subsidiarity: A Reply' (1998) *European Human Rights Law Review*, p 73.
3   (1961) 1 EHRR 15.
4   (1996) 23 EHRR 101 at 129. The European Court of Justice (ECJ) has a similar policy see *Keck* [1993] ECR I-6097.
5   See Lavender, Nicholas 'The Problem of the Margin of Appreciation' (1997) *European Human Rights Law Review*, pp 380-390 for a discussion on the difficulties of the doctrine.
6   See *James v United Kingdom* (1986) 8 EHRR 123.
7   (1976) 1 EHRR 737.
8   The word 'necessary' was interpreted by the Court as implying the existence of a 'pressing social need' which was for the state to assess initially.
9   The margin has been used extensively in justifying violations of Articles 8-11.

the right to the individual and the type of activities concerned.[10] The margin of appreciation is inherently an international law doctrine which recognises the importance of maintaining a concept of 'subsidiarity' if the Court is not to offend national sensitivities by imposing the Court's views on domestic social, economic, cultural and political traditions. As such it should have no direct impact as a domestic interpretative tool. The domestic courts may however develop a concept of discretion similar to the margin doctrine.[11]

All limitations on a Convention right need to have a legitimate aim. The court will assess the legitimacy of the aim which the state claims it was pursuing. In particular Articles 8-11[12] of the Convention set out the legitimate aims that may justify interference with those rights. For example Article 8 provides that the state may not interfere with privacy rights, save where it 'is necessary in a democratic society in the interests of national security, public safety or the economic well-being of the country, for the prevention of disorder or crime, for the protection of health or morals, or for the protection of the rights and freedoms of others.' Legitimate aims are not confined to the aims set out in the Convention. The Court will assess whatever the state claims was its aim in restricting a Convention right to see if it is legitimate. As a result the Court has held that environmental concerns although not specified in the Convention could constitute a legitimate aim.[13]

Should a state wish to restrict a Convention right it will enjoy a margin of appreciation in doing so. The Court will however review the reasons given by the state for the restriction and examine whether they are relevant and sufficient and whether the restriction was 'proportionate to the legitimate aim pursued'.[14] The principle of proportionality allows the Court to assess the context within which a state has restricted a Convention right.[15] The principle applies to the assessment of all restrictions on Convention rights and attempts to achieve a fair balance between individual and community needs. In doing this the court must, even though there is a legitimate aim being pursued by the state, test whether the measure applied to secure it is no more than is strictly necessary to secure that legitimate aim. That test involves assessing the nature of the right involved and whether the measure taken is 'necessary in a democratic society'. The adjective 'necessary' is not synonymous with 'indispensable', nor does it have the flexibility of such expressions as 'admissible', 'ordinary', 'useful', 'reasonable' or 'desirable'; rather, it implies

---

10   See *Olsson v Sweden* (1988) 11 EHRR 259. For a critical analysis of the margin approach see Lavender, N, 'The problem of the Margin of Appreciation' (1997) *European Human Rights Law Review* p 380.

11   See Chapter 7 on the Domestic use of Margin and Proportionality.

12   See Chapter 4.

13   See *Pine Valley Developments v Ireland* (1991) 14 EHRR 319 and *Fredin v Sweden* (1990) 13 EHRR 784.

14   See above p 32, n 20 (van Dijk) p 80. See also *Handyside v United Kingdom* (1976) 1 EHRR 737, *Young, James and Webster v United Kingdom* (1981) 4 EHRR 149, *Dudgeon v United Kingdom* (1981) 4 EHRR 149 and *Moustaquim v Belgium* (1991) 13 EHRR 802.

15   For its use in the EC context see Lord Hoffmann 'A Sense of Proportion' (1998) in Andenas, M and Jacobs, F (Eds), *European Community Law in the English Courts*, p 149.

the existence of a 'pressing social need'.[16] If the measure does not pass this test it is excessive and even though pursuing a legitimate aim it will not be valid.

Both the principle of proportionality and the margin of appreciation are complementary in operation.[17] The margin reflects the fact that it is for the States to make the initial assessment as to the interference with a Convention right and that the court role is supervisory. The principle of proportionality is a tool the court uses to ensure the states do not go too far in exercising their discretion. The Convention provides in Article 1 that it is for the contracting states to 'secure to everyone within their jurisdiction the rights and freedoms defined in section I of this Convention.' Primary responsibility for securing the rights and freedoms of the Convention lies with the states themselves. The principle of proportionality and the margin of appreciation have arisen in recognition of this fact. As Mahoney considered:

> the Convention norm sets a universal minimum standard, which nonetheless incorporates recourse to a principle of subsidiarity in that it allows some scope, albeit not unlimited, for properly functioning democracies to choose different solutions adapted to their different and evolving standards.[18]

The Court's role according to Article 19 of the Convention is to ensure the states observe their obligations under the ECHR. In fulfilling this function the Court sometimes has to balance the state's right to exercise its power for the benefit of the community as a whole, which may be detrimental to an individual's rights and the protection of those individual rights.[19] In doing this it has applied the proportionality principle and the margin of appreciation in an attempt achieve a 'fair balance' between these competing interests.[20] It maintains, however, a strong supervisory role and applies the principle and the doctrine widely or narrowly depending on the context.[1]

As a result, with regard to national security or morality considerations, the state has a wide discretion to restrict rights.[2] If the matter relates to interference with property rights then a more subtle balance is needed and the discretion accorded will very much depend on the consideration of a fair balance between the community and the individual needs.[3] With other rights such as freedom of expression in Article 10, in the context of its impact on a free press[4] or Article 8,

16 See *Handyside v United Kingdom* (1976) 1 EHRR 737, *Sunday Times v United Kingdom* (1979) 2 EHRR 245, *Dudgeon v United Kingdom* (1981) 4 EHRR 149 and *Barthold v Germany* (1985) 7 EHRR 383.

17 For a critical evaluation of the doctrine see Hutchinson, M 'The Margin of Appreciation Doctrine in the European Court of Human Rights' (1999) *International and Comparative Law Quarterly*, Vol 48, pp 638-650.

18 Mahoney, P, 'Universality versus Subsidiarity in the Strasbourg Case Law on Free Speech: Explaining Some Recent Judgments' (1997) EHRLR 364 at 369.

19 See *Rees v United Kingdom* (1986) 9 EHRR 56.

20 On the idea of 'fair balance' see *Sporrong and Lönnroth v Sweden* (1982) 5 EHRR 35.

1   The Canadian courts have a adopted a similar principle of proportionality see *Ross v New Brunswick School District No 15* [1996] 1 SCR 825.

2   See *Leander v Sweden* (1987) 9 EHRR 433.

3   See *James v United Kingdom* (1986) 8 EHRR 123.

4   *Lingens v Austria* (1986) 8 EHRR 407.

privacy in the context of a prisoner's correspondence with his legal adviser[5] the balance will be heavily weighted in favour of protection of the individual right.[6] The state would have to provide very serious justification for the interference with rights of such importance in this context.

In certain cases the Court has refused to accord any discretion to the state. In *Ribitsch v Austria*[7] the case concerned the ill-treatment of a detainee while in police custody. The Court stressed that 'the requirements of an investigation and the undeniable difficulties inherent in the fight against crime cannot justify placing limits on the protection to be afforded in respect of the physical integrity of individuals'. The discretion offered to states is always provisional on the supervision of the Court.

Drittwirkung/horizontal effect, negative and positive rights

The concept of Drittwirkung appears somewhat curiously in most discussions of the interpretation of the Convention rights by the Court. Drittwirkung is a German legal concept that provides that an individual can rely on a national constitutional document to found an action by a private individual against another private individual alleging they have breached rights contained in the constitutional document.[8] Its importance cannot be doubted in terms of the application of the ECHR in the national arena and it is something we return to in Chapter 7 when discussing the horizontal effect of the HRA, but its application in the European Court of Human Rights is extremely limited.[9] This is because none of the rights and freedoms contained in the ECHR can be actioned directly against a private individual through the procedure of the Convention. Article 34 provides that the Court may only receive individual applications about violations of a Convention right committed by a contracting state. No other party, whether an individual or private body, can be held accountable through the Strasbourg machinery. This is not however the end of the matter as a form of indirect Drittwirkung can operate through the states positive obligations under the ECHR.

As explained above written constitutions can contain both negative and positive rights. Negative rights are most closely associated with civil and political rights. Thus the state must not subject an individual to torture (Article 3) or deprive someone unlawfully of their liberty (Article 5). Positive rights are more closely associated with social and economic rights and require the state not just to refrain from interference with rights but to be proactive in securing them.[10]

5   *Campbell v United Kingdom* (1992) 15 EHRR 137.
6   See *Sunday Times v United Kingdom* (1979) 2 EHRR 245 on the narrow discretion accorded to the state when dealing with Article 6 (fair trial).
7   (1995) 21 EHRR 573.
8   For a good general overview of the concept and its applicability see Van Dijk, p and Van Hoof G J H, *Theory and Practice of the European Convention on Human Rights,* (3rd edn, 1998) Kluwer Law, The Hague, pp 22-26.
9   For a detailed consideration Drittwirkung see Alkema, Evert Albert 'The third-party applicability or 'Drittwirkung' of the European Convention on Human Rights' in Matscher, Franz, and Petzold, Herbert (ed) *Protecting Human Rights: The European Dimension, Studies in Honour of Gérard J. Wiarda* (1998) Carl Heymanns Verlag KG, Koeln, pp 33-45.
10   For example the state must protect family life by law see *Marckx v Belgium* (1979) 2 EHRR 330.

For example in *Airey v Ireland*[11] the Court held that Article 6 may sometimes compel the state to provide legal aid when the complexity of the procedure is such that without the assistance of a lawyer it would amount to a denial of access to court.[12] In *Marckx v Belgium*[13] the Court interpreted the right to respect for family life contained in Article 8 (1) as containing positive obligations on the part of the contracting state, to ensure that when operating its domestic legal system it did so in a way that allowed those affected to lead a normal family life.

It is in the positive obligations of the contracting states that we find the indirect application of Drittwirkung. Positive obligations may sometimes impose a duty on the state to protect an individual against infringements of their rights by private parties. Some of the Articles such as Article 4 (freedom from forced labour), Article 8 (the right to respect for private and family life), and Article 11 (freedom of association) are social and economic in nature and require positive acts by the state to secure them.[14] Positive obligations are not just confined to those Articles. The Convention itself either in the wording of the Article or flowing from the nature of the Article provides for positive obligations. Article 2 (1) (right to life), Article 3 (torture), Article 6 (fair trial), Protocol 1, Article 3 (free elections) all fall into this category. Other Articles have in the course of the Strasbourg courts' consideration of these Articles had positive obligations read in. Other rights and freedoms such as Article 10 (expression)[15] have also been held by the Strasbourg court to impose positive obligations primarily because Article 1 of the Convention obliges the contracting states to secure the rights and freedoms contained in the ECHR in their individual jurisdictions. Should they fail to do this or should they default in applying national laws designed to secure the ECHR rights, they may be held responsible by the Court even where the violations have been committed by private parties. In *Young, James and Webster v United Kingdom*[16] the Court held the state responsible for the dismissal of employees by an employer on the grounds that the state had made the dismissal lawful in breach of Article 11. The Court considered that the state had a positive obligation to regulate the conduct of private employers in ensuring the protection of ECHR rights. In *X and Y v Netherlands*[17] the Court found that Dutch domestic law prevented the second applicant from initiating criminal proceedings against a man who had raped her and that this amounted to an infringement of her Article 8 right to respect for private life. There was no effective and practical protection for the applicant in Dutch domestic law and this amounted to a failure on the part of the state to secure respect for her private life.[18] The Court was clear in terms of the positive obligations on the state to secure Convention rights when it stated:

11 (1979) 2 EHRR 305.
12 It also has obligations to provide courts and translators.
13 (1979) 2 EHRR 330.
14 See *Marckx v Belgium* (1979) 2 EHRR 330.
15 *Plattform Arzte fur das Leben v Austria* [1985] 44 DR 65.
16 (1981) 4 EHRR 38.
17 (1985) 8 EHRR 235.
18 See also *Costello – Roberts v United Kingdom* (1993) 19 EHRR 112 and *A v United Kingdom* [1998] 5 BHRC 137.

[t]hese obligations may even involve the adoption of measures designed to secure respect for private life even in the sphere of the relations of individuals between themselves.[19]

With regard to the right in Article 11 to peaceful assembly and freedom of association the Court has held that this is not confined to a minimal duty of non-interference by the state. The obligations of the state with regard to Article 11 extend to protecting those who wish to protest peacefully from interference by private parties who may wish to use violence to oppose the peaceful assembly. The state must take reasonable and appropriate steps to ensure that lawful demonstrations can proceed peacefully.[20]

Derogations[1]

Article 15 of the ECHR allows the contracting states to derogate from the Convention Rights and Freedoms in times of war or other 'public emergency affecting the life of the nation'. This allows the contracting states legitimately to restrict the operation of certain Convention rights without the risk of the ECtHR finding a Convention breach. The ability to derogate is not without limit. The ECtHR will still assess the derogation to see if it is proportionate to the emergency claimed by the contracting state.[2] There are also certain other limits to the contracting states' ability to derogate: a) the derogation must be compatible with other obligations under international law[3] and b) paragraph 2 lists the right to life (Article 2), the prohibition of torture (Article 3) and slavery (Article 4, paragraph 1) and the principles of *nullum crimen, nulla poena sine lege* (Article 7) as non-derogable rights.

Reservations

In 1950 when the ECHR was being drafted it was felt necessary to include a clause allowing the contracting states to express reservations with regard to certain existing national laws which were not compatible with the Convention.[4] As a result Article 57 (formerly Article 64) allows for such reservations as long as they are not of a general character and the reservation contains a brief statement as to the law

---

19   (1985) 8 EHRR 235.
20   *Plattform Arzte fur das Leben* (1988) 13 EHRR 204.
1   See Chapter 4 for Article 15 on derogations.
2   *Aksoy v Turkey* (1996) 23 EHRR 553.
3   For example in the case of obligations under human rights treaties of not merely a regional but worldwide scope such as the International Covenant on Civil and Political Rights (ICCPR). The ICCPR although also containing a derogation clause has a greater number of non-derogable rights listed than the ECHR (eg the freedom of thought, conscience and religion).
4   See generally Frowein, Jochen Abr *'Reservations to the European Convention on Human Rights'* in Matscher, Franz and Petzold, Herbert (ed) *Protecting Human Rights: The European Dimension Studies in Honour of Gérard J Wiarda* (1998) Carl Heymanns Verlag KG, Koeln, pp 193-200.

concerned. Most of the contracting states have made reservations. The UK has one in place with regard to Article 2, Protocol 1 (education).[5]

Occasionally the Court has had to interpret the limits of such reservations. In *Belilos v Switzerland*[6] the Court found that the Swiss government could not rely on a reservation relating to Article 6 because it was too vague and broad to determine its exact meaning and scope. The Court found further that the Swiss reservation had also failed to provide a brief statement as to the law concerned.

Limitations and restrictions

At various times certain contracting states have attempted, while recognising the right of individual petition under Article 34 (formerly Article 25), to limit the scope of the individual petition or, while accepting the compulsory jurisdiction of the Court under Article 32 (Formerly Article 46), to restrict the extent of that competence. Following the Court's decision in *Tyrer v United Kingdom*[7] the UK refused to renew its Article 34 declaration with regard to the Isle of Man. It was only in 1993 that the UK renewed its declaration after changes to the law in the Isle of Man. In 1995 the question of Turkey's Article 34 limitation and restriction of the Court's jurisdiction came under scrutiny. In *Loizidou v Turkey*[8] the Court had to consider whether the Turkish government could rely on a limitation in their Article 34 declaration which excluded the right of individual petition from Northern Cyprus.[9] The Court also considered the validity of certain restrictions placed on the Court's compulsory jurisdiction in Turkey's Article 32 acceptance. The Court found that the limitations and restrictions were incompatible with: a) the nature of the ECHR; b) the provisions of the Convention relating to supervision in light of their object and purpose; and c) the established practice of the contracting states. As such Turkey could not rely on the limitation or restriction.[10]

A European constitution

The ECHR has without doubt impacted greatly on the national laws of the contracting states of the Council of Europe. Individual applicants from all over Europe have challenged state interference with the rights and fundamental freedoms contained in the ECHR and the European Court of Human Rights has on hundreds of occasions upheld those claims. While contracting states have sometimes taken their time in complying with the findings of the Court there have been no cases where a state has refused outright to comply with a ruling of the Court. Despite the lack of any formal mechanism to ensure compliance with a Court judgment, national systems

5   See Chapter 4 for a consideration of Protocol 1, Article 2.
6   (1988) 10 EHRR 466.
7   See *Tyrer v United Kingdom* (1978) 2 EHRR 1.
8   (1995) 20 EHRR 99.
9   The declaration stated that the limitations were not to be considered as reservations.
10 It did allow the restriction on time. Thus a state may restrict petitions before a certain time.

within the contracting states have been adapted to comply with the ECHR as interpreted by the European Court of Human Rights.

The ECHR has over the past 50 years become a European constitutional document of the highest legal order. Convention rights can be claimed by any of the individuals living within a state which has ratified the ECHR.[11] The result has been that since 1950 the treatment of a state's subjects by that state is a matter not just for the individual state but the international community. The existence of a supra-national standard superior to national laws allows the subjects of the state to judge the laws of that state according to the rules of international human rights law and to challenge their legitimacy should they not come up to the superior standard. We turn now in the next chapter to consider the Convention rights themselves.

11   This includes non-nationals of the Council of Europe member states

Chapter four

The Convention rights and freedoms

The convention is drafted in a style very different from the way which we are used to in legislation. It contains wide general statements of principle. They are apt to lead to much difficulty in application; because they give rise to much uncertainty. They are not the sort of thing which we can easily digest.[1]

The ECHR Articles and Protocols

The Articles and Protocols examined below are the complete Rights and Freedoms contained in the ECHR and not just the Convention rights given effect in Schedule 1 of the HRA. We have provided a commentary on all the ECHR Rights and Freedoms for two reasons. First, section 2 of the HRA obliges the domestic courts to take into account the Strasbourg jurisprudence when determining a question concerning a Convention right. As the interpretation of Convention rights often involves a violation of a number of rights the courts will have to have regard to case law which considers rights and freedoms which may not be in Schedule 2. For example it would be very difficult to avoid Article 13 (right to an effective remedy) as it is always combined with other rights and freedoms in seeking a remedy at the Strasbourg level. The government during the course of the debate on section 1 of the HRA recognised that the courts could have regard to the case law on Articles 1 and 13.[2] Second the government may include Protocols 4 and 7 in the Convention rights in the near

---

1   Lord Denning in *R v Chief Immigration Officer, Heathrow Airport and another, ex p Salamat Bibi* [1976] 3 All ER 843 at 847.
2   See Chapter 6 on section 1 HRA 1998.

future. While the UK has yet to ratify Protocol 4 it is presently reviewing it position. The government has ratified Protocol 7 and will introduce it into the HRA once certain family law legislation has been amended.

The ECHR rights and freedoms can generally be categorised into three groups; absolute rights, limited rights and qualified rights. Absolute rights include Article 3 (torture), Article 4 (slavery), Article 7 (no retrospective criminal penalties) and Protocol 6 (abolition of death penalty) from which no derogations or reservations are allowed. Limited rights, for example Article 5 (right to liberty), can be subject to derogations or reservations in certain exceptional circumstances. Articles 8-11 are qualified rights where the rights are conferred subject to qualifications contained in the Articles themselves and additionally derogations or reservations may apply. Interference with these rights will only be allowed if the interference pursues a legitimate aim and it is proportionate to the aim pursued.[3]

> **Article 1- Obligation to respect human rights**: [Not one of the Articles given effect in the HRA]
>
> The High Contracting Parties shall secure to everyone within their jurisdiction the rights and freedoms defined in Section I of this Convention.

Article 1 contains the basic obligation of the contracting parties to 'secure' the rights and freedoms guaranteed in the Convention 'to everyone within their jurisdiction'. It does not form part of the substantive norms guaranteeing specific rights and freedoms, which are contained in section 1 of the ECHR.[4] As such it can only be put forward in Strasbourg in conjunction with one of the other Convention rights. Cases brought before the Court in connection with Article 1 mainly concern two questions: first, with regard to the wording in Article 1 'within their jurisdiction', whether there is an extraterritorial scope of the Convention rights. Secondly, with regard to the wording in Article 1 'obliged to secure', whether a state can be held responsible if domestic legislation does not prohibit private individuals infringing upon the rights of others (horizontal effect/'Drittwirkung').

In the case *Loizidou v Turkey*[5] a Cypriot national living in Nicosia claimed that due to the Turkish occupation of Northern Cyprus in 1974 she was prevented from returning and, thus, could not freely enjoy her property she still owned in the north. The Turkish government argued they could not be held responsible as Northern Cyprus did not form part of Turkey and, therefore, did not fall 'within [their] jurisdiction'. The Court, however, held that Article 1 is not restricted to the national territory of the contracting states. Rather, if violations occur due to control exercised by agents of the state,[6] state responsibility arises regardless of whether this control has been exercised inside or outside national boundaries.

---

3   See Chapter 3 on the interpretation of the ECHR.
4   Section 1(Article 2-18) contains independent substantive rights and freedoms (Articles 2-12) as well as rights of an accessory nature (Articles 13-18).
5   (1995) 20 EHRR 99.
6   In this case the Turkish military.

The case *Young, James v the United Kingdom*[7] concerned the introduction of a closed shop-agreement between British Rail and three trade unions in 1975. The agreement provided that membership in one of these unions was a condition of employment. In the months following the agreement, dozens of employees were dismissed because they refused to comply with the new requirement. The applicants, forming part of this group who were dismissed, could not lodge their complaint against British Rail nor against the trade unions, but only against the United Kingdom as a contracting party to the ECHR.[8] Therefore, the question was whether the UK could be held responsible for the dismissals carried out by a private body. Even though the Court could simply have established that British Rail as a public corporation acted as a state agent being within the control of the UK government, it took another approach: it applied the principle of horizontal effect. In its view, responsibility arose because the British government failed to 'secure' the rights and freedoms through proper legislation prohibiting such agreements.[9]

> **Article 2- Right to life**[10]
>
> 1) Everyone's right to life shall be protected by law. No one shall be deprived of his life intentionally save in the execution of a sentence of a court following his conviction of a crime for which this penalty is provided by law.
>
> 2) Deprivation of life shall not be regarded as inflicted in contravention of this article when it results from the use of force which is no more than absolutely necessary:
> a) in defence of any person from unlawful violence;
> b) in order to effect a lawful arrest or to prevent the escape of a person lawfully detained;
> c) in action lawfully taken for the purpose of quelling a riot or insurrection.

Article 2 imposes upon the national authorities an obligation to protect everyone's right to life, followed by a prohibition on intentional deprivation of life. Through the principle of horizontal effect, this additionally imposes upon the contracting parties a duty to prohibit life-threatening acts and make them punishable by law. It also implies, that the national authorities must abstain from acts which needlessly endanger life. From the formulation of paragraph 1 it is clear that the execution of the death penalty (or extradition to a country where capital punishment is still executed) does not necessarily constitute a violation of this right as long as it is provided for by law.[11] The second paragraph lists several exceptions to the

---

7   (1981) 4 EHRR 38.
8   According to Article 25, paragraph 1 ECHR a petition can only be lodged in the case of a violation of one of the Convention rights 'by one of the High Contracting Parties', ie State Parties.
9   see also Article 11.
10   Further reading: A Sherlock, 'Extradition, Death Row and the Convention' in *European Law Review* 190, pp 87-92; G Williams, 'The Fetus and the 'Right to Life' 'in *Cambridge Law Journal* (1994) pp 71- 80.
11   Note, however, the entering into force of Protocol 6 on 1 March 1985, which prohibits the condemnation to and the execution of the death penalty. The UK has now ratified Protocol 6. See below for a consideration of Protocol 6.

prohibition contained in the first: in situations, where the deprivation of life results from the use of force for a given purpose, and this used force is 'no more than absolutely necessary', the Court will find no violation. Although Article 2 covers a vast range of topics, such as the death penalty, abortion and euthanasia, thus far there have only been a few cases lodged in Strasbourg in connection with Article 2.

The case *McCann v United Kingdom*[12] concerned the killing of three members of the Provisional IRA by soldiers of the British Army. They were suspected of planning a terrorist bombing mission in Gibraltar. Allegedly thinking that the suspects were just about to detonate remote control devices placed in a car, the soldiers shot them at close range. During the examination of both the bodies and the car neither weapons nor detonator devices could be found. In sum, the Court was not persuaded by the UK government's argument that the killings constituted a use of force which was 'no more than absolutely necessary in defence of persons from unlawful violence' within the meaning of Article 2, paragraph 2 (a). Consequently, the UK was found to have acted in breach of the Convention right and had to pay £387,000 (less FF 37,731 legal costs) compensation.

Article 2 has also been invoked in cases concerning extradition to countries where capital punishment is still common practice. The *Soering*[13] case concerned a decision by the British authorities to extradite a German national to the United States where he faced a murder charge in Virginia, a state which still issued death sentences. As Article 2 explicitly permits the death penalty the Court found that an extradition would not amount to a violation of this provision.[14] Article 2 is a non-derogable right, as it is included in the enumeration of Article 15 (2) under which no derogation is allowed in any circumstances whatsoever.

Article 3- Prohibition of torture[15]

No one shall be subjected to torture or to inhuman or degrading treatment or punishment.

Article 3 prohibits torture and inhuman or degrading treatment/punishment. The right is of an absolute character since no exceptions are permitted. As Article 3 covers a wide scope of ill-treatment, numerous cases have been lodged in Strasbourg in connection with this provision. So far, the Court has been very reluctant to find that applications on the basis of a violation of Article 3 amount to torture. In

---

12   (1995) 21 EHRR 97.

13   *Soering v United Kingdom* (1989) 11 EHRR 439.

14   At this time, the UK was not a party to Protocol No 6, which would have prohibited extradition in this case, see below Protocol 6.

15   Further reading: R Alleweldt, 'Protection Against Expulsion Under Article 3 of the European Convention on Human Rights' in *European Journal of International Law* (1993) pp 360-376; A Cassese, 'Prohibition of Torture and Inhuman or Degrading Treatment or Punishment' in Macdonald, R St J/Matscher, F/Petzold, H (eds), *The European System for the Protection of Human Rights* (1993), pp 225- 261; B Phillips, 'The Case for Corporal Punishment in the United Kingdom. Beaten to Submission in Europe?' in *International and Comparative Law Quarterly* (1994) pp 153-163.

Aksoy v Turkey[16] the applicant, allegedly a member of the PKK, had been subjected to so called 'Palestinian Hanging' by the Turkish police. This interrogation method used by the police consisted of blindfolding and stripping the victim naked with his arms tied together behind his back and suspending him by his arms. Electrodes were then connected to his genitals and water was thrown over him while the police electrocuted him. Here, for the first time, the Court found that 'this treatment was of such a serious and cruel nature that it can only be described as torture'. The applicant additionally submitted that in this case the Court should find an 'aggravated violation' of the Convention on grounds of administrative practice in Turkey and his claims for non-pecuniary damage should be doubled. Even though the Court did not give an express opinion as to the question of administrative practice, Mr Aksoy was awarded the full amount sought,[17] which is very rare indeed.

In the case *Ireland v United Kingdom*,[18] the court held that the distinction between the notion of torture and that of inhuman or degrading treatment or punishment derives principally from a difference in the intensity of the suffering inflicted upon the victim.[19] In this case the Court found various practices of the UK government inflicted upon inmates of the Maze and of other Northern Irish prisons, which were commonly referred to as the 'five techniques',[20] in breach of Article 3, but only with regard to inhuman treatment, not torture. Following the judgment, the UK Government gave a solemn declaration not to use these techniques in the future.

The difference between inhuman and degrading treatment and punishment is likewise one of gradation. According to the Court, if ill-treatment is to fall within the scope of Article 3, it 'must attain a minimum level of severity.'[1] The assessment of this minimum will take into account 'all the circumstances of the case, such as the duration of the treatment, its physical or mental effects, and, in some, cases the sex, age and state of health of the victim'.[2]

In the case *Tyrer v United Kingdom*,[3] a 15-year-old boy was sentenced to corporal punishment in the form of three strokes of the 'birch' in accordance with the relevant legislation on the Isle of Man. In defending the actions of the national authorities the UK pointed to public opinion on the island which allegedly strongly supported the retention of corporal punishment. Nevertheless, the Court found that the applicant had been subjected to degrading punishment.

At the time the ECHR was drafted, corporal punishment was still general practice in Europe and Article 3 was intended essentially as a response to the severe atrocities committed by the Nazi-regime. Thus, the Court in finding corporal punishment as falling within Article 3 could only arrive at its finding by neglecting the historical

16   (1996) 23 EHRR 553.
17   Over four thousand million Turkish Lira, an equivalent of £26,000.
18   (1978) 2 EHRR 25.
19   (1978) 2 EHRR 25 at 167.
20   The techniques consisted of forcing the detainee to stand against the wall on their toes for long periods of time, covering their heads with black hoods, subjecting them to constant intense noise, depriving them of sleep and from sufficient food and drink.
1   *Ireland v United Kingdom* (1978) 2 EHRR 25.
2   *Ireland* (n 1 above).
3   (1978) 2 EHRR 1.

interpretation of the Convention. Rather, it observed, that the 'Convention is a living instrument which… must be interpreted in the light of present-day conditions'.[4] Having been informed about the Court's findings, the UK removed the right of individual petition from the Isle of Man: it was only reinstated in 1993. Article 3 is non-derogable under Article 15 (2), as it 'enshrines one of the fundamental values of the democratic societies making up the Council of Europe'.[5]

Article 4- Prohibition of slavery and forced labour[6]

1) No one shall be held in slavery or servitude.

2) No one shall be required to perform forced or compulsory labour.

3) For the purpose of this article the term 'forced or compulsory labour' shall not include:
a)   any work required to be done in the ordinary course of detention imposed according to the provisions of Article 5 of this Convention or during conditional release from such detention;
b)   any service of a military character or, in case of conscientious objectors in countries where they are recognised, service exacted instead of compulsory military service;
c)   any service exacted in case of an emergency or calamity threatening the life or well-being of the community;
d)   any work or service which forms part of normal civic obligations.

Article 4 provides for the protection of freedom from slavery and servitude on the one hand (paragraph 1) and freedom from forced and compulsory labour on the other (paragraph 2).

Slavery indicates that a person is legally owned by another whereas servitude concerns the totality of labour conditions and/or the obligation to work or to service without the person in question having a chance to escape or change the situation.[7] Article 4, paragraph 1 has been invoked only in a few cases, mostly concerning the complaints of detainees who had to perform work in prison. However, the Commission, with special regard to paragraph 3 (a), found the terms slavery and servitude not to be applicable to such situations.[8] Also in this context, the claims of four fifteen- and sixteen-year-old men who were refused a discharge from a nine-year period of Navy service were rejected.[9]

The second paragraph, prohibiting forced and compulsory labour, has played a greater part in the Strasbourg case law. However, so far no complaint has ever

4   *Tyrer v United Kingdom* (1978) 2 EHRR 1.
5   *Soering v United Kingdom* (1989) 11 EHRR 439.
6   Further reading: *Van der Mussele v Belgium* (1983) 6 EHRR 163 as one of the landmark-cases on Article 4; J Andrews, 'Forced Labour at the Belgian Bar' in *European Law Review* (1984), pp 133-135.
7   van Dijk, P/van Hoof G J H, *Theory and Practice of the European Convention on Human Rights*, p 334.
8   Application 7549/76 *X v Ireland* (not published).
9   Applications 3435-3438 *W, X, Y and Z v United Kingdom* (1968) 11 YB 562.

been successful. Two requirements have to be fulfilled in order to amount to a breach of this provision: first, the work performed must be of an involuntary nature and second it must have an unjustifiable or oppressive character.[10] The landmark case on Article 4 is *Van der Mussele v Belgium.*[11] Here, a lawyer complained about his obligation to defend an accused without being entitled to remuneration or reimbursement of his expenses due to the poverty of his client. The Court rejected the alleged breach for two reasons: on the one hand, the applicant, when choosing his profession, knew that this kind of obligation could form part of his tasks. By becoming a defence lawyer, he tacitly consented to the possibility of such obligations arising, this therefore deprived the work of its compulsory character. More importantly, however, when applying the proportionality test, the Court concluded that the burden imposed on the applicant was not excessive or disproportionate to the aim of providing free representation. Under Article 15 (2), no derogations from Article 4, paragraph 1 are permitted under any circumstances. As regards paragraph 2, derogations are allowed.

Article 5 - Right to liberty and security[12] [UK has derogation in place]

1) Everyone has the right to liberty and security of person. No one shall be deprived of his liberty save in the following cases and in accordance with a procedure prescribed by law:

a)   the lawful detention of a person after conviction by a competent court;

b)   the lawful arrest or detention of a person for non-compliance with the lawful order of a court or in order to secure the fulfilment of any obligation prescribed by law;

c)   the lawful arrest or detention of a person effected for the purpose of bringing him before the competent legal authority on reasonable suspicion of having committed an offence or when it is reasonably considered necessary to prevent his committing an offence or fleeing after having done so;

d)   the detention of a minor by lawful order for the purpose of educational supervision or his lawful detention for the purpose of bringing him before the competent legal authority;

e)   the lawful detention of persons for the prevention of the spreading of infectious diseases, of persons of unsound mind, alcoholics or drug addicts or vagrants;

f)   the lawful arrest or detention of a person to prevent his effecting an unauthorised entry into the country or of a person against whom action is being taken with a view to deportation or extradition.

10   Application 4653 *X v Germany* (1974) 17 YB 148.
11   (1983) 6 EHRR 163.
12   Further reading: W. Finnie, ' Anti-Terrorist Legislation and the European Convention on Human Rights' in *Monthly Law Review* (1991) pp 288-293; J Murdoch, 'Safeguarding the liberty of the person: recent Strasbourg Jurisprudence' in *International and Comparative Law Quarterly* (1993) pp 495-522; S Trechsel, 'Liberty and Security of Person' in Macdonald, R St J/Matscher, F/Petzold, H (eds), *The European System for the Protection of Human Rights* (1993), pp 277-344; Eryilmaz, Bedri M *Arrest and detention powers in English and Turkish law and practice in the light of the European Convention on Human Rights* (1999) Nijhoff, The Hague.

2) Everyone who is arrested shall be informed promptly, in a language which he understands, of the reasons for his arrest and of any charge against him.

3) Everyone arrested or detained in accordance with the provisions of paragraph 1.c of this article shall be brought promptly before a judge or other officer authorised by law to exercise judicial power and shall be entitled to trial within a reasonable time or to release pending trial. Release may be conditioned by guarantees to appear for trial.

4) Everyone who is deprived of his liberty by arrest or detention shall be entitled to take proceedings by which the lawfulness of his detention shall be decided speedily by a court and his release ordered if the detention is not lawful.

5) Everyone who has been the victim of arrest or detention in contravention of the provisions of this article shall have an enforceable right to compensation.

Article 5 is aimed at securing for everyone the right to liberty and security of person. According to paragraph 1, a deprivation of liberty is, inter alia, allowed if it is a 'lawful arrest or detention', and if the purpose is to bring the person' before a competent legal authority' on grounds of a 'reasonable suspicion' of having committed an 'offence'.[13] Paragraph 2 entitles the person deprived of his liberty to be informed of the reasons of his detention. Paragraph 3 guarantees the person to be brought 'promptly' before a judicial authority and relates exclusively to detainees on remand as mentioned in Article 3, paragraph 1 (c). This provision ensures that 'no one should be arbitrarily deprived of his liberty'[14] and that the arrest will as short as possible. Article 5, paragraph 4 enshrines the ancient principle of habeas corpus, meaning that everyone who is deprived of his liberty shall be guaranteed that his detention is under the control and supervision of the judiciary. Finally, in the case of an unlawful detention, paragraph 5 obliges the Contracting Parties to grant compensation to the person in question.[15]

In cases concerning Article 5 the Court very often has to strike a balance between the protection of individuals' rights and the need to protect society at large. This becomes especially clear in cases involving terrorism. The case of *Brogan v United Kingdom*[16] concerned the arrest of four men in Northern Ireland. The shortest detention time allowed under the relevant legislation was 4 days and the longest was up to 6 days and 16.5 hours. As a result of the political situation in Northern Ireland in the 1970s and 1980s legislative measures were adopted by the UK governments which gave the police special powers of arrest and detention; these culminated in the 1984 Prevention of Terrorism Act (PTA). The PTA authorised the police to arrest without warrant a person the police officer 'has reasonable grounds for suspecting to be a person involved with acts of terrorism in Northern Ireland'.[17] The applicants, knowing that their arrest was 'lawful' in the sense of

13   Lawson/Schermers, *Leading Cases of the European Court of Human Rights,* p XX.
14   *Schiesser v Switzerland* (1979) 2 EHRR 417.
15   This forms one of the exceptions to section 9 of the HRA.
16   (1988) 11 EHRR 117.
17   Section 12 of the Act.

Article 5, paragraph 1 (c) because of the rules laid down in the Act, claimed the whole Act to be incompatible with Article 5, paragraph 1 (c). They argued that the arrests were not intended to bring the detainees before a competent legal authority, but were only carried out to interrogate the detainees. The Court, however, did not consider it necessary to examine the impugned legislation in abstracto, but confined itself to the facts of the case. It paid special attention to the emergency situation in Northern Ireland and held that the arrests had been made in good faith by the British authorities. The applicants also claimed a breach of Article 5, paragraph 3, as they alleged the British authorities had not brought them before a judge within a reasonable time. Although the Court admitted that the context of terrorism had a prolonging effect on the period during which the authorities may keep a person under arrest before bringing him before a judge, it considered even the shortest period of detention, four days and six hours was too long for the purposes of Article 5, paragraph 3.

As the Convention was at that time not incorporated in the United Kingdom, the applicants could not rely on the violation of Article 5, paragraph 3 before the British courts in order to obtain compensation in the sense of Article 5, paragraph 5. Thus, the Strasbourg court found a violation of paragraph 5 as well. The Court allowed the recovery of the applicants' legal costs. No other claims for compensation had been put forward by the applicant. Following the judgment, the British government took emergency measures under Article 15 (2), reintroducing a derogation from Article 5 it had only withdrawn from in 1984.[18] The derogation is still in place at the time of writing.

Article 6- Right to a fair trial[19]

1) In the determination of his civil rights and obligations or of any criminal charge against him, everyone is entitled to a fair and public hearing within a reasonable time by an independent and impartial tribunal established by law. Judgment shall be pronounced publicly but the press and public may be excluded from all or part of the trial in the interests of morals, public order or national security in a democratic society, where the interests of juveniles or the protection of the private life of the parties so require, or to the extent strictly necessary in the opinion of the court in special circumstances where publicity would prejudice the interests of justice.

2) Everyone charged with a criminal offence shall be presumed innocent until proved guilty according to law.

3) Everyone charged with a criminal offence has the following minimum rights:

---

18   The first notice of derogation from Article 5 was lodged with the Secretary General of the Council of Europe in 1957; the legality of this derogation was discussed in the case *Brannigan and Mc Bride v United Kingdom* (1993) 17 EHRR 539, see below, Article 15.

19   Further reading: Andews, J A, 'Notion of a "tribunal" ' in (1995) *European Law Review*, pp 118-119; van Dijk, P, 'Access to Court' in Macdonald, R St J/Matscher, F/Petzold, H (eds), *The European System for the Protection of Human Rights* (1993), pp 345-379; Wilfinger, Peter, 'Das Gebot effektiven Rechtschutzes' in *Grundgesetz und Europäischer Menschenrechtskonvention* (1995) Lang, Frankfurt/Main.

a)   to be informed promptly, in a language which he understands and in detail, of the nature and cause of the accusation against him;
b)   to have adequate time and facilities for the preparation of his defence;
c)   to defend himself in person or through legal assistance of his own choosing or, if he has not sufficient means to pay for legal assistance, to be given it free when the interests of justice so require;
d)   to examine or have examined witnesses against him and to obtain the attendance and examination of witnesses on his behalf under the same conditions as witnesses against him;
e)   to have the free assistance of an interpreter if he cannot understand or speak the language used in court.

Article 6 guarantees the right to a fair trial, one of the substantial elements of the rule of law. Paragraph 1 contains the right to a fair and public hearing before an independent and impartial tribunal for a person who is charged with a criminal offence, or where civil rights or obligations are being contested. The concept of criminal offence is autonomous. If domestic law describes a particular action as a civil offence it may be considered by the Strasbourg court to be criminal if it has the same effect as a criminal offence.[20] It also includes the requirement that these proceedings must take place within a reasonable time. The following paragraphs are only applicable in cases of criminal proceedings: Paragraph 2 contains the principle of presumption of innocence, and paragraph 3 guarantees several 'minimum rights' to the accused, including the right to information, time and facilities for the defence as well as legal assistance. Additionally the Court has developed several guarantees not expressly mentioned in Article 6 in its case law, such as the right to free legal aid[1] and the right to silence and the privilege against self-incrimination.[2]

In the case *Delcourt v Belgium*[3] the Court held that 'in a democratic society within the meaning of the Convention, the right to a fair administration of justice holds such a prominent place that a restrictive interpretation of Article 6 (1) would not correspond to the aim and purpose of that provision.' This guideline not only applies to the Strasbourg instances, but also to the national courts, which are similarly prohibited from adopting a narrow interpretation of the right to fair trial. Access to the court system is considered by the Strasbourg court to be of fundamental importance. In *Osman v United Kingdom*[4] the ECtHR upheld the applicants claim that their rights under Article 6 of the ECHR had been breached through a blanket immunity against prosecution of the police for carrying out their public functions.

As a result of the importance of this provision, the case law before the Strasbourg court has been immense. Of particular interest is the jurisprudence on the right to a fair and impartial tribunal established by law. In the case *Campbell and Fell v United Kingdom* the Court held that the tribunal need not be 'a Court of law of the

20   See *Engel v Netherlands (No 2)* (1976) 1 EHRR 706. See also Chapter 11.
1   *Airey v Ireland* (1979) 2 EHRR 305.
2   *Funke v France* (1993) 16 EHRR 297.
3   (1970) 1 EHRR 355.
4   (1998) 5 BHRC 293.

classic kind, integrated within the standard judicial machinery of the country'.[5] The notion of independence requires, on the other hand, that the tribunal must function independently of the executive and that there are guarantees in place to enable the Court or tribunal to function independently[6] and that even the semblance of dependence is avoided.[7]

With regard to the freedom to choose a lawyer, the Court has taken the view, that this is not an absolute right, especially where free legal aid is available.[8] However, in *Goddi v Italy*, the Commission took the view, that '[i]n most cases a lawyer chosen by the accused himself is better equipped to undertake the defence. It follows that as a general rule an accused must not be deprived against his will or without his knowledge of the assistance of the defence counsel he has appointed'.[9] This approach was confirmed by the Court in the case *Croissant v Germany*,[10] where it held that the national courts, when appointing defence counsel, must take into account the wishes of the accused. Notwithstanding the importance of Article 6, it does not form part of the provisions enumerated in Article 15 (2) and is therefore a derogable right.

Article 7- No punishment without law[11]

1) No one shall be held guilty of any criminal offence on account of any act or omission which did not constitute a criminal offence under national or international law at the time when it was committed. Nor shall a heavier penalty be imposed than the one that was applicable at the time the criminal offence was committed.

2) This article shall not prejudice the trial and punishment of any person for any act or omission which, at the time when it was committed, was criminal according to the general principles of law recognised by civilised nations.

Article 7 recognises two principles which form essential elements of the rule of law:

First, the principle *nullum crimen sine lege,* prohibiting the (retrospective) incrimination of acts or omissions after they have taken place, and second, the principle of *nulla poena sine lege,* meaning that crimes must not be punished more severely than prescribed by law at the time they were committed. Additionally, the Court has established one further, related principle, namely that criminal laws must not be interpreted expansively by the national authorities, except if such an

5   (1984) 7 EHRR 165.
6   Eg through provisions against discharge at will or on improper grounds. *See Ringeisen v Austria* (1971) 1 EHRR 455.
7   van Dijk, P/ van Hoof, G J H, *Theory and Practice of the European Court of Human Rights,* p 452.
8   Eg Application 6946/ 75, *X v Germany* DR 6 (1977).
9   (1984) 6 EHRR 457.
10   (1992) 16 EHRR 135.
11   Further reading: Beddard, R, 'Retrospective Crime' in *New Law Journal* (1995) p 663; Sherlock, A, 'The nature of a penalty in relation to Article 7 of the Convention' in *European Law Review* (1996), pp 83-86.

interpretation would be advantageous for the accused. As regards the first principle, it lies in the nature of things that applications lodged in Strasbourg often involved common law countries, since by definition common law is developed by the courts and does not always provide for the same degree of legal certainty as a statute. However, rules of common law and also of customary law may provide a sufficient legal basis for a criminal conviction. The conditions are, that the law is adequately accessible and is formulated with sufficient precision so that citizens are able to know the rules and how to abide by them.[12]

The case *SW v United Kingdom*[13] concerned a man who had forced his wife to have sexual intercourse with him against her will. When being tried before the English courts, he invoked marital immunity which up to then existed in traditional English common law but was nevertheless convicted of rape. In his application he claimed, that the decisions of the English courts to lift his immunity and to convict him for rape were in breach of Article 7, paragraph 1. Previously such conduct had been lawful as this was the first case in English legal history in which a husband was convicted of raping his wife with whom he was still living.[14] The court paid special attention to the fact that the law on rape within marriage underwent a fundamental change throughout Europe at that time. Scotland and Ireland had already changed their respective statutes on this matter in 1990, several other countries followed that example shortly after. The court rejected the alleged breach of Article 7, paragraph 1, as in its opinion the criminalisation of forced intercourse between spouses constituted a 'reasonably foreseeable development of law'.[15]

The exception made in the second paragraph has to be seen in the light of the atrocities committed during World War II and the need to legalise the retrospective application of national and international legislation enacted to prosecute those involved in the commission of these atrocities.[16] Put simply the atrocities committed by Nazi officials before and during the war were legal under the Nazi regime. Prosecution for those offences necessarily involved and still involves making something illegal which at the time of the commission of the offence was legal. Accordingly Article 7 (2) does not allow reliance on Article 7 if the crime committed 'was criminal according to the general principles of law recognised by civilised nations' ie genocide. Even though the second paragraph indicates that the guarantees are not absolute, Article 7, paragraph 1 is included in the list of non-derogable rights under Article 15 (2).

12   *SW v United Kingdom* (1995) 21 EHRR 363.
13   A- 335-B (1996) [1996] 1 FLR 434; (1996) 21 EHRR 363; [1996] Fam Law 275.
14   Lawson/Schermers, *Leading Cases of the European Court of Human Rights*, p 614.
15   (1995) 21 EHRR 363.
16   So far, it can not be said with certainty, what kind of offences besides crimes against humanity, such as genocide or apartheid, are covered by Article 7, paragraph 2.

Article 8- Right to private and family life[17]

1) Everyone has the right to respect for his private and family life, his home and his correspondence.

2) There shall be no interference by a public authority with the exercise of this right except such as is in accordance with the law and is necessary in a democratic society in the interests of national security, public safety or the economic well-being of the country, for the prevention of disorder or crime, for the protection of health or morals, or for the protection of the rights and freedoms of others.

Article 8 protects the right to respect for private and family life, the home and correspondence of individuals. As all of the protected rights have been interpreted expansively it is almost impossible to distinguish them clearly and to avoid overlaps; but according to the Strasbourg case law a clear delimitation is not necessary. The Article can therefore be summarised as a right to privacy. Article 8 covers a huge range of issues, such as sexual privacy,[18] registration,[19] medical examination,[20] wiretapping,[1] the principle of allowing families to be united,[2] the search of one's home[3] and the opening and censoring of letters[4] to mention only a few. Under paragraph 2, the right to privacy is subjected to several restrictions. It is therefore not an absolute right.

An example of the negative element of protection guaranteed by Article 8 is the case *Malone v United Kingdom*[5] : here, for several years an antique dealer had been under police surveillance, which included wire tapping, interceptions and recording of conversations on his telephone. He was eventually arrested and charged with the trafficking of stolen goods. However, the conviction failed and he was acquitted. Following his trial he instigated proceedings against the Metropolitan

---

17   Further reading: Cohen- Jonathan, G, 'Respect for Private and Family Life' in Macdonald, R St J/ Matscher, F/ Petzold, H (eds), *The European System for the Protection of Human Rights* (1993), pp 405-444; E Heinze, *Sexual Orientation: A Human Right* Martinus Nijhoff Publishers, Dordrecht; Sherlock, A, 'Article 8 and telephone tapping: *Huvig* case and *Kruslin* case' in *European Law Review* (1990) pp 411-413; Sherlock, A, 'Family life, deportation and the European Convention', in *European Law Review* (1992) pp 79-80; Sherlock, A, (1993) 'Searches and investigations and the Convention; *Niemietz v Germany*' in *European Law Review* (1993) pp 465-468.
18   Eg *Dudgeon v United Kingdom* (1981) 4 EHRR 149 concerning homosexuality.
19   Eg *Leander v Sweden* (1987) 9 EHRR 433 concerning secret police registers.
20   Eg *Herczegfalvy v Austria* (1992) 15 EHRR 437 concerning compulsory administering of food in a hospital.
1   Eg *Klass v Germany* (1978) 2 EHRR 214, concerning German legislation authorising wiretapping.
2   Eg *Abdulaziz, Cabales and Balkandali v United Kingdom* (1985) 7 EHRR 471, concerning the denial of permission of spouses living abroad to join their family in the UK.
3   Eg *Niemietz v Germany* (1992) 16 EHRR 97 concerning the search of a lawyer's office.
4   Eg *Golder v United Kingdom* (1975) 1 EHRR 524 concerning censorship of prisoner's correspondence with his lawyer.
5   (1984) 7 EHRR 14.

Police before the national courts, claiming that the surveillance methods had violated his rights, even if done pursuant to a warrant of the Home Secretary. He claimed not to have an effective remedy and that he therefore had to rely on Article 8 of the ECHR. The Vice-Chancellor, Sir Robert Megarry, dismissed the applicant's claim for the reason that the Convention did not confer any direct rights into English law. As a treaty it was in his words not justiciable in the Court. The Strasbourg court gave extensive consideration to whether the interference with the applicant's rights were justifiable under paragraph 2 of Article 8 of the Convention. It held that 'the phrase "in accordance with the law" relates to the quality of the law, required to be compatible with the rule of law'[6] and eventually observed that 'it cannot be said with any reasonable certainty what elements of the powers to intercept are incorporated in legal rules and what elements remain within the discretion of the executive [in England and Wales]... To that extent, the minimum degree of legal protection to which citizens are entitled under the rule of law in a democratic society is lacking.'[7] Thus, the Court found that there had been a breach of Article 8. Following the judgment, new legislation was introduced to provide stricter guidelines for surveillance activities.[8]

The notion of 'respect' in Article 8 implies that the national authorities are again not only under a duty to refrain from acts that might constitute a violation of Article 8 but also have a positive obligation to secure such 'respect'. An example of the positive element of the rights protected in Article 8 is the case *X & Y v Netherlands*[9] : here the applicants did not claim that the national authorities had violated their right to private and family life but that they had failed to protect their rights from being interfered with by other individuals. Y, a sixteen-year-old, mentally handicapped girl had been sexually abused while residing in a special institution for mentally ill children. Due to a loophole in the Dutch law, it was impossible to institute criminal proceedings against the perpetrator, as Y did not fall within any of the categories of persons protected by law.[10] The Court considered that the contracting parties have a positive obligation to provide criminal legislation which aims to ensure that private individuals respect the private life of others. As the Netherlands had failed to do so, the Court found a breach of Article 8. Y was awarded 3,000 Fl non-pecuniary damages and Dutch laws were amended:[11] it is now an offence in Holland to make sexual advances to a mentally handicapped person. As Article 8 is not included in the enumeration of rights under Article 15 (2), derogations from this provision are allowed.

6   A-82 § 67.
7   A- 82 § 79.
8   However the Regulation of Investigatory Powers Bill 2000 raises serious human rights issues despite a statement of compatibility from the Home Secretary.
9   (1985) 8 EHRR 235.
10   The law at that time only covered offences against minors under the age of sixteen and 'helpless' people, whereby helpless only referred to physical incapacity not mental.
11   They had actually amended them after the Commission decision.

Article 9- Freedom of thought, conscience and religion[12]

1) Everyone has the right to freedom of thought, conscience and religion; this right includes freedom to change his religion or belief and freedom, either alone or in community with others and in public or private, to manifest his religion or belief, in worship, teaching, practice and observance.

2) Freedom to manifest one's religion or beliefs shall be subject only to such limitations as are prescribed by law and are necessary in a democratic society in the interests of public safety, for the protection of public order, health or morals, or for the protection of the rights and freedoms of others.

Article 9, paragraph 1 protects the right to freedom of thought, conscience and religion, without making any restriction. It is, thus, an absolute right, which is aimed at preventing indoctrination by the state. However, the freedom to manifest one's belief, as stated in paragraph 2, is subject to limitations.

The first case before the Strasbourg court involving an alleged breach of Article 9 was *Kokkinakis v Greece*.[13] The applicant, a 74-year old Jehovah's Witness, had been convicted and sentenced to four months' imprisonment for proselytism (converting or attempting to convert someone) a criminal offence under Greek law. Even though the applicant assured the court he had only been engaged in a religious discussion, the Greek courts had found him to have attempted to 'intrude into the religious beliefs' of a member of the Christian Eastern Orthodox Church, the dominant religion in Greece and, thus, guilty of the alleged offence. The Strasbourg court emphasised that, even though Article 9 does include protection of the right to try to convince others of one's beliefs, improper proselytism is not compatible with maintaining respect for the freedom of thought, conscience and religion of others. Apparently the Court balanced these competing rights against each other: since in the Court's view Greece failed to show that the applicant really had used improper means in the first place, Greece could not justify its interference with the applicant's right under paragraph 2 on grounds of a 'pressing social need'. After having found a violation of Article 9, the Court awarded the applicant 400,000 Drachmas non-pecuniary damages and 2,789,500 Drachmas legal costs.

Several cases concerning conscientious objectors to military or substitute service,[14] as well as cases challenging restrictions imposed on prisoners in the manifestation of their religion,[15] have been put forward in Strasbourg but have been dismissed by the Commission at the admissibility stage as manifestly ill-founded. Although

---

12 Further reading: Pannick, D, 'Religious feelings and the European Court' in *Public Law* (1995) pp 7-10; Shaw, M N, 'Freedom of Thought, Conscience and Religion' in Macdonald, R St J/ Matscher, F/ Petzold, H (eds), *The European System for the Protection of Human Rights* (1993), pp 445-463; Sherlock, A, 'Case of *Kokkinakis v Greece*' in *European Law Review* (1994) pp 226-228 Blum, Nikolaus, *Die Gedanken-Gewissens-und Religionsfreiheit nach Art 9 der Europäischen Menschenrechtskonvention* (1990) Duncker und Humbolt, Berlin.

13 (1993) 17 EHRR 397.

14 See eg Application 10600/ 83, *Johansen v Norway* (1985) 44 DR 155 concerning the enforcement of performance of substitute civilian service by contracting states.

15 See eg Application 5947/ 72 *X v United Kingdom* (1976) 5 DR 8 concerning the refusal to take religious belief into account in providing food for prisoners.

Article 9 is not listed in Article 15 (2), and is therefore a derogable right, it should be almost impossible for a state to establish that an interference with the freedom of thought, conscience or religion as regards the private spirituality of a person, is, according to Article 15 (1), 'strictly required by the exigencies of the situation' and therefore justified.

> **Article 10- Freedom of expression**[16]
>
> 1) Everyone has the right to freedom of expression. This right shall include freedom to hold opinions and to receive and impart information and ideas without interference by public authority and regardless of frontiers. This article shall not prevent States from requiring the licensing of broadcasting, television or cinema enterprises.
>
> 2) The exercise of these freedoms, since it carries with it duties and responsibilities, may be subject to such formalities, conditions, restrictions or penalties as are prescribed by law and are necessary in a democratic society, in the interests of national security, territorial integrity or public safety, for the prevention of disorder or crime, for the protection of health or morals, for the protection of the reputation or rights of others, for preventing the disclosure of information received in confidence, or for maintaining the authority and impartiality of the judiciary.

Article 10, paragraph 1 protects freedom of expression, including the right to hold opinions and receive and impart information. The protection of artistic expression is also covered by this provision. Article 10 can be invoked by both natural and legal persons.[17] The Court emphasised on several occasions that Article 10 constitutes 'one of the essential foundations of a democratic society and is one of the basic conditions for its progress',[18] and, thus, adopted a broad interpretation. Applications made under Article 10 have often involved journalists and writers. In order to support the press in playing 'its vital role as a watchdog',[19] the Court has always scrutinised very closely whether restrictions imposed on the publication of information amounted to censorship. Although the right to impart information that the public has a right to receive may justifiably have to be restricted on the basis of

16   Further reading: Andrews, J, 'Freedom of Speech and Government Sensitivities' in *European Law Review* (1992) pp 471-473; Lester, A, 'Freedom of Expression' in Macdonald, R St J/ Matscher, F/ Petzold, H (eds), The European System for the Protection of Human Rights (1993), pp 465-491; Sherlock, A, 'Broadcasting Rights and the Convention' in *European Law Review* (1990) pp 403-404; Sherlock, A, 'Freedom of Expression: how far should it go?' in *European Law Review* (1995) pp 329-337.
17   *Autronic AG v Switzerland* (1990) 12 EHRR 485, Drettman, F,'Wirtschaftswerbung und Meinungsfreiheit' in *Festschrift für Rodolf Lukes zum 65* (1989) Geburtstag, Koeln p 287.
18   *Handyside v United Kingdom* (1976) 1 EHRR 737; *Lingens v Austria* (1986) 8 EHRR 407; *Jersild v Denmark* (1994) 19 EHRR 1.
19   *Observer and Guardian v United Kingdom* (1991) 14 EHRR 153.

the protection of the reputation of others, it will very much depend on the circumstances of each case.[20]

Through the principle of horizontal effect, the contracting states may be under a duty to create a legal obligation for the press to publish replies or rectifications. They may also be under an obligation to protect journalistic resources. In the case *Goodwin v United Kingdom*,[1] a journalist received information about the financial problems of a British company by a person on an unattributable basis. According to the applicant, he had no reason to think that the information had derived from a stolen or confidential document. Thus, before publishing his findings, he contacted the company in question to verify the alleged financial difficulties. It then became clear, that the information had been derived from a confidential draft corporate plan. The British courts then granted an interim injunction to the company restraining the journalist from publishing any of the information he had received. Additionally, the court ordered the journalist to disclose the identity of the source. As the applicant declined to do so, the national courts imposed a fine upon him. The Strasbourg court took the view that 'limitations on the confidentiality of journalistic sources call for the most careful scrutiny by the court'.[2] Notwithstanding the margin of appreciation available to the national authorities, the Court did not regard the restrictions imposed on the applicant as having been necessary in a democratic society. When balancing the company's interest in unmasking a disloyal employee against the interest of a democratic society in securing a free press,[3] the Court found in favour of the applicant. The Court, however rejected the applicant's claim for non-pecuniary damage, but considered the outcome of the case to constitute a just satisfaction. It only awarded him £37,595 for legal costs.

Even though paragraph 2 contains an exceptionally broad range of restrictions to the freedoms guaranteed in paragraph 1, it should be taken into account that, in the words of the Court, these exceptions must be 'narrowly interpreted and the necessity for any restrictions must be convincingly established'.[4] On the other hand, as mentioned above, it very much depends on the subject matter. With regard to the case law, it can be observed that the national authorities enjoy a wide margin of appreciation when commercial speech is involved. In essence commercial expression is not essential to promote a democratic society and so is accorded a lesser level of protection. This is something we return to in greater detail in Chapter 10.

---

20 For example, information or opinions about governing politicians must not be restricted whereas information about private persons not of public concern may be accorded a higher level of protection. Factual accuracy was however emphasised by the House of Lords in *Reynolds v Times Newspapers Ltd* [1999] 4 All ER 609 even where politicians were concerned. See also Young, Alison L 'Fact, Opinion, and the Human Rights Act 1998: Does English Law Need to Modify its Definition of "Statements of Opinion" to Ensure Compliance with Article 10 of the European Convention on Human Rights?' in *Oxford Journal of Legal Studies*, Vol 20 No 1 2000, pp 89-107.
1 (1996) 22 EHRR 123, Reports 1996- II, Volume 7, § 28.
2 Ibid, Reports 1996- II, § 40.
3 Ibid, Reports 1996- II, § 45.
4 *Observer and Guardian v United Kingdom* (1991) 14 EHRR 153.

Article 10 is not enumerated in Article 15 (2) and is therefore a derogable right. However, as it has already been mentioned in connection with Article 9, it should be almost impossible for a contracting state to show that a restriction of the freedom to hold an opinion, which is closely linked to the freedom of thought, might ever be 'strictly required' in the sense of Article 15 (2).[5]

Article 11- Freedom of assembly and association[6]

1) Everyone has the right to freedom of peaceful assembly and to freedom of association with others, including the right to form and to join trade unions for the protection of his interests.

2) No restrictions shall be placed on the exercise of these rights other than such as are prescribed by law and are necessary in a democratic society in the interests of national security or public safety, for the prevention of disorder or crime, for the protection of health or morals or for the protection of the rights and freedoms of others. This article shall not prevent the imposition of lawful restrictions on the exercise of these rights by members of the armed forces, of the police or of the administration of the State.

Article 11, paragraph 1 protects the rights to freedom of peaceful assembly and to freedom of association, including the right to form and join trade unions. In connection with Article 11 it became clear on several occasions in the Strasbourg case law that in order to protect rights effectively, it cannot be enough that states simply do not interfere with these rights. Moreover, the obligation to 'secure' the enjoyment of these rights can go as far as to involve, besides preventing and remedying any breach thereof, the adoption of measures in the sphere of relations between private individuals[7] ('Drittwirkung'/ horizontal effect).

Thus, in the case of *Plattform Ärzte für das Leben v Austria*[8] the applicants, an association against legalised abortion, did not claim that the national authorities had interfered actively in a demonstration held by Plattform, but that the police had failed to protect the peaceful demonstrators against disruptions by counter-demonstrators. Not only did the Court confirm its case law with respect to positive obligations[9] and accept for the first time that such obligations can arise under Article 11 as well, but it held that national authorities can additionally be under a duty to intervene in relations between private individuals. However, in the context of horizontal effect, in the words of the Court, the national authorities enjoy a 'wide

---

5   van Dijk, P and van Hoof G J H, *Theory and Practice of the European Convention on Human Rights*, p 585.
6   Further reading: Andrews, J, 'The Closed Shop Case' in (1981) *European Law Review* pp 412-416; Andrews, J, 'The right to non- association' in *European Law Review* 1994, pp 230-232; Tomuschat, C, 'Freedom of Association' in Macdonald, R St J/ Matscher, F/ Petzold, H (eds), *The European System for the Protection of Human Rights* (1993), pp 493-513; Gallwas, H U ,'Das Grundrecht der Versammlungsfreiheit, Art 8 GG' in (1986) JURA p 484.
7   van Dijk, P and van Hoof G J H, *Theory and Practice of the European Convention on Human Rights*, p 589.
8   *Plattform Ärzte für das Leben v Austria* (1988) 13 EHRR 204.
9   See eg *Marckx v Belgium* (1979) 2 EHRR 330 (p 37 above) with regard to Art 8.

discretion in the choice of means to be used'.[10] It is important to note that this right to protection is not absolute but is limited again by justifications such as 'the protection of the rights and freedoms of others' contained in paragraph 2.[11] Therefore, taking into account that the police actually had taken at least some protective measures, Plattform's complaint under Article 11 was regarded as manifestly ill-founded.

In the case *Young, James and Webster v United Kingdom*[12] Article 11 appeared in quite a different context. Here, the question was whether the applicants could be obliged to join a trade union under the threat of dismissal if they would not do so. The background was a 'closed-shop' agreement between British Rail and three trade unions making membership in one of these unions compulsory for British rail employees. The Court found that Article 11 encompasses a negative right to association, ie the right not to assemble, not to associate or not to join a trade union.[13] Even though the Court did not review the closed-shop system as such, the compulsory membership was found to be in breach of Article 11, as it had been introduced after the applicants had entered into the contract of employment. The applicants in this case were awarded amounts for pecuniary and non-pecuniary loss of between £10,000 and £46,000 and costs of £65,000. While a change of government in the UK had already brought about new legislation strengthening the position of employees who did not wish to join trade unions, the judgment led the UK to introduce further changes in this area.[14]

Article 11 is not an absolute right as it is open to several restrictions under paragraph 2, especially the so called 'necessity-test'.[15] Additionally, special exceptions are made for members of the armed forces, police and for 'the administration of the State'.[16] As Article 11 is not included in the list of non-derogable rights in Article 15 (2), derogations are allowed.

Article 12- Right to marry[17]

Men and women of marriageable age have the right to marry and to found a family, according to the national laws governing the exercise of this right.

---

10 A- 139 § 32
11 Plattform's complaint under Article 11 had already been declared inadmissible by the Commission, but the case was referred to the Court under Article 13. Nevertheless, the Court discussed the scope of Article 11 extensively.
12 (1981) 4 EHRR 38, see also the discussion under Article 1.
13 The court considered that 'a threat of dismissal involving loss of livelihood is a most serious form of compulsion, and, in the present instance, it was directed against persons engaged by British Rail before the introduction of any obligation to join a particular trade union ... such a form of compulsion, in the circumstances of this case, strikes at the very substance of the freedom guaranteed by Article 11' A- 44 § 55.
14 See Resolution DH (83) 3 adopted by the Committee of Ministers under Art. 54 on 23 March 1983.
15 Restrictions are justified, if they are 'necessary in a democratic society', paragraph 2.
16 For the notion of 'administration of a state' see the Case *Vogt v Germany* (1995) 21 EHRR 205 where a teacher was dismissed on grounds of her political activities in the German Communist Party (DKP).
17 Further reading: Armstrong, C/Walton, T 'Transsexuals and the Law' in (1990) *New Law Journal* p 1384; Sherlock, A, 'Case of *F v Switzerland*' in: *European Law Review* (1988) pp 368-370.

Article 12 protects the right of men and women of marriageable age to marry and to found a family. Even though it does not include a separate paragraph for restrictions, Article 12 is limited by its very wording, 'according to the national laws governing the exercise of this right'. Thus, restrictions may result from municipal laws. Of course, these restrictions must be reasonable and may not amount to violations of other provisions of the ECHR or its Protocols.[18]

Clearly, Article 12 prohibits national authorities placing sanctions on marital and/ or parental status,[19] and, through the principle of 'Drittwirkung', obliges them to prevent private individuals from doing so.[20] It is hard to assess, which positive obligations of national authorities may arise under Article 12, especially with respect to financial means that have to be granted in order to enable persons to marry or to found a family.

In the case *Johnston v Ireland*,[1] the question was, whether Article 12 includes a negative element as well, namely the right to divorce, as a marriage at that time could not be dissolved under Irish law. The Court derived from the travaux préparatoires, that the contracting parties did not intend to grant a right to divorce. According to the Court, an evolutive interpretation could in this case not be adopted, as Protocol 7, Article 5 (equality of spouses) introduced in 1984 did not include such a right.

Whether a national law that prohibits marriages between persons of the same sex amounts to a breach of Article 12 was abruptly rejected by the Court in *Rees v United Kingdom*[2] when it stated that 'the right to marry refers to the traditional marriage between persons of the opposite biological sex.'[3] The Court upheld this view four years later, in 1990, in the *Cossey* case.[4] Although the court acknowledged, that some of the contracting states might now regard same sex marriages as valid, the Court observed that 'the developments ... cannot be said to evidence any general abandonment of the traditional concept of marriage'.[5] As it is not included in the enumeration under Article 15 (2), Article 12 is a derogable right.

> **Article 13- Right to an effective remedy**[6] [Not included in the Convention rights given effect in the HRA][7]
>
> Everyone whose rights and freedoms as set forth in this Convention are

---

18   Eg a law permitting compulsory sterilisation would be incompatible with Art 3 of the Convention.

19   van Dijk, P/van Hoof G J H p 58, n 7, p 602.

20   Eg the dismissal of employees on the basis of them becoming a parent or marrying.

1   (1986) 9 EHRR 203.

2   (1986) 9 EHRR 56.

3   A- 106 § 49.

4   *Cossey v United Kingdom* (1990) 13 EHRR 622.

5   A- 184 § 46.

6   Further reading: Hampson, F J, 'The Concept of an "Arguable Claim" under Article 13 of the European Convention on Human Rights' in *International and Comparative Law Quarterly* (1990) pp 891-899; Sherlock, A, 'The guarantee of an effective remedy; case of *Plattform Ärzte für das Leben* in (1988) *European Law Review* p 431.

7   It does however have an effect through the use of the Strasbourg case law in the domestic courts. See the discussion of Article 13 in Chapter 6 in the context of section 1 HRA 1998.

> violated shall have an effective remedy before a national authority notwithstanding that the violation has been committed by persons acting in an official capacity.

According to Article 13, everyone whose Convention rights or freedoms have been violated is entitled to an effective remedy before a national authority. It is clear from the wording, that Article 13 is of an ancillary nature, as it can only be invoked in conjunction with one of the substantive provisions of the Convention.[8] It entitles citizens to obtain control of compliance with the Convention, not only before the Strasbourg court, but rather at the domestic level, as the former only fulfils a supervisory function.

The Court has made clear that the application of the norm does not require that a violation of one of the other rights has already been established. Rather, it introduced an 'arguability-test',[9] which will be applied on a case-by-case basis. In order to fulfil the test criteria, the applicant must have an arguable claim that one of his rights under the Convention has been violated. To have such an arguable claim there must be some factual substantiation leading to a prima face Convention issue. Regarding the wording 'notwithstanding that the violation has been committed by persons acting in an official capacity', both the Commission and the Court have taken the view that this does not include the legislator. Thus there is no Article 13 guarantee where the violation occurs as the direct result of legislation, 'Article 13 does not guarantee a remedy allowing a contracting state's laws as such to be challenged before a national authority on the ground of being contrary to the Convention'.[10] The ECtHR has taken this position because to hold otherwise would be to require the contracting states to incorporate the Convention directly into domestic law. In the case *Observer and Guardian v United Kingdom*[11] it was held that the contracting states are under no obligation to incorporate the Convention into domestic law.

In order for a remedy to be effective it should involve an assessment of the claim and the possibility of rectification. In *Govell v United Kingdom*[12] the Commission took the view that a complaint to the Police Complaints Authority (PCA) was an insufficiently effective remedy because the PCA did not have the requisite level of independence. Thus the standard of review by self-regulating bodies in the UK is likely to come under scrutiny under Article 13 combined with Article 6 (fair trial).

The extent of the effective remedy requirement has been dealt with in the *Aksoy* case.[13] The Court observed that the scope of the obligation under Article 13 varies depending on the nature of the applicant's complaint. The more serious the effect of the breach the stricter the effectiveness requirement. In the instant case, the applicant had been subjected to cruel torture in police custody. The Court paid special attention to the importance of the prohibition of torture. The Court held,

8   Articles 2-12 ECHR.
9   Established in *Silver v United Kingdom* (1983) 5 EHRR 347.
10   *Leander v Sweden* (1987) 9 EHRR 433.
11   (1991) 14 EHRR 153.
12   Appl 27237/95 Commission 14 January 1998: [1999] EHRLR 121.
13   (1996) 23 EHRR 553, see the discussion under Article 3.

that where 'an individual has an arguable claim that he has been tortured by agents of the state, the notion of an effective remedy entails…a thorough and effective investigation capable of leading to the identification and punishment of those responsible…'.[14] Faced with the fact that the Turkish authorities had not instigated any investigation into the subject matter at all, the Court found a violation of Article 13.

Article 14- Prohibition of discrimination

The enjoyment of the rights and freedoms set forth in this Convention shall be secured without discrimination on any ground such as sex, race, colour, language, religion, political or other opinion, national or social origin, association with a national minority, property, birth or other status.

Article 14 contains the prohibition of discrimination on a number of non-exhaustively enumerated grounds. By definition, Article 14 can have no independent meaning, as its applicability is limited to the exercise of other Convention rights or freedoms.[15] However, this linkage-principle does not necessarily presuppose a breach of that other provision. In the *Belgian Linguistic Case,*[16] the Court held that 'a measure which in itself is in conformity with the requirements of the Article enshrining the right or freedom in question may however infringe this Article when read in conjunction with Article 14 for the reason that it is of a discriminatory nature'.[17] The only requirement is that the facts at issue 'fall within the ambit of one or more' of the substantive rights.[18]

The linkage-principle goes even further when it comes to positive obligations of the Contracting Parties. A state may not have to undertake a certain measure in order to give effect to a Convention right.; but once it does take that concrete measure, the state must apply it without discrimination. In the *Abdulaziz* case, three women of foreign birth living permanently and legally in the UK, claimed that the Government had violated Article 8 (Privacy and Family Life) taken in conjunction with Article 14 by denying their foreign spouses permission to join them in the UK. The relevant immigration rules at that time[19] provided for a grant of leave for wives and fiancées seeking to join or remain with their husbands legally settled in the United Kingdom, a fact attributed by the UK government to long-standing commitment to the reunification of the families of male immigrants. However, these rules did not apply to husbands and fiancés of female immigrants. The Court made clear that there is no right to immigration, and that states have authority over their borders. Thus the alleged breach of Article 8 was rejected. Nevertheless, the Court

---

14   P 61, n 13.
15   Confirmed in *Airey v Ireland* (1979) 2 EHRR 305; *Abdulaziz, Cabales and Balkandali v United Kingdom* (1985) 7 EHRR 471; *Rasmussen v Denmark* (1984) 7 EHRR 371, *Karlheinz Schmidt v Germany* (1994) 18 EHRR 513.
16   *Belgian Linguistics v Belgium (No 2)* (1968) 1 EHRR 252.
17   *Belgian Linguistics, A-6* p 33.
18   *Abdulaziz v United Kingdom* (1985) 7 EHRR 471.
19   Immigration Act 1971 and the 'Statement of Changes in Immigration Rules', laid before Parliament at 20 February 1980 (HC 394).

did not accept the UK government's argument, that their generosity towards non-national female spouses was an extra benefit and they were not obliged to give this extra treatment to male spouses as well. Rather, the Court held, that, once such a benefit is granted, it has to be granted in a non-discriminatory way. The legislation in question was therefore found to be in breach of Article 8 in conjunction with Article 14 on grounds of sex. Following the judgment, the UK government had to pay the applicants £28,768 less FF8,825 legal costs and amended its immigration laws. However, rather than equalise the situation by allowing all spouses to join their partners the new provisions removed the difference of treatment by making it equally difficult for wives and fiancées to join their male spouses in the UK.

The categories under which discrimination can be claimed, are not exhaustively enumerated. The use of the wording 'other-status' at the end of Article 14 has enabled the Court to establish new categories without requiring an amendment to the Convention. In the *Marckx* case[20] the Court found Belgium to have violated Article 8 in conjunction with Article 14, as under certain Belgian laws un-married mothers and children out of wedlock experienced serious disadvantages. By following a dynamic interpretation of the Convention and adapting its meaning to the values of the present time, the Court incorporated un-married mothers and so-called illegitimate children into the categories of grounds on which discrimination is prohibited.

It is noteworthy, that Article 14 is only of a subsidiary nature. Once it has found a breach of one of the substantive Convention rights and freedoms, the Court does not deem it necessary to continue to examine a possible violation of Article 14.[1]

Article 15- Derogation in time of emergency[2]

1) In time of war or other public emergency threatening the life of the nation any High Contracting Party may take measures derogating from its obligations under this Convention to the extent strictly required by the exigencies of the situation, provided that such measures are not inconsistent with its other obligations under international law.

2) No derogation from Article 2, except in respect of deaths resulting from lawful acts of war, or from Articles 3, 4 (paragraph 1) and 7 shall be made under this provision.

3) Any High Contracting Party availing itself of this right of derogation shall keep the Secretary General of the Council of Europe fully informed of the measures which it has taken and the reasons therefor. It shall also inform

---

20   *Marckx v Belgium* (1979) 2 EHRR 330.
1   Only very exceptionally, it additionally examines the alleged breach of Article 14, see eg *Marckx v Belgium*, where a breach of Article 8 had already been found.
2   Further reading: Andrews, J, 'Derogation from Article 5 (3) by the United Kingdom' in (1994) ELR, pp 110-112; Hartmann, J F, 'Derogating from Human Rights Treaties in Public Emergencies' in (1981) Harvard International Law Journal, pp 1- 52; Marks, S, 'Civil Liberties at the Margin: the UK Derogation and the European Court of Human Rights' (1995) *Oxford Journal of International Law*, pp 69-95.

the Secretary General of the Council of Europe when such measures have ceased to operate and the provisions of the Convention are again being fully executed.

Under Article 15 the contracting parties are authorised to temporarily derogate from the protected Convention rights and freedoms in times of war or the case of an 'emergency threatening the life of the nation'. There are certain limits to this derogation: it has to be compatible with other obligations under international law[3] and paragraph 2 lists the right to life (Article 2), the prohibition of torture (Article 3) and slavery (Article 4 paragraph 1) and the principles of *nullum crimen, nulla poena sine lege* (Article 7) as non-derogable rights.

A valid derogation is a restriction to the Convention rights and freedoms additional to those already incorporated in the distinct Articles themselves. Thus, even if there is an interference with one of the rights and freedoms protected, the Court will find no violation thereof because the interference is justified. Under Article 15, the contracting parties enjoy a very wide margin of appreciation in assessing, whether there is indeed such an emergency situation. In *Ireland v United Kingdom*[4] the Court held: 'It falls in the first place to each contracting state, with its responsibility for 'the life of (its) nation', to determine whether that life is threatened by a 'public emergency', and, if so, how far it is necessary to go in attempting to overcome the emergency. By reason of their direct and continuous contact with the pressing needs of the moment, the national authorities are in principle in a better position than the international judge to decide both on the presence of such an emergency and on the nature and scope of derogations necessary to avert it. In this matter Article 15 (1) leaves the authorities a wide margin of appreciation'.[5] This wide margin therefore applies to two separate questions: a) is there an objective ground to derogate and b) are there specific measures strictly required by the exigencies of the situation.

In the very first case before the Strasbourg court, *Lawless v Ireland (No 3)*,[6] the Irish government could rely on Article 15, when accused of having breached the applicant's right to freedom from detention by having him arrested for some five months without bringing him before a Court for trial. On 20 July 1957, shortly before the applicant's arrest, the Irish Government had informed the Secretary-General, that the bringing into operation of special powers of arrest and detention which had been proclaimed on 5 July 1957 in the Irish Official Gazette might involve 'derogations from the obligations imposed by the Convention ' and thus invoked their authorisation under Article 15. The court, after having found an interference with the applicant's rights, had to examine the validity of Ireland's derogation. It defined the words 'public emergency threatening the life of the nation' as referring to 'an exceptional situation of crisis or emergency which affects the

---

3   For example, in the case of obligations under human rights treaties of not merely a regional but worldwide scope such as the International Covenant on Civil and Political Rights (ICCPR). The ICCPR, although also containing a derogation clause, has a greater number of non-derogable rights listed than the ECHR (eg the freedom of thought, conscience and religion).

4   (1978) 2 EHRR 25.

5   A- 25 § 207.

6   (1961) 1 EHRR 15.

whole population and constitutes a threat to the organised life of the community of which the State is composed'.[7] Due to the existence of a secret army using violence in and outside the territory of Ireland and therewith 'seriously jeopardising the relations of the state with its neighbour', the Court found the situation to fall within this concept.

Although the discretion given to the member states is not unlimited but 'accompanied by a European Supervision',[8] the lenient attitude of the Court with regard to Article 15 has recently been put into question. The case *Brannigan and McBride v United Kingdom*[9] has to be seen in the light of the outcome of the *Brogan* case.[10] In 1957, the UK government felt compelled to convey a notice of derogation from Article 5 (right to liberty and security) under Article 15 ECHR to the Secretary–General on the same grounds as Ireland had done but withdrew from this notice in 1984 as the situation seemed to have improved. Consequently, a derogation justified by the 'emergency situation' could not be invoked in the case of *Brogan* and the UK was found to have acted in violation of the Convention through the operation of excessive detention times.[11] Within a month the UK again took derogation measures, which raised questions about the genuine need of such steps ie was it a reaction to a genuine emergency or was it a reaction to the judgement of the ECtHR in *Brogan*? When the applicants in *Brannigan and McBride* lodged their complaint, the violation of Article 5 should have been clear, as the individuals concerned had been detained even longer than in *Brogan*. This time, however, the Court found no violation of the Convention due to the valid derogation measures.[12]

Judge Martens, who concurred with the majority opinion 'only after considerable hesitation',[13] considered that in future the Court's traditionally wide margin of appreciation approach with regard to Article 15, as held in *Ireland v United Kingdom* in 1978, could no longer be upheld. In his own words he considered that there was a time when 'the then member States of the Council of Europe might be assumed to be societies which … had been democratic for a long time and, as such, were fully aware both of the importance of the individual right to liberty and of the inherent danger of giving too wide a power of detention to the executive'. This was no longer the case '[s]ince the accession of eastern and central European States that assumption has lost much of its pertinence.'[14] There is some irony in that fact that it is a case involving one of the traditional Western democracies that triggers Judge Martens' opinion. The Strasbourg Court's rejection of Turkey's reliance on derogation measures in the *Aksoy* case[15] with regard to Article 5 may be seen as evidencing a trend towards a more restrictive margin of appreciation,

---

7   A- 3 § 28.
8   A- 25 § 207.
9   (1993) 17 EHRR 539.
10   (1988) 11 EHRR 117.
11   See Article 5 above for a full discussion of the case.
12   Although it had been argued that these measures were mere tactical moves to circumvent consequences similar to Brogan in the future.
13   (1993) 17 EHRR 539.
14   (1993) 17 EHRR 539.
15   See discussion under Article 3.

taking these considerations into account. Article 15 is also applicable to the substantial rights guaranteed in the added Protocols except for Protocol No 6[16] and Article 4 of Protocol No 7.[17]

Article 16- Restrictions on political activities of aliens

Nothing in Articles 10, 11 and 14 shall be regarded as preventing the High Contracting Parties from imposing restrictions on the political activity of aliens.

Under Article 16 the contracting parties are permitted to restrict the rights of aliens guaranteed in Article 10 (freedom of expression), 11 (freedom of assembly and association) and 14 (prohibition on discrimination) of the ECHR. Although originally restricted to Articles 10 and 11 when it was first introduced to the Committee of Ministers, the inclusion of Article 14 in this provision was necessary in order to avoid claims of discrimination.[18]

From the inclusion of Article 14 it follows that Article 16 can be used to justify every discriminatory act of a state which is directed against the political activities of aliens. For example, qualifications on the right to vote on nationality grounds[19] are justified under Article 16, when dealing with Article 14 (discrimination) as read together with Protocol 1, Article 3 (right to free elections). This is a significant encroachment on the Convention system as the Convention rghts are usually guaranteed to everyone within the jurisdiction of a State party, irrespective of one's nationality.[20]

The term 'aliens' originally applied to all non-nationals, without granting a privileged position to those foreigners who are nationals of one of the member states of the Council of Europe. However, in *Piermont v France*[1] the Court acknowledged a privileged status for nationals of the European Union within other member states of this institution. The applicant, a German citizen and at that time a member of the European Parliament, had been invited to French Polynesia in order to take part in a demonstration against nuclear testing. Due to her participation she was expelled from the territory and prohibited from re-entering New Caledonia. The alleged violation of her rights to freedom of expression and her right to peaceful assembly was denied by the French authorities, inter alia, with reference to Article 16. The Court held, that the applicant's 'possession of the nationality of a member state of the European Union and, in addition to that, her status as a member of the European Parliament did not allow Article 16 of the Convention to be raised against her.'[2]

With regard of the scope of 'political activity' it is clear that the concept is a very broad one. Article 16 is evidently intended to protect the interests of the state,

---

16   Concerning the abolition of the death penalty, see Article 3 of the Protocol.
17   Concerning the principle of *ne bis in idem* (freedom from double jeopardy), see Article 4 (4) of the Protocol.
18   Fawcett, J E S, *The Application of the European Convention on Human Rights* (1987) Clarendon Press, p 313.
19   See below, Article 3 of Protocol No 1.
20   Article 1 ECHR.
1   (1995) 20 EHRR 301.
2   A- 314, especially § 64.

including the state's interest in good relations with other states. To take a hypothetical example, Article 16 allows restrictions without any further qualifications, thus a demonstration held by Taiwanese nationals during a visit of the Chinese Prime Minister in one of the contracting parties could be prohibited on the grounds that the persons involved are aliens. This would be the case even if the demonstration's aim is to promote values enshrined in the Convention. The ECtHR has so far had little occasion to deal with the interpretation of 'political activities' as Article 16 has rarely been invoked in the Strasbourg case law.[3]

Article 17- Prohibition of abuse of rights

Nothing in this Convention may be interpreted as implying for any State, group or person any right to engage in any activity or perform any act aimed at the destruction of any of the rights and freedoms set forth herein or at their limitation to a greater extent than is provided for in the Convention.

The prohibition contained in Article 17 is addressed to the contracting parties as well as to groups and individuals. When addressing the national authorities, the object of Article 17 is to make it impossible for states to limit the enjoyment of the rights and freedoms guaranteed in such a way that they would either be limited to a greater extent than is provided for by the ECHR, or ultimately be totally deprived of their essence. When addressed to groups and individuals Article 17 prevents one or more of the Convention rights or freedoms being relied on to the detriment of democracy or in order to subvert the rights of others.

It is important, however, to note that Article 17 is confined to those rights and freedoms which can be abused directly to destroy the Convention rights. The mere fact, that a person is engaged in anti-democratic or for example terrorist activities would not justify depriving this person of all the Convention rights. Rights such as Articles 9 (right to freedom of conscience and religion), Article 11 (freedom of association and assembly, Article 10 (freedom of expression) and Protocol 1, Article 3 (free elections) could be used to subvert Convention rights and freedoms and may thus be limited under Article 17. However rights such as Articles 5 (right to liberty and security) and 6 (right to a fair trial) are not capable of being used to subvert the Convention rights and so cannot be limited. In the *Lawless (No 3)* case,[4] where the applicant was a member of the IRA, the Court held that the interference with the applicant's rights under Articles 5 and 6 could not be justified by reliance on Article 17, as these rights are not directly aimed at destroying the rights of others.[5] Thus, Article 17 is more likely to be invoked successfully by states in connection with Articles 9 (right to freedom of conscience and religion), 10 (freedom of

---

3   As early as 1977 the Council of Europe recommended an amendment of the Convention which would provide for the deletion of Article 16: Recommendation 799 (1977) on the Political Rights and Position of Aliens, 25 January 1977; Council of Europe, Parliamentary Assembly, 28th Ordinary Session, 3rd Part, Texts Adopted (1977).
4   (1961) 1 EHRR 15.
5   A- 3 § 7.

expression) and 11 (freedom of association and assembly) and Protocol 1, Article 3 (free elections) of the Convention.

While originally directed to the threat of communist manipulation,[6] recently Article 17 has focused more on racist, xenophobic and diverse terrorist movements. Article 17 has not so far played a great role in the Strasbourg case law. It has to be seen as an instrument of last resort and will often only be used to reinforce conclusions of justification under the special restrictions such as 'necessary in a democratic society' incorporated in the certain Convention Articles.[7]

Article 18- Limitation on use of restrictions on rights

The restrictions permitted under this Convention to the said rights and freedoms shall not be applied for any purpose other than those for which they have been prescribed.

Article 18 contains the expression of the rule against *détournement de pouvoir*, ie the contracting parties are prohibited from restricting the rights and freedoms guaranteed in the Convention in a manner that would constitute a misuse of powers or be in breach of the principle of good faith implied by this provision. Like Article 14 (discrimination), Article 18 is an accessory right, which can only be invoked in connection with one of the other rights and freedoms. Although not a formal requirement,[8] if there is no violation of the main right the Court will find an examination of a violation in conjunction with Article 18 superfluous.[9] On the other hand, once the Court finds a Contracting party to have violated a Convention right, an additional examination of an alleged violation of Article 18 will not be considered necessary due to the subsidiary nature of this provision.

In the case *De Becker v Belgium*[10] the Commission relied partly on Article 18 when coming to the conclusion that the derogation measures taken by the Belgian authorities under Article 15 were no longer justified as the emergency situation had already ceased to exist. The Court, however, did not deem it necessary to examine the alleged breach of Article 18 but simply did not accept Article 15 as a justification on the side of the Belgian authorities at all.[11]

The formulation of Article 18 has been criticised because it is almost impossible to demonstrate a misuse of powers or bad faith by a national authority, as the burden of proof rests upon either the applicant or in ex officio examinations upon the Court

6   See for instance Application 250/ 57 *Kommunistische Partei Deutschland v Germany.*
7   Eg the 'necessary in a democratic society' requirement will in such cases usually be fulfilled, see eg Application 12194/86 *Kühnen v Germany* (1988) 56 DR 205.
8   According to the Commission, the linkage principle does not require a violation of the linked right invoked, *see Kamma v Netherlands* (1975) 18 YB 300 at 316.
9   *Engel v Netherlands* (1976) 1 EHRR 647.
10   Commission Report of 8 January, B. 2 (1962), p 133.
11   *De Becker v Belgium* (1962) 1 EHRR 43.

itself.[12] This may explain the reason why Article 18 has rarely been successfully invoked.

The additional Protocols to the ECHR[13]

We now turn to examine No 1, No 4, No 6 and No 7 of the 11 Protocols that have entered into force since the adoption of the ECHR.[14] The Court in its case law has repeatedly emphasised that the guarantees provided for in these instruments are to be regarded as an addition to the Convention and, therefore, cannot replace related or similar rights contained therein. Even if they enjoy priority as a *lex specialis*, the provisions in the Protocols will not reduce the scope or protection of the Convention rights. This becomes particularly important in connection with reservations made by a contracting party to one of the Protocols but not to a related provision in the Convention itself. In the case *Burghartz v Switzerland*[15] a married couple complained against restrictions upon the choice of their surname, which allegedly violated their rights under Article 14 (discrimination) in conjunction with Article 8 (right to privacy and family life) of the ECHR. The Swiss government contended that since its entry into force, Protocol 7,[16] Article 5 thereof (equality of the rights of spouses) was the provision exclusively governing rights concerning the choice of surnames of married couples. They therefore argued that the interference with the applicants' rights were justified due to a Swiss reservation which expressly limited the rights under Protocol 7, Article 5. The Court rejected this contention, as in its view a Protocol's purpose is to expand the protection under the Convention system and never to restrict it.[17] Although the growing number of additional Protocols to the Convention indicates a progressive development within the field of regional human rights protection, the provisions are often the result of compromises and not as meaningful and protective as they seem at first glance.

Protocol No 1, Article 1 - Right to property[18]

Every natural or legal person is entitled to the peaceful enjoyment of his possessions. No one shall be deprived of his possessions except in the public interest and subject to the conditions provided for by law and by the general principles of international law. The preceding provisions shall not, however, in any way impair the right of a State to enforce such laws as it deems

12 Article 18 so far only played a minor role in the case law of the Strasbourg court, see eg *Bozano v France* (1986) 9 EHRR 297 in connection with Article 5 (1) and Protocol No 4 Article 2; *Handyside v United Kingdom* (1976) 1 EHRR 737 in connection with Protocol No 1 Article 1.
13 For further reading on the Protocols see Brownlie, I, *Basic Documents on Human Rights* (3rd edn, 1998) Clarendon Press, Oxford.
14 The other Protocols do not confer rights and relate to various procedural changes to the operation of the Convention.
15 (1994) 18 EHRR 101.
16 To which Switzerland is a party.
17 A- 280- B § 23.
18 Protocol No 1 entered into force on 18 May 1954, ratified by the UK on 3 November 1952; for the text and the current status of signatures and ratifications see: http://www.coe. fr/

necessary to control the use of property in accordance with the general interest or to secure the payment of taxes or other contributions or penalties.

According to the Strasbourg court, Article 1 of Protocol 1 is 'mainly concerned with the arbitrary confiscation of property and does not in principle, guarantee a right to peaceful enjoyment of possession in a pleasant environment'.[19] The provision contains a principle of peaceful enjoyment of property, regulates deprivation of property by the state in the public interest and also confers upon the state the right to implement laws as it deems necessary to control the use of property.

The concept of 'possessions' as set out in Article 1 is very broad. It is autonomous, ie not confined to the domestic definition of 'possessions', and the demonstration of an established economic interest by an applicant may be sufficient to establish a right protected by the Convention.[20] Thus, it embraces immovable as well as movable property and corporeal and incorporeal interests, such as shares, patents and even goodwill.[1]

In order to establish, whether the peaceful enjoyment of property has been violated, the Court applies the so called 'fair-balance' test, which it established in the *Sporrong and Lönnroth* case: '[t]he Court must determine whether a fair balance was struck between the demands of the general interest of the community and the requirements of the protection of the individual's fundamental rights. The search for this balance is inherent in the whole of the Convention and is also reflected in the structure of Article 1.'[2]

In accordance with the second sentence of Article 1, deprivation of possessions may only be exercised in the 'public interest'. In the context of Protocol 1, Article 1 the contracting parties enjoy a wide margin of appreciation in deciding what amounts to the 'public interest'. Further, the 'fair balance' test, when applied to Protocol 1, Article 1 requires that 'there must be a reasonable relationship of proportionality between the means employed and the aim sought to be realised by any measure depriving a person of his possessions'.[3] The availability of compensation will be a significant factor in considering this balance.[4] Finally, in

---

eng/legaltxt/9e.htm; for further reading: Andrews, J, 'Leasehold enfranchisement and the public interest in the UK' in (1986) *European Law Review* p 366; Andrews, J, 'Compensation for nationalisation in the UK' in (1987) *European Law Review* p 65; Sherlock, A, 'Council of Europe – Property Rights and the European Convention on Human Rights' in (1987) 8 *Business Law Review*, p 113; Dürig, G., ' Das Eigentum als Menschenrecht' in (1953) *Zeitschrift fuer die gesamte Staatswissenschaft* 109, p 326; Müller, Edgar, *Der völkerrechtliche Eigentumsbegriff, Dissertation Marburg* (1981); Blumenwitz, Dieter, *Das Grundrecht des Eigentums* (2000) Atwerb, Grünwald.

19   *Powell and Rayner v United Kingdom* (1990) 12 EHRR 355.
20   *Gasus Dosier-und Fördertechnik GmbH v Netherlands* (1995) 20 EHRR 403, where the Court considered it immaterial, whether the applicant's right to a concrete-mixer was a right of ownership or a security right in rem; in *Tre Traktörer Aktiebolag v Sweden* (1989) 13 EHRR 309; the Court considered a liquor-licence to fall within the concept of possessions.
1   See *Van Marle v Netherlands* (1986) 8 EHRR 483.
2   *Sporrong and Lönnroth v Sweden* (1982) 5 EHRR 35.
3   *James v United Kingdom* (1986) 8 EHRR 123.
4   *Lithgow v United Kingdom* (1986) 8 EHRR 329.

order to prevent arbitrariness, the measure must have been provided for by law.[5] When imposing restrictions upon the use of property, the national authorities again enjoy a wide margin of appreciation, as they can 'enforce such laws as [they] deem necessary.' Because of it significance with regard to shareholding we consider this Article in detail in Chapter 9.

> **Protocol No 1, Article 2- Right to education** [UK has reservation in place]
>
> No person shall be denied the right to education. In the exercise of any functions which it assumes in relation to education and to teaching, the State shall respect the right of parents to ensure such education and teaching in conformity with their own religious and philosophical convictions.

Rather than the protection of the social and cultural right to education, the primary objective of Article 2 is to guarantee the right to equal access to educational facilities. Thus, Article 2 does not require that the Contracting States ensure at their own expense, or subsidise, education of a particular type, but merely implies for those who are under the jurisdiction of these States 'the right to avail themselves of the means of instruction existing at a given time'.[6]

Further Article 2 does not contain a negative element, ie there is no right to freedom from education.[7] According to the Court, Article 2 has to be read as a whole with the second sentence providing an 'adjunct' to the dominating first part.[8] The second sentence concerns the right of parents to ensure education for their children in conformity with their own religious and philosophical convictions, the latter embracing '... such convictions as are worthy of respect in a 'democratic society'... and are not incompatible with human dignity.'[9] In the case *Campell and Cosans v United Kingdom* the applicants complained that the existence of corporal punishment in the schools they sent their children to violated their rights under the second sentence of Article 2. The parents successfully argued that this way of maintaining school discipline would not be in accordance with their philosophical convictions and that the school authorities had failed to pay due respect to these convictions when they had suspended their child due to his failure to report for corporal punishment. The Court in this case found a second, separate violation of Article 2. Although it has to be read as a whole, the provision is dominated by its first sentence. According to the Court, Jeffrey Cosans could have returned to school only if his parents had been willing to act contrary to their convictions and was thus denied his right to education. The applicants were awarded £3,000 non-pecuniary

---

5   On the origins of the 'by law' criteria see Chapter 1 and for a consideration of its use in the Strasbourg context see Chapter 3.
6   *Belgian Linguistics v Belgium (No 2)* (1968) 1 EHRR 252.
7   In Application 10233/83 *Family H v United Kingdom* (1984) 37 DR 105, the Commission held that ' ... it is clear that Article 2 of Protocol No 1 implies a right for the State to establish compulsory schooling, be it in State schools or private tuition of a satisfactory standard'.
8   *Kjeldsen, Busk Madsen and Pedersen v Denmark* (1976) 1 EHRR 711; *Campell and Cosans v United Kingdom* (1982) 4 EHRR 293.
9   *Campell and Cosans v United Kingdom* (1982) 4 EHRR 293.

damages and £9,787 less FF2,300 legal costs. Following the judgment, the UK government introduced legislation prohibiting corporal punishment in state-funded schools.

When signing the Protocol, the UK government made a reservation which provided that 'in view of certain provisions of the Education Acts in force in the United Kingdom, the principle affirmed in the second sentence of Article 2 is accepted by the United Kingdom only so far as it is compatible with the provisions of efficient instruction and training, and the avoidance of unreasonable public expenditure.'[10]

Protocol No 1, Article 3 - Right to Free elections

The High Contracting Parties undertake to hold free elections at reasonable intervals by secret ballot, under conditions which will ensure the free expression of the opinion of the people in the choice of the legislature.

The Court has held that 'since it enshrines a characteristic principle of democracy, Article 3 of Protocol No 1 accordingly is of prime importance to the Convention system.'[11] As has been noted by the Commission in the *Greek* case,[12] Article 3 of Protocol No 1 'presupposes the existence of a representative legislature, elected at reasonable intervals, as the basis of a democratic society'. Article 3 therefore obliges the contracting parties to hold free and fair elections at reasonable intervals, offering the voters a real choice of the legislature and safeguarding the secrecy of the votes; nonetheless, each state must provide its own Constitutional arrangements allocating legislative power.[13] The Court has held that the provision 'does not create any obligation to introduce a specific (voting) system, such as proportional representation or majority voting with one or two ballots'.[14] As regards the notion of 'reasonable intervals', a five-year period has been accepted to be compatible with this requirement.[15]

Article 3 includes the right for individuals to vote and to stand for election.[16] However, a wide range of restrictions apply to these rights, such as exclusion of prisoners, citizens that are not resident in the country, a minimum age for the exercise of the right to vote or basing the qualifications for the right to vote on nationality.[17] Denying the right to vote for women on the other hand would amount to a violation of Article 3 in connection with Article 14 ECHR.

---

10   See: http://www.coe.fr/tablconv/reservdecl/dr9e.htm UNITED_KINGDOM.
11   *Mathieu-Mohin and Clerfayt v Belgium* (1987) 10 EHRR 1.
12   (1969) 12 YB 1.
13   Harris, D J /O'Boyle, M/ Warbrick, C, *Law of the European Convention on Human Rights* p 553.
14   *Mathieu-Mohin and Clerfayt v Belgium* (1987) 10 EHRR 1.
15   Application 27311/95 *Timke v Germany* (1995) 82 DR 195.
16   A-113 § 51.
17   See *Mathieu-Mohin and Clerfayt v Belgium* (1987) 10 EHRR 1 where the court considered the rights were not absolute and Article 16 ECHR, which expressly allows discrimination of aliens in this respect.

Protocol No 4, Article 1 - Freedom from imprisonment on the ground of inability to fulfil a contractual obligation[18]

No one shall be deprived of his liberty merely on the ground of inability to fulfil a contractual obligation. [UK has signed but not ratified Protocol No 4]

Article 1 of Protocol No 4 guarantees the freedom from deprivation of liberty merely on the grounds of the inability to fulfil a contractual obligation. The terms 'merely' and 'inability' restrict the scope of this provision. Thus, Article 1 is not violated when the debtor acted negligently or in a fraudulent or malicious way or, for example, when the debtor is in fact able but simply refuses to pay. Other examples of cases in which Article 1 is inapplicable are: a person orders food in a restaurant, knowing that he is not able to pay the bill; a person, through negligence, fails to supply goods when he is under a contractual obligation to do so; a person prepares to leave the country in order to avoid meeting contractual obligations.[19] Due to its limited applicability, Article 1 of Protocol No. 4 so far has been of little importance in the Strasbourg case law.[20]

Protocol No 4, Article 2 - Freedom of movement within the territory of a Contracting State, to choose one's residence there and to leave its territory

1) Everyone lawfully within the territory of a State shall, within that territory, have the right to liberty of movement and freedom to choose his residence.

2) Everyone shall be free to leave any country, including his own.

3) No restrictions shall be placed on the exercise of these rights other than such as are in accordance with law and are necessary in a democratic society in the interests of national security or public safety, for the maintenance of ordre public, for the prevention of crime, for the protection of health or morals, or for the protection of the rights and freedoms of others.

4) The rights set forth in paragraph 1 may also be subject, in particular areas, to restrictions imposed in accordance with law and justified by the public interest in a democratic society.

18 Protocol No 4 entered into force on 2 May 1968, signed but not ratified by the UK (the UK is presently reviewing its position); for the text and current status of signatures and ratifications see: http://www.coe.fr/eng/legaltxt/46e.htm; further reading: Hailbronner Kay/ Brinkmann, Gisbert (eds), *30 Jahre Freizügigkeit in Europa* (1998) Müller, Heidelberg Hanum, H, *The Right to Leave and Return in International Law and Practice* (1987).

19 Given in the Explanatory Report to Protocol No 4, which provides guidance as to the meaning of the provisions, see: Explanatory Reports on the Second to Fifth Protocols to the European Convention for the Protection of Human Rights and Fundamental Freedoms, H 71 (11) (1971), pp 39-40.

20 See eg Application 5025/ 71 *X v Germany* (1971) 14 YB 692, where the Commission declared Article 1 to be inapplicable in a case where a person was detained for refusing to make an affidavit on request of a creditor in respect of his property.

Article 4, paragraph 1 protects the freedom of movement within the territory of a contracting state and the freedom to choose one's residence for everybody 'lawfully within the territory'. This includes nationals as well as nationals of other states and stateless persons, as long as persons belonging to one of the latter two groups have abided by the conditions regarding entry into a state's territory and are thus 'lawfully' within it.[1] The second paragraph of Article 4 adds the right to leave the country.

Both of these rights are largely restricted by the third and fourth paragraphs, which allow all sorts of reasons to refuse individuals these rights. According to paragraph 3, such restrictions may be made in the interest of national security or public safety, for the maintenance of the ordre public, for the prevention of crime, for the protection of health or morals, or for the protection of the rights and freedoms of others, when they are in accordance with internal laws and necessary in a democratic society.

In the case *Raimondo v Italy*[2] the applicant, suspected of belonging to a mafia type organisation, had been subjected to a Court supervision order by which he was prohibited from leaving his home without giving notice to the police. While these measures were found to be justified by the 'prevention of crime' requirement by the Court, the applicant's rights had been violated in another context: the national authorities had failed to inform him about the revocation of the order for a period of 18 days, during which the applicant remained restricted in his movements; this was found to be contrary to the 'in accordance with law'- requirement. The court granted 10.0 m lire damages and 5.0 m lire legal costs to the applicant.

Paragraph 4 provides for additional restrictions in particular areas justified by 'the public interest in a democratic society'; this includes the economic welfare of a society as a motive for the imposition of restrictions. It has been suggested that, for example, the transfer of government departments conferring upon employees of those departments a duty to move might be justified on these grounds, even if this included the penalty of loss of the employment.[3]

Protocol No 4, Article 3- Prohibition of expulsion of nationals

1) No one shall be expelled, by means either of an individual or of a collective measure, from the territory of the State of which he is a national.

2) No one shall be deprived of the right to enter the territory of the state of which he is a national.

Article 3, paragraph 1 contains a prohibition on the contracting states from expelling individual or groups of nationals from their territory. Expulsion within the meaning of Article 3 is involved, when a person 'is obliged permanently to leave the territory of a state of which he is a national without being left the possibility of returning later'.[4] Extradition generally does not fall within the scope of Article 3, as has been

---

1   Application 12068/86 *Paramanathan v Germany* (1986) 51 DR 237 at 240.
2   (1994) 18 EHRR 237.
3   van Dijk/van Hoof, *Theory and Practice of the European Convention on Human Rights*, p 670.
4   Application 6189/73 *X v Germany* (1974) 46 CD 214.

held by the Commission in the case *Brückmann v Germany,*[5] which dismissed the West German applicant's claim that his extradition to East Germany would amount to a breach of this provision by the West German authorities. However, the normal definition of expulsion is somewhat too narrow for the purpose of Article 3 (right to freedom from torture) of the ECHR and Protocol 6 (abolition of death penalty) as under these provisions even only temporary expulsion of nationals where there was a risk or torture or death would be prohibited.

Paragraph 2 provides for a person's right to be admitted to the state of which he is a national. It has been suggested that this provision could cause major problems for the United Kingdom with numerous people in the Commonwealth having acquired British citizenship by birth.[6] This may be seen as the main reason why the UK so far has not ratified Protocol No 4.

Protocol No 4, Article 4- Freedom of aliens from collective expulsion

Collective expulsion of aliens is prohibited.

Article 4 contains the prohibition of collective expulsion of aliens without any restrictions.

The Commission defines a 'collective expulsion' as 'any measure of the competent authorities compelling aliens as a group to leave the country, except where such a measure is taken after and on the basis of a reasonable and objective examination of the particular cases of each individual alien of the group.'[7] The criterion that decides whether an expulsion took place collectively is thus the procedure that has been followed in the expulsion.[8] In the case *A v Netherlands*[9] where a group of aliens had been refused asylum, the Commission found that there had been no collective expulsion, as the applicants' arguments against expulsion had all been heard individually, both before the Dutch Minister of Justice and the courts. Cases concerning the individual expulsion of aliens do not fall within the scope of this provision but are considered under Protocol No 7, Article 1, if states are contracting parties thereto, which sets out more expansive restrictions.

Protocol No 6- Concerning the abolition of the death penalty[10]

Article 1, Abolition of the death penalty

The death penalty shall be abolished. No-one shall be condemned to such penalty or executed.

---

5   (1974) 17 YB 458.
6   van Dijk/van Hoof, *Theory and Practice of the European Convention on Human Rights*, p 673.
7   Application 7011/75 *Becker v Denmark* (1975) 4 DR 215 at 235.
8   van Dijk/van Hoof, *Theory and Practice of the European Convention on Human Rights*, p 677.
9   Application 14209/88, (1989) 59 DR 274.
10   Entered into force on 1 March 1985, the UK ratified the Sixth Protocol in 1999, for the text and current status of signatures and ratifications see: http://www.coe.fr/eng/legaltxt/ 114e.htm further reading: Explanatory Report on Protocol No 6 to the Convention for the

The additional Protocols of the ECHR

Article 2 – Death penalty in time of war

A State may make provision in its law for the death penalty in respect of acts committed in time of war or of imminent threat of war; such penalty shall be applied only in the instances laid down in the law and in accordance with its provisions. The State shall communicate to the Secretary General of the Council of Europe the relevant provisions of that law.

Article 3 – Prohibition of derogations

No derogation from the provisions of this Protocol shall be made under Article 15 of the Convention.

Article 4 – Prohibition of reservations

No reservation may be made under Article 57 of the Convention in respect of the provisions of this Protocol.

Article 1 of Protocol No 6 obliges the contracting parties to abolish the death penalty within their jurisdiction and additionally contains the right for every individual not to be sentenced to death or to be executed. However, read in conjunction with Article 2, these guarantees only apply in peacetime. The second sentence of Article 1 may become important in cases where a state party expels or extradites a person who will in the receiving state face the real risk of being sentenced to death or of being executed.[11]

The recent enlargement of the Council of Europe now to include states that still carry out executions or at least contain such provisions in their criminal laws, has made the abolition of the death penalty a matter of primary concern for the Council of Europe. Thus, states that wish to join the Council of Europe must accede within a certain period of time[12] to Protocol No 6.[13] As provided for in Articles 3 and 4 of Protocol 6, the protected rights are non-derogable, and, additionally no reservations may be made.

Protocol No 7, Article 1- Procedural safeguards relating to expulsion of aliens[14]

1) An alien lawfully resident in the territory of a State shall not be expelled therefrom except in pursuance of a decision reached in accordance with law and shall be allowed:

Protection of Human Rights and Fundamental Freedoms concerning the Abolition of the Death Penalty (No. 114) 1983, available from the Council of Europe under http://book.coe.fr/gb/cat/liv/htm/l192.htm.

11   Application 22742/ 93 *Aylor –Davis v France* (1994) 76 DR 164; see also the reasoning in *Soering v United Kingdom* (1989) 11 EHRR 439, and above Article 2.

12   Signature one year from the date of accession, ratification three years from date of accession.

13   See the Report of the Parliamentary Assembly of 25 June 1996 on the abolition of the death penalty in Europe (Document 7589) at: http://stars.coe.fr/index_e.htm.

14   Entered into force on 1 November 1988, neither signed nor ratified by the UK (May 2000). (The UK intends to ratify once Parliamentary time can be found: see White Paper of the HRA

a) to submit reasons against his expulsion,
b) to have his case reviewed, and
c) to be represented for these purposes before the competent authority or a person or persons designated by that authority.

2) An alien may be expelled before the exercise of his rights under paragraph 1.a, b and c of this Article, when such expulsion is necessary in the interests of public order or is grounded on reasons of national security.

Article 1 of Protocol No 7 guarantees that the expulsion of an individual alien lawfully resident in the contracting state will be exercised in compliance with the rule of law.

The protection of Article 1 is rather limited. The residency-requirement ('aliens lawfully *resident*) excludes numerous groups of aliens, for example those who are in transit, who have only been admitted for non-residential purposes or who are waiting for the outcome of a pending decision on a requested residence permit, etc.[15] Further, the words 'lawfully' and 'in accordance with law' contained in Article 1 refer exclusively to domestic law. Thus, it is for the contracting states to determine a) which persons are '*lawfully resident*' and therefore enjoy protection under Article 1, and b) which is the competent authority to decide about the expulsion and which procedures have to be followed. The competent authority does not have to be a judicial organ, unless Article 6 of the Convention additionally applies in the specific case. Once a decision for expulsion has been reached by the competent authorities, the person concerned must be allowed a) to submit reasons against his/her expulsion, b) to have his/her case reviewed, and c) to be represented for these purposes before the competent authority.

This protection, however, is again weakened by several factors: for example, the review provided for in subparagraph b) may be performed by the same authority that considered the case in the first place,[16] the form of representation guaranteed in subparagraph c) will again be determined by domestic law, and does not have to be exercised by a lawyer. Finally, the whole procedure may take a written form, ie there is no right for the person concerned physically to take part in the proceedings.[17]

Protocol No 7, Article 2- Right of appeal in criminal matters

1) Everyone convicted of a criminal offence by a tribunal shall have the right to have his conviction or sentence reviewed by a higher tribunal. The exercise

---

1998. It should then be incorporated into domestic law through an order under section 1 (4) HRA.) For the text and the current status of signatures and ratifications see: http://www.coe.fr/eng/legaltxt/117e.htm; further reading: Explanatory Report on Protocol No 7 to the Convention of Human Rights and Fundamental Freedoms (No 117) 1985, available from the Council of Europe under: *http://book.coe.fr/gb/cat/liv/htm/l194.htm.*

15 For further examples see Explanatory Report on Protocol No 7, p 7.
16 The Explanatory Report on Protocol No 7 states: that Article 1 b) does not require 'a two-stage procedure before different authorities, but only that the competent authority should review the case in the light of the reasons against the expulsion submitted by the person concerned' (p 7)
17 Explanatory Report on Protocol No 7, p 9.

of this right, including the grounds on which it may be exercised, shall be governed by law.

2) This right may be subject to exceptions in regard to offences of a minor character, as prescribed by law, or in cases in which the person concerned was tried in the first instance by the highest tribunal or was convicted following an appeal against acquittal.

Article 2 contains the right for a person convicted of a criminal offence to have his conviction or sentence reviewed by a higher tribunal. The provision is supplementary to Article 6 ECHR and adds the right of appeal for states who are party to the Protocol. Article 2 is only applicable in cases where a person has indeed been convicted and the conviction has been imposed 'by a tribunal', within the meaning of Article 6 ECHR.[18]

The wording 'conviction or sentence' implies that there is not in every case a right to review of both conviction and sentence. If a person, for example, is convicted after having pleaded guilty the right to review may be restricted to the sentence.[19] The second paragraph subjects the right to review to several exceptions. An offence may be regarded as of a minor character, within the meaning of paragraph 2, when it is not punishable by imprisonment.[20] For the last exception to apply, the acquittal must have been pronounced by a judicial body.

Protocol No 7, Article 3- Compensation for wrongful conviction

When a person has by a final decision been convicted of a criminal offence and when subsequently his conviction has been reversed, or he has been pardoned, on the ground that a new or newly discovered fact shows conclusively that there has been a miscarriage of justice, the person who has suffered punishment as a result of such conviction shall be compensated according to the law or the practice of the State concerned, unless it is proved that the non-disclosure of the unknown fact in time is wholly or partly attributable to him.

Article 3 contains the right to compensation in cases where a person has suffered punishment after conviction for a criminal offence as a result of a miscarriage of justice. The person has the right to be compensated according to the law of the state concerned, when all the conditions set out in the provision have been fulfilled. Apart from the suffering of punishment for a criminal offence these conditions include: the person must have been convicted by a final decision;[1] the conviction has been reversed or pardoned and this reversal or pardon has taken place on grounds of new or newly discovered facts; finally, these facts must show conclusively

---

18   Explanatory Report on Protocol No 7, p 10.
19   Explanatory Report on Protocol No 7, p 10.
20   Explanatory Report on Protocol No 7, p 10.
1   According to the Explanatory Report this is the case 'if according to the traditional expression, it has acquired the force of *res judicata*. This is the case when it is irrevocable, that is to say when no further ordinary remedies are available or when the parties have exhausted such remedies or have permitted the time limit to expire without availing themselves of them', p 11.

that there has been a miscarriage of justice, ie 'there (is) acknowledgment that the person concerned was clearly innocent.'[2] In cases where it can be proven that the non-disclosure of the unknown fact(s) in time is wholly or partly attributable to the person concerned, there is no such right to compensation.

Protocol No 7, Article 4- Principle of ne bis in idem (Right not to be tried or punished twice)

1) No one shall be liable to be tried or punished again in criminal proceedings under the jurisdiction of the same State for an offence for which he has already been finally acquitted or convicted in accordance with the law and penal procedure of that State.

2) The provisions of the preceding paragraph shall not prevent the reopening of the case in accordance with the law and penal procedure of the State concerned, if there is evidence of new or newly discovered facts, or if there has been a fundamental defect in the previous proceedings, which could affect the outcome of the case.

3) No derogation from this Article shall be made under Article 15 of the Convention.

Article 4 guarantees freedom from double jeopardy, also known as the principle of *ne bis in idem,* which means that nobody shall be tried or punished more than once for the same criminal offence, once the conviction or the acquittal has become final. According to the provision, the prohibition applies only to repeated trial or punishment in criminal proceedings under the jurisdiction of the same state. Thus, additional proceedings of a different nature, such as disciplinary proceedings, and conviction and/or punishment more than once in two or more different states are allowed.

In the case *Gradinger v Austria*[3] the applicant had driven his car under the influence of alcohol and thereby caused death by negligence. As a consequence, he was not only convicted by a criminal Court under Article 81 § 2 of the Austrian Criminal Code, but subsequently also by the administrative authorities, as driving under the influence of alcohol constituted an offence against section 5 of the Austrian Road Traffic Act. Although the relevant provisions differed with regard to their nature and purpose, the Court found Article 4 of Protocol No 7 as well as Article 6 ECHR to be applicable and to have been violated, as both convictions 'were based on the same conduct'.[4] The applicant was granted 150, 000 Austrian Schillinge (ATS) legal costs. According to its third paragraph, derogations from Article 4 are prohibited.

2   Explanatory Report on Protocol No 7, p 12.
3   Judgment of 23 October 1995, A- 328- C.
4   A- 328- C § 55.

Protocol No 7, Article 5- Equality of rights and responsibilities between spouses during and after marriage

Spouses shall enjoy equality of rights and responsibilities of a private law character between them, and in their relations with their children, as to marriage, during marriage and in the event of its dissolution. This Article shall not prevent States from taking such measures as are necessary in the interests of the children.

Article 5 provides for the right between spouses of equal enjoyment of their rights and responsibilities when they are of a private law character and in their relations with their children. As Article 5 does not apply 'to other fields of law, such as administrative, fiscal, criminal, social, ecclesiastical or labour laws',[5] the basic obligation conferred upon the contracting parties is to provide for the enactment and enforcement of appropriate legislation concerning such matters as personal status with respect to their children and property rights.[6] In the case *Hokkanen v Finland*,[7] the custody of a child had been transferred to the maternal grandparents after the mother's death. The father lodged a complaint, contending that the non-enforcement of his right of custody and access by the national authorities violated his rights under both Article 8 ECHR and Article 5 of Protocol No 7. Although the complaint had been declared admissible under both provisions, the Court held, after having found a violation of Article 8 ECHR that no separate issue arose under Article 5 of the Protocol. The second sentence of Article 5 allows exceptions where legislative or administrative measures are necessary in the interest of the children, even if this leads to inequalities between the spouses.

---

5   Explanatory Report on Protocol No 7, p 13.
6   As complaints can be lodged against states only, Article 5 clearly implies 'Drittwirkung/ Horizontal effect'.
7   (1994) 19 EHRR 139.

Chapter five

The impact of the ECHR on English law prior to the HRA

we were not prepared to encourage our European friends to jeopardise our whole system of law, which we have laboriously built up over the centuries, in favour of some half-baked scheme to be administered by some unknown court.[1]

Introduction

All the contracting states to the ECHR have an obligation under Article 1 to secure the rights and freedoms of the Convention in their domestic systems. The ECtHR has stated that the Convention does not provide any particular method whereby the contracting states are to secure these rights and freedoms in their domestic law.[2] Nevertheless many of the contracting parties such as Germany, Italy, France, Switzerland and others have chosen to fulfil their obligations under the ECHR by variously incorporating the Convention into their domestic law. In *Ireland v United Kingdom*[3] this was something the ECtHR expressly approved of by stating that the original framers of the ECHR:

---

1   The Lord Chancellor, Lord Jowitt in a letter to Hugh Dalton August 3rd 1950, setting out his views and those of other cabinet members on the draft ECHR. LCO 2/5570 quoted in Lester, Anthony 'Fundamental Rights: The United Kingdom Isolated?' (1984) *Public Law* pp 46-72 at 51.
2   See *Swedish Engine Drivers's Union v Sweden* (1976) 1 EHRR 617.
3   (1978) 2 EHRR 25.

intended to make it clear that the rights and freedoms set out would be directly secured to anyone within the jurisdiction of the contracting states. That intention finds a particularly faithful reflection in those instances where the Convention has been incorporated into domestic law.

Until the HRA 1998 or to be more accurate, until the HRA came into force on the 2 October 2000, the UK had not incorporated the ECHR into domestic law. For some 47 years between 1953 when the Convention first came into force and October 2000 the UK had an international obligation to secure the ECHR rights in domestic law but no domestic legislation aimed at doing so. It flows from this that no rights or freedoms under the Convention were directly enforceable in the UK courts during this period. In the absence of such legislation it fell to the judiciary to interpret domestic law in line with the state's international obligations. It is to the judicial interpretation of the ECHR in the national courts prior to the HRA that we turn to consider in this chapter. While the HRA fundamentally changes the way the ECHR operates in domestic law an understanding of its operation prior to the HRA is important for a number of reasons. First, there is some concern about how the judiciary will adapt to a fundamentally different system of interpretation under the HRA. This is discussed in Chapters 6 and 7. Much of this concern cannot be understood unless the reader possesses a knowledge of how the judiciary have tried to deal with the Convention in the past. Second, section 11 of the HRA preserves rights and causes of action that were in existence prior to the HRA. Certain organisations, such as Amnesty International and the BBC, may not be capable of fulfilling 'victim' status for the purposes of the HRA and so may have to rely on the previous operation of the Convention in domestic law.[4] Third, one of the ways the Convention has been given real effect in domestic law prior to the HRA is through European Community law, this will continue to operate under the HRA.

International treaties in domestic law

The ECHR is an international treaty ratified by the United Kingdom but until the HRA not incorporated into domestic law. As such it fell to be considered by the courts alongside the general jurisprudence on the interpretation of treaties in domestic law, most of which has evolved from *The Parlement Belge*.[5] This case concerned the extent of the Crown's prerogative powers. The treaty in question conferred immunity from legal proceeding on foreign ships. The court found that while the Crown had a prerogative power to make treaties the exercise of that power could not diminish the rights of British subjects in the courts of the UK. The case, while it concerns a diminution of the rights of UK subjects, has at times been used to defeat affirmative rights arising from treaties.

In *Salaman v Secretary of State for India*[6] the Court of Appeal found that a treaty, the Terms of Lahore, as an act of state could not confer rights on individuals and

4   See Chapters 6 and 11.
5   (1879) 4 PD 129; on appeal 5 PD 197.
6   [1906] 1 KB 613.

thus no court could consider claims arising from the treaty. In *A-G for Canada v A-G for Ontario*[7] Lord Atkin considered that treaty obligations could only alter existing domestic law if legislation was introduced. In *British Airways Board v Laker Airways Ltd*[8] Sir John Donaldson MR stated that the Court of Appeal had 'no jursidiction to determine the meaning or effect of any treaty to which the government of the United Kingdom is a party and indeed is not equipped to do so...' Considering this same issue Lord Oliver in *Maclaine Watson & Co Ltd v Department of Trade and Industry*[9] stated:

> it is axiomatic the municipal courts have not and cannot have the competence to adjudicate upon or to enforce the rights arising out of transactions entered into by independent sovereign states between themselves on the plane of international law ... as a matter of the constitutional law of the United Kingdom, the royal prerogative, while it embraces the making of treaties, does not extend to altering the law conferring rights on individuals or depriving individuals of rights which they enjoy in domestic law without intervention of Parliament. Treaties, as it is sometimes expressed, are not self-executing. Quite simply, a treaty is not part of English law unless and until it has been incorporated into the law by legislation. So far as individuals are concerned, it is res inter alios acta from which they cannot derive rights and by which they cannot be deprived of rights or subjected to obligations; and it is outside the purview of the court not only because it is made in the conduct of foreign relations, which are the prerogative of the Crown, but also because, as a source of rights and obligations, it is irrelevant.

In *R v Uxbridge Magistrates' Court, ex p Adimi*[10] the Court of Appeal considered the application of the UN Convention on Refugees 1951, to which the UK is a signatory, in UK domestic law. Relying on Lord Oliver's speech above, Newman J concluded 'I am unable to see how an individual asylum seeker who has committed an offence [the offence being the possession of false documents which enabled him to enter the UK] within the jurisdiction can assert any private right to have the law applied to him in a way which differs from other offenders by relying on the terms of an international convention.' A significant body of case law has established that a treaty cannot give rise to rights in domestic law unless legislation has been introduced to effect those treaty rights.

However while a treaty is not part of English law until incorporated the courts will presume that Parliament intends to legislate consistently with it. In *Bloxam v Favre*[11] the court quoted with approval the first part of the following passage from Maxwell[12] on the use of rules of international law:

> [u]nder the general presumption that the legislature does not intend to exceed its jurisdiction, every statute is interpreted, so far as its language permits, so

7   [1937] AC 326 at 347.
8   [1983] 3 All ER 375 at 402, CA.
9   [1989] 3 All ER 523 at 544-545.
10   [1999] 4 All ER 520 at 541-542. .
11   (1883) 8 PD 101 at 107.
12   *Interpretation of Statutes* (12th edn), p 183.

as not to be inconsistent with the comity of nations or the established rules of international law, and the court will avoid a construction which would give rise to such inconsistency unless compelled to adopt it by plain and unambiguous language. But if the language of the statute is clear, it must be followed notwithstanding, the conflict between the municipal and international law which results.[13]

The passage in its entirety has been quoted in numerous cases since.[14] In *Pan-American World Airways Inc v Department of Trade*[15] Lord Scarman considered that a treaty was not part of English law but that there could arise a situation whereby it would be right for the courts to refer to an international convention. That situation appeared when the court was faced with two choices:

one would lead to a decision inconsistent with Her Majesty's international obligations under the convention while the other would lead to a result consistent with those obligations. If statutory words have to be construed or a legal principle formulated in an area of the law where Her Majesty has accepted international obligations, our Courts – who, of course, take notice of the acts of Her Majesty done in the exercise of her sovereign power – will have regard to the convention as part of the full content or background of the law. Such a convention, especially a multilateral one, should then be considered by Courts even though no statute expressly or impliedly incorporates it into our law.[16]

On this quite restrictive basis the ECHR has been utilised by the UK courts on many occasions.

The ECHR as customary international law in the domestic courts

Lord Atkin considered the application of customary international law in the domestic courts in *Chung Chi Cheung v R*[17] where he stated:

[t]he courts acknowledge the existence of a body of rules which nations accept amongst themselves. On any judicial issue, they seek to ascertain what the relevant rule is, and having found it, they will treat it as incorporated into the domestic law, so far as it is not inconsistent with rules enacted by statutes or finally declared by their tribunals.

---

13 For examples on which Maxwell based his opinion see *Madrazo v Willes* (1820) 3 B & Ald 353 and *Niboyet v Niboyet* (1878) 4 PD 1.
14 On the Maxwell quote see *Collco Dealings Ltd v IRC* [1962] AC 1.
15 [1976] 1 Lloyd's Rep 257 at 261.
16 On international law as part of the common law see Lord Denning in *Trendtex v Central Bank of Nigeria* [1977] QB 529 at 554 and on its effect on statutory provisions see Lord Diplock in *Garland v British Rail Engineering Ltd* [1982] 2 All ER 402 at 415.
17 [1939] AC 160 at 168.

In *Trendtex v Central Bank of Nigeria*[18] Lord Denning considered the impact of international law on the common law when he stated:

> [s]eeing that the rules of international law have been changed – and do change – and that the courts have given effect to the changes without any Act of Parliament, it follows to my mind inexorably that the rules of international law, as existing from time to time, do form part of our English law.

The ECHR to the extent that it is part of customary international law formed part of English law prior to the HRA.

Applying the ECHR in the domestic courts[19]

The ECHR has broadly been applied by the courts in five areas: a) the interpretation of legislation both primary and secondary; b) scrutiny of the executive; c) common law[20]; d) the exercise of the court's discretion to grant remedies; and e) European Community law.

Statutory interpretation

Despite the fact that ratification of the ECHR by the UK took place in 1953 and the right of individual petition was subsequently recognised in December 1965, it was not until the 1970s, and in particular after the coming into force of the Immigration Act 1971, that the higher courts in the UK began to outline their thinking on the application of the ECHR in interpreting statutory provisions.

At first it looked as if the Convention could have a broad effect. In *Waddington v Miah*[1] the retrospective effect of the Immigration Act 1971 was considered by the House of Lords. In coming to the conclusion that the Act did not have retrospective effect Lord Reid relied on Article 11 (2) (prohibition on retrospective penal provisions) of the ECHR. Lord Denning MR in *Birdi v Secretary of State for Home Affairs*[2] took a more radical position when he stated that 'if an Act of Parliament did not conform to the Convention, I might be inclined to hold it invalid.' However in *R v Secretary of State for the Home Department, ex p Bhajan Singh*[3] Lord Denning MR retracted his earlier statement in *Birdie* as having gone too far. He continued in that case to consider the Immigration Act 1971 in the light of the ECHR. He found that the court should take the rights and freedoms contained in the ECHR into account when interpreting statutory provisions:

18 [1977] QB 529 at 554.
19 For a complete consideration of the application of the ECHR in the English courts see Hunt, M, *Using Human Rights Law in the English Courts* (1998) Hart, Oxford, Duffy, P J, 'English law and the European Convention on Human Rights' *International and Comparative Law Quarterly* (1980) pp 585- 618 and Dale, William 'Human Rights in the United Kingdom – International Standards' (1976) *International and Comparative Law Quarterly*, pp 292-309.
20 Including equity.
1 [1974] 1 WLR 683.
2 (1975) 119 Sol Jo 322, (1975) Times, 15 February.
3 [1976] QB 198 at 207, CA.

[i]t is to be assumed that the Crown, in taking its part in legislation, would do nothing which was in conflict with treaties. So the court should now construe the Immigration Act 1971 so as to be in conformity with a convention and not against it ... immigration officers and the Secretary of State in exercising their duties ought to bear in mind the principles stated in the convention.

Having set out this position he went on to state that if an aspect of an Act of Parliament was contrary to the ECHR the Act must prevail.

Once again considering the Immigration Act 1971 Lord Scarman stated in *R v Secretary of State for the Home Department, ex p Phansopkar*[4] that the court had a duty, in the absence of clear unequivocal provisions to the contrary, to promote the rights contained in the Convention. When interpreting and applying the law '[p]roblems of ambiguity or omission, if they arise under the language of the Act, should be resolved so as to give effect to, or at least so as not to derogate from, the rights recognised by Magna Carta and the European Convention.'

A more restrictive approach to the ECHR began to arise after *Phansopkar*. In *R v Chief Immigration Officer, ex p S Bibi*[5] Lord Denning MR retracted his earlier statement in *Bhajan Singh* that immigration officers should consider the Convention in the exercise of their duties. In the same case Roskill LJ considered Lord Scarman's statement in *Phansopkar* to be too expansive and that it might need reconsideration.[6] Geoffrey Lane LJ while accepting that the Convention was useful for clearing up ambiguity or uncertainty in statutes, found that it could not override the provisions of the Immigration Act or the Immigration Rules.[7]

In *Brind v Secretary of State for the Home Department*[8] the court found that the ECHR could be used to aid interpretation of primary and secondary legislation where there was ambiguity. In *R v Secretary of State for the Home Department, ex p Norney*[9] the court held that where the UK has been found in breach of the Convention by the ECtHR and has introduced legislation to remedy the breach, the domestic courts, when considering such legislation should place particular weight on the ECHR in interpreting that legislation.[10] By the 1990s the courts had settled upon a minimal use of the ECHR with regard to statutory interpretation. It could be used to aid interpretation where there was ambiguity but once the statute was clear there was no role for the ECHR.

---

4   [1976] QB 606 at 626.
5   [1976] 1 WLR 979.
6   [1976] 1 WLR 979 at 986. Lord Scarman continued to promote a more expensive approach to the use of the ECHR in domestic law, see in particular his dissenting judgment in *Ahmad v ILEA* [1978] QB 36. In Northern Ireland during the late 1970s a number of judges used the ECHR and its surrounding jurisprudence to aid interpretation of statutes, see in particular *R v Deery* (1977) 20 YB 827 and *R v McCormick* [1977] NI 105.
7   [1976] 1 WLR 979 at 988.
8   [1991] 1 All ER 720.
9   (1995) 7 Admin LR 861.
10   See also *SmithKline Beecham Biologics SA v Connaught Laboratories Inc* [1999] 4 All ER 498 and *Ex p Guardian Newspapers Ltd* [1999] 1 All ER 65.

Judicial scrutiny of the executive

In *Fernandes v Secretary of State for the Home Department*[11] the Court of Appeal considered whether the Home Secretary had to take account of the ECHR in the exercise of his powers under statute. The court found that the Home Secretary had no such obligation because the ECHR did not have the force of law in the UK. In *Brind v Secretary of State for the Home Department*[12] the court found that the Secretary of State, when exercising powers deriving from legislation, did not have to consider the Convention.[13] Lord Ackner, having considered the argument that the Secretary of State was bound to comply with the Convention in the exercise of his powers, stated:

> [t]he fallacy of this submission is however plain. If the Secretary of State was obliged to have proper regard to the convention, ie to conform with art 10, this inevitably would result in incorporating the convention into English domestic law by the back door. It would oblige the courts to police the operation of the convention and to ask itself in each case, where there was a challenge, whether the restrictions were 'necessary in a democratic society ...' applying the principles enunciated in the decisions of the European Court of Human Rights. The treaty, not having been incorporated in English law, cannot be a source of rights and obligations and the question – did the Secretary of State act in breach of art 10? – does not therefore arise.[14]

However, where the issue concerned fundamental rights, the English courts established a higher standard of review as part of the general test of irrationality.[15] In *R v Ministry of Defence, ex p Smith*[16] the court considered that '[t]he more substantial the interference with human rights, the more the court [shall require] by way of justification before it is satisfied that the decision is reasonable.' This test while according a higher level of protection to fundamental rights was still part of a search for 'irrationality'.

With regard to the exercise of prerogative powers Lord Woolf suggested in fairly guarded terms in *R v Secretary of State for the Home Department, ex p Ahmed,*[17] that the entering into a treaty could give rise to a legitimate expectation of compliance:

> [s]ubject to any indication to the contrary, it could be a representation that the Secretary of State would act in accordance with any obligations which he accepted under the treaty. This legitimate expectation could give rise to a right to relief, as well as additional obligations of fairness, if the Secretary of State, without reason, acted inconsistently with the obligations which this country had undertaken.

11   [1981] Imm AR 1, CA.
12   [1991] 1 All ER 720.
13   The ECHR may be relevant if it is cited in ministerial guidance see *Jordan Abiodun Iye* [1994] Imm AR 63.
14   [1976] 1 WLR 979 734 –735.
15   See *Council of Civil Service Unions v Minister for the Civil Service* [1985] AC 374 at 410.
16   [1996] 1 All ER 257.
17   30 July 1998, QBCOF 98/0650/4 at 23-24, (1998) Times, 15 October.

Apart from a sort of super irrationality test and Lord Woolf's heavily qualified suggestion that there might be a legitimate expectation that the executive comply with treaty obligations, the courts have firmly ruled out any role for the ECHR in scrutinising decisions of the executive.

Common law[18]

While it has been accepted that the ECHR could aid statutory interpretation where there was ambiguity, the impact on the common law was more uncertain. In *Uppal v Home Office,*[19] a case concerning an application to stop a deportation by the Home Office, Sir Robert Megarry V-C rejected any argument on the basis of Article 8 (respect for family life) of the ECHR and held that obligations in international law are not part of domestic law and could thus not give rise to a declaration. On the other hand in *Whitehouse v Lemon*[20] Lord Scarman expressly relied on the ECHR in deciding a point of common law.

More famously in *Malone v Metropolitan Police Comr*[1] Sir Robert Megarry V-C considered the common law position on the legality of phone tapping with reference to the ECHR. The case is both significant and confusing in that while Megarry V-C referred to his decision in *Uppal* and found that all he could do was 'to hold that the Convention does not, as a matter of English law, confer any direct rights on the plaintiff that he can enforce in the English courts,[2] he also continued to examine the case law of the ECtHR on wire tapping. Having accepted that English law did not conform with Article 8 by referring to the *Klass*[3] judgment of the ECtHR, he considered whether he could base a decision for the plaintiff on rights contained in the ECHR. He concluded:

> [i]t seems to me that where Parliament has abstained from legislating on a point that is plainly suitable for legislation, it is indeed difficult for the court to lay down new rules of common law or equity that will carry out the Crown's treaty obligations, or to discover for the first time that such rules have always existed … to decide this case in the way counsel for the plaintiff seeks would carry me far beyond any possible function of the convention as influencing English law that has ever been suggested; and it would be most undesirable. Any regulation of so complex a matter as telephone tapping is essentially a matter for Parliament, not the courts; and neither the convention nor the Klass case can, I think, play any proper part in deciding the issue for me.[4]

In *Science Research Council v Nassé*[5] the appellants relied on Article 6 (1) (right to a fair hearing) in seeking discovery of documents. Lord Wilberforce in rejecting

---

18 Here for general purposes we include equity, see the judgment of Balcombe LJ in *Derbyshire County Council v Times Newspapers* [1992] 3 All ER 65 at 77.
19 (1978) Times, 21 October.
20 [1979] AC 617 at 665.
1   [1979] 2 All ER 620.
2   [1979] 2 All ER 620 at 647.
3   (1978) 2 EHRR 214.
4   [1979] 2 All ER 620 at 648.
5   [1979] 3 All ER 673.

the application found that it was unnecessary to have recourse to the Convention as the common law standards were designed to achieve the same thing.[6]

The case of *A-G v BBC*[7] involved the Law Lords considering the law on contempt of court. The case was decided shortly after the ECtHR had found that the House of Lord's decision in *A-G v Times Newspapers Ltd*[8] upholding an injunction against *The Sunday Times*, was a breach of Article 10 (freedom of expression).[9] Lord Fraser, having briefly considered the ECtHR's decision in *The Sunday Times*, went on to outline his thoughts on the application of the ECHR in the domestic courts. He stated:

> [t]his House, and other courts in the United Kingdom, should have regard to the provisions of the Convention for the Protection of Human Rights and Fundamental Freedoms… and to the decisions of the Court of Human Rights in cases, of which this is one, where our domestic law is not firmly settled. But the convention does not form part of our law, and the decision on what that law is for our domestic courts and for this House.[10]

Lord Scarman in the same case seemed to feel *The Sunday Times* judgement in the ECtHR more keenly in suggesting that the obligation to consider the ECHR might lead the House to overrule its decision in *A-G v Times Newspapers Ltd*:

> [o]f course, neither the convention nor the European Court's decision in *Sunday Times v United Kingdom* (1979) 2 EHRR 245 is part of our law. This House's decision, even though the European court has held the rule it declares to be an infringement of the convention, is the law. Our courts must continue to look not to the European court's decision reported as *Sunday Times v United Kingdom* but to the House of Lords decision reported *in A-G v Times Newspapers Ltd* for the rule of English law. Yet there is presumption, albeit rebuttable, that our municipal law will be consistent with our international obligations … Moreover, under the practice statement of July 1966 (Note [1966] 3 All ER 77, [1966] 1 WLR 1234), this House has taken to itself the power to refuse to follow a previous decision of its own if convinced that it is necessary in the interest of justice to depart from it. Though, on its facts, the present case does not provide the House with the opportunity to reconsider its Sunday Times decision (and we have heard no argument on the point), I do not doubt that, in considering how far we should extend the application of contempt of court, we must bear in mind the impact of whatever decision we may be minded to make on the international obligations assumed by the United Kingdom under the European convention. If the issue should ultimately be, as I think in this case it is, a question of legal policy, we must have regard to

6   *Science Research Council* [1979] 3 All ER 673 at 682.
7   [1980] 3 All ER 161.
8   [1973] 3 All ER 54.
9   *Sunday Times v United Kingdom* (1979) 2 EHRR 245.
10   *BBC* [1980] 3 All ER 161 at 176.

the country's international obligation to observe the European convention as interpreted by the European Court of Human Rights.[11]

Importantly, Lord Scarman then went on to allow the appeal of the BBC with reference to the tests used by the ECtHR in the *The Sunday Times* case of 'necessary in a democratic society' and 'pressing social need'.[12]

In *A-G v Guardian Newspapers (No 2)*[13] Scott J, sitting in the High Court, examined the precedent on use of the ECHR with regard to the common law, he concluded:

> [t]he courts, in adjudicating on disputes as to the relative weight and requirements of different public interests ought, in my judgment, to endeavour to strike the balance in a manner that is consistent with the convention obligations accepted by the government, the guardian of the public interest in national security. There is, in my view, a clear analogy with the well-known rule of construction of statutes that requires statutes to be construed, if possible, consistently with the government's treaty obligations … if it is right to take into account the government's convention obligations under art 10, the article must, in my view, be given a meaning and effect consistent with the rulings of the court established by the convention to supervise its application. Accordingly, in my judgment, counsel for the Sunday Times is entitled to invite me to take into account art 10, as interpreted by the two judgments of the European Court that I have mentioned. These authorities establish that the limitation of free expression in the interests of national security should not be regarded as 'necessary' unless there is a 'pressing social need' for the limitation and unless the limitation is 'proportionate to the legitimate aims pursued'.[14]

In the Court of Appeal in the same case Sir John Donaldson considered that Article 10 of the Convention had been subsumed into domestic law and that:

> both under our domestic law and under the convention, the courts have the power and the duty to assess the 'pressing social need' for the maintenance of confidentiality 'proportionate to the legitimate aim pursued' against the basic right to freedom of expression and all other relevant factors. In so doing they are free to apply 'a margin of appreciation' based on local knowledge of the needs of the society to which they belong …[15]

In terms of the development of the ECHR and the common law the case is also significant because of the reliance placed on Lord Fraser's quote (above) in *A-G v BBC*[16] by Lord Bingham sitting in the Court of Appeal. Having considered the

---

11   *BBC* [1980] 3 All ER 161 at 177-178. On the use of the ECHR and public policy see also *Blathwayt v Lord Cawley* [1975] 3 All ER 625. .
12   See above Chapter 3.
13   [1988] 3 All ER 545.
14   [1988] 3 All ER 545 at 581, 582.
15   [1988] 3 All ER 545 at 596.
16   [1980] 3 All ER 161 at 176 (BBC).

case law of the ECtHR on Article 10 he found that if 'however, the common law were unclear, it would be appropriate to heed Lord Fraser's observation in *A-G v BBC* ...' that the ECHR and its surrounding jurisprudence should be consulted.

The methodology of the ECtHR is evident in the Court of Appeal decision in *Derbyshire County Council v Times Newspapers*[17] where Balcombe LJ in particular used the authority and language of the ECtHR in his judgment.[18] In the same case, considering the use of the ECHR in the English courts, Butler-Sloss LJ stated:

> the principles governing the duty of the English court to take account of art 10 appear to be as follows: where the law is clear and unambiguous, either stated as the common law or enacted by Parliament, recourse to art 10 is unnecessary and inappropriate. Consequently the law of libel in respect of individuals does not require the court to consider the convention. But where there is an ambiguity, or the law is otherwise unclear or so far undeclared by an appellate court, the English court is not only entitled but, in my judgment, obliged to consider the implications of art 10.[19]

However, despite the finding of Butler-Sloss LJ that the English courts had an obligation to consider the ECHR where there was ambiguity at common law, when the case was appealed to the House of Lords Lord Keith decided the issue exclusively as a common law matter.[20]

Where the common law was certain the use of the ECHR and its jurisprudence to overturn precedent was extremely limited. In *R v Chief Metropolitan Stipendiary Magistrate, ex p Choudhury*[1] the High Court had to consider whether the author Salman Rushdie and his publishers had committed blasphemous/seditious libel by publishing the book entitled *The Satanic Verses*. The court refused to accept that Article 9 (religious freedom) of the ECHR compelled the court to overturn the established common law position on blasphemy as applying to Christianity alone in order to extend it to other religions.

Little can be said with certainty regarding the application of the ECHR at common law prior to the HRA. Some judges accepted that the ECHR and its jurisprudence could be used in a similar way to the established use regarding statutory interpretation as an aid to resolving any ambiguity at common law.[2] Others however did not and continued to base their decisions solely on the established common law position.

---

17 [1992] 3 All ER 65.
18 [1992] 3 All ER 65 at 77, 82. See also Bix, B and Tomkins, A, 'Unconventional Use of the Convention' (1992) *Modern Law Review*, Vol 55, p 721.
19 For a further affirmation of this position see the speech of the Lord Chancellor in *DPP v Jones and Lloyd* [1999] 2 All ER 257.
20 [1993] 1 All ER 1011 at 1021. For an excellent commentary on Lord Kieth's judgment see Bix, B and Tomkins, A, 'Local Authorities and Libel Again' (1993) *Modern Law Review* Vol 56, pp 738-744.
1   [1991] 1 All ER 306.
2   For an example of the use of the jurisprudence of the ECtHR see *John v MGN Ltd* [1996] 2 All ER 35.

The exercise of judicial discretion

Where the courts, as opposed to a government official, were exercising a discretion, in the exercise of that discretion the court should have regard to the ECHR.[3] In particular the House of Lords was keen to emphasise in *R v Khan (Sultan)*[4] the importance of the Convention when a trial judge considered the exercise of the discretion to exclude evidence under the Police and Criminal Evidence Act 1984, s 78.

The ECHR and the European Union

The UK's membership of the European Union (EU) has provided another mechanism whereby the ECHR is applicable in the UK courts. It has long been accepted by the European Court of Justice (ECJ) that the ECHR is a source of law which 'inspires' the protection of fundamental rights as a general principle of community law. In the *Nold*[5] case the ECJ, having considered the ECHR and other treaties, found that 'international treaties for the protection of human rights on which the member states have collaborated or of which they are signatories can supply guidelines which should be followed within the framework of Community law.'[6] In 1992 the Maastricht Treaty on European Union was signed by the member states which included Article F2. Article F2 stated that the European Union:

> shall respect fundamental rights, as guaranteed by the European Convention for the Protection of Human Rights and Fundamental Freedoms… as they result from the constitutional traditions common to the Member States, as general principles of Community law.

Under the Maastricht Treaty on European Union Article F 2 was specifically non-justiciable. This changed post-Amsterdam and Article F became Article 6 of the Treaty on European Union (TEU). Article F2 became Article 6 (2) which is now justicable.[7]

The protection of fundamental rights is thus a general principle of Community law which principally binds the institutions of the EU and is justicable in so far as the acts of the institutions are amenable to judicial review before the ECJ. Where member states act within the scope of Community law, their acts must also comply with such general principles. This happens when a member state legislates to give effect to a Community obligation, or when a member state acts in derogation from Community law. It also has effect where the member state is acting in the administration of Community law (sometimes it is said the member state acts as the 'agent of the Community').

---

3   See the judgment of Lord Templeman in *A-G v Guardian Newspapers Ltd* [1987] 3 All ER 316. See also *Rantzen v MirrorGroup Newspapers* [1994] QB 670.

4   [1996] 3 All ER 289.

5   *J Nold, Kohlen und Baustoffgrosshandlung, Darmstadt v EC Commission* 4/73 [1974] 2 CMLR 338.

6   For an example of the ECJ usage of the ECHR see Case 44/79, *Hauer v Land Rheinland-Pfalz* [1979] ECR 3727.

7   See Article 46 (d) TEU. The ECJ has however held that the EU has no competence to accede to the ECHR; Opinion 2/94 [1996] ECR I-1759.

In interpreting European Community and domestic law relating to Community matters, courts at both the European and domestic level should have regard to the ECHR.[8] The application of EU law at a domestic level is clear. It is directly enforceable in the domestic courts and overrides any contrary national position.[9] As a result the ECHR is influential when applying community law as the domestic courts should attempt to act compatibly with the Convention rights and freedoms.[10] It should also be noted that the influence of the ECHR in Community law also carries the possibility of indirect Drittwirkung or horizontal effect as private parties can rely on ECHR rights regarding Community law.[11] However the influence of the ECHR via Community Law has limitations as it is only applicable to matters affecting European Community law. Therefore in matters falling outside the realm of Community law no obligation arose prior to the HRA to act compatibly with the ECHR.[12] Further the ECJ has recognised that at times it may be legitimate to limit the extent of ECHR rights and freedoms to achieve the overall aims and objectives of the European Community. Because of this the rights and freedoms need not always be respected.[13] This might in theory require the member state to violate the ECHR; this risk of conflict has now been increased by the HRA.

Fundamental rights?

The limited role conferred upon the ECHR by English courts over the past five decades has meant that arguing Convention points in the domestic courts has been a sometimes fruitless task. When dealing with statutory interpretation the ECHR was useless in the face of clear unambiguous statutory provisions. Where there was potential ambiguity the goodwill of the judge was needed in finding that ambiguity existed and that the ECHR applied. Some judges were receptive to finding ambiguity and others not. Decisions of the Executive intentionally ignoring the ECHR obligations could not give rise to review by the courts. With regard to the common law some judges found that it should be interpreted in accordance with the ECHR where there was ambiguity. Others however ignored the ECHR and clung to the pre-existing standards of the common law believing, despite the ECtHR cases to the contrary, that the common law contained the same or higher standards. Limited consideration of the Convention was allowed with regard to judicial discretion and Community

8   See *R v Kirk* [1984] ECR 2689 and *Kremzow v Austria* [1997] ECR I-2629.
9   European Communities Act 1972, s 2 (1) and *R v Secretary of State for Transport, ex p Factortame (No 2)* [1990] ECR I-2433.
10 Indeed some directives refer to the ECHR in their preamble: see *Arbeitsgemeinschaft Deutscher Rundfunkanstalten (ARD) v PRO Sieben Media AG* (Case C-6/98) [2000] All ER (EC) 3. For an example of how the ECHR operates through community law see *R v Hertfordshire County Council, ex p Green Environmental Industries Ltd* [2000] 1 All ER 773.
11 On the possibility of direct Drittwirkung see *Barber v Guardian Royal Exchange Assurance Group* (Case C-262/88) [1990] 2 All ER 660.
12 See Case 149/77 *Defrenne v Sabena* [1978] ECR 1365.
13 See *J Nold, Kohlen und Baustoffgrosshandlung, Darmstadt v EC Commission* 4/73 [1974] 2 CMLR 338 at para 14, and *Otto BV v Post Bank NV* Case C-60/92 [1993] ECR I-5683. See also *Sirdar v Secretary of State for Defence* (Case C-273/97) [1999] All ER (EC) 928.

law matters. The sum total of the ECHR's application in the English courts was considered by Lester in 1984 when he stated:

> [a]t best the Convention is no more than an aid to the interpretation of legal ambiguities and uncertainties so as to ensure, where possible, that United Kingdom law is in conformity with the United Kingdom's treaty obligations. At worst it is so many worthless pieces of paper.[14]

The situation has somewhat changed since Parliament passed the Human Rights Act 1998. In the period between the passing of the HRA in 1998 and its coming into force in October 2000 the courts have paid much closer attention to the ECHR rights, freedoms and precedent in deciding cases. A good example of this is *Reynolds v Times Newspapers Ltd*[15] where there is extensive discussion of the ECHR and its jurisprudence on press freedom.[16] As Lord Steyn considered:

> [n]ow the Human Rights Act 1998, which will corporate the convention into our legal order, is on the statute book. And the government has announced that it will come into force on 2 October 2000. The constitutional dimension of freedom of expression is reinforced. This is the backcloth against which the present appeal must be considered. It is common ground that in considering the issues before the House, and the development of English law, the House can and should act on the reality that the 1998 Act will soon be in force. The new landscape is of great importance inasmuch as it provides the taxonomy against which the question before the House must be considered.[17]

14   Lester, Anthony, 'Fundamental Rights: The United Kingdom Isolated?' (1984) *Public Law*, pp 46-72 at 66.
15   [1999] 4 All ER 609.
16   See also *R v Chief Constable of the North Wales Police, ex p AB* [1998] 3 All ER 310.
17   *Reynolds v Times Newspapers Ltd* [1999] 4 All ER 609 at 628.

Chapter six

The Human Rights Act 1998

Let not England forget her precedence of teaching nations how to live[1]

The history and background to the HRA 1998

The UK's position with regard to the ECHR has been one of almost consistent inconsistency. While the UK is the home of Magna Carta and the Bill of Rights 1688 it is also the home of utilitarianism, positivism and Dicey's concept of parliamentary sovereignty. It has been these latter legal concepts that have prevailed in the legal system of the UK.[2] In a continuation of the ideological schizophrenia, successive Conservative governments, despite their ideological focus on the individual, have opposed the ECHR *per se*, the right of individual petition and the incorporation of the ECHR into domestic law. Equally, successive Labour governments, despite their collectivist ideology, have promoted the individual rights contained in the ECHR. A Labour government negotiated and ratified the ECHR in 1950 and 1951 respectively, a Labour government accepted the individual right of petition in December 1965 and a Labour government incorporated the ECHR into domestic law in the HRA 1998.

The formation of the Council of Europe and the establishment of the ECHR owed a great deal to the political backing of Churchill who believed that civil and political

---

1   Milton, *Areopagitica* quoted by Lord Bingham during the parliamentary debate on the HRA, HL Debates, 3 November 1997: col 1247.
2   See Feldman, D, 'The Human Rights Act 1998 and Constitutional Principles' (1999) *Legal Studies*, p 166 and Singh, R, *The Future of Human Rights in the United Kingdom* (1997) Hart, pp 1-2.

rights offered a bulwark against Communism. However, Churchill's interest in the ECHR was for a convention to be enforced via the state mechanism. Therefore should a state commit a violation of the ECHR it was for the other members of the Council of Europe to take action and not the individuals who had had their rights violated. Churchill and the Conservative party were completely opposed to a Human Rights Convention enforceable by individuals.[3] By 1950, although UK lawyers were instrumental in drafting the ECHR, the opposition of Churchill and certain members of the Labour Cabinet to the right of individual petition[4] led the UK government to lobby successfully for the right of individual petition to be optional.[5] While it was the Attlee Labour government (1945-1951) that negotiated and ratified the ECHR, it fell to the returning Conservative government under Churchill (1951-1955) to decide whether to recognise the right of individual petition. Not surprisingly, given the Conservative party's opposition to the right of individual petition, recognition never materialised.

Four Conservative administrations passed under Churchill, Eden (1955-1957), Macmillan (1957-1963) and Douglas-Home (1963-1964) without any progress on the recognition of the individual right of petition. During this period the Conservative governments' policy remained constant:

> [t]he position which Her Majesty's Government have continuously taken up is that they do not recognise the right of individual petition, because they take the view that States are the proper subject of international law and if individuals are given rights under international treaties effect should be given to those rights through the national law of the States concerned.[6]

It was not until December 1965 that the UK, under the Wilson Labour government (1964-1970), despite the absence of any policy on the matter, accepted the right of individual petition.[7] The acceptance was treated by the Labour government as uncontroversial and unimportant. No Cabinet meeting or House of Commons' debate took place, yet from the moment of acceptance, a supra-national court had been empowered to scrutinise UK law.[8] It was at this point that the debate for incorporation of the ECHR into domestic law began in earnest.

In 1968 the Fabian Society produced a document entitled *Democracy and Individual Rights*[9] authored by one Anthony Lester, now Lord Lester of Herne Hill QC, who argued for limited incorporation of the ECHR into domestic law. He suggested the

---

3   See Lester, Anthony, 'Fundamental Rights: The United Kingdom Isolated?' (1984) *Public Law* pp 46- 72 at 49-50.
4   Lester (n 3 above) pp 49-51.
5   On the UK's role in the preparation of the ECHR see Marston, Geoffrey, 'The United Kingdom's Part in the European Convention on Human Rights, 1950' (1993) *International and Comparative Law Quarterly* pp 796- 826.
6   Selwyn Lloyd Conservative Foreign Minister speaking in the House of Commons on 29 July 1957, HC Debates, vol 574, cols 867-868.
7   In fact what discernable policy there was appeared to be negative see HC Debates, vol 706 col. 194, 9 February 1965.
8   On the background to the acceptance of the individual right of petition see n 3 above (Lester) pp 58-61.
9   Lester, A, *Democracy and Individual Rights* (1968) Fabian Society Pamphlet No 390.

ECHR should not be enforceable in the courts at first but would provide an educative force, which would ultimately lead to a fully enforceable Convention.[10] Over the next few years a number of attempts were made in Parliament to put in place a bill of rights. These attempts met with little success as the Labour government was opposed to a bill of rights.[11]

That opposition hardened with the following Conservative administration under Heath (1970-74) as the situation in Northern Ireland escalated and the Immigration Act 1971 was passed. The first effects of the recognition of the right of individual petition were also beginning to make themselves felt as the first cases fell to the ECtHR for adjudication.[12] The UK was also the subject of two inter-state applications brought by the Republic of Ireland in the early 1970s regarding the exercise of emergency powers in Northern Ireland.[13] However, it was at the domestic level that the next pressure for incorporation of the ECHR arose. The Immigration Act 1971 had spawned a mass of cases before the domestic courts in which the ECHR rights and freedoms were claimed.[14] These cases had the effect of bringing into sharp focus the inferior status of the Convention in domestic law. In 1974 Lord Scarman famously gave his Hamlyn Lectures entitled *English Law – The New Dimension*. He considered that:

> [t]he legal system must now ensure that the law of the land will itself meet the exacting standards of human rights declared in international instruments, to which the United Kingdom is a party, as inviolable. This calls for entrenched or fundamental rights protected by a Bill of Rights – constitutional law which it is the duty of the courts to protect even against the power of Parliament. In other words, there must be a constitutional restraint placed upon the legislative power which is designed to protect the individual citizen from instant legislation conceived in fear or prejudice and enacted in breach of human rights.[15]

The Labour governments that succeeded Heath under Wilson (1974-1976) and Callaghan (1976-1979) inherited the same continuing civil unrest in Northern Ireland and immigration concerns. There were however some limited signs of support for incorporation of the ECHR. In 1975 the Labour party produced a discussion paper on human rights which considered that civil liberties, with their focus on the individual, were compatible with socialism, with its focus on the

10   See also the lecture given on human rights by Tom Sargent, former secretary of Justice, in Bangalore 1968 which is referenced in Anderson, N, *Law Liberty and Justice* (1978) p 56.
11   In 1969 the Conservative Lord Lambton introduced a Bill based on the Canadian Act for the Protection of Human Rights and Fundamental Freedoms 1960. The Bill was defeated by the government. See HC Debates, vol 782, cols 474, 23 April 1969. Lord Wade and Lord Arran also introduced Bills see HL Debates Vol 302 cols 1026, 18 June 1969 and HL Debates Vol 313, col 243, 26 November 1970.
12   See *Donnelly v United Kingdom* (1972) 4 DR 72, *East African Asians v United Kingdom* (1973) 3 EHRR 76, *W, X, Y, and Z v United Kingdom* Appl 3435-38/67 (1968) 11 YB 562 and *X v United Kingdom* (1970) 30 CD 70.
13   *Ireland v United Kingdom* (1972) 15 YB 76 and *Ireland v United Kingdom* (1978) 2 EHRR 25.
14   See Chapter 5.
15   Lord Scarman, *English Law – The New Dimension* (1974) Stevens, pp 19-20. See also Lord Hailsham's Richard Dimbleby Lecture in 1976 entitled the 'Elective Dictatorship' arguing for an entrenched bill of rights and later Lord Scarman *Why Britain Needs a Written Constitution* (1992) London: Charter 88, The Fourth Sovereignty Lecture.

collective, and the incorporation of the ECHR as compatible with the rest of the Labour party's collectivist policies.[16] A discussion paper on the ECHR was also produced by the Labour Home Secretary Roy Jenkins.[17] The Northern Ireland Standing Advisory Commission on Human Rights recommended incorporation[18] as did a Lords Select Committee.[19] However, the Labour government never moved any closer to supporting incorporation of the ECHR nor did the Labour party in opposition under Foot (1980-1983) or Kinnock (1983-1992).

The Conservative government under Thatcher (1979-1990) had an odd relationship with the ECHR. The Conservative party itself during this period seemed either apathetic to the incorporation or actively supportive of incorporation.[20] However, despite the Thatcher administration's rhetoric of small government and returning power to the people, the majority in Cabinet, and crucially Thatcher herself, were opposed to the incorporation of the ECHR. In 1985 Lord Elton, Minister of State at the Home Office announced:

> [t]he question of incorporating such principles [the ECHR] into United Kingdom law raises important constitutional issues which would need to be fully explored between the political parties. The Government do not judge the present time is ripe for further initiative ...[1]

This opposition, combined with a get tough policy on Northern Ireland and immigration, had the knock-on effect of increasing the violations found against the UK by the ECtHR which in turn further hardened the opposition of the government.

In 1986 the Conservative peer Lord Broxbourne, supported by Lord Scarman, introduced a Bill to incorporate the ECHR which narrowly failed to get a second reading.[2] The effect of this activity in Parliament and the increasing cases against the UK in Strasbourg was to raise or at least keep alive public awareness of the ECHR. In 1987 a Cabinet office circular was issued to effect what was known as 'Strasbourg-proofing' because of the number of challenges to government decisions at both the domestic and European level. The circular was not aimed at giving positive effect to the ECHR but rather at minimising the chances of a successful challenge to government decisions.

---

16 See Zander, G, *A Bill of Rights* (1996) Sweet and Maxwell, pp 14-15.
17 Home Office Discussion Paper: Legislation on Human Rights; with particular Reference to the European Convention June 1976.
18 *The Protection of Human Rights by Law in Northern Ireland* (1977) HMSO, Cmnd 7009.
19 (1978) *Report of the Select Committee on a Bill of Rights*, HL 176, para 53, 24 May.
20 See the Conservative Party Election Manifesto 1979 on all-party talks on a Bill of Rights, p 21 and also the letter of the former Conservative Minister Geoffrey Rippon to *The Times*, 30 March 1981 where he argues for a bill of rights and that the Thatcher government should hold all-party talks on the matter as their Election Manifesto had agreed. In June 1984, 107 Conservative MPs supported the incorporation of the ECHR into domestic law see n 16 above (Zander) p 28.
1   HC Debates cols 159 12 March 1985.
2   HL Debates Vol 109, cols 1288, 6 February (1987). The same Bill slightly amended was introduced in the House of Commons by Sir Edward Gardner (Conservative) which similarly failed, see Blackburn, R, *Towards a Constitutional Bill of Rights for the United Kingdom* (1999) Pinter, p 8.

On 30 November 1988 on the 300th anniversary of the Bill of Rights 1688 *The Guardian* newspaper published 'Charter 88', a document proposing the enshrining of a bill of rights to protect civil liberties. It became a rallying point for all those who wished to see the incorporation of the ECHR into domestic law.[3] Mrs Thatcher, as did the Labour party,[4] remained unmoved. In response to a parliamentary question as to whether she would support the incorporation of the ECHR she replied:

[n]o. We are committed to, and support, the principles of human rights in the European Convention on Human Rights but we believe that is for Parliament rather than the judiciary to determine how those principles are best secured.[5]

John Major's (1990-1997) Conservative government, while less aggressive,[6] continued the same policies. In response to a parliamentary question as to whether he intended to incorporate Article 10 of the ECHR into UK law Major replied:

[n]o. Our policy remains not to incorporate the European Convention on human rights into domestic law, since we believe that it is for parliament, rather than the judiciary to determine how the principles of human rights in the convention are best sourced.[7]

The arrival of John Smith (1992-1994) as Labour leader in 1992 signals the beginning of the incorporation of the ECHR into domestic law. As part of the modernisation of the Labour party Smith committed the Labour party to incorporation of the ECHR. In March 1993 he gave a lecture entitled *'A Citizen's Democracy'* in which he stated:

[t]he quickest and simplest way of achieving democratic and legal recognition of a substantial package of human rights would be by incorporating into British law the European Convention on Human Rights.[8]

Official Labour Party policy embracing the ECHR soon followed.

At this point a significant change also occurred in the senior judiciary's support for incorporation of the ECHR. In the 1980s only Lord Chancellors Hailsham and Gardiner, as well as Lords Scarman and Denning, supported the incorporation of the ECHR. The other senior judiciary were either actively hostile as were Lords Diplock and Elwyn-Jones or generally suspicious. By the time the Labour party came to support the incorporation of the ECHR so had a significant group of the senior

---

3   For differing academic views on a bill of rights see Dworkin, R, *A Bill of Rights For Britain* (1990) *Chatto and Windus and Ewing, K D, and Gearty, C A, Democracy or a Bill of Rights* (1991) Society of Labour Lawyers.
4   See Roy Hattersley Deputy Leader of the Labour Party in *The Guardian* 12 December 1988.
5   HC Debates 6 July 1989 Cols WA251-2.
6   For example the Major government reintroduced the right of individual petition to the Isle of Man in 1993.
7   HC Debates Col., 15 January 1993, WA822.
8   See p 98, n 16 (Zander) pp 33-34.

judiciary. In 1994 Lord Lester introduced a Human Rights Bill in the House of Lords.[9] It managed to garner the support of Lords Browne-Wilkinson, Woolf, Bingham, Ackner, Scarman, Lloyd, Simon, Slynn, and Taylor. Further Lord Lester claimed that the Bill had the support of most of the rest of the senior judiciary.[10] However, the Conservative Lord Chancellor Lord Mackay remained totally opposed.[11]

By 1994 the Conservative government's policy while still opposed to incorporation, appeared to be less hostile to the ECHR generally. In response to a parliamentary question by Lord Lester as to whether public officials have a duty to comply with the ECHR and the International Covenant on Civil and Political Rights, Baroness Chalker replied for the government:

> [i]nternational treaties are binding on states and not on individuals, the United Kingdom is party to both treaties and it must comply with its obligations under them. In so far as acts of Ministers and civil servants in the discharge of their public functions constitute acts which engage the responsibility of the United Kingdom, they must comply with the terms of the treaties.[12]

Labour party policy in favour of the incorporation of the ECHR was continued under the leadership of Tony Blair when he succeeded to the Labour leadership on the untimely death of John Smith in 1994. In 1996 in the course of the John Smith Memorial Lecture he stated:

> I believe it makes sense to end the cumbersome practice of forcing people to go to Strasbourg to hold their government to account. By incorporating the Convention into British law the rights and guarantees would be available in courts in both Britain and Northern Ireland. This would make it clear that the protection afforded by the Convention was not some foreign import but that it had been accepted by successive British Governments and that it should apply throughout the United Kingdom.[13]

Later, in 1996, the Labour Shadow Home Secretary Jack Straw produced a consultation paper outlining generally the form that an Act of Parliament incorporating the ECHR would take and the Labour party manifesto going into the 1997 election gave a clear commitment to the incorporation of the ECHR.[14]

In many ways the Labour party's commitment to the ECHR went hand in hand with New Labour's break with its ideological past away from socialism and towards a

---

9   Lord Lester, 'The Mouse that Roared: The Human Rights Bill 1995' (1995), *Public Law* p 198.
10   Lester (n 9 above). Later Lord Taylor as Lord Chief Justice supported the incorporation of the ECHR, see Blackburn, R, *Towards a Constitutional Bill of Rights for the United Kingdom* (1999) Pinter, p 29.
11   Lecture to the Citizenship Foundation, 'Parliament and the Judges: A Constitutional Challenge?' 8 July 1996.
12   HL Debates, 7 December 1994, col WA84.
13   Tony Blair, *John Smith Memorial Lecture* (1996).
14   See 'Bringing Rights Home: Consultation Paper on Labour's plans to incorporate the European Convention on Human Rights into UK law' Labour Party Consultation Paper (1996) and Labour Party Manifesto 'New Labour Because Britain Deserves Better' (1997), p 35.

more centralist liberal position.[15] While the replacement of Clause 4 (commitment to the state ownership of the means of production) of the Labour party's constitution by the Labour party was a high profile break with socialism, the commitment to introduce into domestic law a document devoted not to social and economic rights but to civil and political rights was also a significant step away from socialism and towards liberal constitutionalism.[16]

The Conservative party remained opposed to the incorporation of the ECHR to the last. In their 1997 election manifesto they stated:

> [w]e do not believe that there is a case for more radical reform that would undermine the House of Commons. A new bill of rights, for example, would risk transferring power away from parliament to legal courts – undermining the democratic supremacy of parliament as representatives of the people.[17]

The election of the Labour government in May 1997 was followed soon after by the introduction of the Human Rights Act 1998 as a Bill with accompanying White Paper on 23 October 1997. In introducing the Bill for its reading in the House of Lords the Lord Chancellor set out the reasons for the HRA:

> [t]he traditional freedom of the individual under an unwritten constitution to do himself that which is not prohibited by law gives no protection from misuse of power by the state, nor any protection from acts or omissions of public bodies which harm individuals in a way that is incompatible with their human rights under the convention. Our legal system has been unable to protect people in the 50 cases in which the European Court has found a violation of the convention by the United Kingdom. That is more than any other country except Italy. The trend has been upwards. Over half the violations have been found since 1990 … This Bill will bring human rights home. People will be able to argue for their rights and claim their remedies under the convention in any court or tribunal in the United Kingdom. Our courts will develop human rights throughout society. A culture of awareness of human rights will develop. Before the Second Reading of any Bill the responsible Minister will make a statement that the Bill is or is not compatible with convention rights. So there will have to be close scrutiny of the human rights implications of all legislation before it goes forward. Our standing will rise internationally. The protection

15 It has always been the policy of the Liberal Democrats in their various manifestations as the Liberal party and the Social Democratic Party (SDP) to incorporate a bill of rights into domestic law. See Liberal Democrats *Here We Stand: Proposals for Modernising Britain's Democracy* (1993) Liberal Democrats.

16 For Labour's shift to the centre see, Labour Party, *Social Justice and Economic Efficiency* (1988) Labour Party; Labour Party, *Meet the Challenge Make the Change – Final Report of Labour's Policy Review for the 1990s* (1989) Labour Party; Labour Party, *Looking to the Future* (1990) Labour Party; Anderson, P and Mann, N *Safety First. The Making of New Labour* (1997) Granta Books. Driver, S and Martell, L, *New Labour* (1998) Polity Press.

17 Conservative Party Manifesto *You Can Only Be Sure with the Conservatives* (1997) pp 49-50.

of human rights at home gives credibility to our foreign policy to advance the cause of human rights around the world.[18]

The Bill had a relatively smooth and rapid passage though both Houses of Parliament. The only major opposition came from the Church of England (CE) and the Press. The CE was concerned about its position as the established Church. This meant that it would be part of the state and would be bound to act compatibly with the HRA. The Press were obviously concerned that freedom of expression should not be curtailed by privacy rights. To some extent their lobbying was effective as numerous changes occurred affecting the application of the bill to religious organisations and freedom of the press. Other changes affected the scrutiny of remedial orders in section 10, and the abolition of the death penalty was also added (Protocol 6). On the 9 November 1998, the Bill received the Royal Assent. The Act did not come into force immediately as the government wished time to carry out extensive training of civil servants, and in particular the judiciary, as to the application and interpretation of the Act. After an almost two-year delay it came into force on 2 October 2000.[19]

The general scheme of the HRA 1998

How does the HRA work generally?

Broadly speaking the HRA has incorporated[20] most but not all of the ECHR rights and freedoms into domestic law. Section 1 of the HRA sets out the scope of the Convention rights covered by the Act: Articles 2-12 and 14, Articles 1-3 of Protocol 1 and Articles 1 and 2 of the 6th Protocol, as read with Articles 16-18 of the Convention.[1] Articles 1,13 and 15 have been left out. The reasons for this are discussed below. These Convention rights and freedoms are given effect in the HRA in two distinct ways.

First all public authorities, that is government departments, courts and tribunals and less obviously private bodies who carry out a public function eg privatised utilities and transport companies, must act compatibly with the Convention.[2] If they fail to do so it is an unlawful act for which the victim can bring an action against the public authority alleging a breach of the Convention rights.[3] The HRA has no direct effect on private litigation or on quasi-public bodies acting in their private capacity but it

---

18 HL Debates, 3 November 1997: Col 1229.
19 It came into effect earlier in Scotland via the Scotland Act.
20 Although the Lord Chancellor disagrees that the HRA incorporates the ECHR, for all practical purposes it incorporates those rights and freedoms of the ECHR contained in the HRA: HL Debates Col 850 5th Feburary 1998. The Home Secretary did not seem to share the view of the Lord Chancellor regarding the use of the word 'incorporation': see HC Debates Col 771, 16 February 1998.
1 See Chapter 4 on the ECHR rights and freedoms.
2 Section 6, HRA 1998. Private bodies who carry out public functions must only act compatibly in the exercise of that public function.
3 Section 7, HRA 1998.

will have an indirect effect on private litigation as the courts are public authorities under the HRA and therefore bound to act compatibly with the Convention rights. As a result the courts must interpret statutes, common law, equity and exercise judicial discretion in accordance with the Convention. The HRA also creates a defence for private bodies who are involved in litigation with a public body. One example of this would be to argue that the litigation itself is an interference with the private body's freedom of speech as in *Derbyshire County Council v Times Newspapers.*[4]

In fulfilling its role under the HRA the courts must take into account but are not bound by the jurisprudence of the ECtHR.[5] The courts and tribunals may grant any remedy within their powers which they deem just and appropriate. This could include an award of damages, an order to quash an unlawful decision, or to cease an action or proposed action which affects a Convention right.[6]

The second way in which the Convention rights are given effect is through the legislative process combined with a new power of the courts to scrutinise legislation. All new legislation must have a statement from the relevant Minister stating that the Bill is compatible with the Convention rights or if he is unable to make such a statement, a statement that he cannot do so and that he wishes to proceed with the Bill anyway, is necessary.[7] All legislation, so far as possible must be read and given effect in a way which is compatible with the Convention rights.[8] If that is not possible and the legislation is either primary legislation or subordinate legislation made in the exercise of a power conferred by primary legislation and that primary legislation prevents removal of the incompatibly, a higher court[9] may make a declaration of incompatibility.[10] Should the court choose to do this the legislation still stands and has its full effect. Subordinate legislation outside these criteria may be quashed by the court. If a higher court does issue a declaration of incompatibility the HRA provides that a Minister can make a remedial order amending the incompatible legislation.[11] The HRA does not affect the right of individual petition to Strasbourg but applicants must still show that they have exhausted all the domestic remedies first. The availability of Convention rights at a domestic level should stem the flow of cases to Strasbourg. The Strasbourg court still remains the final arbitrar of ECHR rights and freedoms.

What rights does the HRA incorporate into domestic law?

As noted above, section 1 of the Act incorporates most but not all of the rights and freedoms of the ECHR. The rights and freedoms covered by the HRA are set out in Schedule 1 of the Act and include:

4   [1993] 1 All ER 1011.
5   Section 2, HRA 1998.
6   Section 8, HRA 1998.
7   Section 19, HRA 1998.
8   Section 3, HRA 1998.
9   House of Lords, Court of Appeal, High Court, Privy Council, the Courts-Martial Appeal Court, and in Scotland the High Court of Justiciary.
10 Sections 3 and 4, HRA 1998.
11 Section 10, HRA 1998.

Article 2: The right to life

Article 3: Freedom from torture or inhuman or degrading treatment or punishment

Article 4: Freedom from slavery, servitude or forced or compulsory labour

Article 5: The right to liberty and security of person

Article 6: The right to a fair trial

Article 7: Freedom from retroactive criminal offences and punishment

Article 8: The right to respect for private and family life, home and correspondence

Article 9: Freedom of religion

Article 10: Freedom of expression

Article 11: Freedom of assembly and association

Article 12: The right to marry and to found a family

Article 14: Freedom from discrimination in respect of protected rights

Article 16: Restrictions on the political rights of aliens

Article 17: Restrictions on activities subversive of Convention rights

Article 18: Prohibition of the use of restrictions for an improper purpose

First Protocol: Article 1: The right to property, First Protocol, Article 2: The right to education, First Protocol, Article 3: The right to free election

Sixth Protocol:[12] Articles 1 and 2: Freedom from the death penalty[13]

The HRA does not incorporate Articles 1 (state obligation to secure the rights and freedoms), 13 (the right to an effective national remedy), 15 (derogation in time of war or other public emergency) and Protocols 4 [14] and 7.[15] Neither Protocols 4 nor 7 have been ratified by the UK. The government has promised to ratify and include Protocol 7 in the HRA rights and freedoms once it introduces legislation to amend certain family law provisions.[16] Protocol 4 is presently being reviewed but the government has no plans to include it at present. Section 1 of the Act does not therefore truly incorporate the rights and freedoms of the ECHR into domestic law rather it gives effect to the rights and freedoms contained in Schedule 1 of the HRA.[17]

---

12   The Sixth Protocol was not originally included but after significant pressure in Parliament the government capitulated and included it. The UK ratified the Sixth Protocol in 1999.
13   See Chapter 4 for an analysis of each of the ECHR rights and freedoms.
14   Freedom from imprisonment for non-fulfilment of a contractual obligation; freedom of movement within a state and the freedom to leave its territory; the right of a national not to be expelled from and to enter a state's territory; freedom of aliens from collective expulsion.
15   Freedom from expulsion of individual aliens; the right to review in criminal cases; the right to compensation for miscarriages of justice; *ne bis in idem* (freedom from double jeopardy); equality of rights of spouses.
16   See the accompanying White Paper 'Rights Brought Home' to the HRA 1998 Cm 3782 (1997).
17   Section 1 (4) and (5), HRA 1998 provide for the Minister to add any future Protocols the UK may ratify.

While Article 15 (derogation in an emergency) is not expressly included in section 1 it is given effect through a combination of section 1 (2) and sections 14 and 15 of the Act. Section 1 (2) provides that the rights and freedoms in Section 1 are subject to any designated reservations or derogations. The UK has one derogation in place with regard to Article 5 (3) (right to be brought before a judge within a reasonable time) and a reservation in place with regard to Protocol 1, Article 2 (education).[18] Sections 14 and 15 of the Act provide that these constitute a 'designated' derogation and reservation for the purposes of the HRA.[19] Sections 14 and 15 also provide that should the UK make a derogation or reservation in the future they can be given effect by an order of the Secretary of State.[20] If an existing derogation or reservation is amended, replaced or wholly or partly withdrawn, it ceases to be 'designated' for the purposes of the HRA.[1]

The omission of Articles 1 (obligation to give effect to the Convention rights) and 13 (right to an effective remedy) was the subject of a lively debate in Parliament.[2] The government's position on why the Articles were omitted was outlined by the Lord Chancellor:

> [t]he Bill gives effect to Article 1 by securing to people in the United Kingdom the rights and freedoms of the convention. It gives effect to Article 13 by establishing a scheme under which convention rights can be raised before our domestic courts. To that end, remedies are provided in Clause 8 [HRA section 8]. If the concern is to ensure that the Bill provides an exhaustive code of remedies for those whose convention rights have been violated, we believe that Clause 8 already achieves that and that nothing further is needed. We have set out in the Bill a scheme to provide remedies for violation of convention rights and we do not believe that it is necessary to add to it. We also believe that it is undesirable to provide for Articles 1 and 13 in the Bill in this way. The courts would be bound to ask themselves what was intended beyond the existing scheme of remedies set out in the Bill. It might lead them to fashion remedies other than the Clause 8 remedies, which we regard as sufficient and clear. We believe that Clause 8 provides effective remedies before our courts.[3]

The omission of Article 1 in itself does not provide much of a difficulty as the HRA does indeed secure the majority of the rights and freedoms into domestic law. However there is a difficulty as to the status of Article 13 when the courts come to

---

18   Section 14 (1) and 15 (1), HRA 1998. See Chapter 4 for a full account of the effect of these derogations and reservations.
19   For an interesting view on the operation of a 'designated' derogation or reservation at domestic level which was operable at the Strasbourg level see Feldman D, 'The Human Rights Act 1998 and Constitutional Principles' (1999) *Legal Studies*, pp 194-195.
20   Sections 14 (1) (b) and 15 (1) (b), HRA 1998.
1   Sections 14 (3) and 15 (3), HRA 1998.
2   On Article 13 see HL Debates, 18 November 1997, Columns 466-481, HL Debates, 19 January 1998, Columns 1263-1268, HL Debates, 29 January 1998, Columns 381-388, and HC Debates, 20 May 1998, Columns 975-987.
3   HL Debates, 18 Nov 1997, Column 476.

consider the jurisprudence of the ECtHR, as it is a significant right in itself.[4] The government seemed somewhat concerned that the incorporation of Article 13 would provide the courts with the additional weapon of creating new remedies. They clearly did not wish to allow that to happen.[5] The Lord Chancellor addressed this issue in response to a question by Lord Lester as to whether the courts could have regard to the case law on Article 13:

> the courts may have regard to Article 13. In particular, they may wish to do so when considering the very ample provisions of Clause 8(1). I remind your Lordships of the terms of that provision:
>
> > In relation to any Act (or proposed Act) of a public authority which the court finds is (or would be) unlawful, it may grant such relief or remedy, or make such order, within its jurisdiction as it considers just and appropriate.
>
> Knowing the remedial amplitude of the law of the United Kingdom, I cannot see any scope for the argument that English or Scots law is incapable within domestic adjectival law of providing effective remedies.[6]

It would seem from this that despite the omission of these Articles the courts can rely on the Strasbourg jurisprudence where they are relevant.[7] This does serve to emphasise the point that the HRA is a domestic human rights enforcement mechanism. It operates within the domestic legal system(s). It is distinct from the legal system of the ECHR. This may produce its own incompatibilities between the two systems which require to be resolved. The question is whether the effectiveness of the HRA mechanism may itself end up being challenged before the ECtHR as itself being inadequate. The omission of Articles 1 and 13 does mean that the government in the course of 'bringing rights home' has changed the quality of their operation within the domestic order.

Are the courts bound by the Strasbourg case law?

Section 2 of the HRA 1998 provides that a court or tribunal determining a question in connection with Convention rights must take into account the jurisprudence of the ECtHR, the Commission of the European Court of Human Rights and any decisions of the Committee of Ministers.[8] The effect of this section is that the court is not bound by the jurisprudence of the ECtHR but rather it is of a persuasive authority. Lord Lester set out the advantages of persuasive rather than binding

---

4   See Chapter 4 on Article 13.
5   See the Lord Chancellor above and also the Home Secretary HC Debates 20 May 1998, Column 979.
6   HL Debates 18 Nov 1997: Column 478. The courts have already had occasion to have regard to Article 13 see *Rantzen v Mirror Group Newspapers* [1994] QB 670, CA and *R v Khan* [1997] AC 558, HL.
7   Certainly the Lord Chancellor was aware of the implications of his statement as he alluded to the use of his statement in a *Pepper v Hart* manner to find the intention of Parliament. See HL Debates 18 Nov 1997: Column 477.
8   The Commission and the Committee no longer have a judicial function but their decided cases still have an impact. On the operation of the old and new Strasbourg machinery see Chapter 2.

authority during a debate on an amendment to make the Strasbourg case law binding:

> [t]he only obligation under the convention is in Article 46, paragraph 1, which obliges the United Kingdom to abide by the final judgment of the European Court of Human Rights in any case to which it is party but not otherwise. The amendment seeks to bind our courts by other judgments of the European Court of Human Rights, even though the convention does not compel that conclusion. It is profoundly ironic that the noble Lord, Lord Kingsland, should seek to move an amendment which is more European than the convention requires, especially in view of the Benches on which he sits and the Front Bench from which he speaks since his party has not been conspicuous in urging that European rights should be given great force in our domestic law.
>
> In any event, to give the judgments of the European court great persuasive force in our courts is sufficient. If a judgment of our courts turns out to be incompatible with the convention and is against the applicant, no doubt the European Court of Human Rights will eventually so decide. In the meantime, I believe that our courts, being close to our citizens and our social and political circumstances, are best able to exercise the margin of appreciation enjoyed by our public authorities without being hampered unnecessarily by a doctrine of stare decisis which is not required by the European Convention on Human Rights. [9]

While it is clear from the Act that the domestic courts must draw on the Strasbourg case law, two questions arose in the Parliamentary debates regarding the extent to which the courts should comply with it. First in what circumstances did the government see that the courts could depart from the judgments of the Strasbourg court, and second could the courts draw on the jurisprudence generally or were they to look only at cases where the UK was a respondent? Dealing with both questions the Lord Chancellor stated:

> [t]here may also be occasions when it would be right for the United Kingdom courts to depart from Strasbourg decisions. We must remember that the interpretation of the convention rights develops over the years. Circumstances may therefore arise in which a judgment given by the European Court of Human Rights decades ago contains pronouncements which it would not be appropriate to apply to the letter in the circumstances of today in a particular set of circumstances affecting this country. The Bill as currently drafted would allow our courts to use their common sense in applying the European court's judgment to such a case. We feel that to accept this amendment [to make Strasbourg decisions binding] removes from the judges the flexibility and discretion that they require in developing human rights law. Also in his contribution the noble and learned Lord, Lord Browne-Wilkinson, echoed a point that I believe I made in Committee. Clause 2 requires the courts to pay heed to all the judgments of the European Court of Human Rights regardless of whether they have been given in cases involving the United Kingdom. [10]

9   HL Debates, 18 Nov 1997: Column 513.
10 HL Debates 19 Jan 1998: Column 1272.

The non-binding nature of the Strasbourg case law seems intended to give the domestic courts room to accommodate the law in the UK and Strasbourg rather than make them the same. When the courts can depart from that case law is unclear. They clearly can do so if they wish, but they 'must' consider the Strasbourg jurisprudence before doing so. It is possible that the inclusion of sections 12 and 13 emphasising the importance of freedom of expression and religious expression, which is not contained in the ECHR,[11] could provide cause to depart from the Strasbourg jurisprudence, as will situations where an evolutive approach to interpretation is appropriate.[12] Devolution may also result in different interpretations of rights and freedoms depending on the area of the UK in which the alleged violation takes place.[13] The autonomous meaning of words applied at the Strasbourg level can lead to a different interpretation of rights which can affect whether a violation has occurred. The same is true of the French language text of the ECHR which is not included in Schedule 1. Further, the doctrine of the margin of appreciation will not operate in the same form in the domestic courts.[14]

It is important to note at this point that it is not just the decisions of the Strasbourg court that are being given effect in the UK through the HRA but also the interpretative methods. In order to interpret the Convention rights compatibly with the Strasbourg jurisprudence the courts will have to adopt the interpretative techniques of the ECtHR. This may prove somewhat problematic and so it is a subject we return to later in this Chapter (see below, Will the UK judiciary have to change the way they interpret the law?)

Does all legislation have to be interpreted compatibly with the Convention rights?

Section 3 deals with the interpretation of legislation. It provides that '[s]o far as it is possible to do so, all primary and subordinate legislation must be read and given effect in a way which is compatible with the Convention rights.' It applies to all legislation and so covers legislation enacted prior to the HRA, the HRA itself and legislation enacted after the HRA whether it contains a statement of compatibility or not.[15] If it proves impossible to construe primary legislation in a compatible manner its validity is unaffected by section 3 and it has its full effect even though that may lead to a rights violation. Subordinate legislation which, through the operation of primary legislation cannot be construed in a compatible manner, is also valid and has its full effect.[16]

---

11   Although freedom of expression is one of the most fiercely protected rights in Strasbourg. See Chapter 4 on Article 10.

12   See the consideration of sections 12 and 13 below.

13   Although the Privy Council has the final say on the HRA in the devolved areas of the UK and this should lead to some uniformity.

14   In Community law these types of conflict are solved through a referral to the ECJ.

15   Section 3 (2) (a), (b), HRA 1998.

16   Section 3 (2) (a), (c), HRA 1998. The continuing validity of primary and certain subordinate legislation was considered necessary in order to maintain parliamentary sovereignty and is a continuing theme throughout the HRA. See HL Debates, 18 November 1997: Column 522. Future incompatible primary legislation will require a Minister to produce a statement regarding the incompatibility and will still run the risk of a court issuing a declaration of

Section 3 is clearly a central part of the government's scheme to implement the Convention rights into domestic law. In the words of Lord Cooke '3(1) is a key provision in the proposed legislation, possibly even the most important provision.'[17] It goes beyond the pre-HRA use of the Convention as a guide where there is ambiguity and involves the court in a proactive pursuit of compatibility. As the Lord Chancellor stated in the Tom Sargant Memorial Lecture 1998:

> [t]he Act will require the courts to read and give effect to the legislation in a way compatible with the convention rights 'so far as it is possible to do so…' This as the White Paper makes clear, goes far beyond the present rule. It will not be necessary to find an ambiguity. On the contrary the courts will be required to interpret legislation so as to uphold the convention rights unless the legislation itself is so clearly incompatible with the convention that it is impossible to do so.[18]

The courts will have an obligation where possible to adopt a more purposive approach to statutory construction in order to give effect to the Convention rights. During the course of the Commons debate on section 3 some concern was expressed that this purposive approach would lead to the courts contorting the wording of legislation. The Home Secretary in response set out the government's view on the matter:

> there was a time when all the courts could do to divine the intention of Parliament was to apply themselves to the words on the face of any Act. Now, following *Pepper v Hart*, they are able to look behind that and, not least, to look at the words used by Ministers. I do not think the courts will need to apply themselves to the words that I am about to use, but, for the avoidance of doubt, I will say that it is not our intention that the courts, in applying what is now clause 3 [section 3 HRA 1998], should contort the meaning of words to produce implausible or incredible meanings. I am talking about plain words in what is actually a clear Bill with plain language – with the intention of Parliament set out in Hansard, should the courts wish to refer to it.[19]

This type of interpretive technique is not a novel one and the English courts have already had some experience of this type of statutory construction with regard to European Community (EC) law. This was something the Lord Chancellor considered of great importance:

---

incompatibility under section 4. Should a Minister in the future issue incompatible subordinate legislation he will be acting illegally by virtue of section 6 (1) except where the primary legislation clearly authorises it.

17   HL Debates 18 Nov 1997: Column 535.

18   Lord Irvine of Lairg (1998) 'The Development of Human Rights in Britain under an Incorporated Convention on Human Rights' Justice – Tom Sargant Memorial Lecture, *Public Law* p 224.

19   HC Debates, 3 Jun 1998: Column 423. See also the Lord Chancellor in the House of Lords where he considered that the government 'want the courts to strive to find an interpretation of legislation which is consistent with convention rights so far as the language of the legislation allows and only in the last resort to conclude that the legislation is simply incompatible with them' HL Debates 18 Nov 1997: Column 536.

[w]hilst this particular approach [section 3] is innovative, there are some precedents which will assist the courts. In cases involving European Community law, decisions of our courts already show that interpretative techniques may be used to make the domestic legislation comply with the community law, even where this requires straining the meaning of words or reading in words which are not there.[20]

The classic example of this in UK law is *Litster v Forth Dry Dock and Engineering Co Ltd*[1] where the House of Lord analysed the purpose of the underlying directive in interpreting the regulations intended to give the directive domestic effect. In doing so they implied additional wording into the regulations in order to give effect to the underlying purpose.[2] There are obvious parallels here which the courts could draw on in interpreting domestic legislation compatibly with the Convention rights. However, while the UK judges have shown willingness to adopt Community interpretive techniques, it has been in part because of a strong European Community (EC) law concept of the supremacy of Community actions and a strong supranational court. These are not present in the ECHR context.

In terms of what '[s]o far as it is possible to do so' means for interpreting legislation in conformity with the Convention rights the Lord Chancellor clearly intends that the courts should adopt a broad meaning of that phrase. Further elaborating on how the courts would use Section 3 the Lord Chancellor drew on the New Zealand experience and stated:

> the court will interpret as consistent with the convention not only those provisions which are ambiguous in the sense that the language used is capable of two different meanings but also those provisions where there is no ambiguity in that sense, unless a clear limitation is expressed. In the latter category of case it will be 'possible' (to use the statutory language) to read the legislation in a conforming sense because there will be no clear indication that a limitation on the protected rights was intended so as to make it 'impossible' to read it as conforming.[3]

Thus section 3 should have the effect of requiring the courts to minimise the effect of any legislation which could breach Convention rights, where necessary reading in protections of those rights.

Will the UK judiciary have to change the way they interpret the law?

Sections 2 and 3 place the judiciary clearly in the vanguard with regard to the extent that the HRA will impact on UK law. As Lord Cooke remarked in the parliamentary debate on section 3:

---

20   See n 19, above 137 (Lord Irvine).
1   [1990] 1 AC 546.
2   See also *Marleasing SA v La Comercial Internacional de Alimentación SA* C-106.89 [1990] ECR I-4135.
3   See n 19, above (Lord Irvine).

[t]he clause will require a very different approach to interpretation from that to which United Kingdom courts are accustomed. Traditionally, the search has been for the true meaning; now it will be for a possible meaning that would prevent the making of a declaration of incompatibility... If it is scrupulously complied with, in a major field the common law approach to statutory interpretation will never be the same again; moreover, this will prove a powerful Bill indeed.[4]

The combination of sections 2 and 3 means that when interpreting whether statute or common law is compatible with the Convention rights the courts should have regard not only to the rights themselves but to the case law of the Strasbourg court as guidance. This will necessarily involve adopting the interpretive techniques of the Strasbourg court. It is, however, one thing to look at the cases themselves it is another thing altogether to apply the same reasoning in the English courts. There is some cause for concern as to whether the English courts have sufficient experience of the ECtHR interpretative tools. In terms of protecting human rights in the UK this will by far be the greatest obstacle to overcome. There have been in the past two recurring patterns with regard to the UK judiciary: a) a resistance to drawing on the standards of the ECHR and its jurisprudence; and b); a completely different interpretative method with regard to balancing rights. A brief recap on the record of the UK judiciary's record of rights interpretation provides a good illustration of these patterns and the challenges that lie ahead.

Historically, the difficulty with the use of the ECHR in interpreting statute via the courts' presumption that Parliament would not legislate contrary to its international obligations, was that its intervention was premised on the availability of the presumption. Once Parliament dispelled that presumption with clear unambiguous words, or an official exercising a delegated power decided to act contrary to the ECHR, the court had no role in forcing compliance. The ability of individuals in the UK to claim ECHR rights when a statutory provision was at issue has depended on the willingness of the judiciary to find ambiguity in a statutory provision. Some judges such as Lords Scarman and Denning were more willing to find ambiguity than others. As a result the rights and freedoms under the Convention with regard to statutory interpretation have never operated in the UK in their fundamental character. Unless a judge was willing to find that the statute was ambiguous, the state had no enforceable obligation in domestic law to protect Convention rights.

With regard to the use of the ECHR at common law there was little that one could say with certainty. Some judges would consider the ECHR where there was ambiguity at common law. Others, very often in the same case, would decide the issue exclusively as a common law matter.[5] This is something of a recurring pattern in the upper courts as for every judge who referred to the Convention there was a

---

4   HL Debates 3 November 1997: Column 1273-1274. See also Lord Lester of Herne Hill, 'The Art of the Possible: Interpreting Statutes under the HRA' (1998) *Human Rights Law Review*, p 665.
5   Contrast the judgments of the Court of Appeal with the House of Lords in *Derbyshire County Council v Times Newspapers* [1993] 1 All ER 1011.

judge who referred to the common law as the appropriate or higher standard. In *R v Secretary of State for the Home Department, ex p Brind*[6] Lord Donaldson MR stated:

> [t]here have been a number of cases in which the European Convention on Human Rights has been introduced into the argument and has, accordingly, featured in the judgments. In most of them the reference has been fleeting and usually consisted of an assertion, in which I would concur, that you have to look long and hard before you can detect any difference between the English common law and the principles set out in the convention, at least if the convention is viewed through English judicial eyes.

Perhaps the more famous statement that appears consistently in the case law[7] is that of Lord Goff in *A-G v Guardian Newspapers (No 2)*[8] where he stated:

> [f]inally, I wish to observe that I can see no inconsistency between English law on this subject and art 10 of the Convention for the Protection of Human Rights and Fundamental Freedoms (Rome, 4 November 1950; TS 71 (1953); Cmd 8969). This is scarcely surprising, since we may pride ourselves on the fact that freedom of speech has existed in this country perhaps as long as, if not longer than, it has existed in any other country in the world.

What is surprising about this pattern is the consistency with which the judiciary have maintained that the common law of England and Wales is either consistent with or at a higher standard than the Convention, when the judgments of the English courts have consistently been found to be in breach of the rights and freedoms contained in the ECHR.[9] While the government clearly intends to 'bring rights home' through the mechanism of the HRA this may not necessarily mean a warm welcome. To a large degree the success or failure of a rights culture evolving through the introduction of the HRA depends on the judiciary's willingness to foster such a culture.

A second problem arises with regard to interpretative method and the ECHR. In the first *Sunday Times* case[10] the Strasbourg court expressed some concern about the interpretative method used by the English courts in interpreting rights. The ECtHR stated:

> [w]hilst emphasising that it is not its function to pronounce itself on an interpretation of English law adopted in the House of Lords, the court points out that it has to take a different approach. The court is not faced with a choice between two conflicting principles, but with a principle of freedom of expression that is subject to a number of exceptions which must be narrowly interpreted...

6   [1990] 1 All ER 469 at 477.
7   For example Lord Keith references it in *Derbyshire* [1993] 1 All ER 1011 at 1021.
8   [1988] 3 All ER 545 at 660.
9   See for example *Sunday Times v United Kingdom* (1979) 2 EHRR 245, *Malone v United Kingdom* (1984) 7 EHRR 14, *Observer and Guardian v United Kingdom* (1991) 14 EHRR 153, *Sunday Times v United Kingdom (No 2)* (1991) 14 EHRR 229.
10   *Sunday Times v United Kingdom* (1979) 2 EHRR 245.

The English courts have not traditionally utilised such a rights based approach. As Lord Fraser put it in *A-G v BBC*:[11]

> I agree that in deciding this appeal the House has to hold a balance between the principle of freedom of expression and the principle that the administration of justice must be kept free from outside interference. Neither principle is more important than the other, and where they come into conflict, as they do in this case, the boundary has to be drawn between the spheres in which they respectively operate. That is not the way in which the European Court of Human Rights would approach the question...[i]t is, therefore, not to be expected that decisions of this House on questions of this sort will invariably be consistent with those of the European Court.

On the same issue Lord Goff in *A-G v Guardian Newspapers (No 2)*,[12] continuing from his view on the common law standard quoted above, considered that:

> [t]he only difference is that, whereas art 10 of the convention, in accordance with its avowed purpose, proceeds to state a fundamental right and then to qualify it, we in this country (where everybody is free to do anything, subject only to the provisions of the law) proceed rather on an assumption of freedom of speech, and turn to our law to discover the established exceptions to it.

Using this type of approach the English courts may not even recognise a right as existing at all, as was the situation in *Malone v Metropolitan Police Comr*.[13] Indeed this was recognised by the Lord Chancellor in introducing the Human Rights Bill into the Lords for its second reading:

> The traditional freedom of the individual under an unwritten constitution to do himself that which is not prohibited by law gives no protection from misuse of power by the state, nor any protection from acts or omissions of public bodies which harm individuals in a way that is incompatible with their human rights under the convention. Our legal system has been unable to protect people in the 50 cases in which the European Court has found a violation of the convention by the United Kingdom. That is more than any other country except Italy. The trend has been upwards. Over half the violations have been found since 1990.[14]

The problem illustrated by the concerns of the ECtHR and inherent in statements such as those annunciated by Lords Goff and Fraser is that the English courts are used to weighing various interests in coming to their decision. If a court attempts to balance interests 'the public interest will always carry great weight. The whole point of ascribing rights to individuals is to give them added protection against the power of the state claiming to be acting in the public interest.'[15] When balancing interests

11   [1980] 3 All ER 161 at 176.
12   [1988] 3 All ER 545 at 660.
13   [1979] 2 All ER 620. See the judgment of Lord Diplock in *Harman v Secretary of State for the Home Department* [1983] 1 AC 280 at 299.
14   HL Debates, 3 Nov 1997: Column 1229.
15   Warbrick, C, 'Rights, the European Convention on Human Rights and English Law' (1994) *European Law Review*, p 42.

freedom of speech is just an interest that must be considered alongside the public interest in suppressing free speech. This type of interest balancing prevalent in the English courts will often place individual freedom at a disadvantage to the public interest.[16]

The major effect of the HRA is that it will force the judiciary to apply a more systematically rigorous approach to assessing a public authority's action where the violation of a Convention right is at issue.[17] Starting with an expansive view of the Convention right in question the court should identify the interference with the right and review the reasons given by the state for the restriction. In doing so the court must examine whether those reasons are relevant and sufficient and whether the restriction was 'proportionate to the legitimate aim pursued'.[18] While the margin of appreciation strictly speaking has no application in domestic law it is likely that the courts will accord a measure of discretion to the state on matters of social, economic, cultural and political importance.[19]

The government is alive to this concern regarding the interpretation of the ECHR, as the two-year period before the introduction of the HRA has been devoted to training the judiciary in the interpretative methods of the ECtHR. That training has not gone as well as expected and will only result in an average of one day's training for each judge or tribunal member.[20] As Warbrick considered in 1995 but which is equally applicable today:

> [i]f the courts rely on the Convention, they should try hard to get it right, so that cases which need not reach the Convention institutions may be decided here ... no good is done if the English courts merely pretend to be alive to claims based on the Convention, but ignore the special nature of Convention rights and continue to assert a scarcely modified version of Dicey's utilitarian conception of adjudication. It is not enough that the courts rely on the Convention as a convenient (and quasi-objective) statement of desirable values, to be acknowledged only so long as no public interest is thereby compromised; if they rely on the Convention at all, the judges should take into account the nature of those values as strong, individual rights. Better to avoid the questions altogether and so speed the applicants path to Strasbourg where his rights will be taken seriously.[1]

---

16 For some recent examples of this see *R v Bournewood Community and Mental Health NHS Trust, ex p, L* [1998] 3 All ER 289, HL and *R v Chief Constable of North Wales Police, ex p AB* [1998] 3 All ER 310, CA

17 For a judicial view how the HRA will affect judicial interpretation see Hooper, (Sir) Anthony, 'Current Topic: The Impact of the Human Rights Act on Judicial Decision-making' (1998) *European Human Rights Law Review*, Vol 3, pp 676- 686.

18 See above van Dijk p 80. See also *Handyside v United Kingdom* (1976) 1 EHRR 737, *Young, James and Webster v United Kingdom* (1981) 4 EHRR 38, *Dudgeon v United Kingdom* (1981) 4 EHRR 149 and *Moustaquim v Belgium* (1991) 13 EHRR 802.

19 See Chapter 7 for a detailed analysis of the criteria the courts should apply.

20 Sir Stephen Sedley speaking at the UCL seminar 'The Uses and Abuses of Comparative law' 10 May 2000.

1   Warbrick, C, 'Rights, the European Convention on Human Rights and English Law' (1994) *European Law Review*, pp 43, 46.

However all is not doom and gloom: the judiciary have an excellent track record in interpreting human rights in the Constitutional documents of the states to which the Judicial Committee of the Privy Council is the final court of appeal as well as when interpreting EC legislation in the domestic courts.[2] There is no reason why the judiciary should not be able to bring their ample experience of these areas to the application of Convention rights in the UK.

What will the effect of the HRA be on existing precedent?

The courts are bound under the HRA to comply with the Convention rights as a public authority. Existing precedent must necessarily be reconsidered where a Convention point is at issue. Further, section 3 has a specific effect on the operation of the doctrine of precedent in the UK. As section 3 applies to all legislation past and present, the courts are not bound by previous decisions regarding the meaning of a statutory provision. Should a lower court decide that a House of Lords decision regarding the meaning of a statutory provision is incompatible with the Convention rights it is not bound by that decision. This is not an unlikely scenario as one of the principles the Strasbourg court has adopted is that words should be given an autonomous meaning: therefore there could easily be a difference between the meaning of words at a domestic level and at the Strasbourg level. For example the Strasbourg court takes a different view of what constitutes a civil right than the UK.[3]

What happens when a court finds that legislation is incompatible with the Convention rights?

Section 4 (1) and (2) provide that in any proceedings where a higher court[4] is satisfied that a provision of primary legislation is incompatible with a Convention right it may make a declaration of incompatibility. Section 4 (3) and (4) provide similarly for subordinate legislation where the incompatibility cannot be removed due to the operation of primary legislation. A declaration of incompatibility does not affect the validity of the legislative provision and it continues to operate even though that may involve a rights violation.[5] A declaration 'is not binding on the parties to the proceedings in which it is made.'[6] This wording was inserted to ensure that the government was not bound by the domestic court's decision at the Strasbourg level. Should a declaration of incompatibility be made and the case go to Strasbourg the government would not on the basis of section 4 (6) (b) have to accept that there was a Convention violation.[7]

---

2   See *Minister for Home Affairs v Fisher* [1979] 3 All ER 21 and *Matadeen v Pointu* [1999] 1 AC 98, PC.
3   See *Engel v Netherlands (No 2)* (1976) 1 EHRR 706. See also Chapter 11.
4   House of Lords, Court of Appeal, High Court, Privy Council, the Courts-Martial Appeal Court, and in Scotland the High Court of Justiciary.
5   Section 4 (6) (a), HRA 1998.
6   Section 4 (6) (b), HRA 1998.
7   See Wadham, J. and Mountfield, H, *Blackstones Guide to the Human Rights Act 1998* (1999) Blackstones, p 49.

One of the major traditional objections to a bill of rights in the UK has centred on the role of the judiciary in interpreting those rights.[8] An unelected, unrepresentative judiciary capable of striking down legislation was seen as anathema to the UK's tradition of parliamentary sovereignty.[9] As Lord Bingham stated during the debate in the House of Lords:

> I believe that these are solid reasons for welcoming the Bill. But I do not think that they will turn our world upside down. I do not think so badly of our institutions as to suppose that we have been routinely violating human rights and undermining fundamental freedoms all these years. I am aware, as are your Lordships, of a number of objections in principle to incorporation. The first is that it involves, so it is said, a major transfer of power from Parliament to the judiciary. While I respect those who advance that argument, it is not one I accept. The mode of incorporation does not empower judges, as the noble and learned Lord the Lord Chancellor made clear, to overrule, set aside, disapply, or – if one wants to be even more dramatic – strike down Acts of Parliament. That is a power which throughout the recent debates the judges have made clear they do not seek. The mode of incorporation adopted is that which most fully respects the sovereignty of Parliament. Following incorporation, nothing will be decided by judges which is not already decided by judges. The difference is that British judges will in the first instance have an opportunity to provide a solution.[10]

Section 4 of the HRA has been designed to deal at least in part with this objection. The judiciary are still unelected and unrepresentative but at least cannot under section 4 strike down legislation.

Section 4 allows the higher courts (House of Lords, Judicial Committee of the Privy Council, Court of Appeal, High Court, the Courts-Martial Appeal Court, and in Scotland the High Court of Justiciary sitting otherwise than as a trial court or the Court of Session) to make a declaration of incompatibility where primary or certain subordinate legislation is found to be incompatible with the Convention rights. By confining the ability to make declarations to the higher courts the government intended to emphasise the importance of such declarations as well as remove the possibility of upsetting criminal trials by such declarations.[11] A declaration of incompatibility will not have any effect on the operation of the legislation at issue and so in that sense the sovereignty of Parliament is preserved. While the lower courts are not empowered to make declarations they have to comply with gections 2 (use ECtHR case law) and 3 (interpret legislation compatibly) and thus in the course of their judgments it will be apparent that legislation is incompatible. Unfortunately, when this happens there is no procedure for notifying the Government.

---

8   For a defence of the judiciary see Loveland, Ian 'Incorporating the European Convention on Human Rights into UK Law' (1999) *Parliamentary Affairs*, Vol 52, pp 113-127.

9   See the accompanying White Paper to the HRA 1998, para 2.13 and also the Home Secretary, HC Debates 16 February 1998: Column 773.

10   HL Debates, 3 November 1997: Column 1247.

11   HL Debates, 18 November 1997: Column 551.

In the course of the parliamentary debates on section 4 an amendment was tabled which would have allowed the courts to make a declaration of incompatibility where the issue was an absence of legislation. The idea behind this amendment was to give effect to the UK's positive obligations under the ECHR. For example the Strasbourg court has found that in *Malone v United Kingdom*[12] the absence of law was a violation of convention rights. In *X & Y v Netherlands*[13] a failure of Dutch law to criminalise the sexual abuse of a mentally handicapped 16-year-old was a violation of Article 8. In *A v United Kingdom* the failure of the UK to legislate to prohibit the abusive beating of a child by a parent was found to violate Article 3. In rejecting this amendment the Lord Chancellor considered:

> [i]f a person believes that his convention rights have been violated as a result of action by a public authority which is not governed by legislation the right course is for him to bring legal proceedings against the authority under Clause 7 of the Bill or to rely on his convention rights in any other legal proceedings to which he and the authority are a party. If the court finds in his favour it will be able to grant whatever remedy is within its jurisdiction and appears just and appropriate. The fact that there is no specific legislation for the court to declare incompatible with the convention does not affect the ability of the person concerned to obtain a remedy... There is no corresponding need to make a declaration of incompatibility in cases where the problem is an absence of legislation, because there is nothing to stop the courts providing a remedy in those cases. There is no legislative bar or block on the courts doing so.[14]

The making of a declaration of incompatibility should trigger the 'fast track' procedure provided in section 10 of the HRA for the amendment of legislation where a declaration of incompatibility has been made.[15] The government is not compelled to amend legislation but a declaration of incompatibility will create both a moral and public pressure to amend the offending legislation. This does not however guarantee that the government's view of the amendment needed will necessarily meet the remedy needed. Should the government repeatedly provide inadequate legislation in response to declarations of incompatibility the judiciary may become very specific as to the extent of the amendments necessary to avoid a violation.

The making of a declaration is discretionary and so even though there may be an incompatibility the court is not obliged to make such a declaration. During the parliamentary debate on the issue, the government made it clear that they considered that a court would generally make a declaration where there was an incompatibility but the judiciary should be allowed a discretion to consider the appropriateness of such a declaration given the circumstance of the case.[16]

12   (1984) 7 EHRR 14.
13   (1985) 8 EHRR 235.
14   HL Debates 24 November 1997: Column 815-816.
15   See below.
16   See HL Debates 18 November 1997: Column 546.

The major effect of section 4 will not necessarily be the use of declarations of incompatibility but rather the rarity of such declarations. The declarations are likely to be used as a last resort and only when the court cannot find a compatible effect under section 3 will they make such a declaration. Section 4's major effect will be to reinforce section 3 and ensure that the judiciary do give effect to legislation in a manner compatible with the Convention rights.

Does the government have to be notified if a court is going to make a declaration of incompatibility?

Where the court is considering making a declaration of incompatibility the Crown must be notified under section 5 at any time during the proceedings and the Crown is entitled to be joined as a party.[17] If the proceedings are criminal the Crown once joined as a party 'may, with leave, appeal to the House of Lords against any declaration of incompatibility made in the proceedings.'[18]

In cases where either the Crown is already a party or where it is clear that there is a possibility of a declaration of incompatibility this section causes no real difficulty as the Crown can be notified in advance.[19] However where the possibility of a declaration of incompatibility arises during the course of the case there would have to be a significant delay while the proceedings are adjourned and the Crown is given a chance to consider being joined to the proceedings.[20]

In the course of the parliamentary debate on section 5 there was some concern as to the issue of costs when the Crown was joined to proceedings. It was felt that the threat of having to pay the Crown's costs could deter meritorious litigants. Lord Lester put the matter to the government:

> [i]n the past year I have known public authorities – in one case the Official Solicitor and in the other the Human Embryo and Fertilisation Authority – to seek costs orders against a meritorious applicant – in one case as a condition for leave to appeal to the Court of Appeal, and in the other where an amicus curiae had been appointed. In both cases it happened that the same judge – a compassionate and commonsense judge – refused the application for costs, but the deterrent effect of the possibility of a costs order being made against those litigants was extremely severe. Had they not had confident counsel who encouraged them to take the substantial risk, they might never have been able to get their cases finally determined. My question is: granted that the courts need to have wide discretion in deciding costs matters, will the Minister assure the Committee that, so far as concerns this Administration, the Crown

17 Section 5 (1), (2) and (3). A Minister may also nominate someone to represent him. The Lord Chancellor gave the example of the Director General of Fair Trading see HL Debates 18 November 1997: Column 555.

18 Leave here refers to leave granted by the court that has made the declaration or the House of Lords (section 5 (5)). The section only covers criminal appeal because civil cases confer the same rights of appeal on joined parties as any other party. Appeal under this section only applies to issues relating to the declaration.

19 The appropriate government representation can then be arranged.

20 Even where the Crown is a party there may be a delay as for example the Crown Prosecution Service may not feel competent to deal with the matter of declarations under the HRA.

would not normally seek a costs order against a litigant where there was a strongly arguable case, properly brought, on a genuine issue of public importance, because, with that assurance, the deterrent effect to which I referred would be much less?[1]

Lord Williams of Mostyn responding for the government refused to be drawn on the matter, while noting Lord Lester's concerns he considered:

[i]t would be quite improper for me to give any indication of Crown policy generally which would attempt to bind my colleagues for the future. After all, any government is the steward of public funds and ought not legitimately to say, 'This is going to be our policy in these matters.'[2]

Lord Lester's concerns remain and it is for the courts to use their discretion to decide the matter of costs. The South African Constitutional Court has reflected Lord Lester's concerns by adopting a 'cautious' but not 'inflexible' approach to awarding costs against a failed applicant in a constitutional matter because of the inhibiting effect of such orders on legitimate constitutional litigation.[3] Should the English Courts award costs against a legitimate applicant who fails in his claim it may prove a grounding for an appeal to Strasbourg on the basis of Article 6 as access to the courts must be effective.

Does the government have to do anything about a declaration of incompatibility?

Section 10 and Schedule 2 of the HRA set out what is known as the 'fast track' procedure. Section 10 provides the government with the power to take remedial action should a declaration of incompatibility have been made and the avenues of appeal have expired, been determined, abandoned or all parties who may appeal have indicated in writing that they have no intention of doing so.[4] The government can also take remedial action under section 10 (1) (b): where it appears to a Minister as a result of a judgment of the ECtHR, that is only judgments involving the UK, made after the HRA came into effect, a legislative provision is incompatible with Convention obligations.[5] Should the Minister take the view that there are compelling reasons[6] for remedial action to amend legislation to bring it into conformity with the Convention the Minister may make a remedial order. Section 20 (1) of the HRA provides that remedial orders are in the form of a statutory instrument. The

---

1   HL Debates, 18 November 1997: Column 560-561.
2   HL Debates, 18 November 1997: Column 561.
3   *Motsepe v IRC* (1997) (6) BCLR 692 at 705.
4   Section 10 (1) HRA 1998.
5   While other judgments of the ECtHR are not covered it is unlikely that following a judgment of the ECtHR where the UK is not involved but similar laws are at issue the UK would do nothing.
6   During the debate in the Commons the Home Secretary explained that the government considered the 'compelling reasons' criteria in the section to set a very high test. See HC Debates 24 June 1998: Column 1138.

order may have retrospective effect save that no one can be guilty of an offence solely as a result of the retrospective effect.[7]

While the government is not compelled to use the 'fast track' procedure under the HRA it intends that a declaration of incompatibility should trigger a 'fast track' amendment.[8] As the Lord Chancellor stated:

> [i]t is for Parliament to decide whether there should be remedial legislation. Parliament may, not must, and generally will, legislate. If a Minister's prior assessment of compatibility (under Clause 19) is subsequently found by declaration of incompatibility by the courts to have been mistaken, it is hard to see how a Minister could withhold remedial action. There is a fast-track route for Ministers to take remedial action by order ... This is the logic of the design of the Bill. It maximises the protection of human rights without trespassing on parliamentary sovereignty.[9]

Originally the 'fast track' procedure was designed to make it easy to remedy legislation which was incompatible with the Convention rights and freedoms. However both in the Commons and the Lords there was some disquiet as to the constitutionality of the government's scheme. As it was put during the Commons debate:

> [w]e start from the position where even the Government recognise that their proposals for the fast-track procedure – for the diminution of Parliament – are wrong in principle, yet they persist with them. I question whether they understand why they are wrong in principle. I am not sure that they do. The European convention on human rights is not a system for making laws: it is not a substitute for Parliament. It is a broad framework within which all our laws should be framed and with which our laws must comply. The courts will tell us, after due argument, whether some aspect of our law is incompatible, but it is not for the courts to redesign those laws. They are not equipped to do so. It would be wholly undemocratic if they were to attempt to do so. That is the role of Parliament. What possible justification is there for the Government to diminish the role of Parliament? What are the compelling reasons which are to entitle Ministers to override the rights of the people and of our electorates to be represented in these matters by their chosen representatives? We are not told.[10]

This pressure from MPs who were concerned that remedial orders without reference to Parliament were unconstitutional, eventually forced the government to amend section 10.[11] As Wadham and Mountfield have observed the amendment may have unfortunate consequences as:

7   Schedule 2, para 1 (3).
8   See the White Paper accompanying the HRA 1998, para 2.9.
9   HL Debates, 3 November 1997: Column 1229-1230.
10   Mr. Garnier, HC Debates, 21 October 1998: Column 1327.
11   See the Lord Chancellor on the need for parliamentary scrutiny HL Debates, 3 November 1997: Column 1231 and on the introduction of Schedule 2 see HC Debates, 24 June 1998: Columns 1130-1143.

a breach of human rights may go uncorrected for want of Parliamentary time or because it relates to an unpopular group or a controversial cause. But it is precisely this domination of majority over minority interests which human rights law is designed to prevent. The amendment therefore had the unfortunate effect of weakening the structure of the Act: it makes it far less likely that people will litigate with a view to seeking declarations of incompatibility.[12]

Schedule 2 of the Act provides two procedures for making a remedial order. The 'standard procedure' under Schedule 2, para (2) (a) and the 'emergency procedure' under Schedule 2, para (2) (b). If the standard procedure is followed the Minister must lay before Parliament a draft of the proposed order as well as an explanation of the incompatibility including any court declaration, finding or order. The Minister must also provide both a statement as to the reasons for seeking an order and for making the order in that particular form.[13] The draft and the 'required information' must be placed before Parliament for at least 60 days and during that time representation can be made to the Minister by interested parties. After the 60-day period the draft, amended or not, must be laid before Parliament a second time accompanied by any representations made. For the order to have effect it must be approved by both Houses of Parliament within 60 days of being laid for the second time.

The emergency procedure provides that the Minister can make the order without laying the order before Parliament. If the Minister decides to do this the order must state that because of the urgency of the situation prior parliamentary approval was unnecessary. After the order has been made the same requirements as in the standard procedure must be followed save that unless the order is approved by both Houses within 120 days of being laid before Parliament the second time it will cease to have effect.[14] If it ceases to have effect any acts done under the order remain valid and the government could if it wishes introduce a new remedial order for approval.

Does everybody have to act compatibly with the Convention rights?

Section 6 makes it unlawful for a public authority to act incompatibly with a Convention right unless they are compelled to do so by primary legislation or provisions made under primary legislation.[15] In such a case of compulsion a higher court could make a declaration of incompatibility under section 4. An act is defined in section 6 (6) as including a failure to act but not a failure to '(a) introduce in, or lay before, Parliament a proposal for legislation; or (b) make any primary legislation

12 Wadham, J and Mountfield, H, *Blackstones Guide to the Human Rights Act 1998* (1999) Blackstones, p 49.
13 Schedule 2, para (5) (a) and (b).
14 Schedule 2, para (4).
15 The sovereignty of Parliament is thus preserved; section 6 (1) and (2), HRA 1998. A 'public authority' exercising a discretion under such legislation would have to make sure that there was no possibility of construing the legislation compatibly with Convention rights before it exercised its discretion to violate a right.

or remedial order.'[16] A 'public authority' in section 6 (1) is left undefined. However in section 6 (3) a 'public authority' includes '(a) a court or tribunal, and (b) any person certain of whose functions are functions of a public nature.' However, a person is not a public authority by virtue only of section 6 (3) (b) if the nature of the act is private.[17] A 'public authority' does 'not include the House of Parliament or a person exercising a function in connection with proceedings in Parliament' but does include the House of Lords acting in its judicial capacity.[18]

Section 6 covers three types of 'public authority' i) obvious public bodies, covered directly by section 6 (1), ii) courts and tribunals covered by section 6 (3) (a), and iii) quasi-public bodies covered by sections 6 (3) (b) and 6 (5). Everyone else is private and so not bound by the HRA. Should any of these bodies act incompatibly with regard to Convention rights it will be an unlawful act. As the Lord Chancellor explained:

> [Section] 6(1) refers to a 'public authority' without defining the term. In many cases it will be obvious to the courts that they are dealing with a public authority. In respect of government departments, for example, or police officers, or prison officers, or immigration officers, or local authorities, there can be no doubt that the body in question is a public authority. Any clear case of that kind comes in under [section] 6(1); and it is then unlawful for the authority to act in a way which is incompatible with one or more of the convention rights. In such cases, the prohibition applies in respect of all their acts, public and private. There is no exemption for private acts such as is conferred by [section] 6(5) in relation to [section 6(3)(b)]. [Section 6(3)(b)] provides further assistance on the meaning of public authority. It provides that 'public authority' includes, 'any person certain of whose functions are functions of a public nature'. That provision is there to include bodies which are not manifestly public authorities, but some of whose functions only are of a public nature. It is relevant to cases where the courts are not sure whether they are looking at a public authority in the full-blooded [section] 6(1) sense with regard to those bodies which fall into the grey area between public and private. The Bill reflects the decision to include as 'public authorities' bodies which have some public functions and some private functions.[19]

The government's position here seems a little odd. The basis for the distinction between an 'obvious' and 'quasi' public authority seems to be that the former *only* carry out public functions. If this is not the distinction how is section 6 (5) kept away from an obvious public authority? The Lord Chancellor here seems to accept that obvious public authorities have private functions. If so why doesn't section 6(5) apply? This distinction may come back to haunt the Lord Chancellor.

Obvious state bodies such as Ministers, government departments, health authorities and trusts, police forces, army, navy, air force, prison authorities, immigration

---

16   Again this provision is aimed at the preservation of parliamentary sovereignty.
17   Section 6 (5), HRA 1998.
18   Section 6 (3) (b) and (4), HRA 1998.
19   HL Debates, 24 Nov 1997: Column 812.

officials or local authorities are clearly covered by the definition of 'public authority' in section 6 (1).[20] The courts must, as a 'public authority', under section 6 (3) (a) act compatibly with the Convention rights. This will affect not only the role in dealing with public authorities but also private individuals as the court must interpret statute and common law compatibly with Convention rights.[1] Where the matter is between two private individuals the court additionally has, where the Strasbourg court has found that positive obligations exist, an obligation to protect individuals from a violation of their rights.[2]

These 'public authorities' must, subject to section 6 (2) (compulsion by legislation), act consistently with the Convention. The nature of the transaction is unimportant for these bodies as both private and public acts must be compatible with the Convention. They will be committing an unlawful act should they fail to do so. This new form of action therefore makes it imperative to identify 'public authorities'. Section 6 (3) (b) covers certain companies and bodies which carry out functions, some of which are of public in nature. When carrying out these functions they will be a 'public authority' for the purposes of the HRA. These companies are for the most part the privatised utilities and transport companies such as British Gas, British Telecom and Railtrack. They must act compatibly with the Convention in the carrying out their public functions. The extent to which they must act compatibly with the Convention rights is complex and so it is a subject we return to in Chapter 7.

Section 6 has the effect of making unlawful acts of a 'public authority' which are not in conformity with the Convention rights and freedoms. It is likely to lead to significant amounts of litigation. Should a 'public authority' act incompatibly, a victim would have number of options depending on the context: judicial review on the basis of an illegal action in breach of section 6 (1); a private law action for breach of statutory duty; or as a defence in an action brought by the 'public authority'.[3] Section 6 puts under strain the public-private law divide exhibited in cases such as *O'Reilly v Mackman*.[4] In litigating against an obvious 'public authority' the question will arise as to which form of action is the most appropriate as a 'public authority' can act unlawfully with regard to a private law matter as well as a public law matter.[5]

If you think here has been a violation of a Convention right by a public authority what can you do about it?

Section 7 (1) (a) provides that a person who claims that a public authority has acted or proposes to act in a manner incompatible with the Convention may bring proceedings against the authority under the HRA in the appropriate court or tribunal.

20 See Chapter 7 for a further consideration of public authority status.
1   See the Lord Chancellor on this matter HL Debates, 24 Nov 1997: Column 783.
2   On the state's positive obligations see *Costello-Roberts v United Kingdom* (1993) 19 EHRR 112 see also Chapter 3.
3   See below on section 7, HRA 1998.
4   [1983] 2 AC 237 although it has already been put under strain in *Mercury Communications Ltd v Director General of Telecommunications* [1996] 1 WLR 48.
5   See the proceedings provided in section 7.

Alternatively they may rely on the Convention right or rights in any legal proceedings, including proceedings brought by a public authority and an appeal against a court or tribunal.[6] In any proceedings reliance is conditional on fulfilling the victim test under Article 34 of the ECHR.[7] Proceedings under section 7 (1) (a) where section 6 illegality by a public authority is alleged must be brought within one year of the date of the act complained of or longer period as the court deems equitable subject to any rule imposing a stricter time limit.[8] Reliance on the Convention in other legal proceedings does not carry any time limit. Section 7 (11) allows the Minister to make rules in relation to particular tribunals in order to ensure an appropriate remedy is available.[9] Nothing in the Act creates a criminal offence.[10]

Section 7 allows the Convention rights to operate in the courts in two ways. First in any legal proceedings Convention points may be raised and second as a free standing action alleging section 6 illegality. Unfortunately while it allows the Convention rights to operate in this manner section 7 is also generally agreed to contain the two major weaknesses in the Act. First the time limit in section 7 (5) (a) restricts the availability of the section 6 action and second the use of the ECHR victim test restricts the number of potential litigants.

The original Bill introduced to Parliament in 1997 did not contain any limitation period on actions brought alleging section 6 illegality. It was only during the course of its passage through both Houses that the government introduced the limitation. It establishes a standard one year limit with a discretion on the part of the court to extend subject to stricter time limits. As there is certainly the possibility that many actions alleging section 6 illegality will be brought by way of judicial review, which has a three-month time limit, the time limits for section 7 (1) (a) either three months or at most a year appear very tight. The government's explanation for introducing such short time limits was simply that there had to be a limit and that one year was a sufficient period.[11] In the House of Lords, Lord Lester tabled an amendment to section 7 which would have increased the time period to two years. In introducing his amendment he stated:

> [w]hat troubles me, first, about the time limit of one year is that it will cause confusion and uncertainty because the scheme of the Act will be to bind convention rights into the fabric of the common law. Therefore, there will be a whole variety of claims, some of which have time limits appropriate to an ordinary tort action but some of which will have time limits appropriate to this one-year constitutional tort action. Perhaps I may give your Lordships an example. Let us suppose that there is the tort of misfeasance in public office,

6   Section 7 (1) (b) and 7 (6). Section 7 (1) (b) has retrospective effect in relation to proceedings brought by a public authority. The appeal provision ensures that a Convention violation can be claimed for the first time alleging that the initial court decision was incompatible with the Convention rights.
7   Section 7 (1) (a) and (b), 7 (3), 7 (4) and 7 (7).
8   Section 7 (5) (a) and (b).
9   Sections 7 (9)–(13) concern the making of rules. The sections are intended to provide short-term solutions to remedy problems as they arise. See the government's explanation HL Debates, 19 Jan 1998: Columns 1360-1362.
10   Section 7 (8).
11   See Home Office Minister Mike O'Brien, HC Debates 24 Jun 1998: Column 1096.

which might have a convention element added to it. That would be subject to a longer time limit. Alternatively, there could be an *Entick v Carrington* claim based upon common law notions of personal privacy which would be subject to a different time limit. Somehow the unfortunate litigant will have to sort out what the true position will be about time limits. Therefore, I am troubled that it may cause confusion and uncertainty to introduce this unique one-year limit. I say "unique" in the sense that I know of nothing like it in any constitutional Bill of Rights. The Minister referred to the three-month time limit in judicial review, but that does not deal with a claim of right – a tort claim – indeed, it is dealing with a separate issue about judicial review ... It is easy to imagine a situation where someone with a potentially meritorious claim is unaware for a year that his or her rights have been infringed, especially if the person has had no effective access to legal services and little knowledge about the impact of the new legislation. In such a situation, the Minister will no doubt say that we can trust the judges to extend the time limit. I agree that that seems to be probable. However, I am still concerned that this new one-year time limit will have a chilling effect upon the vulnerable and underprivileged in deciding whether to invoke the Act.[12]

It is almost certain that the one-year time limitation will cause some difficulties. First, potential applicants may not realise they had a cause of action in time. This is particularly likely during the initial period after the HRA comes into force. Second, confusion is likely to occur where mixed proceedings take place involving differing time limits which may lead to actions failing. For example an action brought by a victim of a rail disaster against Railtrack alleging negligence and section 6 illegality with regard to the carrying out of their public safety function.[13] If they do not bring the action within one year they could not obtain a remedy for a breach of a Convention right and can only rely on the negligence claim. However where the act complained involves a cause of action other than a section 6 allegation of unlawful action by a public authority, for example a tort action combining Convention arguments, the court as a public authority under section 6 would have an obligation regardless of time limits to act compatibly with the Convention rights.

It may be that as the government have suggested the courts will use their discretion sensibly in section 7 (5) (b) to extend time limits.[14] However, overall the one-year limit seems an odd restriction on the right to take an action for breach of a Convention right by a 'public authority'. Wadham and Mountfield have suggested that section 7 (5) may itself be a breach of Article 6 (fair trial) combined with Article 14 (disrimination) because it limits access to the courts.[15] Might we one day see a declaration of incompatibility regarding section 7 (5) (a)?

12 HL Debates, 29 October 1998: Column 2097-2098.
13 A failure to carry out their safety function leading to injury could be an violation of Article 8 (private life).
14 The courts have a similar discretion under the Sex Discrimination Act 1975. For a consideration of how the courts' discretion operates under that Act see *Mills and Crown Prosecution Service v Marshall* [1998] IRLR 494.
15 Wadham, J and Mountfield, H, *Blackstones Guide to the Human Rights Act 1998* (1999) Blackstones, p 36.

The second major restriction on access to Convention rights contained in section 7 is the need for any potential applicant to establish victim status under Article 34 (formerly Article 25) of the ECHR.[16] While we deal extensively with standing in Chapter 8 we make some general observations here.

In general establishing victim status should not cause great difficulty for private law as it is focused on the individual anyway. There will usually be someone who can claim that they were directly affected by the Convention violation as is necessary for the Strasbourg victim test. However the major effect of the imposition of victim status will be on public interest litigation. As Lord Lester explained:

> [t]he present sensible and satisfactory position under English law is to be changed. The law of standing is concerned with who can invoke the judicial process. Issues of standing can arise in private law or public law … When one is dealing with private law claims – that is to say, tort actions for damages or damages and injunctions in relation to a public nuisance or a breach of statutory duty – someone claiming has to show that he or she was personally affected. That is similar to the European victim test. So I am not troubled about using the European victim test in a private law context, because in a private law context there is a focus on the individual. That is the central quality of what we call private law. It is concerned, above all, with the rights of private individuals and corporations. As regards judicial review, the position is entirely different. Mr Justice Sedley observed in a recent judgment that public law is not at base about rights, even though abuses of power may and often do invade private rights. He pointed out: 'it is about wrongs – that is to say, misuses of public power', and the courts have always been alive to the fact that a person or organisation with no particular stake in the issue or outcome may, without in any sense being a mere meddler or a busybody, wish and be well-placed to call the attention of the court to an apparent misuse of public power. Mr. Justice Sedley also pointed out that our courts will not permit busybodies or mere troublemakers to apply for judicial review. The basic English rule of standing is that the applicant for judicial review must have a sufficient interest in the matter to which the application relates. That includes cases of representative or associational standing, where an association seeks standing, either to represent a group of interested parties or to represent the public interest. So our courts have accepted that bodies such as the Child Poverty Action Group, Greenpeace, the EOC [Equal Opportunities Commission], the Immigration Law Practitioners' Association or the Joint Council for the Welfare of Immigrants all have standing to bring judicial review proceedings, regardless of whether the people whose interests they seek to represent are their members or are identified and joined as individual victims. As it stands, Clause 7 alters that sensible English legal test of standing for cases of judicial review involving alleged breaches of convention rights by requiring the applicants to be victims within the meaning of Article 25 of the European convention. That is a test devised for the entirely different purpose of deciding who is entitled to have recourse to the European Commission and the European Court of Human Rights.[17]

16   Section 7 (1), (3), (4), and (7).
17   HL Debates 5 Feburary 1998: Column 806-807.

Victim status under the ECHR is a narrower concept than 'standing' as it presently exists in RSC Order 53 for the purposes of judicial review. The Strasbourg case law which the courts must take account of under section 2 provides that a victim is a person who is at risk of or is actually and directly affected by the act or omission complained of.[18] Relatives of individuals who have been directly affected can also fulfil victim status.[19] Professional associations, non-governmental associations and trade unions can all fulfil victim status as long as they can identify a member or member directly affected and show evidence of their authority to act for them.[20] Companies are considered to fulfil victim status without having to show that a member has been affected by an act.[1] Although sometimes non-governmental organisations have been able to claim victim status themselves it has been on the basis of an assumption that the claim is brought on behalf of its members.[2] For example in *Christians Against Racism and Fascism v United Kingdom*[3] an association of religious groups was held to fulfil victim status after a march planned by the association was banned. However, in general, public interest groups cannot in themselves claim victim status unless they can show a member has been directly affected.[4] Pure public interest litigation does not exist at the Strasbourg level. This is very different than the position in domestic law.

In the past decade the domestic courts have expanded the concept of 'standing' under Order 53 to include public interest groups who, although not directly affected, were considered to have 'sufficient interest' to bring an action.[5] Section 7 (3) changes this with regard to the HRA by providing 'the applicant is to be taken to have sufficient interest in relation to the unlawful act only if he is, or would be, a victim of that act.' The section creates a strange situation where for general judicial review purposes a public interest group would have 'standing' under Order 53 but should they wish to advance argument based on the HRA they may not be a victim. In particular, organisations such as Amnesty International who represent others who have suffered could be badly affected by the victim requirement. The courts will then be placed in a confusing situation when deciding to what extent Convention points can be raised.[6]

If the public interest group is not a victim they clearly cannot rely on the HRA. The courts will, however, be reluctant to preclude public interest litigants from relying on Convention rights and are likely either to adopt an expansive view of victim status or find another way to allow Convention rights to be argued.[7] For example

18 See *Marckx v Belgium* (1979) 2 EHRR 330.
19 See *McCann v United Kingdom* (1995) 21 EHRR 97.
20 See *Confederation des Syndicats Medicaux Francais v France* (1986) 47 DR 255.
1   See Chapter 8.
2   However see *Council of Civil Services Unions v United Kingdom* (1987) 50 DR 228 where a trade union was a victim.
3   (1980) 21 DR 138.
4   See *Klass v Germany* (1978) 2 EHRR 214.
5   See for example *R v Lord Chancellor, ex p Child Poverty Action Group* [1998] 2 All ER 755.
6   The Law Lords were particularly concerned with this issue see HL Debates, 5 Feb 1998: Column 807.
7   The definition of victim status is not found in the Convention itself but rather in the case law of the Strasbourg court; therefore a domestic court, because of section 2 of the HRA, is not bound to follow the case law rather it must take it into account.

any matters raising EC law points will still include the ECHR rights and freedoms as part of the values to be given effect to by the court.[8] If they cannot expand the concept of victim to cover public interest litigation they may allow litigants to rely on the Convention as it applied prior to the HRA. As section 11 of the HRA 1998 preserves pre-existing rights of action this is one possible way of including Convention points or expanding common law protections.[9] This would be a limited form of access to the Convention rights as ambiguity is needed[10] but the Courts position as a public authority under the HRA could then allow the court to expand the pre-HRA common law and statutory position on use of Convention rights. One of the more interesting views on how victim status will operate has been put forward by de la Mare. He has argued that the victim test does not apply:

> to actions brought for the sole purpose of obtaining a declaration of incompatibility. The s 7 AJR [applications for judicial review] victim test only applies to the 'proceedings' referred to in s 7 (1), which proceedings are in turn intended to prevent s 6 (1) infringements of Convention rights. In other words the victim test only applies where the party is arguing that a public authority is acting in a fashion incompatible with a Convention right. Expressly exempted from a s 6 (1) illegality is where the primary or secondary legislation in question compels the public authority to act in breach of the ECHR... It may therefore be arguable that the victim test does not apply to an AJR whose sole purpose is to seek a declaration of incompatibility.[11]

In most cases public interest organisations such as the Child Poverty Action Group, Greenpeace, the Equal Opportunities Commission, trade unions and gay rights groups will be able to find someone who fulfils victim status, but for organisations such as Amnesty International, the Immigration Law Practitioners' Association or the Joint Council for the Welfare of Immigrants it may be more difficult as the victims may be outside the jurisdiction. For those organisations, even under an expansive approach to the pre-HRA use of Convention rights the HRA armory of section 6 illegality and declarations of incompatibility will be unavailable.[12] In dismissing similar concerns in Parliament the Lord Chancellor stated:

> [t]here is a flexible Strasbourg jurisprudence on the victim test which I suggest the English courts would have no difficulty applying. Although I hesitate to take up time, and indeed abstain from doing so, I could cite example after example of an expansive approach by the Strasbourg court to the victim test. As we have said a number of times, the purpose of the Bill is to give further effect in our domestic law to our convention rights, and it is in keeping with that approach that a person should be able to rely on those rights before our courts in the same circumstances that they can rely upon them before the

---

8   See below on the application of the ECHR on EC law.
9   See *R v Lord Chancellor, ex p Witham* [1998] QB 575, QBD where at common law freedom of expression and access to the courts are given effect.
10   See Chapter 5.
11   de la Mare, Tom, 'The Human Rigths Act 1998: The Impact on Judicial Review' (1999) *Judicial Review*, Vol 4, Issue 1, p 33.
12   However see de la Mare above on declarations of incompatibility.

Strasbourg institutions, and not in different circumstances. Bringing rights home means exactly what it says – to mirror the approach taken by the Strasbourg court in interpreting convention rights. I acknowledge that as a consequence, and despite the flexibility of the Strasbourg test, a narrower test will apply for bringing applications on convention grounds than in applications for judicial review on other grounds. But I venture to think that interest groups will plainly be able to provide assistance to victims who bring cases under the Bill, including, as I mentioned in Committee, the filing of amicus briefs. Interest groups themselves will be able to bring cases directly where they are victims of an unlawful act. I do not believe that different tests for convention and non-convention cases will cause any difficulties for the courts or prevent interest groups providing assistance to victims of unlawful acts.[13]

What remedies are available for a violation of a Convention right by a public authority?

Section 8 (1) provides that where a court finds that a 'public authority' has acted or proposes to act unlawfully 'it may grant such relief or remedy, or make such order, within its powers as it considers just and appropriate.'[14] Only a court which has power to award damages or compensation may award damages in relation to section 8.[15] The same applies for injunctive relief. As a result a criminal court could not award damages or an employment tribunal grant injunctive relief. Damages under section 8 are discretionary and not awarded as of right, unlike the normal position in private law for breach of statutory duty. As the definition of court in section 8 includes tribunals, section 8 (2) also expands the remedies available to those tribunals, once compensation is within its power it can also award damages. In making an award of damages the court must be satisfied that an award is necessary to afford just satisfaction to the person affected.[16] In doing so the court is compelled, by virtue of section 8 (3), to consider all the circumstances of the case before making such an award. In particular the court must consider '(a) any other relief or remedy granted, or order made, in relation to the act in question (by that or any other court), and (b) the consequences of any decision (of that or any other court) in respect of that act'. Section 8 (4) further compels that court to consider the ECtHR's principles in relation to the award of compensation under Article 41 (just satisfaction) of the ECHR when considering damages.[17]

13 HL Debates, 5 Feb 1998: Column 811. For a less optimistic view see the explanation given by the Home Office Minister, Mike O'Brien, who states that the purpose of the victim test is specifically to exclude these types of groups from bringing test cases: HC Debates, 24 June 1998: Column 1086. Additionally the use of the victim test may cause extreme difficulty for the BBC: see Chapter 10.

14 This wording is similar to section 6 of the Hong Kong Bill of Rights 1991 and the Canadian equivalent in section 24 (1) of the Canadian Charter of Fundamental Rights.

15 Section 8 (2), HRA 1998.

16 Section 8 (3), HRA 1998.

17 Article 41 is considered below.

The types of remedies available to the courts will be those already in existence: injunctions, damages, declarations and relief available in judicial review cases. In discussing the impact of section 1 of the HRA we noted that Article 13 (right to an effective remedy) had not been included in the rights and freedoms contained in the HRA.[18] In the parliamentary debates there was some concern that this would undermine the effective remedy requirement by the ECHR. The Lord Chancellor's response to criticism of this omission was that Article 13 would be given effect through section 8 as the courts would provide an effective remedy. As he explained during the debate on Article 13:

> [the Act] gives effect to Article 13 by establishing a scheme under which convention rights can be raised before our domestic courts. To that end, remedies are provided in [section] 8. If the concern is to ensure that the Bill provides an exhaustive code of remedies for those whose convention rights have been violated, we believe that [section] 8 already achieves that and that nothing further is needed. We have set out in the Bill a scheme to provide remedies for violation of convention rights and we do not believe that it is necessary to add to it.[19]

In the debate the Lord Chancellor seemed to misunderstand the concerns expressed about the omission of Article 13. The concern was not that no remedies were available under the HRA scheme, which is in effect a procedural obligation (a right to a remedy), but rather that Article 13 is aimed at achieving a substantive standard (the remedy must be effective). The remedy scheme as it stands in the HRA may indeed not be adequate to achieve the substantive standard required by Article 13. The White Paper that accompanied the Bill considered that the courts would apply the various remedies available depending on the context. Sometimes it would be right for a decision of a 'public authority' to be quashed, on another occasion an award of damages would be the appropriate remedy, sometimes both would be applicable.[20] In doing so the courts must take into account the Strasbourg case law on remedies, which will necessarily involve an assessment of the Article 13 case law.

However, the remedies under section 8 (1) will not be available where primary or certain secondary legislation has caused the breach.[1] In such a case a higher court can make a declaration of incompatibility but that is unlikely to fulfil the requirement for an effective remedy under Article 13. The individual in question has still had their rights violated and no remedy will be available unless the government acts to change the legislation. Even where the government does act to remove the incompatibility in the legislation this may not involve compensating the individual

---

18   See Chapter 4 for an examination of the operation of Article 13.
19   HL Debates, 18 Nov 1997, Column 476. See also the Lord Chancellor at HL Debates, 29 January 1998: Column 386. Should the Government need to extend the relief available to courts or tribunals the Act provides for rules to be made under section 7 (9)–(13).
20   Rights Brought Home: The Human Rights Bill, Cmnd 3782, para 2.6.
1   Section 6 (2), HRA 1998.

for the loss suffered by virtue of the violation.[2] As some two-thirds of the violations of Convention rights in the UK to date have involved primary or secondary legislation this is likely to be a significant problem.[3] This may be one area where the Strasbourg court will see some applications as a result of a gap in the HRA.

Section 8 (4) compels the court to consider the principles by which the Strasbourg court awards compensation under Article 4. Article 41 reads:

> [i]f the Court finds that there has been a violation of the Convention or the Protocols thereto, and the internal law of the High Contracting Party concerned allows only partial reparation to be made, the court shall, if necessary afford just satisfaction to the injured party.

It is immediately obvious that Article 41 is of little help in outlining the principles of compensation by which the ECtHR operates. The trouble is that the case law is equally unhelpful. In short there are no principles applied by the court or if there are they have never set them out. Having said that there is some very broad (and we mean very broad) guidance that can be gleaned from the case law.

Separate claims for compensation arise under Article 5 (5) of the ECHR for deprivation of liberty and in Protocol 7, Article 3 regarding a miscarriage of justice.[4] Generally speaking compensation at the Strasbourg level is of secondary importance and no right exists to compensation. Aggravated and exemplary damages have never been awarded by the ECtHR. The Court regards its role primarily as a supervisor of the Convention rights and not as an ordinary court with a role in awarding such damages.[5]

The wording of Article 41 (just satisfaction) and the ECtHR's refusal to interpret it as including aggravated damages will probably exclude the domestic courts awarding such damages. Other jurisdictions have taken the view that the idea of a penalty was inappropriate when dealing with a public authority that had breached constitutional rights.[6] However the domestic courts are not constitutional courts but ordinary courts with, unlike the Strasbourg court, a private law role in awarding damages, and so it is not beyond the realm of possibility that aggravated and

---

2   A remedial order under section 10 could contain a provision for compensation. The government has to some extent recognised this problem and the Lord Chancellor expected that in appropriate circumstances compensation would be paid through the exercise of prerogative powers or ex gratia actions. See HL Debates, 27 November 1997: Column 1108.

3   Justice, (1998) The Human Rights Bill: Briefing for the second reading in the House of Commons' Monday 16 February, p 1.

4   The UK has not yet ratified Protocol 7 and so it has not as yet been included in the HRA. See Chapter 4 on Protocol 7.

5   See Reid, K, *A Practitioners Guide to the European Convention on Human Rights*, (1998) Sweet and Maxwell, p 398 see also pp 399-420 on the awards made by the ECtHR.

6   For a consideration of how other jurisdictions have awarded damages for breach of constitutional rights see *Simpson v A-G* [1994] 3 NZLR 667 where the New Zealand Court of Appeal allowed damages to be claimed even though the New Zealand Bill of Rights does not provide for any specific remedies. See also the South African approach in *Fosse v Minister of Safety and Security* (1997) (2) BHRC 434.

exemplary damages could be available against a 'public authority' for breach of a Convention right.[7]

Just satisfaction claims fall under three headings: 'pecuniary loss', 'non-pecuniary loss' and 'costs'.[8] In order to be awarded pecuniary loss such as loss of earnings, opportunity, inheritance, and property there must be some causal link between the act complained of and the loss. Generally the awards are conservative[9] the largest amounts paid have been with regard to property interference.[10] Non-pecuniary loss is awarded for harm, suffering, pain and distress generally. In such cases the court has generally taken the view that proof of such feelings is not necessary.[11] Again, awards for non-pecuniary loss are generally conservative[12] except that where the violation involved police brutality and/or false imprisonment,[13] fair trial,[14] privacy,[15] or children[16] the court has made higher awards. The conduct of the individual will affect the amount awarded and so if the individual has contributed to the violation the amount of damages will be reduced.[17] If the domestic courts follow the Strasbourg general pattern of awards the amounts awarded for breach of a Convention right are likely to be low. It should be noted, however, that section 8 should not reduce the amounts that have been awarded in the past for similar actions such as police brutality or false imprisonment because section 11 of the Act operates to preserve pre-existing claims.[18]

Costs at the Strasbourg level are likely to be fairly unhelpful as guidance for the domestic courts. Costs are awarded where they are necessary and reasonable. The applicant must prove additionally that the costs claimed were actually incurred. At the domestic level the costs issue is unclear. The government has left it for the courts to decide on a case by case basis. For a discussion on costs see above on section 5 of the HRA.

If you think a court or tribunal has violated a Convention right how do you challenge the decision?

Section 9 (1) provides that proceedings under section 7 (1) (a) (claiming unlawfulness on the part of a public authority) where the act complained of is a judicial act, can only be brought: '(a) by exercising a right of appeal; (b) on an

---

7   At common law exemplary damages are available against a public body acting in a high handed manner: see *Rookes v Barnard* [1964] AC 1129. The German courts also allow such punitive damages see BGH November 15, 1994, BGHZ 128, 14-16.

8   Interest on compensation has also been awarded see *Stran Greek Refineries v Greece* (1994) 19 EHRR 293.

9   See *Lingens v Austria* (1986) 8 EHRR 407 and *Open Door Counseling and Dublin Well Woman v Ireland* (1992) 15 EHRR 244 (£25,000 loss of income).

10   See *Pine Valley Developments v Ireland* (1993) 16 EHRR 379 (£1,200,000 award).

11   See *Abdulaziz, Cabales, and Balkandali v United Kingdom* (1985) 7 EHRR 471.

12   See *Artico v Italy* (1980) 3 EHRR 1 (3 million Lire).

13   See *Aksoy v Turkey* (1996) 23 EHRR 553 (£25,040)

14   See *Delta v France* (1990) 16 EHRR 574 (100,000 FF).

15   See *Halford v United Kingdom* (1997) 24 EHRR 523 (£10,000).

16   See *Eriksson v Sweden* (1989) 12 EHRR 183 (200,000 SEK to the Mother and 100,000 SEK to the Daughter).

17   See *Johnson v United Kingdom* (1997) 27 EHRR 296.

18   See below on section 11.

application (in Scotland a petition) for judicial review; or (c) in such other forum as may be prescribed by rules.' This does not affect any rule of law which prevents the court from being the subject of judicial review.[19] Judicial acts done in good faith cannot give rise to damages otherwise than to the extent required by Article 5 (5) (compensation for arrest or detention in breach of right to liberty and security) of the Convention.[20] Should a court consider making such an award of damages the Minister responsible must be joined to the proceedings.[1] For the purposes of section 9: court includes a tribunal; judge includes a tribunal member, justice of the peace, clerk or other officer entitled to exercise the jurisdiction of the court; judicial act means a judicial act of a court and includes an act done on the instructions, or on behalf, of a judge.[2]

Section 9 sets out the mechanism by which a judicial act can be challenged by way of the HRA. It is also designed to preserve the traditional immunities of the courts in the UK.[3] In particular, section 9 (3) is designed to preserve the common law and statutory rules which provide that the Crown is not liable in tort in respect of judicial acts. Judges and magistrates acting within their jurisdiction, or outside their jurisdiction if doing so in good faith, are also immune from having proceedings brought against them personally. Section 9 represents a significant restriction on the remedies available should a court itself violate a Convention right. In only two circumstances, bad faith and Article 5 (5), are damages payable. Where the only effective remedy would be damages it is possible that the appeal court could have recourse to the Article 13 (right to an effective remedy) case law in fashioning an award of damages.[4] Should they fail to do so section 9 is likely to be the subject of appeal to the Strasbourg court.

Originally section 9 (3) did not contain any recognition of the right to compensation in Article 5 (5) (compensation for arrest or detention in breach of right to liberty and security) of the ECHR. The UK has been found by the Strasbourg court to be in breach of Article 5 (5) in virtue of the court's traditional immunity.[5] During the course of the parliamentary debates on section 9 the government introduced an amendment to allow compensation.[6]

Does the HRA diminish any greater protection of rights UK law already offers?

Section 11 provides that reliance on a Convention right does not restrict: '(a) any other right or freedom conferred on him by or under any law having effect in any part of the United Kingdom; or (b) his right to make any claim or bring any

---

19 Section 9 (2), HRA 1998.
20 Section 9 (3), HRA 1998 this may require amendment if the UK ratifies Protocol 7 as Article 3 provides for compensation for a miscarriage of justice.
1   Section 9 (4), HRA 1998.
2   Section 9 (5), HRA 1998.
3   See for example the immunity of magistrates in sections 51-52 of the Justices of the Peace Act 1997.
4   See the discussion of Article 13 in section 1 above and section 8.
5   See *Santa Cruz Ruiz v United Kingdom* [1998] EHRLR 208.
6   See HL Debates, 24 Nov 1997: Column 857.

proceedings which he could make or bring apart from sections 7 to 9.'[7] The section is designed to ensure two things.

First, that where the UK has more developed protections of rights and freedoms they are not restricted by the incorporation of the Convention rights which may in some cases adopt a more restrictive approach to those rights or freedoms.[8] As the courts are not bound by section 2 to follow the Strasbourg jurisprudence, in areas where the UK has more developed rights and freedoms section 11 may have the effect of developing a more expansive UK version of those ECHR rights. Alternatively section 11 could have the negative effect of allowing judges to form the opinion that the UK has a more sophisticated protection of certain rights and thus apply the pre-existing law, much as some judges have done in the past when dealing with Convention rights. As we have discussed above with regard to sections 2 and 3 the domestic case law which led to successful Strasbourg judgments such as *Sunday Times v United Kingdom,*[9] *Observer and Guardian v United Kingdom,*[10] *Sunday Times v United Kingdom (No 2)*[11] all have the similar characteristic of a claim that the English common law protected rights to an equal or higher standard than the ECHR.

Second where the UK recognises a right to a claim or to bring proceedings this should also remain unaffected by the introduction of the HRA. In awarding damages it should also allow the courts to maintain the levels of damages awarded prior to the HRA for pre-existing actions.[12] As we discussed regarding victim status in Section 7, section 11 may allow the court to protect public interest litigation. There seems to be an inherent tension between section 11 and the attempt in section 7 to limit locus standi. A public interest body despite the lack of victim status could now bring a judicial review on Wednesbury grounds arguing that fundamental human rights were at issue and that the principles in *R v Ministry of Defence, ex p Smith*[13] require the court to apply a higher standard of review. Section 11 would seem to preserve this but how would the court assess this without looking at the human rights infringed – which seems to be precluded by section 7?

Will the HRA affect the ability of the press and media to operate?

Section 12 applies in any case where the court is considering granting relief which might affect the right to freedom of expression. The section therefore applies even though freedom of expression may not be directly at issue. It does not however

---

7   The section is very similar in form to Article 53 of the Convention which ensures that domestic laws which confer rights should not be limited or restricted by the Convention.

8   In the UK the word 'family' includes same sex partners but not as interpreted under the ECtHR see *Sterling Housing Association Ltd v Fitzpatrick* [1999] 4 All ER 705, [1999] 3 WLR 1113.

9   (1979) 2 EHRR 245.

10   (1991) 14 EHRR 153.

11   (1991) 14 EHRR 229.

12   See section 8 on damages.

13   [1996] 1 All ER 257.

apply to criminal cases.[14] Section 12 (2) provides that if the respondent is not present nor represented, the court should not grant relief unless it is satisfied that the applicant has taken all practicable steps to notify the respondent or there are compelling reasons[15] why the respondent should not be notified. Therefore, under the HRA, there will be a presumption against granting ex parte injunctions unless the above criteria are filled.[16]

Relief is not to be granted to restrain publication before trial unless 'the court is satisfied that the applicant is likely to establish that publication should not be allowed.'[17] Therefore there must be an assessment of the applicant's case before a grant can be made.[18] Section 12 (4) further provides that the court must have regard to the importance of the right to freedom of expression. If the proceedings relate to journalistic, literary or artistic material or conduct related to such material[19] the court must have regard to: '(a) the extent to which – (i) the material has, or is about to, become available to the public;[20] or (ii) it is, or would be, in the public interest for the material to be published;[1] (b) any relevant privacy code.'[2]

Section 12 was introduced late in the Bill's passage through Parliament as a result of pressure from the press because of fears that Article 8 (right to privacy) would interfere with the operation of the free press in the UK. Lord Wakeham in championing the press as Chairman of the Press Complaints Commission (PCC) introduced an amendment to address press concerns. He explained the aim of the amendment as follows:

14 Section 12 (5), HRA 1998. This was because of concern over reporting restrictions and so the section 12 duty to have 'particular regard' to Article 10 does not apply. However in its general function as a 'public authority' the court must act compatibly with Convention rights including Article 10, and so while 'particular regard' is unnecessary some regard will in any case be needed. What difference this will make if at all to the court's deliberations when imposing restrictions remains to be seen. See the Home Secretary HC Debates, 2 July 1998, Column 540.
15 The Home Secretary gave the example of an issue of national security and considered that it would be rarely used. See HC Debates, 2 Jul 1998: Column 536.
16 See the Home Secretary at HC Debates, 2 Jul 1998: Column 537.
17 Section 12 (3), HRA 1998.
18 This is in line with the Convention case law see *Observer and Guardian v United Kingdom* (1991) 14 EHRR 153.
19 This would include the investigation of a story by a journalist see *Godwin v United Kingdom* (1996) 22 EHRR 123.
20 The availability of the information or its imminent availability is one of the considerations applied by the ECtHR. In such cases it is unlikely that an injunction would be allowed: see *Sunday Times Ltd v United Kingdom (No 2)* (1991) 14 EHRR 229. See also Chapter 4 on Article 10.
1   See Chapter 4 (Article 10) for the ECtHR view on the circumstance when a restriction on Article 10 will be justified.
2   Section 12 (4), HRA 1998. What the impact of this part of the section will be is unclear. The government intended that it should emphasise the importance of self-regulation when Article 10 matters fell to the court to adjudicate. See the Home Secretary HC Debates, 2 July 1998: Column 541. Presumably one of the considerations of the court will be whether the newspaper has complied with the PCC guidelines. That in itself would not be the end of the matter as the guidelines themselves, and any actions of the PCC, would necessarily fall under scrutiny if the court is to comply with its section 6 duty.

[m]y amendment aims to stop the development of a common law of privacy. Such a law could never be as effective as self-regulation in safeguarding the rights of individuals … If there is a law of privacy, fashioned by the courts, I fear that the newspapers will simply say to complainants, 'Use it'. That will be fine for the rich and the powerful, but it will be a remedy out of the reach of ordinary people. Indeed, where there is a problem with intrusion into the privacy of ordinary citizens, a law will simply make it worse than under tough self-regulation, not better. I fully expect that the noble and learned Lord the Lord Chancellor will tell me – indeed, he has never sought to make any bones about it – that a judge-made law of privacy is on its way and that it may happen in a year or two anyway as the courts seek to advance, without Parliament's express approval or scrutiny, the law of confidence. With great respect, if I may say so as one who believes in the sovereignty of Parliament and has been Leader of both its Houses, that is no justification. If Parliament wants a law of privacy – which would be a fundamental change in our constitutional balance, to which I am, of course, opposed – it should pass one, not just acquiesce in the courts' creating one without its approval or scrutiny.[3]

Despite the operation of section 12 the right to privacy contained in Article 8 is one of the rights that is likely to have a major effect on the present non-existent state of a right to privacy in the UK.[4] First the tort of breach of confidence could certainly be extended by the courts when combined with Article 8 even where the matter is a dispute between private individuals.[5] Second the PCC had a right to be concerned about the effect of the Convention rights on its operation. As a 'public authority' it is not inconceivable that a dissatisfied complainant, having been through the PCC mechanism, could allege section 6 illegality on the basis of a positive obligation to protect Article 8 (privacy) and an insufficiently independent procedure leading to a breach of Article 6 (fair trial).

Section 12 has been formulated to curb the interference with freedom of expression by emphasising the importance of Article 10 in any hierarchy of rights the court may have to consider. Given that the Strasbourg jurisprudence has always regarded Article 10 as carrying great weight, section 12 on one interpretation does no more than set out the status quo regarding freedom of expression.[6] On another

3   HL Debates, 24 Nov 1997: Column 773
4   During the debate on section 12 the Lord Chancellor stated: 'I say as strongly as I can to the press: "I understand your concerns, but let me assure you that press freedom will be in safe hands with our British judges and with the judges of the European Court". I add this, "You know that, regardless of incorporation, the judges are very likely to develop a common law right of privacy themselves. What I say is that any law of privacy will be a better law after incorporation, because the judges will have to balance Article 10 and Article 8, giving Article 10 its due high value".' HL Debates, 3 Nov 1997: Column 1231.
5   See *Hellewell v Chief Constable of Derbyshire* [1995] 1 WLR 804. On Article 8 and its use in conjunction with other actions see the Home Office Minister Mike O'Brien HC Debates, 2 July 1998 : Column 561.
6   On the basis of the importance of freedom of expression the Commission has held that the present UK position where there is no actionable right of privacy did not breach Article 8: see *Winer v United Kingdom* (1986) 48 DR 154.

interpretation it may lead to a more protective view of Article 10 than the Strasbourg court which may lead to divergent UK case law on Article 10. Should the courts do this to the detriment of other important rights such as privacy in Article 8 it may lead to challenges to the court's decision first at the domestic level on appeal and eventually at the Strasbourg level.[7] Should such an application be successful the UK would have to amend or remove section 12.

Another effect section 12 may have is on rights of commercial expression. While we consider this matter in greater detail in Chapter 11 we make the following observation here. When dealing with Article 10 the Strasbourg court has always regarded expression in the context of the press as a right of the highest order. However with regard to commercial expression the Strasbourg court has accorded only secondary protection allowing a large margin of appreciation to the domestic authority. Section 12 (4) draws no distinction between expression in the context of the press and commercial expression. All expression is potentially of the same importance and the court must work out its own order of primacy. In taking account of the Strasbourg jurisprudence under section 2 the courts must also have regard to the special place accorded to Article 10 in section 12 (4), which may lead to a higher level of protection for commercial expression.

Is the Church of England affected by the HRA?

Section 13 provides that on any question before a court under the HRA where the exercise by a religious organisation (itself or the members collectively) of the right to freedom of thought, conscience and religion in Article 9 of the ECHR might be affected the court must have particular regard to that right.

The background to section 13 is similar to that of section 12 in that it was a late amendment to the Act introduced to placate the Lords Spiritual in the Upper House. The Bishops were concerned that Convention rights, in particular Article 14 (discrimination), would cause difficulty for the operation of religious based schools as to their employment practices[8] or that they might be compelled to perform same sex marriages. As the Home Secretary explained section 13:

> would come into play in any case in which a court's determination of any question arising out of the Bill might affect the exercise by a religious organisation of the convention right of freedom of thought, conscience and religion. In such a case, it provides for the court to have particular regard – not just to have regard, going back to the earlier debate, but to have particular regard – to the importance of that right. Its purpose is not to exempt Churches and other religious organisations from the scope of the Bill – they have not sought that – any more than from that of the convention. It is to reassure them against the Bill being used to intrude upon genuinely religious beliefs

---

7   The Home Secretary seemed to suggest that the Article 10 would have a higher priority in a clash with Article 8: see HC Debates, 2 July 1998: Column 543.
8   The fear was that they might be compelled to employ an unbeliever or, worse, a believer in a different faith.

or practices based on their beliefs. I emphasise the word 'practices', as well as 'beliefs'.[9]

In itself the section does no more than state the present position in the Strasbourg case law. Its effect is likely to be neutral and it serves largely as a balm for those who opposed the HRA in the misguided belief that it would interfere with the present operation of religious organisations in the UK.[10] However should, for example, the Strasbourg court in the future find that state refusal to allow same sex marriages was in breach of the Convention it might provide reason for departure from that decision at a domestic level. This would however only lead to an appeal to the ECtHR who would hold section 13 to be a breach of the Convention which would compel the UK government to remove or amend the section thus adding further to its irrelevance.

Does the UK have any restrictions in place with regard to the Convention rights and can it enter further restrictions?

Sections 14 to 17 are concerned with derogations from, and reservations to, articles of the Convention.[11] The UK has one derogation and one reservation in place, relating to Article 5(3) (right to be brought before a judge within reasonable time) of the Convention and Protocol 1, Article 2 (education), respectively, and those articles have effect in domestic law subject to them.[12] This means the state does not have to give effect to those parts of the articles in domestic law. For a full consideration of the effect of this section see the discussion in section 1 above and Chapter 6 on Article 5 and Protocol 1. Additionally the text of the derogation and reservation is set out in Schedule 2 to the Act (see Appendix 1). Future derogations and reservations may also be given domestic effect under the Bill.[13] For domestic purposes they will be subject to periodic renewal in the case of derogation, or review in the case of reservations.[14]

Will the HRA mean that more senior judges will want to go to Strasbourg?

Section 18 simply provides for the appointment of judges to the European Court of Human Rights.[15] The major effect of section 18 is to change the situation pre-HRA where a judge would have to resign his office in the UK in order to take up an appointment at Strasbourg, with no guarantee of reinstatement on return from Strasbourg. Section 18 removes that bar, and so if a judge is appointed to the European Court he will have the right to return to the bench in the United Kingdom after his term of office in Strasbourg. The effect of this section should be to see

9   HC Debates, 20 May 1998: Column 1021.
10   As the Secretary of State for Scotland pointed out in the Commons whatever effect the Church feared has been in place since the UK ratified the Convention in 1953. See HC Debates, 20 May 1998: Column 1036.
11   On derogations and reservations generally see Chapter 3 and Chapter 6.
12   Section 14-15, HRA 1998.
13   Section 14-15, HRA 1998.
14   Section 16-17, HRA 1998.
15   It also makes certain pension provisions for judges serving in the ECtHR.

more senior judges coming forward to take up a post in Strasbourg. Given that Convention rights will become a major part of the judge's domestic interpretative role, over time it is likely that spending time in Strasbourg will become an essential part of the career path of the senior judiciary rather than the exalted chalice of exile it presently is.

Does the HRA affect the way legislation passes through Parliament?

Section 19 requires a Minister in charge of a Bill in either House of Parliament to make a statement in writing, before the Second Reading,[16] that in his view the provisions of the Bill are compatible with the Convention rights (statement of compatibility). If the Minister cannot make such a statement he must make a statement that even though the Bill is incompatible the government wishes to proceed with the Bill.[17] While section 19 will reinforce the courts' interpretative obligation in section 3 as it acts as a sort of supercharged *Pepper v Hart* [1993] AC 59 statement, its main impact will be on the legislative process. As the Lord Chancellor explained:

> [Section] 19 imposes a new requirement on government Ministers when introducing legislation. In future, they will have to make a statement either that the provisions of the legislation are compatible with the convention or that they cannot make such a statement but nevertheless wish Parliament to proceed to consider the Bill. Ministers will obviously want to make a positive statement whenever possible. That requirement should therefore have a significant impact on the scrutiny of draft legislation within government. Where such a statement cannot be made, parliamentary scrutiny of the Bill would be intense.[18]

However, there is nothing to stop the government introducing an incompatibility after the second reading? The initial test of how parliamentary scrutiny will operate under the present Labour government has not been exemplary. In November 1998 an ad hoc Committee of both Houses of Parliament was formed to consider the Financial Services and Markets Bill (FSMB). The Joint Committee reported in April 1999 and again in June 1999. On both occasions the Committee found that the FSMB contained provisions which raised serious human rights issues, in particular with regard to Article 6 (1) (fair trial). While the government has amended the FSMB to take account of some of these concerns there is still a major question surrounding the compatibility of the FSMB (now the FSMA) with Convention rights. The government ignored these concerns and the Chancellor of the Exchequer issued a statement of compatibility for the FSMA even thought it is doubtful whether certain provisions of the Act are compatible.[19] The same has happened with regard to the statement of compatibility on the face of the Regulation of Investigatory Powers Bill 2000 signed by the Home Secretary despite serious human rights concern about

16 The idea of a statement at such an early stage is to provide time for Parliament to consider properly the human rights implications of a Bill.
17 Section 19 came into force on the passing of the HRA.
18 HL Debates, 3 Nov 1997: Column 1234.
19 See his statement on the front of the Bill printed on 17 June 1999.

its contents. There is no obligation on the part of a Minister to accept that a Bill has inconsistencies and as Parliament is not a 'public authority' for the purposes of section 6 it does not give rise to a right of action. However the government's actions over the FSMB have damaged the credibility of statements of compatibility as a mechanism to ensure compatibility. Curiously for a government often accused of pandering to lobbyists, the government refused to accept there were human rights problems with the FSMB even when faced with the immense lobbying power of the financial sector. Ultimately it will be a matter for the courts to decide on the issue of compatibility.

How is the power to make orders exercisable under the HRA?

Section 20 provides that the power to make orders under the HRA is exercisable by statutory instrument and that various orders exercisable under the Act must be laid before Parliament.

Is there an interpretive section of the HRA?

Section 21 is the interpretative section of the HRA. It additionally includes procedural references to the Convention and the abolition of the death penalty and its substitution with a lesser penalty for military offences.

Did all the sections of the HRA come into force on the 2 October 2000?

Section 22 provides that the HRA is to be given the title Human Rights Act 1998 and that it only comes into force on such day in the future as the Minister appoints (2 October 2000). Different days may be appointed for different sections.[20] However, sections 22, 18 (judicial appointment), 20 (orders under the Act) and 21 (5) (amending death penalty for military offences) came into affect on the passing of the HRA. It also provides that section 7 (1) (b) (ability to rely on the Convention rights in any legal proceedings) has retrospective effect but only in relation to proceedings brought by a public authority. Section 22 (5), (6) and (7) provide that the Act binds the Crown, applies to Northern Ireland and with regard to the abolition of the death penalty for military offences applies in any place those offenses apply. The HRA does not apply to the Isle of Man or the Channel Islands but the government has stated that the authorities there intend to incorporate the ECHR themselves.[1]

During the Lords debate Lord Monson tabled an amendment, which he later withdrew, objecting to the title of the bill. He explained his objection as follows:

> [w]hether by accident or by design – I am sure it is the former – this is a propagandistic title. Faced with this title, the sort of voter who reads only the tabloids and watches only commercial television could be forgiven for being

---

20   Section 19 (statement of compatibility) came into force on the 24 November 1998 as a result of the Human Rights Act 1998 (Commencement) Order 1998, SI 1998/2882.

1   See HC Debates, 3 June 1998: Column 471. For a consideration of how the HRA will operate in Northern Ireland, Scotland and Wales see Lord Lester and Pannick, D, *Human Rights Law and Practice* (1999) Butterworths.

persuaded that prior to 1 May 1997 the United Kingdom was in a state of semi-tyranny compared with the liberal paradise to be found on the Continent of Europe. The Members of this Chamber, Members of another place, those who have a university education and broadsheet readers in general are well aware that this is the reverse of the truth and that Britain, with its Magna Carta, jury system, equality before the law, its House of Commons with power to refuse to vote funds to the Monarch, the Glorious Revolution and so on, has always been – despite many imperfections – far freer than almost any continental nation. Most of those people know that the Soviet Union had rights written in black and white into its constitution right through the Lenin terror, the Stalin terror and the enduring Gulags and that it is the underlying attitudes and instincts of a nation's people that count just as much as what is written on paper. They know too that most people from third countries would far rather find themselves in the hands of the British police than the French police, whatever the theoretical safeguards in France. Moreover, the title as it stands may give the public the impression that the rights conferred by this Bill are so comprehensive that nothing more needs to be done, ever. Of course we know better. For example, the European Convention on Human Rights is weak on property rights, as the European Court's judgments on the confiscatory aspects of the 1977 Aircraft and Shipbuilding Industries Act demonstrate. This is not surprising as the convention was formulated in the late 1940s when western Europe was going through a decidedly socialist phase.[2]

What do the Schedules to the HRA deal with?

The HRA contains four schedules. Schedule 1 lists the Convention rights included in the Act. These are Articles 2-12 and 14, Articles 1-3 of Protocol 1 and Articles 1 and 2 of the 6th Protocol, as read with Articles 16-18 of the Convention.[3] Schedule 2 sets out further provisions for remedial orders under Section 10.[4] Schedule 3 contains the text of the UK derogations and reservations in respect of Article 5 (3) and Protocol 1, Article 2 respectively.[5] Schedule 4 contains the provisions regarding judicial pensions for those serving in the ECtHR.

Does the HRA provide for a Human Rights Commission?

The government ruled out introducing a standing Commission on Human Rights in the HRA.[6] While not ruling it out in the future the government proposed instead a joint committee of both Houses to scrutinise legislation for human rights issues.[7] As the Lord Chancellor explained:

[a]lthough we have given this proposal much thought, we have concluded that a human rights commission is not central to our main task today, which

2   Lord Morison, HL Debates, 27 Nov 1997: Column 1167.
3   See section 1 for a full consideration of Schedule 1.
4   See section 10 for a full consideration of Schedule 2.
5   See section 1 and Chapter 4 on Article 5 and Protocol 1.
6   There is one in place in Northern Ireland since the Northern Ireland Act 1998.
7   On the role of such a Commission see Spencer, S and Bynoe, I, 'A Human Rights Commission for the United Kingdom – some options' (1997) *Human Rights Law Review* p 152.

is to incorporate the convention as promised in our election manifesto. There are questions to be resolved about the relationship of a new commission with other bodies in the human rights field; for example, the Equal Opportunities Commission and the Commission for Racial Equality. Would a human rights commission take over their responsibilities, or act in partnership with them, or be an independent body independent of them? We would also want to be sure that the potential benefits of a human rights commission were sufficient to justify establishing and funding for a new non-governmental organisation. We do not rule out a human rights commission in future, but our judgment is that it would be premature to provide for one now. We have, however, given very positive thought to the possibility of a parliamentary committee on human rights. This is not in the Bill itself because it would not require legislation to establish and because it would in any case be the responsibility of Parliament rather than the Government. But we are attracted to the idea of a parliamentary committee on human rights, whether a separate committee of each House or a joint committee of both houses. It would be a natural focus for the increased interest in human rights issues which Parliament will inevitably take when we have brought rights home. It could, for example, not only keep the protection of human rights under review, but could also be in the forefront of public education and consultation on human rights. It could receive written submissions and hold public hearings at a number of locations across the country. It could be in the van of the promotion of a human rights culture across the country.[8]

Does the HRA have any special constitutional status?

Section 3 of the HRA provides that '[s]o far as it is possible to do so, all primary and subordinate legislation must be read and given effect in a way which is compatible with the Convention rights.'[9] This includes the HRA itself as primary legislation and may provide the courts with reason to expand on ambiguities in the Act, for example, to widen the remedies available utilising the Article 13 (right to an effective remedy) case law and taking a broader view of victim status in the cause of interpreting the HRA in a manner to give effect to Convention rights.[10]

The HRA is additionally a document of Constitutional importance and as such may be treated differently than ordinary primary legislation for interpretative purposes.[11] The Privy Council has some experience of interpreting constitutional documents from the Commonwealth and has taken the view that such documents will be

8   HL Debates, 3 Nov 1997: Column 1234.
9   The preamble to the HRA also makes the purpose clear as it is an 'Act to give further effect to rights and freedoms guaranteed under the European Convention on Human Rights'.
10   The Convention does not define the concept of victim and so the victim criteria is contained only in the Strasbourg case law which the courts must take into account but are not bound by: see sections 7 and 2 of the HRA 1998.
11   However it is always possible that even though it is a document of constitutional importance the courts could take the view that, as the government did not entrench the Act, as such it is just an ordinary Act of Parliament, subject to ordinary rules of interpretation.

interpreted generously so as to give effect to rights contained within.[12] As Lord Hoffman stated with regard to the Mauritian constitution:

> [t]he background of a constitution is an attempt, at a particular moment in history, to lay down an enduring scheme of government in accordance with certain moral and political values. Interpretation must take these purposes into account ... They may expressly state moral and political principles to which the judges are required to give effect in accordance with their own conscientiously held views of what such principles entail.[13]

Lord Wilberforce observed similarly that the Bermudan Constitution must be provided:

> a generous interpretation avoiding what has been called 'the austerity of tabulated legalism', suitable to give individuals the full measure of the fundamental rights and freedoms referred to.[14]

The same generous approach to constitutional documents avoiding technical legalism is evident in the Canadian[15] and New Zealand[16] courts' approach to their respective Charter and Bill of Rights.

This generous approach does not however mean that the judiciary can ignore clear intention in the constitutional document or clear unambiguous language in legislation intended to limit rights. As Lord Hoffman, quoting from the South African case of *State v Zuma*,[17] stated '[i]f the language used by the lawgiver is ignored in favour of a general resort to 'values', the result is not interpretation but divination.'[18]

Should the courts treat the HRA as such a constitutional document a court would adopt an expansive approach and when determining the validity of limitations on rights by the state the court will have regard to their fundamental nature and only allow limitations if such limitations are clear and unambiguous.

Is EC law affected by the HRA?

In Chapter 5 we set out the ways in which the ECHR operated in the UK law prior to the HRA. One of the ways in which the ECHR was given a more rigorous effect was through European Community law.[19] As we explained above it has long been accepted by the European Court of Justice (ECJ) that the ECHR forms part of the influences on Community law.[20] As such the domestic courts must consider the

---

12 See *A-G Hong Kong v Lee Kwong-Kut* [1993] AC 951, *A-G of Gambia v Momodou Jobe* [1984] AC 689, PC.
13 *Matadeen v Pointu* [1999] 1 AC 98, PC.
14 *Minister for Home Affairs v Fisher* [1979] 3 All ER 21.
15 *R v Big M Drug Mart Ltd* (1985) 18 DLR (4th) 321.
16 *R v Grayson and Taylor* [1997] 1 NZLR 399.
17 (1995) (4) BCLR 401 at 412.
18 *Matadeen v Pointu* [1999] 1 AC 98, PC.
19 It will still operate in this manner. See p 92 'The ECHR and the European Union'.
20 *J Nold, Kohlen und Baustoffgrosshandlung, Darmstadt v EC Commission* 4/73 [1974] 2 CMLR 338.

Convention rights when interpreting EC law. There is one important difference between the operation of the Convention rights through EC law prior to the HRA and post-HRA, that is, since the HRA came into force the court has a duty to interpret all legislation, even legislation of EC origin, compatibly[1] and to act compatibly[2] with the Convention rights. This has the potential to lead to conflict as Community law allows wide exceptions to human rights where there are Community interests at stake. The ECJ has recognised that at times it may be legitimate to limit the extent of ECHR rights and freedoms to achieve the overall aims and objectives of the European community. Because of this the rights and freedoms need not always be respected.[3] Domestically the courts will have to work out the balance between acting compatibly with the Convention rights and Community law. Community law should win out but clashes are likely to take some time to resolve. The domestic courts may be faced with Community law which is incompatible with the Convention rights. What would a domestic court do in such a situation faced with section 6 (duty to act compatibly with the Convention rights) and section 2 (compulsion to take account of relevant Strasbourg case law) of the HRA, and the courts' obligations under the European Communities Act 1972. This presents the court with a Constitutional dilemma, does it protect the fundamental rights of its citizens or does it follow Community law? While the court might try to find a compromise between the opposing compulsions, clearly the obligation under the European Communities Act 1972 is the stronger. In which case could the court even issue a declaration of incompatibility under section 4 of the HRA regarding domestic legislation of Community origin? What would be the point as the government has no power to change Community legislation? While the court has no power to disapply a Community act because it violates a Convention right it could grant interim relief and refer the case to the ECJ to determine the validity of the Community act. It is entirely possible, however, that a victim of a violation of their Convention rights could be left without any remedy for the violation once it is based on Community law. The victim could attempt to bring an action under section 6 of the HRA alleging the court as a 'public authority' had committed an unlawful act by acting incompatibly with the Convention. This, however, would not get the victim very far as section 6 exempts a public authority from liability where because of primary legislation it could not have acted differently.[4] The only recourse for the victim would be bring an action at the Strasbourg level. This again would not result in a change in the domestic law if the applicant was successful as the government has no power to change Community law. It would provide some remedy in that compensation could be awarded.

However there may be advantages to be gained from Community law for a victim of a rights violation. If, using a combination of Convention arguments and EC law, primary domestic legislation can be shown to be incompatible with the EC provisions

---

1   Section 3, HRA 1998.
2   The court is a public authority under section 6, HRA 1998.
3   See *J Nold, Kohlen und Baustoffgrosshandlung, Darmstadt v EC Commission* 4/73 [1974] 2 CMLR 338 at para 14, and *Otto BV v Post Bank NV* Case C-60/92 [1993] ECR I-5683. See also *Sirdar v Secretary of State for Defence* (Case C-273/97) [1999] All ER (EC) 928.
4   Section 6 (2) HRA 1998.

the EC provisions will override any incompatible domestic legislation. Using the HRA alone this could only lead to a declaration of incompatibility. Relying on EC law would also open the possibility of a remedy for a failure to give proper effect to legislation which would not be allowable under the HRA.[5]

The domestic courts' experience of EC law is likely to be of great assistance to the courts in terms of the interpretative methods that need to be brought to bear on the ECHR rights and freedoms. For example the ability to 'read in' wording to legislation intended to give effect to EC directives and regulations as in *Litster v Forth Dry Dock and Engineering Co Ltd*[6] will prove an invaluable tool in interpreting legislation compatibly with Convention rights under section 3 of the HRA.[7] Additionally the concept of 'appropriate and necessary' which accords a discretion to the state in the EC context derives from the same French and German administrative law concept of discretion as the margin of appreciation that operates at the Strasbourg level. The domestic courts' experience of 'appropriate and necessary' in the EC context should be helpful in developing a similar concept of discretion to accord to the state when interpreting human rights.[8]

5   *See Francovich v Italy* [1991] ECR I-5357.
6   [1990] 1 AC 546.
7   See also *Marleasing SA v La Comercial Internacional de Alimentacion* SA C-106.89 [1990] ECR I-4135 and the commentary on section 3 above.
8   See Chapter 3 on the margin of appreciation and *R v Chief Constable of Sussex, ex p International Trader's Ferry Ltd* [1999] 2 AC 418; *R v Ministry of Agriculture, ex p First City Trading* [1997] 1 CMLR 250; R *v Secretary of State for Employment, ex p Equal Opportunities Commission* [1995] 1 AC 1 and *Stoke-on-Trent City Council v B and Q plc* [1991] Ch 48.

Part two

Companies and the Human Rights Act 1998

Chapter seven

Companies and the HRA

The rights we seek to protect are those of the individual against the state. The Human Rights Act would therefore provide that its protections could only be relied on by individuals, not by companies or organisations. We do not want to repeat here the confusion and injustice that has occurred in some other countries, where companies and commercial organisations have tried to resist social legislation controlling their activities by claiming that it infringes their 'human' rights.[1]

The special issues raised by companies and human rghts

The Labour party originally intended the HRA to exclude companies from relying on rights contained in any document incorporating the ECHR. First John Smith and

1   Speech of John Smith (1993) 'A Citizens Democracy'.

then Lord Irvine set out a view of the HRA which could only be relied upon by natural persons.[2] Their main concern in excluding corporations was a fear of companies attacking progressive legislation if they had access to human rights.[3] This policy however was quietly dropped probably because 'victim' status at the Strasbourg level has always included companies and the sky has not as yet fallen in.[4] A 'victim' test at the domestic level which excluded companies would quickly have been challenged at the Strasbourg level. Such fears of attacks on progressive legislation are misplaced as we would hope to demonstrate in the following chapters. The introduction of the HRA and its application to corporations is both a burden and an opportunity for corporations. It is a burden in that companies that carry out public functions will be considered a 'public authority' for the purposes of the HRA and therefore have to comply with the Convention rights for all or part of their activities. As we will see below, where we discuss public authority status, the ability of companies to comply with the Convention rights has been hampered by the way public authority status has bee defined in the HRA. The horizontal effect of the HRA may also prove to some extent to be an additional burden. However the HRA is also an opportunity for companies in that the Convention rights will be available to companies to use as they can to prevent violations of their rights by public authorities and also to some extent other private parties.

The fact there was consideration of excluding companies from utilising the HRA illustrates a certain discomfort about the idea of an artificial entity having 'human' rights.[5] While the idea of corporations being accorded human rights may seem a contradiction in terms the issue of whether companies can rely, or the extent to which companies can rely, on law essentially designed for humans is nothing new. The courts and the legislature have had to deal with this issue since the beginning of modern company law in the 19th century. A company is an artificial legal entity and not generally considered to be 'human'. This artificial entity by its nature poses legal problems, ie it is difficult to describe or define the rights and duties of an artificial entity without using human metaphors. The question is however to what extent are those metaphors appropriate? Can a corporation have human rights? Is it a 'human'? Is it a 'person'? Can it be a 'victim'? In the UK it appears clear that a corporation has to some extent a separate existence from its members. The principle expounded by the House of Lords in *Salomon v Salomon & Co*[6] makes it clear that the company is a legal person separate and distinct from its members. The courts though, when dealing with directors' fiduciary duties, have defined the

---

2   See John Smith (1993) 'A Citizens Democracy' and Lord Irvine 'The Legal System and Law Reform under Labour' in D Bean (ed) *Law Reform for All* (1996).

3   In the US see *Buckley v Valeo* 424 US 1 (1976) and *Miami Herald Publishing Co v Tornillo* 418 US 241 (1974) where companies have successfully utilised constitutional rights to strike down legislation. In Canada companies have used Charter rights to strike down Sunday trading legislation: *R v Big M Drug Mart Ltd* (1985) 18 DLR 4th 321.

4   Liberty also drafted a bill of rights excluding companies from relying on those rights see National Council for Civil Liberties *A Peoples Charter* (1991).

5   Note, however, that in other jurisdictions the term 'human rights' is often substituted by the term 'basic rights' or the approach of Romano Prodi at the Cologne European Council on 3 and 4 June 1999 to draft a European Charter of 'Fundamental' Rights to be applied at the Union Level.

6   [1897] AC 22, HL.

'interests of the company' in terms of shareholders. The entity itself has no separate interest. So for liability purposes the corporation is a separate entity from the members but for fiduciary purposes the shareholders' interests are the entity's interests.[7]

Within the sphere of criminal law the courts have had great difficulty applying laws designed for natural persons to an artificial entity. Companies have no physical being and so punishment such as imprisonment is inapplicable. The ability of the criminal law to find a corporation's mens rea has been hampered by the complexity of corporate decision making.[8] To take an extreme example, in the UK a corporation cannot commit rape as the Sexual Offences Act 1956, section 1 (1) requires 'a man to rape a woman' a corporation has no gender and so it could not fulfil the criteria. In New Zealand consideration was given to whether a corporation was a 'human being', as homicide was defined by statute as the killing of a 'human being' by another 'human being'.[9] The court determined that a company was not a 'human being' and thus could not commit the offence.

On the other hand sometimes the English courts have treated the corporation as having characteristics which could be described as 'human'.[10] A company can be a 'person' depending on the context but is not an 'individual'.[11] The corporation has also been held to have acquired the attributes of an 'enemy'.[12] In *Winkworth v Edward Baron Development Co Ltd*[13] Lord Templeman considered that the company had a 'conscience'. In *Re Lindsay Bowman Ltd*[14] Megarry J considered the corporation's emotional state:

> I must assume that the artificial and impersonal entity that we know as the limited company has been endowed with the capacity not merely of having feelings but also of feeling aggrieved ...

The corporation could as a result of these 'feelings' take an action for defamation.

Jurisdictions with written constitutions have had to grapple with whether a corporation can hold rights under such a constitution. If a constitution uses words such as 'citizen' or 'human' the question arises as to whether a corporation is a 'citizen' or 'human'. If it is a 'citizen' or 'human' it could claim constitutional rights, if not such protections would be denied the corporation. For example, until 1995 the corporation in Ireland

7   See Lord Wedderburn of Charlton, 'Companies and Employees: Common Law or Social Dimension?' (1993) *Law Quarterly Review*, Vol 109, April, pp 220-262 and the comments of Dillon LJ *Multinational Gas and Petrochemical Co v Multinational Gas and Petrochemical Services Ltd* [1983] Ch 258.

8   See *Lennard's Carrying Co v Asiatic Petroleum* [1915] AC 705; *R v IRC Haulage Ltd* [1944] 1 All ER 691; *DPP v Kent and Sussex Contractors Ltd* [1944] KB 146 and *Tesco Supermarkets v Nattrass* [1972] AC 153.

9   *R v Murray Wright Ltd* [1970] NZLR 476.

10 For a wider consideration of when associations take on a form substantially different from its component parts see Laski, The Personality of Associations (1916) 29 *Harvard Law Review* 404, and Dicey, *Law and Public opinion in England* (3rd edn, 1920).

11 *Pharmaceutical Society v London Supply Association Ltd* (1880) 5 App Cas 857, HL see also the Interpretation Act 1978, section 5 and Schedule 1.

12 *Daimler Co Ltd v Continental Tyre and Rubber Co (Great Britain) Ltd* [1916] 2 AC 307.

13 [1987] 1 All ER 114 at 118.

14 [1969] 3 All ER 601 at 604.

was thought to be unable to exercise property rights guaranteed to 'citizens' in the Irish Constitution. If such rights were to be exercised they had to be exercised by the shareholders of the company as their individual rights.[15] Since 1995 the corporation can exercise such rights qua 'citizen'.[16] The length of time it took the Irish courts to confer such constitutional rights on companies illustrates the difficulty inherent in adapting human rights for corporate use. The German Basic Law or 'Grundgesetz' (GG)[17] expressly provides for the applicability of the 'basic rights' to corporations. Article 19, paragraph 3 GG states '[t]he basic rights shall also apply to domestic artificial persons to the extent that the nature of such rights permits.' The question of which right is accessible to which organisation has been and still is resolved on a case-to-case basis.[18]

However, just because the courts and legislature have some experience of the difficulties of applying law designed to protect elements of human personality to companies, does not mean that the HRA does not present challenges with regard to the application of the Convention rights to companies. It is to a large extent the special issues that companies raise when claiming human rights that we explore in this part of the book. We start in this chapter by looking at general issues with regard to companies that the HRA raises. In the next chapter we move to consider whether the corporation can be a victim of a human rights violation and how the Strasbourg court has balanced the rights of not only the corporation but also the shareholders, employees and creditors behind the corporate veil. We then turn in the following chapters to examine the application of certain key Convention rights to the corporation. These include the application of: Article 6 (fair trial) which impacts mostly on those regulating companies but which is important for companies to know what standards they can expect those regulators to come up to when they are the subject of investigations;[19] Article 8 (privacy) which protects officers of the company but raises special issues as to whether a company itself can rely on a right to privacy; Article 10 (expression) which protects commercial expression and how the regulation of that expression will be effected by the HRA; Protocol 1, Article 1 (property) and the potential impact this has on the operation of company law in England and Wales; and the impact generally of the Convention rights on companies as employers.

---

15 See *Quinn's Supermarket Ltd v A-G* [1972] IR 1 *and Chestvale Properties Ltd and Hoddle Investments Ltd v Glackin* [1993] 3 IR 35.

16 *Irish Rail and Bernard Patrick Dowling v A-G HC,* Judgment delivered 28 April 1995, Keane J.

17 The complete text can be found in the German Law Archive (GLA) under http://www.iuscomp.org/gla/

18 With regard to artificial persons in private law see the following decisions of the German Constitutional Court (so called 'Bundesverfassungsgericht' or BVerfG): BVerfGE 3, 359 (363); 3, 383 (390f); 4, 7 (12); 10, 89 (99); 13, 174 (175); 46, 73 (82); 80, 124 (131). Generally on the applicability of basic rights to artificial entities of private law (whether applicable and which rights) see: Bethge, H: Grundrechtsträgerschaft juristischer Personen' in: Archiv des öffentlichen Rechts (AöR) 104 (1979) 54, Commentary on Art. 19 III GG (ie applicability of human rights to artificial persons) GG in: von Muench, Ingo/ Kunig, Philip (applicability of human rights to artificial persons) Grundgesetz-Kommentar, Band 1 Beck, Muenchen 2000, p 1055.

19 It is also dealt with in Chapter 13 on employment issues.

How does the HRA affect companies?

The HRA impacts on companies in three ways. First the regulatory agencies such as the DTI, FSA, Competition Authority and the utility regulators will all be 'public authorities' according to the definition in section 6 (1) and have to act compatibly with the Convention rights. Other regulatory agencies such as the Panel on Takeovers and Mergers and the Stock Exchange will also fall within either the section 6 (1) definition or section 6 (3) (b) as bodies certain of whose functions are public in nature. To this extent the economic regulatory agencies of the state will have to change their operation to ensure that they do not interfere with Convention rights. This will mean two major changes. First when dealing with companies as part of their supervisory role these agencies will have to be careful to act compatibly with Convention rights. The most likely Convention rights the regulatory agencies could violate in this role are Article 6 (fair trial), Article 8 (privacy) Article 10 (expression) and Protocol 1 Article 1 (property). Second the regulatory agencies will also have to ensure the regulatory regime they operate gives effect to their positive obligation to protect Convention rights from violation by private parties. This may mean over time the development of more extensive regulation than exists at present. OFTEL for example, in anticipation of the HRA, has already issued guidance to companies regarding the recording of employee's private telephone calls which would breach the employees' Article 8 (privacy) rights. Interestingly the regulator presumed a high level of horizontal effect of the HRA in taking the view that the Convention rights would affect all companies and not only those that were a 'public authority' under the Act.[20]

Second certain companies which carry out functions of a public nature are included in the section 6 (3) definition of a 'public authority'. These companies are for the most part the privatised utilities and transport companies and must also act compatibly with the Convention in the carrying out certain of their functions. While as we discuss below there is some difficulty assessing the extent to which these quasi-public bodies have to comply with the Convention rights, it is certain that their safety functions will have to operate in a way that is compatible with the Convention rights. Therefore should Railtrack or British Gas be responsible for property loss, personal injury or death through a failure of their safety systems this could be an unlawful act under section 6 of the HRA as it could interfere with Protocol 1, Article 1 (property) and Article 8 (private life). A victim of such interference has a directly enforceable right to a remedy against those companies.[1] These companies will not however be able to rely on the Convention rights with regard to their public function because a public authority cannot fulfil victim status.[2] Only in their private capacity will they be able to rely on the HRA. So for example British Gas could not use Convention rights to defend or instigate an action arising from the carrying out of its public function.

---

20   Singleton, Susan 'Business Recording Telephone Calls: New Oftel Guidance' in *Justice of the Peace,* Vol 16, 3 October 1999, pp 833-834. See also chapter 13.
1   See Chapter 10.
2   See *Ayuntamiento de M v Spain* (1990) 68 DR 209.

Third all companies will be affected by the Convention because of the indirect horizontal effect of the HRA. Whether the HRA has a high level of indirect horizontal effect or a minimal one remains to be seen but one thing is for certain: there will be some horizontal application because of the court's section 6 duty to act compatibly with the Convention rights.[3] In terms of the corporation's ability to raise argument on the basis of Convention rights it can do so alleging illegality against a 'public authority' if it has been the victim of a violation. It may also use Convention rights in any litigation against another private party arguing that the court must as a 'public authority' act compatibly with the corporation's Convention rights.[4] As we explain below when discussing horizontal effect, the company is not enforcing Convention rights against the other party to the dispute but rather against the court as 'public authority' by arguing that the court must give effect to its Convention rights. There is however some difference between the concept of victim status in the HRA and the common law position on corporate standing contained in *Foss v Harbottle*. This is something we return to in Chapter 8.

In terms of the use of Convention rights against companies there is a twofold effect. First it is important to be clear that should a company violate a Convention right it would not give rise directly to a cause of action under the HRA unless the company falls within section 6 (3) (b) and is a 'public authority' for the purposes of the HRA. However if we take the example of a company operating a chemical plant under licence from the local authority which pollutes the air in the local area, an individual who has suffered some ill-health as a result of the pollution would have two possibilities of redress using the HRA. First, to allege section 6 illegality by the local authority for its failure to protect the individuals Article 8 right to private life despite its positive obligation do so. Over time actions like this are likely to lead to more stringent licensing regimes where there is any possibility of affecting Convention rights. Second the individual could also raise a combined action in tort against the company directly, perhaps alleging negligence or nuisance and arguing that the court as a public authority under section 6 of the HRA has an obligation to interpret the common law compatibly with the Convention rights, in particular Article 8, and that additionally the court has a positive obligation to ensure respect for the applicants Article 8 right to private life from violation by a private company relying on the Article 8 environmental case law.[5]

Whether companies are operating under a licensing regime or not, if their actions have the potential to affect Convention rights, then they should review their procedures and policies to ensure that they are at least aware of the risks and where they judge it to be necessary assess the proportionality of their action. In the following sections we explore the implications of public authority status for companies, regulatory bodies and courts.

3   See below on the horizontal effect of the HRA.
4   That is unless the company is a 'public authority' in which case it cannot rely on the Convention rights or if it is a quasi-public body it can only be a 'victim' in relation to its private functions.
5   See Chapter 10.

How do you know if something is a 'public authority' under the HRA?

Obvious public athorities

Obvious state bodies such as Ministers, government departments, health authorities and trusts, police forces, army, navy, air force, prison authorities, immigration officials or local authorities are clearly covered by the definition of 'public authority' in section 6 (1) of the HRA.[6] The courts are also a 'public authority' according to section 6 (3) (a) and must act compatibly with the Convention rights in carrying out their function.

Self-regulating bodies

Identifying other public authorities for the purposes of the HRA is not necessarily an easy task as there is long tradition of self-regulation in the UK. The Panel on Takeovers and Mergers is a self-regulatory body which sets and enforces standards for takeovers and mergers in the form of the City Code on Takeovers and Mergers. The accountancy profession regulates accounting standards, which are recognised by statute and used as the standard of skill and care by the courts. This tradition can be seen outside conventional industry, in the operation of bodies such as the Football Association, the Jockey Club, the Press Complaints Commission[7] and in the General Medical Council,[8] who similarly set and enforce professional standards. Determining whether these bodies are a 'public body' under the HRA and if so whether they are covered by section 6 (1) and are obvious public bodies, or whether they are quasi-public bodies under section 6 (3) (b) is not an easy task.

In dealing with whether these types of bodies are public or not the English courts have traditionally sought to find some ultra vires ground upon which to base judicial review decisions.[9] On this basis the court must find a statutory, prerogative, contract or common law power to review.[10] The European Court of Justice (ECJ) has adopted a similar test. In *Foster v British Gas plc*[11] the ECJ described a public body as 'a body, whatever its legal form, which has been made responsible, pursuant to a measure adopted by the state, for providing a public service under the control of the state and has for that purpose special powers beyond those which result from the normal rules applicable in relations between individuals'.[12]

---

6   See Chapter 6 for a consideration section 6 HRA 1998.
7   For its Code of Practice see, Bailey, S H; Harris, D J, and Jones, B L, *Civil Liberties: Cases and Materials* (4th edn, 1995) Butterworths, p 565.
8   Mason, J K and McCall Smith, R A, *Law and Medical Ethics* (5th edn, 1999) Butterworths. See pp 10-13.
9   See *R v Cobham Hall School, ex p S* [1998] ELR 389.
10 Older cases suggest that if the activity is carried on for a profit it will not be a 'public authority'. See *R v Woods and Forest Comrs, ex p Budge* (1850) 15 QB (Adolphus and Ellis) 761 and *Griffiths v Smith* [1941] AC 170.
11 [1991] 1 QB 405.
12 See *Foster v British Gas plc* [1991] 1 QB 405 at 427.

Sometimes however where the courts have been unable to find traditional statutory, prerogative, contract or common law powers upon which to base decisions for judicial review they have focused on the nature of the power exercised. In *R v Panel on Take-overs and Mergers, ex p Datafin*[13] the Court of Appeal found that a self-regulating body was judicially reviewable essentially because of the public nature of the power exercised. In *R v Disciplinary Committee of the Jockey Club, ex p Aga Khan*[14] the court found that the Jockey Club was not judicially reviewable because it was not exercising powers which were 'governmental' in nature.[15] De Smith, Woolf and Jowell have described a public body in the context of judicial review as one that 'seeks to achieve some collective benefit for the public or a section of the public and it is accepted by the public or that section of the public as having authority to do so'.[16] Hunt has offered a more expansive approach to the nature of power exercised and argued that:

> [t]he test for whether a body is 'public', and therefore whether administrative law principles presumptively apply to its decision-making, should not depend on the fictional attribution of derivative status to the body's powers. The relative factors should include the nature of the interests affected by the body's decisions, the seriousness of the impact of those decisions on those interests, whether the affected interests have any real choice but to submit to the body's jurisdiction, and the nature of the context in which the body operates. Parliament's non-involvement or would be involvement, or whether the body is woven into a network of regulation with state underpinning, ought not to be relevant to answering these questions. The very existence of institutional power capable of affecting rights and interests should itself be sufficient reason for subjecting exercises of that power to the supervisory jurisdiction of the High Court, regardless of the its actual or would be source.[17]

If the courts are to consider self-regulating bodies under section 6 (1) of the HRA and determine in the Lord Chancellor's words whether they are a 'full-blooded'[18] 'public authority' the court must under section 2 of the HRA take into account the Strasbourg jurisprudence. State responsibility for public bodies has an expansive meaning when interpreted by the Strasbourg court. Through a combination of direct responsibility for the exercise of public functions, whether by a public authority or by a private body and positive obligations, it is very difficult for the state to avoid responsibility for the acts or omissions of public bodies when Convention rights are affected. State claims of ultra vires,[19] or that private bodies were carrying out the

13   [1987] QB 815.
14   [1993] 1 WLR 909.
15   See the judgment of Bingham MR in *R v Disciplinary Committee of the Jockey Club, ex p Aga Khan* [1993] 1 WLR 909 at 923. See also the judgment of Hoffman LJ at 932.
16   De Smith, Woolf and Jowell 'Judicial Review of Administrative Action' (1995) London: p 167.
17   Hunt, M, 'Constitutionalism and the Contractualisation of Government in the United Kingdom' in Taggart, M, *The Province of Administrative Law* (1997) Chapter 2.
18   HL Debates, 24 November 1997: Column 812.
19   *Ireland v United Kingdom* (1978) 2 EHRR 25.

public function[20] or that the act was a purely private act,[1] will not absolve the state of responsibility for a violation of Convention rights.

In formulating section 6 in such broad terms it would appear that the government intended to incorporate the same expansive approach to state responsibility into domestic law. During the Commons debate the Home Secretary set out the government's thinking:

> I must briefly explain the principles underlying that clause. Under the convention, the Government are answerable in Strasbourg for any acts or omissions of the state about which an individual has a complaint under the convention. The Government have a direct responsibility for core bodies, such as central Government and the police, but they also have a responsibility for other public authorities, in so far as the actions of such authorities impinge on private individuals. The Bill had to have a definition of a public authority that went at least as wide and took account of the fact that, over the past 20 years, an increasingly large number of private bodies, such as companies or charities, have come to exercise public functions that were previously exercised by public authorities. Under UK domestic common law, such bodies have increasingly been held to account under the processes of judicial review. As was generally acknowledged in debates in another place, it was not practicable to list all the bodies to which the Bill's provisions should apply. Nor would it have been wise to do so. What was needed instead was a statement of principle to which the courts could give effect. Clause 6 therefore adopts a non-exhaustive definition of a public authority. Obvious public authorities, such as central Government and the police, are caught in respect of everything they do. Public – but not private – acts of bodies that have a mix of public and private functions are also covered.[2]

The Strasbourg jurisprudence, an evolving nature of the power test in judicial review, combined with the government's intention to copy the Strasbourg position should lead to the courts taking an expansive approach to whether a self-regulating body is a 'public authority' within the meaning of section 6 (1).[3] This would have the effect of making it a 'public authority' with regard to all its functions both public and private. This would mean that the Accounting Standards Board, the Jockey Club, the Panel on Take-Overs and Mergers and the Press Complaints Commission would all have to act compatibly with the Convention rights not just when carrying out their public function but also when dealing in what are traditionally viewed as private functions such as employment and other contractual matters.

The determination of whether these bodies are covered by section 6 and if so whether 6 (1) applies or 6 (3) (b) is extremely important. If a body falls within

---

20   See *Van der Mussele v Belgium* (1983) 6 EHRR 163.
1   See Chapter 3 on positive obligations and Chapter 4 on Article 1.
2   HC Debates, 16 Feb 1998: Column 776 see also the Lord Chancellor at HL Debates 24 Nov 1997: Column 809.
3   Indeed during the debate in parliament on the definition of a 'public authority' the government considered the Jockey Club would be 'public authority'. See HC Debates 20 May 1998: Column 1018.

section 6 (1) all its functions, private and public, will have to be carried out in a manner compatible with the Convention rights. Should any of its actions be incompatible with a Convention right it will be an unlawful act and therefore actionable under the HRA. Additionally, it will not be capable of fulfilling 'victim' status for the purposes of the HRA as a public authority cannot be a 'victim' according to the Strasbourg jurisprudence.[4] This would mean that the body has no standing to claim Convention rights in court. Alternatively the courts may decide that self-regulating bodies are primarily private in nature with some public functions and thus fall under Section 6 (3) (b) and 6 (5).[5] As a result only in the operation of its public function would it have to act compatibly with the Convention rights. In respect of its private functions the body would not have to act compatibly with the Convention rights and could claim to be a 'victim' of a Convention violation. Either way the test for a 'public authority' in section 6 is likely to emphasise the nature of the power exercised in a manner much closer to Hunt's formulation than to a 'source of power' based test. It is likely that the majority of the self-regulatory bodies in the UK will fall within the definition of 'public authority' under the Act and give rise to a new cause of action against them should they act contrary to the Convention.

Companies and quasi-public body status

Some uncertainty arises when attempting to determine the interaction of section 6 (3) (b) and section 6 (5) of the HRA. A quasi-public body is defined in section 6 (3) (b) as 'any person certain of whose functions are functions of a public nature' but, according to section 6 (5), a person is not a 'public authority' if the nature of the act is private. The combination of section 6 (3) (b) and 6 (5) is intended to deal with bodies who carry out both public and private functions. This affects those companies that carry out such functions. As the Lord Chancellor explained:

> Railtrack would fall into that category because it exercises public functions in its role as a safety regulator, but it is acting privately in its role as a property developer. A private security company would be exercising public functions in relation to the management of a contracted-out prison but would be acting privately when, for example, guarding commercial premises. Doctors in general practice would be public authorities in relation to their National Health Service functions, but not in relation to their private patients.[6]

The intention of section 6 (5) is to exempt quasi-public bodies operating in a private capacity but the dividing line of such operation may be more difficult to determine that the government thinks.[7] To take Railtrack as an example, in its operation as a

4   See *Ayuntamiento de M v Spain* (1990) 68 DR 209. This causes particular problems for the BBC and C4: see Chapter 11.

5   For the purposes of judicial review there is already a recognition of the fact public bodies carry out private functions. In *R v BBC, ex p Lavelle* [1983] ICR 99 the BBC was not subject to judicial review in an employment dispute. See also *Mass Energy Ltd v Birmingham City Council* [1994] Env LR 298, CA.

6   HL Debates, 24 Nov 1997: Column 812.

7   Although the government seems to have learned its lesson about such ambiguity from the HRA experience and has introduced a list of public authorities for the Freedom of Information Bill.

property developer it is not entirely acting privately as it has certain planning privileges only state bodies possess eg planning exemptions and compulsory purchase powers. It also receives a subsidy from the government to maintain its operation.[8] In using that subsidy to maintain its general operation does that qualify its general operation as a public function and therefore all transactions flowing from that operation are public in nature? Are all areas where that subsidy is used public in nature? If British Gas appoints an employee to the position of safety inspector is British Gas bound to act compatibly with the Convention in relation to that employment contract or is it a purely private act? Are all contracts arising from British Gas's safety function public in nature? Another question is whether all aspects of the safety function are covered on the basis that all are public, or only those functions that are ancillary to a public function such as providing a rail network in the case of Railtrack. If the former then are all functions of all businesses under health and safety legislation public functions?

Presumably these quasi-public authorities will only be able to fulfil 'victim' status with regard to their private functions but not their public functions for which they are a 'public authority'.[9] Many former state companies and private companies carrying out public functions such as security firms running prisons have overlap functions between the public and private and it may take some time to firm up the dividing line. In the meantime at least with regard to their clear public role they should review all aspects of that activity to ensure compatibility.

In all, bodies such as government departments and Ministers, local authorities, British Telecom, Railtrack, the privatised utility companies, the BBC, C4, regulatory agencies like the Press Complaints Commission, the Advertising Standards Authority, the Broadcasting Standards Authority, the Independent Television Commission, the Panel on Takeovers and Mergers, the utility regulators, the Office of Fair Trading, the Financial Services Authority and the Competition Commission, to name but an obvious few, will have section 6 'public authority' status conferred upon them either for all or part of their functions.

What factors are relevant in deciding whether a body is a 'public authority' under the HRA?

In determining whether a body is likely to be considered a 'public authority' under section 6 the following are significant elements drawn from the case law and literature on the subject. We don't suggest that each element will give rise to 'public authority' status but rather that they are considerations to take into account depending on the context:

8   See the consideration of 'public authority' in *Hong Kong Polytechnic University v Next Magazine Publishing Ltd* [1996] 2 HKLR 185 where a university was held to be a 'public authority' for the purposes of the Bill of Rights Ordinance 1991. There was no government control of the university but rather public funding and the nature of its function were the determining factors.

9   See *Ayuntamiento de M v Spain* (1990) 68 DR 209.

a)   Does the body form part of a statutory framework operating in the public arena carrying out public law duties?

b)   Does it have statutory powers including powers to penalise?

c)   If the body is non-statutory is there government involvement in its formation?

d)   Does its function have a significant impact on the public or a part of the public?

e)   Do the individuals have any choice but to submit to the jurisdiction of the body?

f)   Could the carrying out of its function deprive an individual of a legitimate expectation?

g)   Are individual rights and obligations affected by the operation of its function?

h)   If the body did not exist would the government have to carry out its function?

i)   Is it required to act judicially in the exercise of its function?

j)   Does it receive a state subsidy?

k)   Is it subject to any form of state control?

l)   Does it have any State privileges, such as special powers, immunities or exemptions in the carrying out of its function eg powers of compulsory purchase or exemptions from planning control etc?

m) Does it carry out functions formerly carried out by the state?

n)   Is its primary function to make a profit for its shareholders?

The government appeared to learn its lesson from the uncertainty surrounding 'public authority' status under the HRA when it came to draft the Freedom of Information Bill (FOI). Instead of leaving the status of 'public authority' under the FOI to the courts to decide the government decided to list all the companies and bodies it considered to carry out public functions. The list is fairly comprehensive and offers a good guide to the companies and bodies likely to have public authority status conferred on them by the courts.

If a company or body is a 'public authority' what impact does it have?

Essentially there are two major impacts. First if a company or body is a 'public authority' it must act compatibly with the Convention rights for all or part of its function depending on whether it is an obvious public authority or a quasi-public body. If it does not it will have committed an unlawful act which give rise to an action under the HRA for which a remedy such as damages can be claimed. Second if a company or body is a 'public authority' it either cannot fulfil the 'victim' test necessary to claim a Convention right was violated at all or can only fulfil that test with regard to its private function. This is because the Strasbourg interpretation of 'victim status' precludes a public authority from fulfilling that test of standing. The idea behind this prohibition being that Article 34 of the ECHR allows only applications from 'any person, non-governmental organisation, or group of individuals'. A public authority as part of the state cannot bring an action alleging a violation of a Convention right.

As a result a 'public authority' has no enforceable Convention rights.[10] This causes particular problems for the BBC and C4 as they are likely to be public authorities under the HRA and so will have difficulty raising human rights arguments, in particular Article 10 (expression), in court.[11] Because the boundaries of the state are somewhat fuzzy in the UK and companies and bodies carry out public functions with a high degree of independence from government this position with regard to 'victim status' may need modification by the courts.

If a company or body is a public authority will there still be a certain discretion or 'margin of appreciation' to interfere with Convention rights?

As we explained in Chapter 3 the margin of appreciation is an international law concept aimed at maintaining a respect for the contracting states' social, economic, cultural and political traditions. It accords a measure of discretion to national authorities when interfering with Convention rights. As such it has no application in the domestic courts.[12] However English public law has traditionally accorded the state a degree of discretion when a state action has been challenged.[13] This is unlikely to change due to the HRA.[14] The courts are likely to develop something similar to the margin of appreciation recognising a measure of discretion to be accorded to public authorities on rights violations which concern a delicate balance between competing social, economic, cultural or political aims.[15] Indeed the Canadian courts have developed such as concept of discretion when interpreting their Charter of Rights and Freedoms. The Supreme Court explained this was necessary because:

> courts are not specialists in the realm of policy making, nor should they be. This is the role properly assigned to the elected representatives of the people ...[16]

10 See *Ayuntamiento de M v Spain* (1990) 68 DR 209.
11 See Chapter 11 for a detailed analysis of this problem.
12 On this see Pannick, D, 'Principles of Interpretation of Convention Rights Under the Human Rights Act and the Discretionary Area of Judgment' (1998) *Public Law* p 545, Singh, R, Hunt, M and Demetriou, M, 'Is there a Role for the Margin of Appreciation in National Law after the Human Rights Act' (1999) *European Human Rights Law Review* p 14 and Lord Lester and Pannick, D, *Human Rights Law and Practice* (1999) Butterworths, p 74.
13 Lord Irvine, [1996] 'Judges and Decision Makers: The Theory and Practice of Wednesbury Review' Public Law p 59.
14 See Supperstone, Michael and Coppel, Jason, 'Judicial Review after the Human Rights Act 1998' (1999) *European Human Rights Law Review* pp 318-319.
15 This is certainly what the Home Secretary thinks will happen see HC Debates, 3 June 1998: Column 424-426. Indeed it has already made an appearance in English law in *R v Ministry of Defence, ex p Smith* [1996] 1 All ER 257 at 263 and for the rationale for the development of such a concept see *R v Somerset County Council, ex p Fewings* [1995] 1 WLR 1037.
16 *Libman v A-G of Quebec* (1998) 3 BHRC 269 at 289 note though that the Charter is not an ordinary Act of Parliament and so is accorded a higher level of protection, the Canadian courts were much less generous with the 1960 Bill of Rights.

The question for the domestic courts is whether the discretion they accord will be less than is presently accorded the executive where fundamental rights are at issue, the same or more.

The absence of a margin of appreciation or the operation of a lesser discretion at a domestic level has two consequences of note. First, case law where violations of Convention rights by the contracting state have been allowed by the Strasbourg court on the basis of the margin of appreciation should be treated as suspect in the domestic arena. In particular numerous cases on Articles 8-11 violations have been decided on the basis of the margin of appreciation. Therefore interferences which were justifiable at the Strasbourg level may cease to be justifiable at the domestic because there can be no equivalent application of the margin of appreciation.

This brings us to our second point. Because the government can rely on the margin of appreciation at the Strasbourg level and not at the domestic it is more likely to be able to justify an interference with a Convention right at that level. Should, for example, a violation of primary legislation be found at the domestic level and a declaration of incompatibility be issued by the House of Lords the government could choose not to amend the legislation in the knowledge that should the applicant appeal to Strasbourg the violation is within the state's margin of appreciation.[17] There is therefore the temptation on the part of the government not to accept the domestic court's view as it knows it will have a better chance of winning in the Strasbourg court.

If your company or body is a 'public authority' what does it have to do to ensure that it acts compatibly?

All procedures, policy, acts and omissions of an obvious public authority under section 6 (1) must be compatible with the Convention rights. A quasi-public body under section 6 (3) (b) must ensure the same with regard to its public functions. While this means that the public authority must review its operation to consider the Convention implications it does not mean that all the acts of the public authority must not interfere with Convention rights. Should a public authority identify an area where an interference with Convention rights is likely it should consider two things. First whether the courts will accord the public authority a discretion or 'margin of appreciation' with regard to the interference.[18] As we explained above the courts are likely to develop something similar to the 'margin of appreciation' at the domestic level, recognising a measure of discretion to be accorded to public authorities on rights interferences which concern a delicate balance between competing social, economic, cultural or political aims. The extent of this discretion will become clear over time.

17 The government has no right of appeal to Strasbourg only a victim can apply. On this see the Home Secretary HC Debates, 24 June 1998: Columns 1121-1123.

18 See the detailed explanation of the margin of appreciation and proportionality concepts in Chapter 3.

Second the public authority should consider the proportionality of its action. This involves adopting a similar systematic approach to the Strasbourg court when measuring the proportionality of an interference with Convention rights by a public authority. The following are the criteria for measuring whether an interference with a Convention right can be justified as proportionate to the legitimate aim pursued by the public authority.

a) Identify the right in question, adopting an expansive approach to the scope of the Convention rights. This is part of the purposive approach adopted by the ECtHR in fulfilling the object and purpose of the Convention, that purpose being the protection of individual human beings.[19] Additionally a public authority under section 6 of the HRA has an obligation act compatibly with Convention rights.

b) Having identified the right in question the public authority should then turn to identify the interference with the right and whether it can be justified. The following are the considerations when assessing whether an interference can be justified:

   i) Is it provided for by law which is clear, accessible and foreseeable?[20] For companies this may mean being able to identify a particular part of the employment contract or company policy. Do any derogations or reservations apply to the Convention right in question? Is there any provision in the HRA that affects this right ie section 12 of the HRA emphasises the importance of Article 10 (expression)?

   ii) Does it serve a legitimate aim or purpose?[1] Interference can be legitimate on differing grounds and these change from Article to Article and depending on the context.[2]

   iii) Is it necessary in a democratic society? Three-stage test:
      • Is there a pressing social need?[3]
      • Is the policy, action or procedure proportionate to the aims pursued, ie is the effect excessive or disproportionate on the affected person?[4]
      • Are the reasons for the interference relevant and sufficient?[5]

   iv) Is it discriminatory?[6]

   v) Does the violation at issue involve a government policy of social, economic cultural or political importance in which case the court may allow a margin of discretion in interfering with Convention rights?[7]

---

19 *Niemietz v Germany* (1992) 16 EHRR 97. The purpose of the HRA is to give further effect to the Convention rights see the preamble to the HRA.
20 *Sunday Times v United Kingdom* (1979) 2 EHRR 245.
1   See n 20 above.
2   See Chapters 3 and 4.
3   *Handyside v United Kingdom* (1976) 1 EHRR 737.
4   See *F v Switzerland* (1987) 10 EHRR 411.
5   See *Goodwin v United Kingdom* (1996) 22 EHRR 123, *Jerslid v Denmark* (1994) 19 EHRR 1 and *Vogt v Germany* (1996) 21 EHRR 205.
6   See Chapter 4 on Article 14.
7   We recognise that the margin of appreciation applied at the Strasbourg level will not operate in the domestic courts but also think that the courts will develop a similar concept of discretion on delicate social, cultural and political matters.

c) General considerations to bear in mind when dealing with Convention rights:

i) The margin of appreciation will not operate in the same way, if at all, in the domestic courts. This is important to bear in mind when using the Convention case law as precedent.

ii) The Convention is to be interpreted as a 'living' instrument and so is not bound by the values of the 1950s founders rather it is to be interpreted in light of present day conditions. Therefore the older a Convention case is, the less reliable. When interpreting issues such as 'necessary in a democratic society' attention should be paid to the evolving standards of the UK and the other member states of the Council of Europe.[8]

iii) The Strasbourg court has placed great emphasis on the effective protection of the rights and freedoms contained in the ECHR. This means that the courts are to give effect not to rights that are 'theoretical or illusory but rights that are practical and effective.'[9] Therefore Article 6 requires not just the availability of a court system but effective access to it. Emphasising this point in the context of how the English courts would operate under section 3, Wadham and Mountfield found 'they are required, if possible to find one of a range of possible interpretations which in fact affords real and effective protection to the Convention right, as it applies in the present state of society.'[10]

Assessing an interference on the basis of the criteria above is likely to provide an idea of whether an interference is justifiable.

Will the courts adopt the same criteria when assessing an interference with a Convention right?

The Courts are required by section 2 of the HRA to take into account the Strasbourg case law where it is relevant to the question before the court. The criteria above are drawn from the Convention case law on proportionality and so will be applied in assessing the proportionality of an interference with a Convention right. However, adopting such a systematic approach is likely to cause a profound change to the traditional assessment by the courts of the actions of public authorities.[11] The ability to challenge the action of a public authority prior to the HRA was limited by the need to show unlawfulness or irrationality on behalf of the decision maker. Lord Diplock summed the test up as:

a decision which is so outrageous in its defiance of logic or accepted moral standards that no sensible person who had applied his mind to the question to be decided could have arrived at it.[12]

---

8   See *Tyrer v United Kingdom* (1978) 2 EHRR 1.
9   *Airey v Ireland* (1979) 2 EHRR 305.
10 Wadham, J and Mountfield, H, *Blackstones Guide to the Human Rights Act 1998* (1999) Blackstones, p 31.
11 See also Chapter 3 on proportionality.
12 *Council of Civil Service Unions v Minister for the Civil Service* [1985] AC 374 at 410.

This test made it very difficult to challenge successfully an action of a public authority. However, where the issue concerned fundamental rights, the English courts established a higher standard of review. In *R v Ministry of Defence, ex p Smith*[13] the court considered that '[t]he more substantial the interference with human rights, the more the court [shall require] by way of justification before it is satisfied that the decision is reasonable.' This test, while according a higher level of protection to fundamental rights, was still part of a search for 'irrationality'.

The Strasbourg test of proportionality is of a very different character, requiring a higher level of justification from a public authority where its action has prima facie interfered with a Convention right. As we explained in Chapter 3, the ECtHR starts with the presumption that the Convention rights and freedoms should be respected. It does however recognise occasions when restrictions on rights are allowable. The Court will review the reasons given by the state for the restriction and examine whether they are relevant and sufficient and whether the restriction was 'proportionate to the legitimate aim pursued'.[14] In doing this the Court must, even though there is a legitimate aim being pursued by the state, test whether the measure applied to secure it is no more than is strictly necessary to secure that legitimate aim. That test involves assessing the nature of the right involved and whether the measure taken is 'necessary in a democratic society' which in turn has been taken by the ECtHR to mean that there is the existence of a 'pressing social need'.[15] If the measure does not pass this test it is excessive and even though pursuing a legitimate aim it will not be valid.

For example in *Barthold v Germany*[16] the applicant was a vet who as a result of a newspaper interview in which he had highlighted the deficiencies of his competitors' practices and the merits of his own practice, had an injunction imposed on him. The injunction prohibited him from repeating the original or any new remarks of the same character. The Court found that while there was a legitimate aim being pursued, 'the protection of the rights of others' ie his competitors, the action was not proportionate because it was more than was necessary to achieve the legitimate aim. Thus it was in breach of his Article 10 (expression) rights.

In *Dudgeon v United Kingdom*[17] the applicants challenged a law in Northern Ireland which criminalised buggery between consenting men alleging it was in violation of Article 8 (privacy). While finding that the law in question was pursuing a legitimate aim in upholding a particular moral position the court found that 'on the issue of proportionality, the Court considers that such justifications as there are for retaining the law in force unamended are outweighed by the detrimental effects which the very existence of the legislative provisions in question can have on the life of a person of homosexual orientation like the applicant.'[18]

13 [1996] 1 All ER 257
14 See above (van Dijk) p 80. See also *Handyside v United Kingdom* (1976) 1 EHRR 737, *Young, James and Webster v United Kingdom* (1981) 4 EHRR 38, *Dudgeon v United Kingdom* (1981) 4 EHRR 149 and *Moustaquim v Belgium* (1991) 13 EHRR 802.
15 See *Handyside v United Kingdom* (1976) 1 EHRR 737, *Sunday Times v United Kingdom* (1979) 2 EHRR 245 *and Dudgeon v United Kingdom* (1981) 4 EHRR 149.
16 (1985) 7 EHRR 383.
17 (1981) 4 EHRR 149.
18 Dudgeon n 15 above, *A-45* para 60.

The concept of proportionality is not something alien to the English courts as they have had to work with the concept of proportionality in the context of Community law.[19] Further proportionality was being developed outside the Community context in common law cases such as *R v Barnsley Metropolitan Borough Council, ex p Hook*[20] and *R v Highbury Corner Magistrates' Court, ex p Uchendu*[1] until the judgment in *ex p Brind*.[2] The examination of the proportionality of a public authority's interference with Convention rights is likely to lead to a greater duty on the part of the public authority to provide reasons for interference and a concomitant limitation of the exceptions upon which the public authority could rely in not providing reasons.[3] As part of any justification for the limitation on Convention rights the public authority will have to demonstrate that it considered the proportionality test and that each part was satisfied. In all, the courts' use of proportionality should lead it to a greater examination of the public authority's decision making process especially where the interference with the Convention right has a significant effect on the victim.[4] As the Lord Chancellor explained, a court:

> will only accept an interference with that right where a justification allowed under the Convention, is made out. The scrutiny will not be limited to seeing if the *words* of an exception can be satisfied. The court will need to be satisfied that the *spirit* of this exception is made out. It will need to be satisfied that the interference with the protected right *is* justified in the public interests in a free democratic society. Moreover, the courts will in this area have to apply the Convention principle of proportionality. This means that the Court will be looking *substantively* at that question. It will not be limited to a secondary review of the decision making process but at the primary question of the merits of the decision itself.[5]

Where the court itself as a 'public authority' under section 6 is faced with taking an action which might interfere with a Convention right it will also have to set out the legitimate aim it is trying to achieve and to examine the proportionality of its action. This should lead to a fuller explanation of policy oriented decisions.[6] In particular policy decisions such as flood gates arguments will be harder to justify and may lead to a greater reliance on empirical evidence.

---

19   Although primarily concerned with economic rights see *R v Chief Constable of Sussex, ex p International Trader's Ferry Ltd* [1998] 3 WLR 1260, *R v Ministry of Agriculture, ex p First City Trading* [1997] 1 CMLR 250, R *v Secretary of State for Employment, ex p Equal Opportunities Commission* [1995] 1 AC 1 and *Stoke-on-Trent City Council v B and Q plc* [1991] Ch 48.

20   [1976] 1 WLR 1052.

1   (1994) 158 LGR 481.

2   [1991] 1 AC 696. Although see the use of a proportionality type analysis by Auld LJ in *Holley v Smyth* [1998] 1 All ER 853.

3   For example the UK's protective position with regard to policy or national security is likely to be inconsistent with the ECtHR case law. See *Leander v Sweden* (1987) 9 EHRR 433.

4   See de la Mare, Tom, ' The Human Rights Act 1998: The Impact on Judicial Review' *Judicial Review* (1999) Vol 4, Issue 1, pp 34-36.

5   Lord Irvine of Lairg, 'The Development of Human Rights in Britain under an Incorporated Convention on Human Rights' (1998) *Public Law* p 229.

6   See *Osman v United Kingdom* (1998) 5 BHRC 293.

What is the effect of the HRA on companies that are not 'public authorities'?

The HRA does not make Convention rights directly enforceable against private companies[7] or individuals. Its focus is primarily to ensure that public authorities act compatibly with the Convention rights and that should they fail to do so, a victim can pursue an action based on section 6 of the HRA alleging an unlawful act on the part of the 'public authority'. However it does have a horizontal effect which impacts on private companies, in that section 6 (3) (a) of the HRA includes courts and tribunals in the definition of 'public authority'. This means that the court in carrying out its function must act compatibly with the Convention rights. As part of the court's section 6 obligation it may have to give effect to Convention rights even where the matter is between private parties. This does not mean that there is a new action based on a violation of the Convention rights, rather it means that existing common law or statutory rights must be given effect in a manner compatible with the Convention. Should the domestic court as a 'public authority' fail to give effect to Convention rights the court itself will, according to section 6 of the HRA, be acting unlawfully. Therefore, whether interpreting statute or common law or dealing with public or private bodies, the court must interpret the law compatibly with the Convention rights. This include the courts as public bodies having a positive obligation to protect individuals from having their rights violated by other private individuals where the Strasbourg court has already found positive obligations to exist.[8]

In litigation between private parties, the parties themselves will therefore not be seeking to use Convention rights against each other, because they have no Convention rights exercisable against each other, but rather to ensure that the court as a 'public authority' acts compatibly with such Convention rights as they can show are capable of violation by the court. This will obviously involve the court balancing the competing rights the private parties claim the court should give effect to and a decision for one party will horizontally impact on the Convention rights of the other.

Despite the fact that Lord Wilberforce was of the opinion during the parliamentary debate on this issue that the HRA 'is aimed entirely at public authorities and not at private individuals'[9] the government made it clear that some horizontal effect was intended. As the Lord Chancellor explained:

> [w]e also believe that it is right as a matter of principle for the courts to have the duty of acting compatibly with the Convention not only in cases involving

---

7   We use the phrase 'private companies' here to mean all companies that are not public authorities or quasi-public bodies acting in their private capacity.

8   See Chapter 3. The Convention itself either in the wording of the Article or flowing from the nature of the Article provides for positive obligations. Article 2 (1) (right to life), Article 3 (torture), Article 6 (fair trial), Protocol 1, Article 3 (free elections) all fall into this category. Other Articles have in the course of the Strasbourg Court's consideration of these Articles had positive obligations read in. The word 'respect' in Article 8 has been interpreted as conferring a positive obligation on the state to ensure such respect: *Marckx v Belgium* (1979) 2 EHRR 330. The same is true of Article 11: see *Young, James and Webster v United Kingdom* (1981) 4 EHRR 38.

9   HL Debates, 24 November 1997: Column 781.

other public authorities but also in developing the common law in deciding cases between individuals. Why should they not? In preparing this Bill, we have taken the view that it is the other course, that of excluding Convention considerations altogether from cases between individuals which would have to be justified.[10]

There is however considerable debate as to the extent of this horizontal effect on private parties. At one extreme Kentridge has argued that the HRA will only have limited effect horizontality because it only gives rise to procedural rights.[11] Most commentators however agree that Kentridge is incorrect as section 6 (1) of the HRA clearly goes further than protecting rights with regard to legal procedures as it makes it unlawful for courts and tribunals to act incompatibly with all the Convention rights in Schedule 1.[12] At the other extreme is Sir William Wade QC who has consistently argued that the distinction between private and public bodies is an artificial one and that the HRA has a direct horizontal effect. In his own words:

> is there any significance in distinguishing between direct and indirect effect, or in speaking of new private causes of action? A claimant pleads the facts of his case, and he may claim any relief to which the facts, if proved, entitle him. He may argue that they show a violation of a Convention right, and if the court agrees, the court has no option but to obey section 6 and enforce the right. Whether this is called direct or indirect effect or a new cause of action seems to be a matter of words and makes no intelligible difference. The court must be an effective agent in all cases alike.[13]

In many ways Wade does the argument for the possibility of direct horizontal effect a disservice in ignoring the clear distinction drawn in the HRA between public and private bodies. Most commentators agree that there is no direct horizontal effect but we prefer Phillipson's analysis of the problem with Wade's argument:

> [s]uch an outcome – the effective collapsing of the distinction between public and private applicants – would be startling indeed. It would mean that the apparent basic scheme of the HRA – to bind public authorities only and to provide procedures and remedies for this purposes [sic] – would be radically undercut. The carefully worded definition of 'public authority' in section 6 would become largely redundant and the HRA would instead effectively bind *both* public and private bodies to follow the Convention but – with no apparent justification for the distinction – make provision for proceedings and remedies

---

10   HL Debates, 24 November 1997: Column 783.
11   Kentridge, S, 'The Incorporation of the European Convention on Human Rights' in University of Cambridge Centre for Public Law (ed) *Constitutional Reform in the United Kingdom: Practice and Principles* (1998) Hart p 69. See also Buxton, Richard 'The Human Rights Act and Private Law' (2000) 16 LQR 48.
12   Feldman, David, 'The Human Rights Act 1998 and Constitutional Principles' (1999) *Legal Studies,* p 200.
13   Sir William Wade, QC 'Horizons of Horizontality' (2000) *Law Quarterly Review* Vol 116 p 222.

in relation to the former only. If such an interpretation were to have been approved by the Lord Chancellor it would be surprising, to say the least.[14]

It is without doubt the case that neither the Home Office officials nor the government intended direct horizontality to operate with regard to the Convention rights. Indeed, the Home Office officials had hoped for a speedy implementation of the HRA to avoid the danger that commentators would attempt to distort the intention of the framers. This however is exactly what the two-year gap between the HRA's passage through Parliament and its entry into force on 2 October 2000 has achieved.

Most commentators agree with the government and see either a low level of horizontality as Phillipson[15] does, where the Convention rights are treated as guiding principles only,[16] or a high level of indirect horizontal effect, where the courts will offer high levels of protection for Convention rights in interpreting the law. Arguing for a high level of indirect horizontality Hunt considers that:

> the Convention will be regarded as applying to all law, and therefore relevant in proceedings between private parties, but will fall short of being *directly* horizontally effective, because it will not confer any new private causes of action against individuals in respect of Convention rights. This requires a distinction to be drawn between the evolution of existing causes of action over time and the creation of entirely new causes of action against private parties. It is beyond argument that the Human Rights Act does not do the latter, but the courts will undoubtedly develop over time causes of action such as trespass, confidence, and copyright, as the Lord Chancellor himself accepted in Parliament. Law which already exists and governs private relationships must be interpreted applied and if necessary developed so as to achieve compatibility with the Convention. But where no cause of action exists, and there is therefore no law to apply, the courts cannot invent new causes of action, as that would be to embrace full horizontality which has clearly been precluded by Parliament.[17]

The reality is that no one is sure to what extent the courts will allow the indirect horizontal effect of the HRA to operate. It is however clear that it is for the courts to work this one out over time. For our part Hunt's argument is the one which closest matches our interpretation of the HRA's indirect horizontal effect.

---

14   Phillipson, Gavin, ' The Human Rights Act, 'Horizontal Effect' and the Common Law: a Bang or a Whimper?' (1999) *Modern Law Review* p 828.

15   Phillipson, n 14 above, pp 824-849.

16   Somewhat like the Canadian and South African values model where the common law must be developed according to the values in their respective constitutional documents. However neither jurisdiction has an equivalent of section 6, HRA 1998 whereby the court would be acting unlawfully if it acts in a way which is incompatible with the Convention rights. See *Hill v Church of Scientology of Toronto* [1995] 2 SCR 1130 and *Du Plessis v De Klerk* (1996) 5 BCLR 658.

17   Hunt, Murray, 'The 'Horizontal Effect' of the Human Rights Act' (1998) *Public Law* pp 421-422.

The one comparative point we would make in favour of the judicial development of a high level of indirect horizontality is that the Irish Supreme Court[18] when interpreting the Irish Constitution began to allow rights to give rise to a cause of action exercisable directly against private parties.[19] The reason the Irish Supreme Court developed direct horizontal rights was because in certain cases there was no other way to protect the constitutional rights of an individual from interference.[20] The focus of the Supreme Court of the common law system most closely matching the English common law system[1] on the necessity to provide an effective remedy may have been one of the reasons the government did not include Article 13 (right to an effective remedy) in the Convention rights in Schedule 1 of the HRA. Certainly one of the reasons given by the Home Secretary for the exclusion of Article 13 was to discourage judicial valour in creating new remedies.[2] Article 13 does not cease to be applicable because of its absence from Schedule 1 of the HRA. It is given effect through the section 2 obligation of the court to consider relevant case law of the ECtHR.[3] It is not inconceivable that the English courts could over time rely on the Article 13 case law to develop a high level of indirect horizontal effect where there is no other possible way of providing an effective remedy. In such a case the Convention rights would still not be enforceable against the other private party but against the court which arguably has an obligation to provide an effective remedy under Article 13.

Our final point here is to observe that in the case of primary legislation or certain secondary legislation where the court finds incompatibility the use of a declaration of incompatibility in section 4 limits the ability of the court to give full effect to the Convention rights. The HRA does not accord the common law a similar protection and as such the court can give full effect to the Convention rights when incompatibility between common law rules and the Convention arises.

Can the Convention rights be waived?

It is possible within very confined limits to waive Convention rights. Such waivers must be unequivocal[4] and are always subject to the requirement that the waiver must not be contrary to important public interest matters. Because of this procedural requirements such as those contained in Article 6 (fair trial) are considered to be minimum guarantees pursuing an important public interest and cannot be waived.[5] The High Court in 1999 considered the impact of a scheme of arrangement for

---

18 While Hunt does consider the Irish Constitutional position he does not take the comparative point far enough.

19 See *Meskell v Córas Iompair Éireann* [1973] IR 121.

20 *Lovett v Grogan* [1995] ILRM 12.

1   We say this because the Irish legal system continues to look to English case law and statutes for guidance. Indeed the similarity of legal systems has led the Irish Law Commission to work closely with the UK on the introduction of European legislation into both countries.

2   HC Debates, 20 May 1998: Column 979.

3   See Chapter 6.

4   *Pfeiffer and Plankl v Austria* (1992) 14 EHRR 692.

5   See n 4 above.

an insurance company in provisional liquidation on creditors' access to the court. The scheme provided for the appointment of an independent adjudicator to resolve disputes between the creditors and the administrators of the scheme. The High Court initially refused to sanction the scheme because it involved the creditors' having to waive any right to appeal. After further argument the court accepted that the ability to sue the adjudicator for negligence, breach of trust or fraud was sufficient to provide access to the courts under the scheme.[6] It is however highly likely that such an accommodation would offend the requirements of Article 6.[7]

While the ECtHR has consistently held that employees' rights may be curtailed in their employment contract on the basis of confidentiality, loyalty or national security, for example restricting a school teacher from expressing religious belief in a non-denominational school, it has also exercised a supervisory role over such waivers.[8] In *Vogt v Germany*[9] the ECtHR held that the dismissal of a language teacher because of the teacher's membership of the Communist Party was a breach of Article 10 (expression). The deciding factor in this case was the absolute nature of the restriction on political activity imposed by the German state. The teacher was not a security risk nor had she attempted to indoctrinate her students. The case law on restrictions of Convention rights is difficult to predict and very much depends on the context. A waiver is however never concrete and always subject to court supervision.

6   *Re Hawk Insurance Co Ltd* (13 January 1999, unreported).
7   See Chapter 9.
8   *Stedman v United Kingdom* (1997) 23 EHRR CD 168.
9   (1995) 21 EHRR 205.

Chapter eight

Companies and victim status

We are neither human nor European: whether we have European human rights is a matter for the Court.[1]

Can a company be a 'victim' of a violation of Convention rights?

Despite the historical struggle of our domestic courts in according human characteristics to companies, the Strasbourg court has never seen any problem with companies fulfilling the 'victim' criteria necessary to claim in respect of a human rights violation.[2] The court has always accepted that the corporation is a 'person' for the purposes of Article 34 victim status and accordingly has human rights.[3] This in itself illustrates the difference in approach to corporate standing the ECtHR has taken compared with the English courts. The Strasbourg court has never engaged in a technical legal sense with the question of whether the artificiality of the corporation imposes limitations on its ability to be the victim of a rights violation.

1   The opening submissions of counsel for Air Canada in *Air Canada v United Kingdom* (1995) 20 EHRR 150.
2   Similarly the Canadian courts extended the protections of the Charter of Rights and Freedoms to companies without too much fuss: see Ison, Terence G, 'A Constitutional Bill of Rights – The Canadian Experience' in: 60 *Modern Law Review* 1997, pp 499-512.
3   See, for example, in the context of freedom of expression *Autronic AG v Switzerland* (1990) 12 EHRR 485.

The locus standi for an application to the Strasbourg court is based on Article 34 (previously Article 25) which allows complaints by a 'person, non-governmental organisation or a group of individuals claiming to be the victim of a violation' of a right contained in the Convention.[4] The Strasbourg court has accepted that a company is a person for the purposes of Article 34.[5] Therefore under the ECHR a corporation can lodge an application alleging it is the victim of a state action which interfered with rights guaranteed under the ECHR. The fact that the Strasbourg court has allowed companies to be victims does not mean that a corporation will be able to claim a rights violation with regard to all of the Convention rights. The artificial nature of a corporation does mean that rights such as Article 2 (the right to life), Article 12 (right to marry) and Article 3 (freedom from torture) cannot be claimed[6] but other rights which are of a less human orientation are applicable to companies, the most important being Article 6 (fair trial), Article 8 (privacy),[7] Article 10 (expression) and Protocol 1, Article 1 (property). The application of these Articles to companies is considered in the following chapters.

Can shareholders be victims where the act complained of is aimed at the company's property?

The issue of whether shareholders can be a victim of an act aimed at the corporation is a complex one to which there is presently no easy answer. Essentially, it all turns on the Convention right it is alleged has been violated. If the Article in question is Protocol 1, Article 1 (property) then the shareholders are unlikely to be able to claim that they are Article 34 'victims'.[8] If the act complained of concerns any other Convention Article, the shareholders have a better chance of fulfilling 'victim' status for the purposes of Article 34.[9]

The case law of the Strasbourg court on victim status for corporations has at times demonstrated a significantly different view of the corporate vehicle than the English courts. While the English courts have over the last decade been reluctant to interfere with the principle contained in *Salomon v Salomon & Co*[10] the Strasbourg court has at times had no such reluctance in casting aside the veil of incorporation when attempting to balance the parties' rights before it.[11] The Strasbourg court's position

---

4   The Human Rights Act 1998, section 7 allows the same right to complain.
5   See *Yarrow v United Kingdom* (1983) 30 DR 155.
6   On the difficulty the US courts have had in according standing to companies where similar issues have arisen see R N S 'Corporate Standing To Allege Race Discrimination In Civil Rights Actions' in: 69 Virginia Law Review 1983, pp 1153-1181.
7   The Strasbourg court has never considered whether the company can have a right of privacy but its officers do have such a right. See Chapter 10 for a detailed explanation of how privacy applies to companies.
8   *Agrotexim v Greece* [1996] 21 EHRR 250.
9   *GJ v Luxembourg* Application No 00021156/93 (1996).
10   [1897] AC 22, HL. See *Adams v Cape Industries plc* [1990] Ch 433.
11   See *Pine Valley Developments Ltd v Ireland* (1993) 16 EHRR 379.

on minority rights also diverges from the established position in *Foss v Harbottle*[12] in that it confers Convention rights on minority shareholders, majority shareholders, employees and the company at times.[13]

Salomon v Salomon: The company as separate legal entity in the UK

In the UK it is clearly established that a company is a legal person in its own right which is a legal entity quite separate from that of its members. This is the position that the House of Lords laid down in *Solomon v Solomon & Co.*[14] A registered company obtains its own separate personality on incorporation by complying with the formal requirements of the Companies Act. It is one of the most fundamental characteristics of a company that it is an entity separate from its members. This characteristic allows the company to hold property in its own right and has the advantage for the members that the debts of the company are also its own.[15] As a result, the principle in *Salomon* has endured as a core element of company law in the UK for a little over a century.

Over the past decade the English courts have demonstrated a reluctance to interfere with the *Solomon* principle and look behind the separate personality of the company to the members. As a consequence claims against a parent company for the actions of its subsidiaries can fail, as was illustrated by the Court of Appeal in *Adams v Cape Industries plc.*[16] When asked to rule that an English company was 'present' in the jurisdiction of a Texas court on the basis of the presence of one of its subsidiary companies, the Court refused to lift the veil of incorporation and set out the limited circumstances when an English court would allow such an act. As Davies comments:

> [t]here seem to be three circumstances only in which the courts can do so. These are:
> (1) when the court is construing a statute, contract or other document;
> (2) when the court is satisfied that a company is a 'mere façade' concealing the true facts;
> (3) when it can be established that the company is an authorised agent of its controllers or its members, corporate or human.[17]

Cases following *Adams* reveal that in English courts the position is now reaffirmed that the veil of incorporation is a solid construct which will only be brushed aside in very limited circumstances.[18]

---

12   (1843) 2 Hare 461.
13   See *Bramelid and Malmstrom v Sweden* (1982) 29 DR 64, Applications 8599/79 and 8589/79.
14   [1897] AC 22.
15   *Macaura v Northern Assurance Co. Ltd* [1925] AC 619.
16   [1990] Ch 433.
17   Davies, P L, *Gower's Principles of Modern Company Law* (1997) Sweet and Maxwell p 173.
18   See for example *Yukong Line Ltd of Korea v Rendsburg Investments Corp of Liberia, The Rialto (No 2)* [1998] 4 All ER 82, [1998] 1 WLR 294, [1998] 1 Lloyd's Rep 322 and Lord Cooke of Thornton, *Turning Points of the Common Law – The Hamlyn Lectures* (1997) Sweet and Maxwell. See also Chapter 9 for a more detailed analysis of the trend.

Foss v Harbottle: standing for the corporation

The existence of a separate legal entity which limits the liability of the shareholders is thought a double-edged sword. While it enables the separation of legal and real personalities creating a separate corporate interest and allowing shareholders to claim limited liability, it has also meant that the internal power structure of the corporation is focused on the corporate exercise of power rather than the individual shareholders' exercise of rights. At the heart of this is the case of *Foss v Harbottle*[19] .

It was in the 19th century that the domestic courts had to decide for the first time what rights should properly be accorded to an aggrieved minority of members trying to resolve disputes with the majority or with the management of a company. The modern development of the larger scale corporations and the resulting diversion between ownership and control, meant that the law of partnership and agency were no longer sufficient to cope with the problems of the modern corporation, particularly where a minority party was involved. The courts therefore developed the rule first set out in *Foss v Harbottle,*[19] which was one of the first cases to consider the 'proper plaintiff' principle in the context of companies.

In *Foss v Harbottle*[19] the company in general meeting refused to take an action against the directors who were alleged by the minority shareholders to have wronged the company. The court dismissed an action by the minority shareholders who sought to force the directors to put right the wrong to the company and held that only the company had a right to bring such an action. It lies with the organs of the company to instigate an action. Such an action should be brought by the board of directors as the control organ,[20] if the directors cannot, or will not bring an action, the power reverts to the general meeting.[1] The general rule that the company itself was the proper plaintiff in proceedings concerning its rights had a considerable influence on later judicial decisions in adopting an increasingly restrictive attitude when dealing with minority actions.

In *Burland v Earle*[2] the court described the policy as forming distinct principles. First, the court will not interfere with the internal management of companies acting within their powers and in fact has no jurisdiction to do so. Second, in order to redress a wrong done to the company or to recover moneys or damages alleged to be due to the company, the action should be brought by the company itself. Third no mere informality or irregularity which can be remedied by the majority will entitle the minority to sue, if the act when done regularly would be within the powers of the company and the intention of the majority of the shareholders is clear.[3]

The courts, although familiar with commercial risks, benefits, ideas and policies are reluctant to intervene and decide on matters which affect genuine management

---

19   (1843) 2 Hare 461.
20   *Shaw and Sons (Salford) Ltd v Shaw* [1935] 2 KB 113, CA.
1   *Pender v Lushington* (1877) 6 Ch D 70.
2   [1902] AC 83, at pp 93-94.
3   Per Lord Davey citing *Mac Dougal v Gardiner* (1875) 1 Ch D 13 at 25.

policies.[4] The Courts prefer for companies to decide their own policies and settle their own disputes by majority decision[5], and there is no doubt that a concern to prevent a torrent of actions (the 'floodgates' argument) is probably the most oft quoted justification for the rule in *Foss v Harbottle*. The Court of Appeal explained in *Prudential Assurance Co Ltd v Newman Industries (No 2)*[6] that it is an:

> elementary principle that A cannot, as a general rule, bring an action against B to recover damages to secure other relief on behalf of C for an injury done by B to C. C is the proper plaintiff because C is the party injured, and therefore, the person in whom the cause of action is vested. This is sometimes referred to as the rule in *Foss v Harbottle* (1843) 2 Hare 461 when applied to corporations, but it has a wider scope and is fundamental to any rational system of jurisprudence.

There are exceptions to this fundamental rule, and the courts have in certain circumstances, allowed derivative actions to be brought by members to enforce the right of action of the company. The exceptions were set out by Jenkins LJ in *Edwards v Halliwell*.[7] No majority vote can be effective to sanction an act of the company which is ultra vires or illegal.[8] If procedures either required by law or by the company's articles are not observed, then the majority must follow that procedure or else the decision is invalid.[9] If a member is deprived of his individual membership rights then he may sue to enforce that right.[10] If those who control the company defraud the company the minority may bring an action against the majority.[11] In practice the exceptions have been very difficult to establish and most minority actions are now taken alleging unfairly prejudicial conduct under section 459 of the Companies Act 1985.[12]

The rule in *Foss v Harbottle* is an indication of the importance the judiciary place on the corporation as a collective rather than the individual shareholders. It represents a sacrifice of the individual rights of shareholders to the group rights exercised through the organs of the company, the aim being that through the denial of those rights the corporate good is enhanced by maintaining the directors' freedom

---

4   Especially the Commercial and Chancery courts.
5   See *Cooper v Gordon* (1869) LR 8 Eq 249 per Stuart V-C.
6   [1982] Ch 204 at p 210.
7   [1950] 2 All ER 1064 at 1067 cited in *Prudential Assurance Co. Ltd. v Newman Industries (No 2)* (supra) as the best modern formulation of the rule in F*oss v Harbottle*.
8   *Ashbury Railway Carriage And Iron Co v Riche* (1875) LR 7 HL 653.
9   *Jackson v Munster Bank* 13 LR (Ir) 118.
10 *Pender v Lushington* (1877) 6 Ch D 70 there Jessel MR stated '[t]his is an action by Mr Pender for himself. He is a member of the company, and whether he votes with the majority or the minority he is entitled to have his vote recorded – an individual right in respect of which he has the right to sue'.
11 See *Foss v Harbottle* (1843) 2 Hare 461. Whether or not these exceptions are fixed, or could in fact be expanded is a matter of unsettled controversy. Jenkins LJ in *Edwards v Halliwell* stated that the rule is not an inflexible one and could be relaxed where warranted by the interests of justice. However the decision in *Prudential Assurance Co Ltd v Newman Industries (No 2)* [1982] Ch 204 seems to have closed off such an avenue.
12 See Chapter 12 on section 459 and the HRA.

to manage without having to deal with interference from individual shareholders which would stifle the operation of the company.[13] As Davies explains:

> [t]he rule in *Foss v Harbottle* has been vigorously criticised by commentators over the years … It has been said to restrict too narrowly the individual shareholder's power to enforce the company's rights; to have resulted in an overly complex body of rules; to pursue inconsistent policies; and to have been extended beyond its proper scope…Yet it is a body of law to which the courts are attached, not simply because it is well established but because it is seen as performing a valuable function. That function can perhaps best be expressed as the preservation of the corporate and collective nature of the company.[14]

The early Strasbourg case law on shareholder standing

The concepts of standing in Strasbourg and domestic case law have developed quite independently of each other and this independent development provides prima facie scope for tension between the two bodies of case law. As outlined above there is no controversy about the corporation being able to fulfil the requirement of 'victim' status on the facts of any given case. The issue of standing for shareholders is somewhat more complex. The early Strasbourg case law on shareholder standing is important in that it reveals a significant difference in approach to that of the English Courts which continues into the later case law.

In *Yarrow v United Kingdom*[15] the Commission held that minority shareholders would not normally fulfil the requirements of victim status, as the acts complained of were directed against the company and not against the shareholders personal interests. The minority shareholders' interests were sufficiently protected by the standing of the company itself to complain of a Convention violation if so advised. However the Commission also considered the position of majority shareholders with regard to victim status. The Commission found that majority shareholders could fulfil victim status as their direct personal interest had been affected by an act directed at the company and the reality of the situation was that that the majority shareholders were merely carrying on a business through the medium of the company. While the first part of the judgment is entirely consistent with English law, recognising the distinction between the shareholders' property and the companies' property and setting out a proper plaintiff solution, the second part contrasts sharply with English law as the Commission ignored the proper plaintiff principle and swept away the veil of incorporation.

From this case the following conclusions can be drawn. First, minority shareholders cannot fulfil the requirements of 'victim' status as their interests are protected through the corporate ability to exercise Convention rights. Second, there is no distinction between the corporation's property and the majority shareholder's property as the company is just a vehicle through which the majority shareholders carry on a

---

13   For a judicial consideration of the rule see *Prudential Assurance Co Ltd v Newman Industries (No 2)* [1982] Ch 204 and *Barrett v Duckett* [1995] 1 BCLC 243, CA.
14   See p 175, n 17 (Davies) above 659-660.
15   (1983) 30 DR 155.

business. *Ex hypothesi,* a violation aimed at the company will mean that the majority shareholders will qualify as 'victims'.

In *Pine Valley Developments Ltd v Ireland*[16] the Commission considered in the context of applications by related companies and an individual shareholder, the 'victim test'.[17] The case concerned the speculative purchase of land for gain by development. There were three applicants, all of which were 'interested' in the land the subject matter of the case, in a loose sense, at the time of their application. The first applicant, Pine Valley Ltd, had owned the land in question but, at the time of the application, had sold the land to the second applicant, Healy Holdings Ltd. Pine Valley Ltd has also been struck off the Register of Companies by the time of its application. Healy Holdings Ltd was in receivership at the time of the application, and the Receiver was not a party to the proceedings. Mr Healy was the third applicant: he was the sole beneficial shareholder of Healy Holdings and was bankrupt at the time of the application. The complaint concerned the purchase of property by the first applicant, and the subsequent sale by it of the second applicant, both on the basis of a grant of outline planning permission for industrial use. It was subsequently decreed by the Irish Supreme Court that the Minister for Local Government had acted ultra vires when granting the permission, and the permission was revoked ab initio. Without outline planning permission, the property was worth substantially less, but the applicants had no effective remedy under their national (Irish) law. The three applicants applied to the Strasbourg court alleging interference with their property under Protocol 1, Article 1. The Irish government objected to the claim, amongst other reasons, on the basis of standing.[18] The Irish government pointed out that the first applicant had sold the land prior to the Supreme Court decision which found that the grant of outline planning was unlawful. Moreover, the company had been struck off and dissolved, and did not, strictly speaking, exist and no attempt was made to resurrect it for the purposes of this action. The second applicant was in receivership, and the Receiver took no part in the action. The third applicant was a mere shareholder in the second applicant company (although it is fair to say that he was the only beneficial shareholder) and was a bankrupt.

On these facts, it is difficult to imagine that an English court would find that any of the applicants had locus standi as a matter of English law. The European Commission were not so troubled and held:

> Pine Valley and Healy Holdings were no more than vehicles through which Mr Healy proposed to implement the development for which outline planning permission had been granted. On this ground alone it would be artificial to draw a distinction between the three applicants as regards their entitlement to claim to be 'victims' of a violation.[19]

16 (1991) 14 EHRR 319.
17 At the time of the case in 1991 the standing requirement was contained in Article 25 which is now Article 34 of the Convention.
18 *Pine Valley Developments Ltd v Ireland* (1991) 14 EHRR 319 at p 350-351, paragraphs 40 to 43.
19 (1991) 14 EHRR 319 at 350 paragraph 41.

This finding by the Commission once again contains the view of the corporation as mere vehicle simpliciter through which shareholders do business. The company as an artificial entity was therefore ignored and the shareholder conferred with the status of 'victim'. Here therefore is a real distinction between the approach to standing under domestic law, and the approach taken when applying the ECHR concept of 'victim'.

The Commission went on to find with more specificity:

> with respect to Pine Valley, neither its sale of the land nor the later dissolution alters the fact that it was for a certain period of time … the Owner of the property to which the planning permissions attached …. In the Court's view, this suffices to permit a claim of violation to be made on its behalf. The Government's remaining pleas all turn, directly and indirectly on the financial status of Healy Holdings and Mr. Healy. Whilst that status may, of course, be of importance or have effects on the domestic level, it is in the Court's opinion, of no relevance as far as entitlement to claim to be a victim of a violation is concerned. Insolvency cannot remove the right which Article 25 [now Article 34] of the Convention confers on 'any person'.[20]

While it is not entirely clear from the case what the Commission meant when they referred to the financial status of the applicants having implications at the domestic level (it may purely have been an observation of fact) but not at Strasbourg, the Commission's opinion it is in line with the principle applied by the Strasbourg court that victim status does not contain a requirement of legal capacity. As such, the mentally ill and children can bring actions alleging they have been the victim of a rights violation. The same it would seem is true for companies in liquidation, receivership and for individual bankrupts. These early cases indicate that corporate standing in terms of victim status should be pragmatic and inclusive.

The recent Strasbourg cases on corporate standing

Since the mid-1990s the Strasbourg court has adopted a more restrictive approach to victim status in relation to shareholders, echoing more the English approach to corporate standing. In *Agrotexim v Greece*[1] six Greek limited companies with a shareholding in another Greek company with limited liability (the Fix Brewery) claimed violation of Article 1 of Protocol 1 of the ECHR. Fix Brewery was in liquidation with the liquidators appointed by its biggest creditor, the National Bank of Greece. The company was ultimately wound up by the bank and its possessions were taken by the state (under a scheme expropriating the company's land) and by the bank. The complaint made was that in all the circumstances of the case, the expropriation of the land offended Article 1 of Protocol 1. When the Commission considered the case it noted that:

> the term 'victim' in Article 25 (Art 25) of the Convention denotes the person directly affected by the act or omission which is at issue (cf Eur Court HR, Eckle judgment of 15 July 1982, Series A No 51, p 30, para 66). The

---

20   See p 179, n 18 (*Pine Valley*).
1   (1995) 21 EHRR 250.

Commission has held that an individual who held a substantial majority shareholding in a company could, under certain circumstances, claim to be victim of measures directed against the company (No 1706/62, Dec. 4.10.66, Collection 21, p. 26 and No 7598/*76 Kaplan v United Kingdom* (1980) 4 EHRR 64, 21 DR 5). In the case of *Yarrow v United Kingdom* (No 9266/81, (1983) 30 DR 155) the Commission held that the applicants, who did not hold a majority or controlling interest in the company in question, were not directly and personally affected by the nationalisation of the company, although this measure undoubtedly affected the value of their shares. In that case the Commission found that the applicants could not claim to be victims of the measure of nationalisation. The Commission finds that, the question whether a shareholder may claim to be victim of measures affecting a company cannot be determined on the sole criterion of whether the shareholder detains [sic] the majority of the company shares. This element is an objective and important indication but other elements may also be relevant in view of the circumstances of each particular case. In this respect the Commission recalls that it has previously taken into account the fact that an applicant shareholder was carrying out his own business through the medium of the company and that he had a personal interest in the subject-matter of the complaint (cf above-mentioned Applications No 1706/62 and 9266/81). It has also considered whether it was open to the company itself, being the direct victim, to lodge an application with the Commission.

In the present case the Commission notes that, although none of the applicants separately holds the majority of the company's shares, the group of the applicant companies holds 51.35% of the Karolos Fix Brewery SA shares. It is moreover apparent that the applicant companies have an interest in the subject-matter of the application ... In these specific circumstances, the Commission finds that the applicant shareholders are entitled, by lifting the veil of the company's legal personality, to claim that they are victims of the measures affecting the company's property, within the meaning of Article 25 para 1 (Art 25-1) of the Convention. In this respect the Commission recalls that not only substantive rights under Section I of the Convention or its Protocols but also Article 25 (Art 25) of the Convention, which confers upon individuals and non-governmental organisations a right of a procedural nature, must be interpreted as guaranteeing rights which are practical and effective as opposed to theoretical and illusory (cf Eur Court HR, *Cruz Varas v Sweden* (1991) 14 EHRR 1).[2]

However, the ECtHR found that the complainant shareholders had no locus standi to bring their claim before the Court, finding that:

[t]he piercing of the 'corporate veil' or the disregarding of a company's separate legal personality will be justified only in exceptional circumstances, in particular where it is established that it is impossible for the company to

2   *Agrotexim Hellas SA, Biotex SA, Hymofix Hellas SA, Kykladiki SA, Mepex SA and Texema SA v Greece* Application No 00014807/89 (1992).

apply to the Convention Institutions through the organs set up under its articles of incorporation or – in the event of liquidation – through its liquidator. [3]

The obstacles that a shareholder must overcome, on test of 'impossibility' appear on the face of it high. In the *Agrotexim* case, although the liquidator had the power to bring an action he failed to do so. Quite what the position would be if a liquidator failed or refused to take an action which he objectively should do, is not clear from the decision.

It is not hard to imagine an English court delivering a similar ruling to the Strasbourg court in *Agrotexim* on the same facts. The case has been subsequently applied in the context of violations of Protocol 1, Article 1. In *JW v Poland*[4] the Commission in finding that a shareholder was not a victim set out the reasoning of the Court in *Agrotexim:*

> the Court held that the fall in the value of the shares cannot be automatically considered as conferring locus standi on the shareholders. To adopt such position would be to run the risk of creating difficulties in determining who is entitled to apply to the Strasbourg institutions, regard being had to possible differences of positions and interests between the shareholders. This would also engender considerable problems concerning the requirement of exhaustion of domestic remedies. Concerned to reduce such risks and difficulties the Court considered that the piercing of the corporate veil or the disregarding of a company's legal personality would be justified only in exceptional circumstances, in particular where it was clearly established that it was impossible for the company to apply to the Convention institutions through the organs set up under its articles of incorporation (Eur Court HR, *Agrotexim v Greece* (1995) 21 EHRR 250, paras 65-66).

In 1998 it fell to the Commission in *Penton v Turkey*[5] to decide on the victim status of a shareholder in a Cypriot company who complained of an interference with his property as a result of the Turkish occupation of Northern Cyprus. While not ruling out the possibility of a shareholder qualifying for victim status the Commission relied on the decision in *Agrotexim* in rejecting the admissibility of the claim. In *Credit and Industrial Bank and Moravec v Czech Republic*[6] the Commission again applied the *Agrotexim* test in declaring a majority shareholder to have an insufficient interest in his company to fulfil victim status.[7] In conclusion therefore, the present Strasbourg case law is such that where the shareholders are complaining of a breach of Protocol 1, Article 1 in relation to an act aimed at the company, they

3   *Agrotexim v Greece* (1995) 21 EHRR 250, para 65-66.
4   Application No 00027917/95 (1997).
5   Application 24463/94 (1998).
6   Application 00029010/95 (1998).
7   See also *Tee v United Kingdom* Application No 00026663/95 (1996) where the fact that the company had withdrawn from the litigation at the domestic stage proved fatal to the applicant's claim to be a victim.

have no standing as they cannot be 'victims' within the meaning of Article 34.[8] Only the corporation has standing in relation to such acts.

Shareholder standing for other Articles of the ECHR

The extent to which *Agrotexim* applies outside the context of Article 1, Protocol 1 is uncertain. Despite the fact that the court in *Agrotexim*[9] held that 'Article 6 . . . [does not] imply that under the national law of the contracting states shareholders in a limited company should have the right to bring an action seeking an injunction or damages in respect of an act or omission that is prejudicial to "their" company' the judgment has not been as influential where the Article at issue is not Protocol 1, Article 1. Here again the earlier decisions of the Strasbourg court are important. In contrast to the Commission's decision in *Yarrow,* the Court in *Neves e Silva v Portugal,*[10] rejected Portugal's submissions that Mr Neves failed to qualify as a victim on the ground that he was a minority shareholder. The Portuguese government had claimed that the owner of 30% of the shares in a company could not claim to have the status of a victim and pointed to *Yarrow* as authority for this proposition. The court considered this claim but differentiated the case from the *Yarrow* decision as *Yarrow* concerned solely Article 1 of Protocol No 1. The Court held that in the separate context of Article 6:

> its task is to determine not whether Mr Neves e Silva met with an unlawful refusal to grant him the authorisation sought, but whether the case was heard within a 'reasonable time' as is required under Article 6 para 1 (art 6-1). In this respect, he is entitled to claim the status of 'victim' for the purposes of Article 25 [now Article 34]. The fact that he was a minority shareholder is immaterial in this connection.

It is not easy to decipher from the judgment in the *Neves e Silva* case why it was immaterial to the Court that Mr Neves was a minority shareholder. The fact the Court found that Neves's case was determined within a reasonable time, and considered the factual enquiry, it ex hypothesi determined that the claimant had standing to bring his claim. In *Groppera Radio AG v Switzerland*[11] the Court found in the context of Article 10 that for the purposes of 'victim' status there was no ground:

> for distinguishing between the different applicants, despite obvious dissimilarities of status or role and the fact that Groppera Radio AG alone joined the co-operative's appeal to the Federal Court. All had a direct interest in the continued transmission of Sound Radio's programmes by cable: for the company and its sole shareholder and statutory representative, it was essential to keep the station's audience and therefore to maintain its financing

---

8   The same applies for policy holders in relation to insurance companies. See *Wasa Liv Omsesidigt, Forsakringbolaget Varlands Pensionsstiftelse v Sweden* (1988) 58 DR 163.
9   (Op cit) paragraph 73.
10   [1989] 13 EHRR 535.
11   (1990) 12 EHRR 321.

from advertising revenue; for the employees, it was a matter of their job security as journalists.[12]

On this basis not only shareholders but employees fulfilled 'victim' status even though the act of the state was aimed at the company.[13] In *Ruiz-Mateos v Spain*[14], a case involving the expropriation of shares and Article 6, the Court again regarded the company as a mere vehicle through which the shareholders did business. It held that the applicants, who together owned all the shares in the relevant company, were victims of a violation of ECHR, Article 6 (1), having regard to the length of the proceedings and an absence of fairness on the part of the Spanish Constitutional Court.

In *GJ v Luxembourg*[15] the applicant complained that the proceedings concerning the liquidation of the limited liability company, in which he owned 90% of the shares, were not terminated within a reasonable time within the meaning of Article 6 (1) of the Convention. The liquidation proceedings took six years during which time the applicant was debarred from being a director, shareholder or employee of a Luxembourg company for a period of two years, and his freedom of movement was restricted.

The majority shareholder also complained under Article 8 of the Convention, that the proceedings interfered with his right to respect for his family life as it allegedly resulted in the dissolution of his marriage. The applicant further alleged that he has been treated in a discriminatory manner in the proceedings against his company because he was a foreigner, in breach of Article 14. The Commission considered the position on shareholders' standing and opined:

> [t]he Government point out that the insolvency proceedings were directed against the limited liability company and, therefore, had no effect on the applicant's civil rights and obligations.
>
> To the extent the Government suggest that the applicant cannot claim to be a victim within the meaning of Article 25 (Art 25) of the Convention the Commission recalls that the term 'victim' in Article 25 (Art 25) of the Convention denotes the person directly affected by the act or omission which is at issue. The Commission furthermore recalls that disregarding a company's legal personality as regards the question of being a 'victim' will be justified only in exceptional circumstances, in particular where it is clearly established that it is impossible for the company to apply to the Commission through the organs set up under its articles of incorporation or – in the event of liquidation – through its liquidators (cf Eur Court HR, *Agrotexim v Greece* (1995) 21 EHRR 250).
>
> In the present case the company was under liquidation and the complaint brought before the Commission relates to the activities of the liquidators – the official receiver and the Commercial Court. In these circumstances the

12   See p 183, n 11 (*Groppera*) para 49.
13   See also *Purcell v Ireland* (1991) 70 DR 262.
14   (1993) 16 EHRR 505.
15   Application No 00021156/93 (1996).

Commission finds it established that it was in all practicality impossible for the company, as a legal personality, to bring the case before the Commission.

After discussing the position in *Agrotexim* the Commission continued:

[o]n the other hand the Commission considers that the applicant is entitled to claim to be a 'victim' within the meaning of Article 25 (Art 25) of the Convention of the measures directed against the company as he held a substantial majority shareholding of 90% in the company, was in effect carrying out his business through the medium of the company and has a direct personal interest in the subject-matter of the complaint (cf No 11189/84, Dec 11.12.86, DR 50 p 121 with further references).

A number of propositions arise from this case. First, while recognising the judgment in the *Agrotexim* case, the Commission found that shareholders can fulfil victim status where the complaint is about the actions of a liquidator, receiver or court. This may indicate that the 'impossibility' criteria set in *Agrotexim* for when shareholders can fulfil victim status with regard to Protocol 1, Article 1[16] are fulfilled where the company is in liquidation, receivership or subject to a court order. Second, where the complaint arises outside of the context of Protocol 1, Article 1, the Commission seems more prepared to ignore the separate legal entity of the company.[17] This may be because of the importance placed on Article 6, which figures in many of the cases, by the Strasbourg court.[18] Third, the case although recognising the *Agrotexim* judgment follows the analysis of the earlier Commission decisions on corporate standing where the company was held merely to be a vehicle through which the shareholder does business. These three propositions cast some doubt on the reliability of *Agrotexim* even in the context of Protocol 1, Article 1.[19]

How will corporate victim status operate in the domestic courts?

The HRA 1998 provides its own definition of standing under section 7(1):

7. Proceedings

(1) A person who claims that a public authority has acted (or proposed to act) in a way which is made unlawful by section 6(1) may

16 See above.
17 See *Pafitis v Greece* (1998) 27 EHRR 566 where the ECtHR allowed minority shareholders to fulfil 'victim' status with regard to a rights violation in the context of Article 6. The fact that the company had been placed under the control of a state administrator was also significant.
18 See Chapter 9 on Article 6 and companies.
19 See also *JW v Poland* Application No 00027917/95 (1997) the Commission seemed to continue to draw a distinction between standing in the context of Protocol 1, Article 1 and other ECHR rights and freedoms by stating that 'as regards the locus standi of shareholders of limited liability companies before the Convention organs, in particular in respect of complaints under Article 1 of Protocol No 1 (P1-1) to the Convention the Court held [in *Agrotexim*] that the fall in the value of the shares cannot be automatically considered as conferring locus standi on the shareholders'.

(a) bring proceedings against the authority under this act in the appropriate court or tribunal, or

(b) rely on the convention right or rights concerned in any legal proceedings.

But only if he is (or would be) a victim of the unlawful act.

The concept of 'victim' in section 7 of the HRA is taken from ECHR, Article 34, as amended by Protocol 11. A person who would have standing as a 'victim' to bring proceedings in the European Court of Human Rights is a victim for the purpose of HRA, section 7. By virtue of section 2 of the HRA, the Courts will have to have regard to the Strasbourg case law when deciding who is and who is not a 'victim'. The Strasbourg case law leaves no doubt that the corporation can be a 'victim'. In turn the domestic courts should find that the corporate entity is capable of being a 'victim' for the purposes of section 7. The real difficulty for the court lies in how to apply 'victim' status in the context of shareholders when the violating act is aimed at the company's property.

While the domestic courts are likely to favour a restrictive approach to interpreting 'victim' status under section 7 for shareholders, there are two considerations at the domestic level which may push the courts towards a more expansive view of 'victim' status. First, the courts are likely to want to expand the Strasbourg concept of 'victim' to include public interest groups. Second, where previously a court was only concerned with the rights and obligations of the parties before it, the indirect horizontal effect of the HRA will mean that the courts as a 'public authority' under section 6 of the HRA must consider not only the Convention rights of those before it, but the rights of those who might be affected by any decision the court may make.

The pressure to expand victim status

As outlined in Chapter 6, there is a significant difference between the Strasbourg test of 'victim' and the domestic test of standing for the purposes of judicial review. In English law, standing for a judicial review application is determined by establishing that an applicant has 'sufficient interest' as stipulated under section 31(3) of the Supreme Court Act 1981 and, in similar terms, by RSC Order 53, rule 3. These provisions expressly refer to the Court refusing leave to apply unless the applicant has standing.

Rules 3(1) and 3(7) of RSC Order 53 puts the requirement of sufficient interest in the following terms:

(1) No application for judicial review shall be made unless the permission of the Court has been obtained in accordance with this rule ...

(7) The Court shall not grant permission unless it considers that the applicant has a sufficient interest in the matter to which the application relates.

Section 31(3) of the Supreme Court Act 1981 restates these provisions in similar words:

(3) No application for judicial review shall be made unless the leave of the court has been obtained in accordance with the Rules of Court; and the court

shall not grant leave to make such an application unless it considers that the application has a sufficient interest in the matter to which the application relates.

The words used in Order 53 and section 31(3) make it clear that the statutory requirement that the applicant has a 'sufficient interest' is the test of standing which the applicant must satisfy to apply for judicial review, but there is no guidance in the terms of the Act or Order 53 as to precisely what will be regarded as a 'sufficient interest'. It is, however, clear that the courts have been keen to give the wording a generous interpretation.[20]

The House of Lords gave careful consideration to the 'sufficient interest' test in the case of *IRC v National Federation of Self-Employed and Small Businesses Ltd.*[1] The Federation, a limited company, represented members of the public who were either self-employed or ran a small business. The Federation's concern involved an arrangement between the Inland Revenue and employers of some 6,000 casual workers in Fleet Street and their union. The arrangement centred around casual workers agreeing to end a practice of using false names to avoid paying tax, in return the Revenue agreed not to look into the practice in previous years. The Federation complained that the Revenue was treating casual workers differently from other taxpayers who evaded paying their tax. It sought a declaration that the Revenue had acted unlawfully in allowing such an 'amnesty', and asked for an order of mandamus directing the Revenue to assess and collect the income tax due from the casual workers in previous years.

In the Divisional Court the question of the Federation's locus standi was taken as a preliminary issue. The Court dismissed the application on the basis that the Federation did not have sufficient interest to support its application. An appeal by the Federation to the Court of Appeal was allowed, but it was not until the appeal was heard by the House of Lords that the Federation was successful.

In judicial review, the Court is not so much concerned with a dispute between two parties, but is instead concerned with decisions of public authorities. In the circumstances, the Courts have allowed and have been keen to allow interest groups who, have not *themselves* suffered from an unlawful or unreasonable action, to bring proceedings. This was made clear in *National Federation* by Lord Diplock:

> [i]t would, in my view, be a grave lacuna in our system of public law if a pressure group like the federation, or even a single public-spirited taxpayer, were prevented by outdated technical rules of locus standi from bringing the matter to the attention of the court to vindicate the rule of law and get the unlawful conduct stopped.[2]

Subsection 7(3) of the Human Rights Act specifically provides that where proceedings are brought on an application for judicial review, an applicant will have a 'sufficient

20 On this development see Gledhill, K, 'Standing, Capacity and Unincorporated Associations' (1996) *Judicial Review* p 67.
1   [1982] AC 617.
2   [1982] AC 617 at 644.

interest' in the unlawful act only if he is or would be a victim of that act, so displacing the ordinary interpretation of the sufficient interest test under domestic law. This latitude to allow interest groups to intervene in proceedings will therefore not be open to the courts where the Convention rights are at issue. The HRA requires the litigant intervening to prove that it is a 'victim', within the meaning applied by the Strasbourg court. Pure public interest litigation does not however exist at the Strasbourg level.[3]

The English courts would be concerned if, for example, Help the Aged, Child Poverty Action Group or Amnesty International could not acquire standing under the HRA because of the narrowness of the definition of 'victim'.[4] Yet it is difficult to imagine how these organisations could be 'victims' in the sense envisaged by the HRA. It seems clear that third party interest groups will not be able to commence actions under the HRA if they are not 'victims' themselves.[5] The victim test is such that organisations such as Amnesty International who represent others who have suffered could be badly affected by the victim requirement. The courts will then be placed in a confusing situation when deciding to what extent Convention points can be raised.[6]

If the public interest group is not a 'victim' they clearly cannot rely on the HRA. The courts will however be reluctant to preclude public interest litigants from relying on Convention rights and are likely either to adopt an expansive view of victim status departing from the Strasbourg jurisprudence or find another way to allow Convention rights to be argued. For example any matters raising EC law points will still include the ECHR rights and freedoms as part of the values to be given effect to by the court.[7] If they cannot expand the concept of victim to cover public interest litigation could they allow litigants to rely on the Convention as it applied prior to the HRA? As section 11 of the HRA 1998 preserves pre-existing rights of action this is one possible way of including Convention points or expanding common law protections.[8] The court's position as a public authority under the HRA could then allow the court to expand the pre-HRA common law and statutory position on use of Convention rights.

In most cases public interest organisations such as the Child Poverty Action Group, Greenpeace, Equal Opportunities Commission, trade unions and gay rights groups will find someone who fulfils victim status, but for organisations such as Amnesty International, the Immigration Law Practitioners' Association or the Joint Council for the Welfare of Immigrants it may be more difficult as the victims may be outside the jurisdiction. For those organisations, unless the courts adopt an expansive

3 See Chapter 6 on section 7.
4 See for example the intervention of Amnesty International in *R v Bow Street Metropolitan Stipendiary Magistrates, ex p Pinochet Ugaite* [2000] 1 AC 61 (1st HL); [2000] 1 AC 119; [2000] 1 AC 147 (HL No 3).
5 See Hansard, House of Commons, 20 May 1998, column 1084.
6 The Law Lords were particularly concerned with this issue see HL Debates, 5 Feb 1998: Column 807.
7 See chapter 6 on the application of the ECHR in EC law.
8 See *R v Lord Chancellor, ex p, Witham* [1998] QB 575, QBD where at common law freedom of expression and access to the courts are given effect.

approach to 'victim' status the HRA armoury of section 6 unlawful act and the remedies that flow from it will be unavailable.

Our point here in terms of corporate standing is that the courts will be pulled from both ends regarding victim status for a section 6 action.[9] They are likely to want to expand victim status for public interest litigation yet restrict it for corporate standing purposes. The 'victim' test as it is called is not actually defined in Article 34 but rather is the product of the Strasbourg court's interpretation of Article 34. As the definition of victim is found only in the case law of the ECtHR the domestic courts could if they wished depart from the Strasbourg interpretation of 'victim'.[10] However, an expansive approach to public interest groups might also allow shareholders, creditors and employees standing.

Indirect horizontal effect and interested third parties

The indirect horizontal effect of the HRA is also likely to have an impact on corporate victim status. The ability of private parties to raise Convention points will arise not only in the context of a challenge to the action of a public authority but also in actions between private parties seeking to exercise Convention rights they may have against the court as a public authority. As Feldman has pointed out, the courts will in those situations have to be aware that there may be parties other than the private parties in court who may have Convention rights exercisable against the court in relation to the matter at hand and the court should allow interested third parties to intervene.[11]

While in areas such as family law third parties and the effect on them may be obvious, as disputes between parents over children may clearly impact on grandparents, with corporations this is a more complex issue. In any legal dispute involving the corporation, the shareholders may also have a claim to be represented as their rights under the Convention may be affected by a decision adverse to the company. Unions, employees and creditors could similarly have a right to be represented in court in a dispute primarily involving the company but which could adversely affect their Convention rights should the decision go against the company. For example, in *Groppera Radio AG v Switzerland* the Court found in the context of Article 10 that for the purposes of 'victim' status there was no ground:

> for distinguishing between the different applicants, despite obvious dissimilarities of status or role and the fact that Groppera Radio AG alone joined the co-operative's appeal to the Federal Court. All had a direct interest in the continued transmission of Sound Radio's programmes by cable: for the company and its sole shareholder and statutory representative, it was essential to keep the station's audience and therefore to maintain its financing from advertising revenue; for the employees, it was a matter of their job security as journalists.[12]

9   See chapter 6 for how section 6 operates.
10 Section 3 of the HRA only requires that the court take account of the Strasbourg case law.
11 Feldman, David 'The Human Rights Act 1998 and Constitutional Principles' (1999) *Legal Studies,* p 200.
12 (1990) 12 EHRR 321 para 49.

As such employees fulfilled 'victim' status even though the act (banning a radio transmission) was aimed at the company. The employees' interest in maintaining their jobs placed them at risk from a state act which primarily affected the company.

Conclusion

As can be seen from the above the Strasbourg case law divides into two streams when considering the ability of shareholders to fulfil victim status for an act aimed at the company. The decision in *Agrotexim* represents one stream which is not dissimilar to the domestic position regarding shareholders' standing when the act is aimed at the company. *Agrotexim*, however, applies to cases involving an allegation that Protocol 1, Article 1 rights have been violated. Where the matter concerns a violation of other Convention rights, the Strasbourg court has allowed shareholders to fulfil 'victim' status.[13]

Whether the ECtHR applies one stream or another depends on a number of factors. If the matter at hand solely concerns Article 1 of Protocol 1 then *Agrotexim* is the most likely but not altogether certain precedent should the company be in liquidation, receivership, administration or subject to a court order. If the action complained of violates Protocol 1, Article 1 in conjunction with another ECHR right or freedom or solely another ECHR right or freedom the decision in *GJ v Luxembourg* would indicate that shareholders, employees and creditors may fulfil victim status. If the case concerns the actions of a liquidator, receiver or court action aimed at the company which affects a Convention right, the shareholder should be able to fulfil victim status. More specifically the following conclusions can be drawn:

1. The *Agrotexim* model is substantially the same as the domestic position on corporate standing. The application of the *Agrotexim* case appears limited to cases solely involving Protocol 1, Article 1. However as Protocol 1, Article 1 is the Article most likely to be claimed by shareholders regarding a violating act aimed at the company, this should maintain the position established in *Foss v Harbottle.*

2. However, the *Agrotexim* exception of impossibility appears to cover situations where the company is in liquidation, receivership, or subject to a court order. In such circumstances where the violating act concerning a Convention right of the company is committed by the liquidator, receiver or court the shareholders can fulfil victim status even in regard to Protocol 1, Article 1.

3. The case law on shareholder 'victim' status where the violation concerns a Convention right other than Protocol 1, Article 1 indicates a significant difference between the rules of corporate standing in domestic law and the ECHR rules of standing regarding corporate 'victim' status as applied in the *GJ v Luxembourg* stream of case law. Applying the approach of the Commission in *GJ v Luxembourg* and *Groppera Radio AG* the scope of victim status for acts aimed at the company which violate Articles other than Protocol 1, Article 1 encompasses shareholders and employees.

4. It is important to note that the Strasbourg model of the corporation is not focused on the preservation of the collective rights subsumed into the corporate form

13   See *GJ v Luxembourg* Application No 00021156/93 (1996).

but on the recognition of all of the individual rights within the collective. There is a consistent theme in the Strasbourg case law that the company is merely a vehicle for the shareholders to do business through. As such, there is at times no difference between the company's property and the shareholder. A violating act aimed at the property of the company will violate the company's Convention rights and those of the shareholders.

5) The insolvency or placing in receivership of a company or bankruptcy of an individual has no bearing on whether that company or person can be a victim within the meaning of Article 34. Legal capacity is not necessary to fulfil 'victim' status.

6) The lack of public interest litigation at the Strasbourg level attributable to a restrictive victim test is likely to put pressure on the judiciary to expand victim status. Additionally the courts will have to be increasingly aware of the rights that third parties may be able to exercise against them should a decision interfere with a third party Convention right. These factors may allow other parties such as shareholders, creditors and employees access to litigation primarily involving the company.

Chapter nine

Corporations and fair trial

Distrust all in whom the impulse to punish is powerful.[1]

Right to a fair trial

Article 6 of the ECHR provides as follows:

(1) In the determination of his civil rights and obligations or of any criminal charge against him, everyone is entitled to a fair and public hearing within a reasonable time by an independent and impartial tribunal established by law. Judgment shall be pronounced publicly but the press and public may be excluded from all or part of the trial in the interest of morals, public order or national security in a democratic society, where the interests of juveniles or the protection of the private life of the parties so require, or to the extent

1   Freidrich Wilhelm Neitzsche (1883-1892) *Thus Spake Zarathustra.*

strictly necessary in the opinion of the court in special circumstances where publicity would prejudice the interests of justice.

(2) Everyone charged with a criminal offence shall be presumed innocent until proved guilty according to law.

(3) Everyone charged with a criminal offence has the following minimum rights:
(a)   to be informed promptly, in a language which he understands and in detail, of the nature and cause of accusation against him;
(b)   to have adequate time and facilities for the preparation of his defence;
(c)   to defend himself in person or through legal assistance of his own choosing or, if he has not sufficient means to pay for legal assistance, to be given it free when the interests of justice so require;
(d)   to examine or to have examined witnesses against him and to obtain the attendance and examination of witnesses on his behalf under the same conditions as the witnesses against him;
(e)   to have the free assistance of an interpreter if he cannot understand or speak the language used in court.

Article 6 generally

Article 6 guarantees a right to a fair and public hearing within a reasonable time before an independent and impartial tribunal established by law to determine the individual's civil rights and obligations or criminal liability. The intention of Article 6 is to ensure procedural fairness in the determination of those civil rights and obligations or criminal charges. The fair administration of justice is considered fundamentally important in the interpretation of the Convention, and there is a corresponding broad and purposive interpretation of Article 6.[2] As appears from the express words used, Article 6(1) applies to both criminal and civil proceedings, whilst the application of Articles 6(2) and 6(3) is restricted to criminal proceedings. Articles 6(2) and 6(3) are supplementary to Article 6(1), but they are not intended to describe exhaustively the requirements for fairness in proceedings, instead, they describe the minimum guarantees which must be provided by the member states of the Council of Europe.

Article 6 is, by an appreciable distance, the most frequently invoked Article of the ECHR.[3] While it was, no doubt, drafted primarily with the intention of protecting the rights of individuals the Article has been developed to protect companies and their officers when they themselves face criminal charges or are sued in the civil division.[4] Article 6 impacts on companies in four ways. First, the regulatory agencies such as the FSA, the Panel on Take-overs and Mergers and the DTI as well as the courts will all have to ensure that the standards necessary to comply with Article 6 are applied in the carrying out of their functions. Second, companies and their officers are often the subjects of those regulatory bodies' investigations and as such

2   *Moreira de Azevedo v Portugal* (1990) 13 EHRR 721.
3   Sir Nicolas Bratza, *The Implication of the Human Rights Act 1998 for Commercial Practice* (2000) *European Human Rights Law Review*, Issue 1, p 7.
4   *Saunders v United Kingdom* (1996) 23 EHRR 313.

need to be aware of the standards they can expect to be applied in the course of those investigations and adjudications. Third certain companies such as British Gas, BNFL, Railtrack and British Telecom will be public authorities for the purposes of the HRA. As such where they are carrying out investigatory and adjudicatory functions affecting civil or criminal liability, as public authorities they must comply with Article 6 or else they will commit an unlawful act actionable under the HRA by those affected.[5] Four, the horizontal effect of the HRA will mean that the fair trial standards contained in Article 6 will impact on private parties wherever a court or tribunal is involved.[6]

Access to the courts

Central to the operation of Article 6 is access to the courts. On this basis a public authority can never restrict or eliminate judicial review and it is even questionable whether judicial review instead of a full hearing on the facts is a sufficiently effective remedy for the purposes of the Convention.[7] In general the ECtHR has found that judicial review is an effective remedy for the majority of Convention rights.[8] However in the context of Article 6 (1) the Strasbourg court has consistently held that a fair hearing requires a hearing of the facts unless the matter is purely one of law or policy.[9] As a result, in *W v United Kingdom*[10] the ECtHR found a breach of Article 6 because the High Court in the course of judicial review proceedings could not consider the merits of the case. In the context of Article 6 the court has been more willing to allow shareholders to fulfil victim status for acts aimed at the company's property.[11]

Similarly, alternative dispute resolution or administrative schemes where there is no appeal to a court on the facts of the matter run the risk of breaching Article 6 (1). Generally an individual can waive their right of access to the court through a voluntary submission to arbitration. However, should there be any element of compulsion present (for example a court order), the arbitrator must comply fully with Article 6 or else there will be a violation of Article 6.[12] This issue arose recently in the High Court regarding a scheme of arrangement for an insurance company in provisional liquidation. The scheme provided for the appointment of an independent adjudicator to resolve disputes between the creditors and the administrators of the scheme. The High Court initially refused to sanction the scheme because it involved the creditors having to waive any right to appeal. After further argument the court accepted that the ability to sue the adjudicator for negligence, breach of trust or fraud was sufficient to provide access to the courts under the

5   Bodies such as the Ladbroke Grove Rail inquiry into the Paddington rail disaster would not have to apply Article 6 standards as they are not determining civil rights and obligations or criminal liability.
6   In particular it has an effect on employment policy, see Chapter 13.
7   *See Golder v United Kingdom* (1975) 1 EHRR 524.
8   See *D v United Kingdom* (1997) 24 EHRR 423.
9   *Bryan v United Kingdom* (1995) 21 EHRR 342.
10 (1987) 10 EHRR 29.
11 See Chapter 8.
12 *Malmstrom v Sweden* (1983) 38 DR 18.

scheme.[13] It is doubtful whether this decision is sufficient for the purposes of Article 6 (1). Should the arbitrator fail to comply with Article 6 in the determination of any dispute it will be a breach of Article 6 regardless of the ability of the parties to sue in negligence, breach of trust or fraud.

Immunity from suit, such as that previously conferred on barristers is as a consequence questionable, and that conferred on the police force has already been held to be a breach of Article 6.[14] While access to the court must be practical and effective the imposition of a fee in order to have access to the courts will not necessarily be in breach of Article 6.[15] However the absence of legal aid has been held to constitute a violation of Article 6 in certain circumstances.[16] Similarly, the courts will have to consider the parties' Article 6 rights in considering its discretion to order security for costs. Should it order too large an amount as security it would run the risk of violating Article 6.[17]

What do the courts and regulators have to do in order to ensure a fair trial?

Over time the Strasbourg court has identified certain key components necessary to ensure a fair trial. These consist of equality of arms, a public hearing, an independent and impartial tribunal, determination within a reasonable time frame, presumption of innocence from criminality and the privilege against self-incrimination.

Equality of arms

The idea of equality of arms equates to the principle that each party to the action should have an equal chance to present their case. This means the parties must have equal access to documents and to have evidence put before the court.[18] The court as a 'public authority' under the HRA must be careful to balance the need to use its trial management powers in limiting evidence or access to witnesses against its obligation to respect the parties' Article 6 rights. A breach of those rights by the court is an unlawful act under the HRA for which the parties can claim a remedy.[19] As a general principle the parties should be present and in a fit state to take part in the proceedings.[20]

---

13   *Re Hawk Insurance Co Ltd* Ch D (13 January 1999, unreported).
14   See *Osman v United Kingdom* (1998) 5 BHRC 293.
15   See *R v Lord Chancellor, e p Lightfoot* [1999] 4 All ER 583.
16   *Airey v Ireland* (1979) 2 EHRR 305 at 314. The government eventually agreed, because of human rights concerns, to provide legal aid for offences under the FSMA 2000. In the UK companies are precluded from being the subject of a grant of legal aid. This might in certain circumstances constitute a breach of Article 6.
17   See *Tolstoy Miloslavsky v United Kingdom* (1995) 20 EHRR 442.
18   See *Mc Michael v United Kingdom* (1995) 20 EHRR 205 on access to documents and *Mantovanelli v France* (1996) 24 EHRR 370 on the exclusion of expert witnesses.
19   See Chapter 6 on section 6.
20   See X *v Germany* (1963) 6 YB 520.

Public hearing

The right to a public hearing is a relatively straightforward part of providing a fair trial but is described by the ECtHR as one of 'fundamental importance'.[1] It can be restricted to some extent in the interests of justice, public order, national security, morals, the private lives of the participants and juveniles, by excluding the press and public from all or part of the trial. The parties can agree to waive their right to a public hearing but such waiver must be unequivocal and must not be contrary to any important public interest.[2] Judgments must, however, be pronounced in public.

Independent and impartial tribunal

The Strasbourg court set out in *Langborger v Sweden*[3] that independence meant independence from the executive and the parties. In order to ensure this regard should be had to whether the appointment and remuneration system ensures independence, whether there was a guarantee against outside pressure and there was the appearance of independence. Independence also means that the investigating authority is separate from the adjudicatory body.[4] Impartiality involves no actual bias being present or even the appearance of bias.[5]

These criteria have already begun to have an effect at the domestic level. The fact the Secretary of State appoints and pays lay members of employment tribunals has been held to be insufficiently impartial for the purposes of Article 6 of the ECHR.[6] The ECtHR has similarly found that the Bailiff of Guernsey is in breach of Article 6 because of his combined role as the executive, administrative and judicial function on the island.[7] This would also cast doubt on the ability of the Lord Chancellor to continue his role as a member of the Cabinet, the Judicial Committee of the House of Lords and the House of Lords. The claim that a body is insufficiently independent and impartial is often combined with a claim that Article 13 (right to an effective remedy) has also been breached. In *Govell v United Kingdom*[8] the Commission took the view that a complaint to the Police Complaints Authority (PCA) was an insufficiently effective remedy because the PCA did not have the requisite level of independence. All regulatory bodies that are 'public authorities' under the HRA and that carry out investigatory and adjudicatory functions in the determination of civil rights and obligations or criminal liability, such as the FSA, the Panel on Take-overs and Mergers, the Press Complaints Commission,[9] the Law Society and the

1   *Schuler-Zgraggen v Switerland* (1993) 16 EHRR 405 para 58.
2   See n 1 above (*Schuler*).
3   (1989) 12 EHRR 416 at para 32.
4   See *Fayed v United Kingdom* (1994) 18 EHRR 393.
5   Requirements of impartiality have been set down recently by the House of Lords in *Re Pinochet Ugarte* [1999] 1 All ER 577, [1999] 2 WLR 272; and guidelines on bias can be found in *Locabail (United Kingdom) Ltd v Bayfield Properties Ltd* (1999) [2000] 1 All ER 65, [2000] 2 WLR 870. See also Chapter 4 Articles 6 and 13.
6   *Smith v Secretary for State for Trade and Industry* (1999) [2000] ICR 69; [2000] IRLR 6. In Scotland temporary sheriffs have been held to be insufficiently impartial on the same basis which in turn casts doubt on the operation of part-time recorders in the English courts.
7   *McGonnell v United Kingdom* (2000) Times, 22 February, Application No 00028488/95.
8   Appl 27237/95 Commission 14 January 1998: [1999] EHRLR 121.
9   See Chapter 11 on the questionable independence and impartiality of the PCC.

General Medical Council must comply with the independence and impartiality requirements of Article 6. If they do not their decisions are challengeable for being in breach of Article 6.

Reasonable time frame

The length of time necessary to constitute a violation of Article 6 varies depending on the context of the proceedings. The more complex the issue, the importance of the determination for the applicant, the conduct of the authority and the applicant will all be considered as to whether a violation of Article 6 has occurred in relation to a reasonable time.[10] Criminal trials are required to be determined quicker than civil proceedings. Some examples of the courts' findings with regard to time are: nine years was too long for an employment dispute;[11] two years and eight months was too long for a pension appeal;[12] four years and four months in the context of a director's disqualification case was too long;[13] four years for a costs dispute was too long;[14] where the issue is compensation for injury the court has required much more speed in determining issues; two years and three months was too long where the issue was contamination with the HIV virus.[15]

The presumption of innocence from criminality

Article 6 (2) provides that '[e]veryone charged with a criminal offence shall be presumed innocent until proved guilty according to law.' This places the burden of proof on the prosecution.[16] There are two qualifications to this general proposition. First that the state can sometimes provide defences which move the burden of proof such as requiring the defendant to show that he acted reasonably and/or truthfully.[17] Second that certain presumptions of law or fact may operate against the defendant in limited circumstances as long as they are not contrary to the Convention. For example smuggling offences often carry a presumption of guilt when found in possession of controlled substances.[18]

Privilege against self-incrimination

Article 6 does not contain a specific restriction on self-incrimination in its wording. However, the Strasbourg court has interpreted Article 6 expansively so that the right to a fair trial in a criminal case includes a right 'to remain silent and not to contribute to incriminating himself'.[19] This freedom means that the prosecuting authorities in a criminal trial cannot rely on evidence obtained through compulsion

---

10   See *König v Germany* (1978) 2 EHRR 170.
11   *Obermeier v Germany* (1990) 13 EHRR 290.
12   *Styranowski v Poland* [1998] HRCD 1001.
13   *EDC v United Kingdom* (unreported, 1995) commented on in EHRLR 1996, 2, 189-191.
14   *Robins v United Kingdom* (1997) 26 EHRR 527.
15   *A v Denmark* (1996) 22 EHRR 458; see also speed with regard to personal injury cases in *Silva Pontes v Portugal* (1994) 18 EHRR 156.
16   *Austria v Italy* (1963) 6 YB 740.
17   *Lingens v Austria* (1981) 26 DR 171.
18   See *Salabiaku v France* (1988) 13 EHRR 379.
19   *Funke v France* (1993) 16 EHRR 297.

contrary to the defendant's wishes. In the case of *Funke v France,*[20] the applicant complained of rights violations in connection with an investigation by the state into alleged customs irregularities. The applicant failed to produce bank statements relevant to an investigation being carried out by the French customs authorities. As a consequence, the applicant was charged and convicted with the offence of failing to produce the relevant documents, although no substantive customs charge was ever made against him. The European Court held that the attempt by the French authorities to compel the applicant to produce incriminating documents contravened his Article 6 right. At paragraph 44 the Court held:

> [t]he Court notes that the customs ... [officials] ... secured Mr Funke's conviction in order to obtain certain documents which they believed must exist, although they were not certain of the fact. Being unable or unwilling to procure them by some other means, they attempted to compel the applicant himself to provide the evidence of offences which he had allegedly committed. The special features of customs law cannot justify such an infringement of the right to anyone 'charged with a criminal offence', within the meaning of this expression in Article 6, to remain silent and not to contribute to incriminating himself.

However complications arise as to the application of Article 6 where, in the course of a regulatory investigation, evidence is obtained under compulsion and is subsequently used in a criminal trial. These circumstances generally arise under the wide range of statutory provisions requiring companies and their officers to participate and assist statutory investigations of a regulatory nature. So far as companies and their officers are concerned, statutory bodies are empowered to investigate and interrogate under section 43A of the Insurance Companies Act 1982 (insurance investigations), sections 431, 432, 434, and 442-444 of the Companies Act 1985 (relating to investigations into the companies' affairs), sections 218, 235, 236, 433 of the Insolvency Act 1986 (relating to provision of information to office-holder or court),[1] sections 94, 105, 177 and 178 of the Financial Services Act 1986 (unit trusts, investment business and insider dealing investigations), sections 82–91 of the Companies Act 1989 (investigation in co-operation with an overseas regulatory authority), section 2 of the Criminal Justice Act 1987 (relating to investigations of serious fraud), sections 39, 41 and 42 of the Banking Act 1987 (banking investigations) and the Financial Services Authority's (FSA) powers under Part XI of the Financial Services and Markets Act 2000.

The application of the Article 6 privilege against self-incrimination in the face of regulatory investigation was examined by the Strasbourg court in the case of *Saunders v United Kingdom*[2]. The case concerned the competition in early 1986

---

20   *Funke v France* (1993) 16 EHRR 297.
1   The Insolvency Bill 2000 amends section 219 of the Insolvency Act 1986 so that answers given by an individual under a power of compulsion conferred by section 218 (5) cannot be used against him by the prosecution in subsequent criminal proceedings except in very limited circumstances.
2   *Saunders v United Kingdom* (1996) 23 EHRR 313.

between Guinness plc and Argyll Group plc to take over a third company, Distillers Company plc. The take-over battle resulted in victory for Guinness. Guinness' offer to the Distillers shareholders, like Argyll's, included a substantial share exchange element and, accordingly, the respective prices at which Guinness and Argyll shares were quoted on the stock exchange were of a critical factor for both sides. During the course of the bid, the Guinness share price rose dramatically, but once the bid had been declared unconditional, it fell significantly.

The substantial increase in the quoted Guinness share price during the bid was, it was discovered, achieved as a result of an unlawful share support operation. This involved 'supporters' purchasing Guinness shares in order to maintain or inflate its quoted share price. Supporters were offered secret indemnities against future losses and, in some cases, secret fees contingent upon the Guinness bid being successful. These inducements were not disclosed to the market as required by the City code and the indemnities and fees were to be paid out of Guinness assets in breach of section 151 of the Companies Act 1985, which prohibits a company assisting third parties in the acquisition of its own shares. Allegations and rumours of misconduct during the course of the bid led the Secretary of State for Trade and Industry to appoint Inspectors pursuant to sections 432 and 442 of the Companies Act 1985. The Inspectors took the view in December 1987 that there was 'concrete evidence' of criminal offences having been committed and informed the Crown Prosecution Service on 12 January 1987. On 14 January 1987, the applicant was dismissed from Guinness. Between February and June 1987, the applicant was interviewed on nine separate occasions by DTI inspectors.

The applicant was eventually tried in a case involving 75 days of evidence, 10 days of speeches and 5 days of summing up by the trial judge. The applicant gave evidence denying any knowledge of wrongdoing, and saying that he was not consulted about the facts and matters complained of at the time. The Crown relied on the statements given by the applicant to the DTI inspectors, under compulsion. The transcripts of those interviews were read to the jury over a three-day period. They were used by the Crown to establish the state of the applicant's knowledge and to refute evidence given by the applicant to the jury. In his summing up, the trial judge compared and contrasted the evidence the applicant had given to the DTI inspectors, and the evidence he had given at the trial. On 22 August 1990, the applicant was convicted of 12 counts in respect of conspiracy, false accounting and theft. He received a prison sentence of five years.

The applicant, relying upon Article 6(1) of the Convention, complained to the Strasbourg court that he was denied a fair hearing because of the use at his criminal trial of the statements obtained from him by the DTI inspectors in exercise of their statutory powers of compulsion. The Commission considered the complaint that statements obtained under compulsion were used in criminal proceedings and found:

> that the applicant was in effect compelled to incriminate himself and that the incriminating material furnished a not insignificant part of the evidence against him at his trial. While the Government contest that the reason for the applicant deciding to give evidence was the necessity for him to counter the evidence

of the DTI interviews, the Commission notes that on the Government's own submissions, it is not denied that, though the real value of the transcripts was in cross examination … the evidence contained admissions in itself. In these circumstances, the Commission considers this must have exerted additional pressure on the applicant to take the witness stand rather than exercise the right to remain silent at the trial and leave it to the prosecution to prove its case.

In light of the above, the Commission finds that the use at the applicant's trial of incriminating evidence obtained from him under compulsory powers was oppressive and substantially impaired his ability to defend himself against the criminal charges facing him. He was therefore deprived of a fair hearing within the meaning of Article 6(1) of the Convention.

The Commission concludes, by 14 votes to 1, that there has been a violation of Article 6(1) of the Convention.[3]

The matter went to the ECtHR for final adjudication, there the court held that it did:

not accept the Government's argument that the complexity of the corporate fraud and the vital public interest in the investigation of such fraud and the punishment of those responsible could justify such a marked departure as that which occurred in the present case from one the basic principles of fair procedure. Like the Commission, … [the Court] … considers that the general requirements of fairness contained in Article 6, including the right not to incriminate oneself, apply to criminal proceedings in respect to all types of criminal offences without distinction, from the most simple to the most complex. The public interest cannot be invoked to justify the use of answers compulsorily obtained in non-judicial investigation to incriminate the accused during the trial proceedings … Accordingly, there has been an infringement in the present case of the right not to incriminate oneself.[4]

It is important to note that cases like *Saunders* and *Funke* do not strike at the investigative regimes themselves, but at the subsequent use of the evidence obtained under compulsion. In *Saunders* the court was unconcerned about the use of compulsory evidence for the purposes of a regulatory investigation.[5] As a general rule the court has been particularly protective of investigatory regimes where it considers them to be pursuing an important public interest. In *Abas v Netherlands*[6] the applicant had been under a legal obligation to provide information to a Dutch tax inspector in default of which he could have been fined or imprisoned, but no criminal proceedings were actually pursued against him. In the circumstances, the Commission took the view that the applicant's right not to incriminate himself was not infringed. The Commission found that to subject ordinary tax investigations to

3   (1997) 23 EHRR 313, paras 75 to 77.
4   (1997) 23 EHRR 313, paras 74 and 75.
5   (1997) 23 EHRR 313, para 67.
6   *Abas v Netherlands* Appl 27943/95 [1997] EHRLR 418.

the rigour of Article 6 would unnecessarily hamper a process which is in the public interest.[7]

Following the decision by the European Court in *Saunders* the Court of Appeal observed in *R v Morrissey* and *R v Staines*[8] that it had no power to exclude evidence under section 78 of PACE 1984, as this was contrary to plain statutory intent. This situation was described by Bingham LCJ as 'very unsatisfactory'. Similarly in *R v Hertfordshire County Council, ex p Green Environmental Industries Ltd*[9] a waste regulation authority suspected that the defendant had disposed of controlled clinical waste without a licence. The authority sent a requisition under the Environmental Protection Act 1990, s 71(2) requiring the defendant to provide information about the waste operation. The defendant would not comply with the requisition unless the waste authority agreed their replies would not be used to incriminate them. The waste authority would not agree and brought criminal proceedings against the defendant for non-compliance with the requisition. The defendant made an application for judicial review of the original decision against him and the Court of Appeal found that the fact that information provided under s 71(2) of the 1990 Act might incriminate its provider was not a reasonable excuse for failing to comply with it. The protection against self-incrimination afforded by s 69(8) of the 1990 Act only extended to an individual giving oral answers to an inspector on company premises pursuant to s 69(3) and would not protect the company or other individuals. Information provided in circumstances other than those outlined in s 69(3) was not subject to the protection of s 69(8). It was clear that Parliament intended that a waste regulation authority should be able to use its powers under s 71 to obtain evidence which could then be used in criminal proceedings, subject only to the court's power to exclude evidence under the Police and Criminal Evidence Act 1984, s 78.

As a result of cases such as these the Attorney General issued guidance in February 1998 that prosecutors should not use evidence obtained under compulsion. However the guidance does not constitute an absolute ban and contains a discretion to use evidence obtained under compulsion which is introduced by the defendant, is based on the silence of the defendant or where the answers to questions are untrue. Since then where the proceedings are criminal in nature the domestic courts have been careful to exclude evidence obtained under compulsion. In *R v Faryab*[10] the Court of Appeal held that evidence obtained under section 433 of the Insolvency Act 1986 could not be used in relation to a prosecution for handling stolen goods. The DTI also failed successfully to prosecute Kevin Maxwell for contempt of court over his refusal to answer inspectors questions because they would not agree to confine the questions to matters unrelated to evidence at his criminal trial and insolvency investigations.[11]

---

7   See also *K v Austria* A/255-B (1993).
8   *R v Morrissey* and *R v Staines* (1997) Times, 1 May.
9   [1998] Env LR 153.
10   [1999] BPIR 569, CA.
11   See Mason, John 'Maxwell cleared of contempt in Mirror inquiry' *Financial Times* 12 March 1999, p 9.

As a result of the HRA, the government has introduced section 59 of the Youth Justice and Criminal Evidence Act 1999 in order to clarify the position with regard to the use of compulsory evidence in criminal trials. Section 59 amends section 434 of the Companies Act 1985, section 433 of the Insolvency Act 1986, s 20 of the Company Directors' Disqualification Act 1986, ss 105 and 177 of the Financial Services Act 1986, ss 39, 41 and 42 of the Banking Act 1987 and section 2 of the Criminal Justice Act 1987. The amendments prohibit the prosecuting authorities in criminal proceedings relying on evidence obtained by compulsion by the regulatory agencies. Additionally, the Insolvency Bill 2000 amends s 219 of the Insolvency Act 1986 so that except in limited circumstances answers given by an individual under compulsion cannot be used in subsequent criminal proceedings.

These amendments, while they do deal with the main areas of compulsion, still provide exceptions and do not cover all the circumstances whereby evidence is required from individuals under compulsion. Additionally, while currently there exists a discretionary bar on the transfer of documents from the statutory investigators to the Serious Fraud Office, there is no legal prohibition. A similar scheme exists in the context of evidence given by freezing (formerly Mareva) order defendants in compulsory cross examination which goes to substantive issues.[12] The use of compulsory evidence is an area which is likely to see continued challenge by companies and their directors following the implementation of the HRA. Challenges are likely to be made where evidence obtained in statutory investigations is used either in the context of criminal proceedings, or when such evidence provokes criminal proceedings and the use of other legitimate investigatory powers. As Sir Nicholas Bratza observed,[13] our courts are likely to be confronted with difficult questions as to the precise scope of the right to silence of the case of company and other investigations. In particular, the courts must decide whether a right is violated in any case where a person is punished for refusing to answer incriminating questions, or whether such a violation only results where the investigation in which the refusal occurred may be regarded as part of a broader criminal investigation.

Does the privilege apply to documents?

The common law recognises a privilege with regard to documents.[14] However the position at the Strasbourg level is far from clear where documents are at issue. In *Funke v France*,[15] in overruling the Commission, the Court found that a conviction for failure to produce documents was a violation of Article 6.[16] In finding this the Court drew no distinction between the compulsion with regard to the production of documents and compulsion with regard to answering questions. However in

12   *Yukong Line Ltd of Korea v Rendsburg Investments Corpn of Liberia* [1996] 2 Lloyd's Rep 604.
13   *The Implications of the Human Rights Act 1998 for Commercial Practice* (p 194, n 3) pp 11-12.
14   See *AT & T Istel Ltd v Tully* [1992] 3 All ER 523 and s 14 of the Civil Evidence Act 1968.
15   *Funke v France* (1993) 16 EHRR 297.
16   See Reid, Karen *A Practitioner's Guide to The European Convention on Human Rights* (1998) Sweet and Maxwell pp 133-135.

Saunders the Court considered that the privilege against self-incrimination was primarily concerned with the ability to remain silent and not to 'the use in criminal proceedings of material which may be obtained from the accused through the use of compulsory powers but which has an existence independent of the will of the suspect such as, inter alia, documents acquired pursuant to a warrant, breath, blood and urine samples and bodily tissue for the purpose of DNA testing'.[17] Given that the Strasbourg position is unclear and that the domestic courts already recognise the privilege in domestic law it is unlikely that the HRA would diminish the pre-existing protection given to documents.[18]

Companies and their directors are often defendants in proceedings where the claimant seeks against them interim remedies, often in the various forms of injunctions which can be granted by the courts. The Commercial Court in England and Wales often presides over applications previously known under the Rules of the Supreme Court and in case law as Anton Pillar orders, but which are now known as search orders and governed by Part 25 of the CPR and the relevant *Practice Direction*.

Since their 'invention' in the mid-1970s, a very significant volume of authority has built up concerning search orders[19]. The causes behind what has been described as 'the most remarkable example of judicial creativity this century'[20] are significant to the understanding of this wealth of English authority. In the 1960s, it became apparent that civil law remedies were often found to be inadequate against defendants who actively sought to avoid the enforcement of judgments by disposing of assets, or who actively destroyed evidence to diminish the risk of judgments being made against them. In response, the courts devised interlocutory powers to permit claimants to search a defendant's premises and seize material prior to a trial. Having created these remedies out of necessity, the courts have been careful to protect them when threatened by applications from search order defendants.[1] On the other hand, the courts have also recognised, on more than one occasion, that

17 (1997) 23 EHRR 313 at para 69.
18 However in the US and Australia where the documents are corporate in nature the courts have accorded a lower level of protection: see Scherb, Katherine: 'Administrative Subpoenas for Private Financial Records: What Protection for Privacy does The Fourth Amendment Require?': (1996) *Wisconsin Law Review* pp 1075-1099 and Hill, Jennifer, 'Corporate Rights and Accountability – The Privilege Against Self-Incrimination And The Implications Of *Environment Protection Authority v Caltex Refining Co Pty Ltd* Corporate and Business Law *Journal* (University of Adelaide) Vol 7 No 2, Special Issue – orporate Theory (1994) pp 127-148. On the other hand the Canadian courts have protected companies from search and seizure: Tollefson, Chris 'Constitutional Law – Charter of Rights – Strict Liability Offences – Reverse Onus Clauses – Standing of Corporations – Charter of Rights and Freedoms, ss 1, 7, 11(1)(d) – Competition Act, RSC 1970, c C-23, ss 6(1)(a), 37.3(2): *R v Wholesale Travel Group Inc* in (1992) 71 *Canadian Bar Review* pp 369-383.
19 See generally Steven Gee QC, *Mareva Injunctions and Anton Pillar Relief* (4th edn).
20 Lord Hoffmann, foreword to the 4th edn of *Mareva Injunctions and Anton Pillar Relief* (above).
1   See, for example, *Yukong Line Ltd of Korea v Rendsburg Investments Corpn of Liberia*, [1996] 2 Lloyd's Rep 604 where the Court of Appeal permitted the interrogation of a defendant against his will in freezing order proceedings, even though the questions trespassed on substantive matters in circumstances where the freezing order defendant was not going to provide substantive evidence at trial.

search orders can be extremely draconian, and there is a consequent need to ensure that the search order defendant's rights are protected so far as they can be bearing in mind that the requirement for these orders is seen as a necessary remedy in the modern commercial world where data can be deleted at the touch of a button.[2]

While the Article 6 privilege against self-incrimination only operates where the proceedings are criminal in nature, Article 8 offers protection even where the search order is in the context of civil proceedings.[3] In considering whether to grant such orders the impact of both Article 6 and Article 8 (private life) should be significant. In *Niemietz v Germany*[4] the Strasbourg court held that the words 'private life', 'home' and 'correspondence' in Article 8 include, in some circumstances, professional and business activities, so that a search order made by a German court had to satisfy the requirements of proportionality. Similarly, in *Miailhe v France*,[5] customs officers seized some 15,000 documents from premises housing the head office of companies managed by the Applicant. The court found that the search breached Article 8 as there were few legal safeguards to protect the applicant defendant and the seizure of documents was, to a large extent, indiscriminate. That is not to say that search orders necessarily contravene the ECHR.

It seems clear from these cases search orders can satisfy the requirements of the ECHR, providing that the courts act to safeguard the Convention rights of the Search order defendants, in so far as they can be protected. In this respect, the courts already have safeguards in place in that the provisions of CPR Part 25 and the previous case law do seek to protect the interest of these defendants. The Commercial and Chancery Courts do already scrutinise applications to search to ensure that there is no unnecessary interference and to ensure that the only items covered by the terms of the order are removed. However, the courts will have to be even more vigilant in supervising such orders under the HRA. Applications for search orders are almost invariably made ex parte without notice. As such the court as 'public authority' under section 6 of the HRA must act compatibly with the Convention rights. Should it make an order in breach of an individual or a company's Convention rights it will be an unlawful act actionable under the HRA.

It will also be incumbent on lawyers acting for the search order applicants to ensure that the orders sought and the manner in which they are executed do not contravene the ECHR. This will serve to protect not only the interests of the Search order defendant, but also the interests of their own clients as it is one thing to obtain such orders ex parte, quite another to maintain them inter partes. Moreover, lawyers acting for search order applicants owe a duty to the court to ensure that their clients disclose all matters relevant to the court at the time of the *ex parte* application. This is taken very seriously by solicitors and counsel alike. If there is any matter

2   For example in *AT&T Istel Ltd v Tully* [1992] 3 All ER 523 the privilege against self-incrimination was successfully invoked in order to defeat a freezing order and in *Rank Film Distributers Ltd v Video Information Centre* [1981] 2 All ER 76 the privilege was used to defeat a search order.
3   See below.
4   *Niemietz v Germany* (1992) 16 EHRR 97.
5   *Miailhe v France* (1993) 16 EHRR 332.

which, when considered objectively, might adversely affect the search order claimant's application, it should be brought expressly to the judge's attention, who very often will have to consider search order applications under pressure of time.

It must be the case therefore, that lawyers must positively consider whether there is a danger that the order(s) sought may contravene the ECHR and, if so, counsel will be duty bound to bring this expressly to the attention of the court, so that unlawful orders are not made. Judicial scrutiny coupled with the honest diligence of the applicant's lawyers should ensure that search orders are framed in a way which satisfies the provisions of the HRA. If there is a risk that the order(s) sought would contravene a Convention right, then the orders ought not be made.[6]

Does the privilege against self-incrimination apply outside the criminal context?

The privilege does not apply outside the criminal context, however where the proceedings are civil in nature Article 6 requires a general standard of fairness.[7] As such, investigations by regulatory authorities are subject to Article 6 scrutiny. In *Fayed v United Kingdom*[8] the applicants complained that a report of the DTI into the take-over of the House of Fraser contained a statement that they had lied about their origins and that they could not challenge that finding because of a statutory immunity for the DTI inspectors. The court found that this did engage Article 6 and the court examined the investigatory regime to see if it came up to the standards required by the court. The court found that the function of the inspectors was to investigate and not to adjudicate. The ability of independent inspectors to investigate without fear was an important aim of the regulatory regime. Businessmen conducting the affairs of large companies should expect to tolerate a wider degree of criticism than was the case with private individuals. As a result the inspectors' immunity was justifiable.[9]

Where the proceedings are civil in nature the domestic courts have already considered that Article 6 allows evidence to be used even though it was obtained under compulsion. In *Re Westminister Property Management Ltd*[10] the court held that compulsory evidence obtained under section 235 of the Insolvency Act 1986 was available in directors' disqualification proceedings because they were civil and not criminal in character. In the case of *Official Receiver v Stern*,[11] the Court of

6   On the New Zealand experience see Butler, Andrew S, 'The scope of s 21 of the New Zealand Bill of Rights Act 1990: Does it provide a general guarantee of property rights' in (1996) *New Zealand Law Journal* February, pp 58- 64.

7   This is consistent with the ECJ's view on the matter. See *Otto BV v Postbank NV* [1993] ECR I-5683 where the ECJ held that the privilege did not apply in competition proceedings which were civil in nature.

8   (1994) 18 EHRR 393.

9   The Canadian courts considering the fair trial provisions contained in the Canadian Charter of Rights and Freedoms has been careful not to exclude its use in civil proceedings applying it on a case by case basis rather than an overall blanket approach. See *R v Fizpatrick* (1995) 129 DLR (4th) 129.

10   [2000] 05 LS Gaz R 33.

11   *Official Receiver v Stern* (unreported judgment delivered 2 February 2000).

Appeal considered a first instance decision of a preliminary issue that the making of a director disqualification order or the use of material obtained under compulsion would not be contrary to the right to a fair trial under Article 6(1) of the ECHR. The Official Receiver had commenced disqualification proceedings under section 6 of the Company Directors Disqualification Act 1986 against two directors in relation to the affairs of a company. A preliminary issue was ordered to be tried, namely whether in the circumstances of the case the making of a disqualification order or the use against the respondents of evidence provided by them under section 235 of the Insolvency Act 1986 would be contrary to Article 6. The Court of Appeal held that the issue of a fair trial was to be determined having regard to all of the relevant factors including (a) the fact that disqualification proceedings were not criminal proceedings but nonetheless carried serious allegations and subsequent stigma; (b) there was a hierarchy of coercive powers used to obtain information in corporate insolvency, resulting in different degrees of prejudice arising from any admissions; and (c) section 235 was less formal and rigorous than other powers in the hierarchy and was not directed exclusively at obtaining material of a self-incriminatory nature. The Court of Appeal held that the use of statements under section 235 of the Insolvency Act in disqualification proceedings did not necessarily involve a breach of Article 6(1) of the ECHR.[12]

How can companies or their directors tell whether proceedings brought against them are defined as either civil or criminal within the meaning of the ECHR?

As the protections given to civil and criminal proceedings differ the proper definition of proceedings as either criminal or civil will be of primary importance to companies and their officers who find themselves as defendants in proceedings. The Strasbourg court has made it clear that the classification of proceedings by member states as either criminal or civil will not be finally determinative, at least not when domestic law classifies the proceedings as civil.[13] In *Engel v Netherlands*,[14] the court held that the meaning of 'criminal charge' in Article 6 of the Convention is an 'autonomous' concept. As a result the Strasbourg court will not necessarily accord the same meaning to the phrase 'civil proceedings' as the domestic authority.

How then are the domestic courts to resolve a dispute as to the status of proceedings brought against a company or its directors? It is submitted that the Court must for the first time have regard to the way in which the Commission and ECtHR have previously determined whether proceedings are either criminal or civil rather than simply referring to the domestic classification as the final arbiter. This will involve considering the issues set out below and according the various considerations proper weight:

12   See also *R v Secretary of State for Trade and Industry, ex p McCormick* [1998] BCC 379 and *Hinchcliffe v Secretary of State for Trade and Industry* [1999] BCC 226.
13   See Reid, Karen, *A Practitioner's Guide to The European Convention on Human Rights* (1998) Sweet and Maxwell, pp 60-62.
14   *Engel v Netherlands (No 2)* (1976) 1 EHRR 706.

Are the proceedings classified as 'criminal' or 'civil' in domestic law?

If the proceedings are defined as a matter of domestic law as 'criminal', then it is submitted that this will be sufficient for the court to determine that the proceedings are also 'criminal' for the purposes of Article 6 of the ECHR. However, if the proceedings are defined as 'civil' the court should consider this and give it proper weight, but it is not determinative and the court will continue to consider the factors set out below.[15]

What is the nature of the offence or conduct in question?

Very often, the nature of the offence or conduct in question will point clearly to the classification of the charges brought as being either civil or criminal. If an individual is sued for damages flowing from an alleged breach of contract, the charge concerns the private rights between two individuals, and this fact points strongly towards the classification of the proceedings as being civil. By contrast, if the individual is charged with murder, the charge concerns, primarily, a public offence, and this fact points strongly towards the classification of the proceedings as being criminal. The Commission has previously considered how the different member states have classified the offence in question and have considered whether the alleged offence could apply to the population as a whole, or only part of it.[16]

What is the greatest severity of any possible penalty?

The maximum penalty which could be imposed upon an applicant has been a key factor in determining whether proceedings are criminal or civil in the pre-HRA Strasbourg authority, and understandably so. If the applicant could lose his liberty, then the charge will almost certainly be classified as criminal within the meaning of Article 6, even if the initial sanction is a low level fine, and imprisonment could only follow the non-payment of that fine.[17]

Problem areas

Where the proceedings in question are at or near the extremities of criminal or civil proceedings, classification of proceedings for the purposes of Article 6 becomes more difficult. It is envisaged that companies and their officers can easily become involved in litigation in this middle ground of uncertainty. There is at present no definitive answer as to where the boundaries of the extremities lie but the following is intended to provide some useful indicators.

---

15   *Benham v United Kingdom* (1996) 22 EHRR 293.

16   See above where the offence was the alleged non-payment of the community charge which was found to be criminal within the meaning of Article 6. However the fact that the proceedings could only affect a part of the population is not finally conclusive, especially if the sanction could be loss of liberty. For example, prison disciplinary proceedings, which ex hypothesi can only affect those in prison have been classified as criminal by the Commission: see *Campbell and Fell v United Kingdom* (1984) 7 EHRR 165 (a case concerning the possible loss of remission).

17   For example see *Umlauft v Austria* (1995) 22 EHRR 76.

a) *Injunction proceedings*: if a company or director is a defendant in proceedings where a remedy sought and granted to the claimant on an interim basis is an injunction, and the court has the power to impose fines and sequestrate the assets of the injunction defendant, the proceedings are unlikely to be classified as criminal proceedings for the purposes of Article 6 for those reasons alone.[18]

b) *Forfeiture*: if a company is the subject of a statutory seizure order executed by a government body, the courts have not previously found that the proceedings concern the determination of criminal proceedings against the applicant.[19] In *Air Canada v United Kingdom*,[20] one of Air Canada's fleet was seized following the discovery of an unlawful consignment of drugs after previous warnings to the airline as to its preventative responsibilities. However, the European Commission declined to accede to Air Canada's submission that the proceedings were criminal and relied upon the fact that the UK government had not laid or threatened any criminal charges against Air Canada. The seizure was permitted under the Customs and Excise Act 1979, a power which Air Canada must have been aware of when deciding to trade within the UK's territory and jurisdiction.[1]

c) *Proceedings relating to the suspected or actual non-payment of taxes*: whether proceedings relating to the actual or suspected non-payment of taxes by a company or individual are to be classified as civil or criminal depends entirely on the nature of the proceedings brought. If non-payment is suspected, and the state interrogates the applicant, the proceedings by which the interrogation takes place have previously been held not to form part of a criminal process, even in circumstances where the applicant was obliged to answer the questions put to him and failure to do so could result in a custodial sentence.[2] It is clear that policy considerations have affected the Commission's interpretation of tax cases, and there has been a recognition by the Commission that the application of Article 6 to tax proceedings generally could act to prohibit the effective functioning of the state.[3] Where tax evasion is found and penalties have been imposed, the Strasbourg court has focused on the proportionality of the penalty imposed when determining whether the proceedings brought were classified as criminal or civil. If the court found that the penalty was proportionate the

18 *Krone-Verlag GmbH and Mediaprint Anzeigen GmbH and Co KG v Austria* (1997) 23 EHRR 152.

19 *AGOSI v United Kingdom* (1986) 9 EHRR 1 (a case concerning the seizure by Her Majesty's Customs and Excise of the applicant company's Kruggerands. The reasons for the court finding that the proceedings were not of a criminal nature were not provided by the High Court on this occasion).

20 *Air Canada v United Kingdom* (1995) 20 EHRR 150.

1 On forfeiture generally see Burke, Christopher '"…and shall be liable to forfeiture" – The Detention, Seizure and Condemnation of "Guilty" Goods Under the Customs and Excise Management Act 1979 Part 2' (1999) *Justice of the Peace* Vol 163, October pp 829-832.

2 *Abas v Netherlands* Appl 27943/95 [1997] EHRLR 418.

3 *Abas*, n 2 above; see also Smyth, Michael 'The United Kingdom's Incorporation of the European Convention and Its Implications for Business' (1998) *European Human Rights Law Review* Issue 3, pp 273- 291.

proceedings are likely to be civil. In *Smith v United Kingdom*[4] , the surcharge (Community Charge) was only 10% with no prospect of a custodial sentence the proceedings were found not to be criminal within the meaning of Article 6. However, in *Perin v France*[5] , where the penalties of 30% and 50% of the amounts due were imposed, the proceedings were considered to be criminal because of the severity of the punishment. Similarly, in *Bendenoun v France*[6] where the penalty surcharge amounted to half a million francs the court found the proceeding to be criminal in character.[7] In these cases, the sanctions against the defendant must be fairly low for the proceedings to be found to be civil.

The Financial Services and Markets Act 2000 (FSMA)

The FSMA has proved somewhat of a moving target with regard to the government's position on the human rights implications of the FSMA as it passed through Parliament.[8] In November 1998 an ad hoc Committee of both Houses of Parliament was formed to consider the Financial Services and Markets Bill (FSMB). The Joint Committee reported in April 1999 and again in June 1999.[9] On both occasions the Committee found that the FSMB contained provisions which raised serious human rights issues, in particular with regard to Article 6 (1) (fair trial) and Article 7 (certainty). The government made some amendments to the FSMB to take account of some of these concerns but there was still a major question surrounding the compatibility of the FSMB with the Convention rights. The government ignored these concerns and the Chancellor of the Exchequer issued a statement of compatibility for the FSMB even though it was doubtful whether certain provisions of the Act were compatible.[10]

The main issue of concern was the proposed FSMB disciplinary proceedings which included the civil offence of 'market abuse'.[11] The proceedings were designed originally to work as follows. The Financial Services Authority (FSA) would issue a 'warning notice' to the individual who was the subject of the disciplinary proceedings proposing a penalty or public censure. The individual could then make representations to the FSA. The FSA then would decide whether or not to carry out

4   *Smith v United Kingdom* (1996) 21 EHRR 74.
5   *Penin v France* Appl 18656/91 1992.
6   *Bendenoun v France* (1994) 18 EHRR 54.
7   On the favourable treatment of tax issues see Reid, Karen, *A Practitioner's Guide to the European Convention on Human Rights* (1998) Sweet and Maxwell, pp 372-375.
8   See the Treasury website for the numerous consultation papers. www.hm-treasury.gov.uk
9   Standing Order number 137. The committee was also able to consider the Treasury's Progress Report published in March 1999. The Joint Committee published its first report on 29 April 1999 (Draft Financial Services and Markets Bill: First Report; House of Lords, 50 I – II; House of Commons, HC328 I – II) and its second report on 2 June 1999 (Draft Financial Services and Markets Bill: Second Report; House of Lords, 66; House of Commons, HC465). The Government response to the reports of the Joint Committee on Financial Services and Markets was published in June 1999.
10   See his statement on the front of the Bill printed on 17 June 1999. See also George Graham 'Banking Editorial' *Financial Times*, 18 June 1999.
11   See Part VIII of the FSMA.

the sanction it had proposed. If the FSA saw fit it would publish information about the proceedings and in any case would inform the individual of its decision. The individual could then appeal to the Appeal Tribunal which was independent of the FSA. The main objections to this procedure on Convention grounds was the lack of certainty as to whether the proceedings were civil or criminal in nature.[12] The offence of market abuse was extremely wide and did not provide that intention was needed or a defence that the individual had made reasonable efforts to comply with established practice. As such it was in danger of breaching Article 7 (certainty) and Article 6 (fair trial).

The government eventually capitulated and agreed a number of amendments to address these human rights concerns. The word 'appeal' was removed from the Tribunal name and it was made an independent first instance tribunal with power to re-hear the proceedings. Additionally Part IV of the FSMA provides a right to appeal against a decision of the tribunal on a point of law. The government also conceded an 'Enforcement Committee' under the auspices of the FSA made up of practitioner and public members. The committee would start proceedings with a fully reasoned decision to issue a 'warning notice' provided to the person at issue.[13] The individual would then either settle the matter or put forward a response. The individual would have 28 days to choose to go before the tribunal after which time if the individual had not taken this option the penalty would take effect.[14] In order to create more certainty about market abuse Part VIII of the FSMA sets out the kinds of behaviour which constitutes market abuse and requires the FSA to produce a code aimed at assisting individuals to determine whether particular behaviour amounts to market abuse. Evidence obtained under compulsion may not be used by the FSA in regard to market abuse and some legal aid will be available.[15] The Financial Services and Markets Act 2000 received its Royal Assent on the 14 June 2000

Does Article 6 make it easier to sue the auditor?

The Companies Act 1985, section 384 requires all companies, unless they are dormant or small companies (and thus exempt from audit), to appoint an auditor. If no appointment is made the DTI must be informed within one week and it may if it wishes appoint an auditor.[16] The statutory audit regime imposes both statutory

12 On Offences see Part XXVII of the FSMA which creates certain offences, including making misleading statements and supplying false information to the Authority. It also makes general provision about offences under the Act and contains provision about the institution of proceedings, for example under Part V of the Criminal Justice Act 1993 (insider dealing) and in relation to money laundering.
13 See Part XXVI of the FSMA on Notices.
14 On penalties see Part XIV of the FSMA.
15 Part XI of the FSMA sets out the powers of the Authority and of the Secretary of State to require the production of information and documents, to require reports to be prepared, to conduct investigations and to gain access to premises with a warrant. For the various consultation papers the FSA has proposed on its operation see www.fsa.gov.uk
16 Section 387.

duties on the auditor and confers certain rights. Section 237 of the Companies Act 1985 imposes certain statutory duties with regard to the preparation and content of the audit report. Sections 389A and 390 confer on the auditor certain rights to information and to attend meetings of the company respectively. In the carrying out of their statutory function an auditor has a certain degree of protected legal status with regard to negligent misstatements contained in an audit report.[17] For the purposes of the HRA the auditor in the course of his statutory function may fulfil the criteria necessary to be considered a 'public authority' under section 6 of the HRA.[18] As such the auditor in the carrying out of his function is required to act compatibly with the Convention rights. Should an act or omission of the auditor interfere with a Convention right, this will give rise to a claim under the HRA by a victim alleging that the auditor acted unlawfully in interfering with their Convention rights.[19] The company could certainly fulfil 'victim' status with regard to the auditor's act or omission, and potentially the shareholders (if the company was in liquidation or receivership)[20] could bring an action against the auditor alleging an unlawful act under section 6 of the HRA in violating Protocol 1, Article 1 (property). For example if the auditor failed to notice that the company was insolvent and allowed the directors to declare a dividend,[1] the company could claim that the auditor had acted unlawfully by violated the company's Protocol 1, Article 1 rights and seek damages under the HRA. How this will operate in practice is somewhat of a mystery. Rights are not really designed for litigation that is essentially about a wrong. A careless act should attribute liability to a public authority under the HRA just as any other type of act. It does however raise interesting issues. As we consider in Chapter 10, in the context of environmental actions under Section 6,[2] the question arises as to whether the action amounts to no-fault liability or would there have to be a process of establishing fault on the part of the public authority? Even where you could show fault could the public authority defend the action with reference to discretion, legitimate aim and proportionality? The applicability of those interpretative tools seems odd where a careless act is at issue. Where is the legitimate aim or the proportionality? In terms, let us say, of the Article 8 (privacy) case law on environmental hazards[3] it is possible to see a careless act leading to an interference with Article 8 being at least arguably justifiable as pursuing a legitimate aim (BNFL producing electricity for the public grid) and that the act was proportionate (the escaping radioactivity had to be released in order to stop a larger explosion). However with a careless act of an auditor a justification is more difficult to find. The legitimate aim might be the necessity of the audit in maintaining standards for the shareholders. Unfortunately the careless act itself may not have upheld those standards. Proportionality however is beyond us.

---

17   See *Caparo Industries plc v Dickman* [1990] 2 AC 605 below.
18   See Chapter 7 for the considerations in determining a public authority.
19   See Chapter 6 on section 6.
20   With regard to Protocol 1, Article 1 the shareholders have difficulty fulfilling victim status. See Chapter 8.
1   See *Sasea Finance Ltd (In Liquidation) v KPMG (formerly KPMG Peat Marwick McLintock) (No 2)* [1999] BCC 857.
2   See Chapter 10.
3   See Chapter 10.

Whatever the solution in terms of a section 6 action regarding a careless act it will probably not displace negligence as the main form of action. This is because the damages payable for a section 6 unlawful act are a) not compulsory and b) likely to be low. Section 8 of the HRA does not compel the court to award a remedy and so a public authority breach of a Convention right might not lead the court to award damages. There are essentially two reasons why awards of damages for section 6 unlawful acts are likely to be low. First, the courts have as we explained in Chapter 6 an obligation to look at the Strasbourg court's[4] principles on compensation. The Strasbourg court has historically been conservative in its awards. Second if the fault criteria is no-fault or a lesser degree of fault than negligence then the amounts payable in damages will correspondingly be lower. For example the damages for successful deceit actions are higher than those available for negligence because of the degree of fault attributable to the wrongdoer.[5]

A further impact of the HRA on the statutory audit is that the Auditing Practices Board (APB) will also be a 'public authority' for the purposes of the HRA. In which case it has an obligation to respect the Convention rights in the carrying out of its function. As a result the accounting standards produced by the APB must be compatible with the Convention rights. In the course of fulfilling its obligation to respect the Convention rights of those affected by audit standards it will have to review continuously those standards in the light of changing circumstance.

Negligent misstatement in the audit and the HRA

The auditor in the carrying out of his statutory duty has in the past had a privileged position with regard to negligent misstatement. The established authority for this is contained in *Caparo Industries plc v Dickman*[6] where the House of Lords found that the category of individuals who could claim to be proximate to the auditor for the purposes of negligent misstatement was extremely limited. Specifically, the House of Lords found that a relationship of proximity did not exist between the auditor and everybody entitled to copies of the audited accounts. The company itself had such a relationship of proximity as did the existing shareholders and possibly debenture holders; everyone else was insufficiently proximate. However the existing shareholders were only owed a duty with regard their ability to exercise informed control over their shares and this duty did not extend to the purchase of further shares in reliance on the audited accounts. The HRA will have a particular effect on this position established in *Caparo*.

In *Osman v United Kingdom*[7] the ECtHR applicants claimed that their rights under Article 6 of the ECHR had been breached. They had attempted to bring proceedings in the UK against the police alleging negligence in the prevention and pursuit of crime. Those proceedings were struck out by the Court of Appeal[8] applying the

4   Section 8 (4) HRA 1998.
5   See the judgment of Lord Steyn in *Smith New Court Securities Ltd v Scrimgeour Vickers (Asset Manegement) Ltd* (1996) 4 All ER 769 at 790 .
6   [1990] 2 AC 605.
7   (1998) 5 BHRC 293.
8   *Osman v Ferguson* [1993] 4 All ER 344.

Does Art 6 make it easier to sue auditor

decision of the House of Lords in *Hill v Chief Constable of West Yorkshire*[9] Considering the applicants' experience in the domestic courts the ECtHR stated:

> the court considers that the applicants must be taken to have had a right, derived from the law of negligence, to seek an adjudication on the admissibility and merits of an arguable claim that they were in a relationship of proximity to the police, that the harm caused was foreseeable and that in the circumstances it was fair, just and reasonable not to apply the exclusionary rule outlined in *Hill v Chief Constable of West Yorkshire*. In the view of the court the assertion of that right by the applicants is in itself sufficient to ensure the applicability of art 6(1) of the convention.
>
> 140. For the above reasons, the court concludes that art 6(1) is applicable. It remains to be determined whether the restriction which was imposed on the exercise of the applicants' right under that provision was lawful.[10]

Having set out the scope of Article 6, the Strasbourg court held that there was in the applicant's case a breach of a right of access to the English court. The breach lay in the application of a blanket exclusionary rule covering litigation against the police force which excluded all claims against the police for negligent failure to investigate or protect from crime. As a result of this, the Strasbourg court held that the English court was in breach of Article 6 by striking out the applicants' claim without hearing any evidence by reference to which the proportionality of the rule in that particular case could be judged. The granting of a 'blanket immunity' was a disproportionate and therefore an unjustifiable restriction on the applicants' right of access to the court.[11] If the domestic courts wished to apply such an exclusionary rule it would involve the court deciding its application afresh in each individual case. If the court did not do this each time it could not determine whether the public interest in an efficient police force is or is not proportionate to the seriousness of the harm suffered by the plaintiff in the individual case.[12]

While the case in general terms has enormous implications for the operation of binding precedent in the UK[13] it has a particular impact on the restrictive view of proximity taken by the House of Lords in *Caparo Industries plc v Dickman*.[14] Shareholders who have suffered loss as a result of a negligent act of an auditor will under the HRA be able to argue in the course of a negligent misstatement action that the court has an obligation under section 6 (3) (a) of the HRA to act compatibly with Article 6. The court can only fulfil its obligation in a negligent misstatement case involving the auditor if it considers afresh each time the proportionality of the decision to exclude shareholders and others from being owed a duty of care. This would involve re-examining why shareholders are only owed a duty with regard

---

9   [1989] AC 53, [1988] 2 All ER 238.

10   5 BHRC 293 at 327 paras 139 and 140.

11   Note 10 above, paras 151 and 152.

12   Note 10 above, para 150.

13   The *Osman* case is a very odd case in that it would appear that counsel for the UK incorrectly stated the law on the police immunity from prosecution in negligence to the ECtHR. The matter may be resolved when a similar application reaches the court in the near future.

14   [1990] 2 AC 605.

to informed control as it operates as a significant bar to an effective remedy for loss. Policy weighs heavy in the *Caparo* decision as the court recognised the need to protect the auditor in the carrying out of his statutory function. If the courts wish to maintain that protection the HRA will make little difference to their ability to do so. It will however require the courts to explain the proportionality of their decision to a much greater extent than they do at present. As a result the courts will have to explore the reasons for protective policy decisions to a much greater extent than they do at present.

Does Article 6 affect the ability to lift the corporate veil?

Up to this point we have looked at the impact of the principle in *Salomon v Salomon & Co*[15] from the viewpoint of 'victim' status. We turn now to consider the impact of the HRA generally on the common law principle in *Salomon*. In the UK it is clearly established that a company is a legal person in its own right with a separate existence from its members. A registered company obtains its own separate personality on incorporation by complying with the formal requirements of the Companies Acts. It is one of the most fundamental characteristics of a company that it is an entity separate from its members.[16] In particular the domestic Courts have over the past decade demonstrated an extreme reluctance to interfere with the *Salomon* principle and look behind the separate personality of the company to the members. This often has the affect of defeating claims against a parent company for the actions of its subsidiaries.

The principle in Salomon has had a number of distinctive periods of interpretation. From the late 19th century until the 1960s the veil of incorporation was a fairly solid one which was not easily displaced.[17] Positivism generally formed the framework within which the judiciary operate.[18]

In the 1960s things began to change. The war had had a significant effect on the judiciary which was beginning to filter through to the senior Law Lords. Rights and ideas of justice were becoming increasingly important in the decision making process of the judiciary to the detriment of certainty.[19] As Allen commented at the time:

---

15   [1897] AC 22.
16   *Macaura v Northern Assurance Co Ltd* [1925] AC 619.
17   It should be noted that it was not until the 1966 practice direction that the House of Lords could overrule its own judgments. Thus any judicial intervention in the *Salomon* principle had to be indirect.
18   For an in-depth examination of when the veil of incorporation will be 'lifted', 'peeped behind', 'penetrated', 'extended' or 'ignored', see Ottolenghi, S, 'From Peeping Behind the Corporate Veil to Ignoring it Completely' (1990) *Modern Law Review*, Vol 53, No 3, pp 338-396.
19   Patterson's work reveals in his chapter on 'Who Influences Law Lords?' that the Law Lords paid little attention to academics and were really only influenced by their experiences as barristers and by their fellow Law Lords. Patterson, A, *The Law Lords* (1982) Macmillan, Chapter 2. Both the changing academic and judicial views at this time may be reflective of the shared experiences of the nation during the war years and the shock of the atrocities committed by the Nazis which were perfectly legal within a utilitarian/positivist framework.

[t]here seems to be less reluctance than formerly in superior courts either to overrule previous, and sometimes old, precedence, or else to sterilise them by the semi-fictions of 'distinguishing' them on tenuous grounds of fact or law by recourse to the doctrine of incuria. With the help of a certain degree of 'judicial valour', new opportunities seem to be opening up of escaping from the bondage which carries 'consistency' or 'loyalty' to unprofitable extremes ...[20]

The principle in *Salomon* was one such certainty which was affected by this trend. In *Littlewoods Stores v IRC* [1969] 1 WLR 1241 Lord Denning stated:

[t]he doctrine laid down in Salomon's case has to be watched very carefully. It has often been supposed to cast a veil over the personality of a limited company through which the courts cannot see. But that is not true. The courts can, and often do, pull off the mask. They look to see what really lies behind. The legislature has shown the way with group accounts and the rest. And the courts should follow suit.[1]

He continued to develop his interventionist approach in *DHN Ltd v Tower Hamlets* [1976] 1 WLR 852 at 860 where he stated:

[t]his group is virtually the same as a partnership in which all three companies are partners. They should not be treated separately so as to be defeated on a technical point. They should not be deprived of the compensation which should justly be payable for disturbance. The three companies should, for present purposes, be treated as one, and the parent company D.H.N. should be treated as that one.

The influence of these cases continued right into the 1980's and can be seen in *Re a Company* (1985) 1 BCC 99.421, CA where the Court of Appeal stated at 99.425:

[i]n our view the cases before and after *Wallersteiner v Moir* [1974] 1 WLR 991 [another Lord Denning case] show that the court will use its power to pierce the corporate veil if it is necessary to achieve justice irrespective of the legal efficacy of the corporate structure under consideration.

The cases which pierce the veil represent a different view of the corporate model where the balance of rights before the court are weighed and a decision given on the justice of the case. The corporate veil will be lifted in the sectional interests of those whom the judiciary perceive to be disadvantaged by the pre-existing corporate model, usually creditors, minority shareholders and employees. These cases look at the motives of those behind the corporate veil and decide on the merits of what they find there if the separation of personalities is to be maintained. The presumptions

---

20   Allen, C K, *Law in the Making* (1964) Clarendon p 357.
1   In the 1960s at least, Lord Denning had some like minded colleagues but in the early 1950s his approach caused some disquiet. Lord Simmons in *Magor and St Mellons RDC v Newport Corpn* [1952] AC 189 at 191 famously described it as 'a naked usurpation of the legislative function under the thin guise of interpretation'.

of Parliament that investment will be encouraged and the directors' freedom to take risks enhanced through limited liability are subsumed into a sometimes ad hoc application of public policy perspectives.

These interventionist cases had a significant impact on the development of the *Salomon* principle over this period, drawing criticism from a number of commentators.[2] As Lowry concluded when examining the judicial practice of lifting the veil:

> [t]he problem that can naturally arise from this approach is the uncertainty which it casts over the safety of incorporation. The use of the policy to erode established legal principle is not necessarily to be welcomed.[3]

The difficulty with lifting the veil in such an organised fashion was that the judiciary were electing to replace the *Salomon* model with its focus on the sanctity of the corporate body, with another model, that of a series of individual arrangements variable at the dictate of judicial intervention.

The 1990s, however, saw the rise into the higher courts of a large number of commercial and chancery judges bathed in the private law norms of those courts. Of the 15 Law Lords presently sitting in the House 11 are from a commercial/chancery background. The other four include the Scottish and Irish Lords (Lords Hope, Clyde and Hutton) and the Master of the Rolls, Lord Woolf, who normally sits in the Court of Appeal. In the Court of Appeal where 13 of the 35 judges are from a commercial/chancery background the panels are generally chosen according to their expertise. A commercial/corporate case would usually have at least two judges from the three presiding from that specialist background.[4]

Foremost amongst those private law norms is the concept of certainty being favoured over justice. As the great commercial judge Lord Mansfield stated in *Vallejo v Wheeler* (1774) 1 Cowp 143 at 153:

> [i]n all mercantile transactions the great object should be certainty: and therefore, it is of more consequence that a rule be certain, than whether the rule be established one way or the other. Because speculators in trade then know what ground to go upon.[5]

The progress of *Salomon* over the 1990s illustrates the ascendancy of certainty and the retreat of interests of justice decisions.

2   See Gallagher, L and Ziegler, P 'Lifting the Corporate Veil in the Pursuit of Justice' (1990) *Journal of Business Law*, July, pp 292-313 for an examination of when the courts will at common law lift the veil of incorporation. They conclude that the lifting of the veil impacts on other aspects of the law such as the directors' duty to the company as a whole, individual taxation principles, and the rule in *Foss v Harbottle* (1843) 2 Hare 461.

3   Lowry, John P, 'Lifting the Corporate Veil' (1993) *Journal of Business Law*, January, pp 41-42.

4   Source Lord Chancellors Department.

5   See the judgment of Lord Salmon in *Mardorf Peach and Co Ltd v Attica Sea Carriers Corpn of Liberia, The Laconia* [1977] AC 850 at 878 for his views as to the immense importance of certainty in commerce. See also Lord Goff on the importance of certainty in Goff, R, 'Commercial Contracts and the Commercial Courts' (1984) *Lloyds Mercantile and Commercial Law Quarterly* 382.

The Court of Appeal in *Adams v Cape Industries plc*[6] considered the concept of lifting the veil in great detail and produced a judgment which considerably reduced the courts ability to pierce the veil. This view of incorporation continued in *Ord v Belhaven Pubs Ltd*[7] where the Court of Appeal confirmed that as far as the common law was concerned the veil of incorporation was a rigid construct which was not easily demolished. The Court of Appeal considered that they had no role in interpreting the justice of the case save the application of the Act. They singled out Lord Denning's highly interventionist judgment in *DHN Food Distributers v Tower Hamlets London Borough Council*[8] for criticism, narrowed the application of *Wallersteiner v Moir*[9] specifically overruled *Creasy v Breachwood Motors*[10] (a highly interventionist High Court judgment) and affirmed the view of the court in *Adams v Cape Industries* that the exceptions to the rule in *Salomon* were few and far between.[11] A month later in *Williams v Natural Life Health Foods Ltd*[12] the House of Lords emphasised the *Salomon* principle in the context of the tortious liability of corporate actors. Lord Steyn at 835 stated:

> [w]hat matters is not that the liability of the shareholders of a company is limited but that a company is a separate entity, distinct from its directors, servants or other agents. The trader who incorporates a company to which he transfers his business creates a legal person on whose behalf he may afterwards act as director. For present purposes, his position is the same as if he had sold his business to another individual and agreed to act on his behalf. Thus the issue in this case is not peculiar to companies. Whether the principal is a company or a natural person, someone acting on his behalf may incur personal liability in tort as well as imposing vicarious or attributed liability upon his principal. But in order to establish personal liability under the principle of *Hedley Byrne,* which requires the existence of a special relationship between plaintiff and tortfeasor, it is not sufficient that there should have been a special relationship with the principal. There must have been an assumption of responsibility such as to create a special relationship with the director or employee himself.

Despite the occasional lapse from this position of inelasticity regarding the veil of incorporation, the 1990s can be characterised by a return to a more certain approach to the *Salomon* principle.[13]

---

6   [1990] Ch 433.
7   [1998] BCC 607.
8   [1976] 1 WLR 852.
9   [1974] 1 WLR 991.
10 [1992] BCC 638.
11 See *also Yukong Line Ltd of Korea v Rendsburg Investments Corpn of Liberia (The Rialto) (No 2)* [1998] 4 All ER 82, [1998] 1 WLR 294, [1998] 1 Lloyd's Rep 322.
12 [1998] 1 WLR 830.
13 Given the stated opinion of both the Court of Appeal and the House of Lords on this matter the decision of the House of Lords in *Connelly v RTZ Corp Plc* [1998] AC 854 where the veil of incorporation is swept aside solely in the interests of justice is a curious one. See also Deakin, S, 'Lifting the Veil – Illustrations from Labour Law' (1995) *Cambridge Law Journal* 512 for indications of a softer approach to the Salomon principle in labour law.

In terms of the judicial view of the corporation the principles annunciated in *Salomon* are significant. By subscribing to the corporation each individual shareholder subsumes his or her rights into the corporation and gains limited liability – they become members. As Ireland described it:

> [f]ollowing the 1862 Companies Act, people no longer 'formed themselves' into incorporated companies, they 'formed' incorporated companies, objects external to themselves, made *by* them but not *of* them. In short the company was reified ... This conceptual change was accompanied by a decline in the right of shareholders to intervene in the day-to-day running of companies and by the steady shift of power from general meeting to board. As their 'ownership' rights were steadily eroded, shareholders 'surrendered a set of definite rights for a set of indefinite expectations'.[14]

The ensuing history of the judicial interpretation of the power relationship between shareholders and the corporate personality resonates this distinction between the corporate interest and the individual rights of shareholders. The courts have recognised that the Companies Acts allow the creation of a separate legal entity because of the wider public interest in such an arrangement, ie encourage investment, allow directors greater freedom to take risks and to discourage fraud. By recognising the existence of a corporate personality with interests separate from the shareholders the courts have sacrificed the private rights of shareholders and outsiders, such as creditors, on the basis of the greater good served by affirming the corporate personality.[15]

The HRA causes some difficulty for the strict application of the *Salomon* principle. In considering whether to lift the veil of incorporation the court will have to act compatibly with the Convention rights. In refusing to lift the veil the court could violate Article 1 of Protocol 1 (property), Article 13 (right to an effective remedy) and, most significantly, Article 6 (fair trial). For example, if *Ord v Belhaven Pubs Ltd*[16] were to be decided utilising the HRA a number of additional arguments could be raised in favour of lifting the veil of incorporation. Belhaven had appealed against the granting of leave to substitute an associated company of Belhaven as defendant in a contractual dispute brought by Ord against Belhaven. The reason for the substitution was that Belhaven no longer had sufficient assets to meet the damages payable should Ord win the contractual dispute. The court allowed the appeal and found that the substitution as defendant of either a company in the same ownership as, or a company which was a shareholder in, the defendant company, did not fall within the scope of RSC Ord15 r 7(2). The court reasoned that it would be an incorrect application of the principle of piercing the corporate

---

14 Ireland, P 'Company Law and the Myth of Shareholders Ownership' (1999) 62 *MLR* 42-43. See also Ireland, P 'The Rise of the Limited Liability Company' (1984) 12 *International Journal of the Sociology of Law* p 239.

15 The same logic can be seen in the origin of the concept of ultra vires, where the upholding of the shareholders' contract with the company takes precedence over the outsiders' contract with the company. See in particular the judgments of Willes and Blackburn JJ, in *Taylor v Chichester and Midhurst Rly* (1867) LR 2 Ex 356.

16 [1998] BCC 607.

veil to allow such a substitution and an inappropriate use of the discretionary power granted to the court by RSC Ord15 r 7(2).

The additional arguments that could be raised under the HRA by Ord for the court exercising its discretion under RSC Ord 15 r 7 (2) in substituting a parent company are as follows. First the court has a duty under section 6 of the HRA to act compatibly with the Convention rights which would include the exercise of its discretion compatibly with the Convention rights and freedoms. Second should the court refuse to exercise its discretion in favour of the substitution it could arguably amount to a violation of:

a)   Ord's property rights contained in Article 1 of Protocol 1, as the ECtHR has found that property for the purposes of Article 1 of Protocol 1 includes contractual rights including rights in leases,[17] judgment debts[18] and unestablished legal claims[19];

b)   Article 6 (right to a fair trial) which includes real and effective access to a fair and public hearing. This right creates a significant obligation of the court where the effect of the exercise or negative exercise of the court's discretion would deny an individual effective access to the courts. In 1996, when the Convention rights were not part of domestic law, Sir Thomas Bingham MR considered that Article 6 (1) of the ECHR should be kept 'in mind when the court is invited to make an order which would have the practical effect of preventing a plaintiff pursuing his rights anywhere.'[20] He then went on to lift the veil of incorporation in that particular case. In *Osman v United Kingdom*[1] the ECtHR found that the application of a blanket immunity from prosecution for the police force breached the applicant's Article 6 right to effective access to the courts. The restrictive application of the *Salomon* case could similarly amount to such an immunity for parent companies;[2] and

c)   Article 13 (the right to an effective remedy) which although not part of the Convention rights included in the HRA has an impact through the court's obligation to consider relevant Strasbourg case law. In the *Aksoy* case[3] the Strasbourg court found that the extent to which the effective remedy requirement impacts depends on the effect of the violation. The more serious the effect of the breach the stricter the effectiveness requirement. The court should, in deciding whether to exercise its discretion, consider whether not exercising its discretion has the effect of denying individual the ability to pursue his rights which in turn denies him an effective remedy.

---

17   *A, B and Co AS v Germany* (1978) 14 DR 146; *Mellacher v Austria*, Series A, No 169; (1990) 12 EHRR 391.

18   *Stran Greek Refineries and Stratis Andreadis v Greece* (1994) 19 EHRR 293.

19   *Pressos Compania Naviera SA v Belgium*, Series A, No 332; (1995) 21 EHRR 301.

20   *Edward Connelly v RTZ Corpn plc* [1997] IL Pr 643 at 651.

1   (1998) 5 BHRC 293.

2   Lord Bingham in *Schalk Willem Burger Lubbe v Cape plc* judgment of the House of Lords [2000] 1 WLR 1545 allowed employees of a South African subsidiary standing in the UK to sue a parent company based in the UK. Although not determinative Lord Bingham used Article 6 to support his finding.

3   (1996) 23 EHRR 553: see the discussion in Chapter 4.

Even where the court refuses to exercise its discretion it will have to address the Convention points raised. It is always feasible that the court might not accept that there is a Convention point at issue but, should it accept that its action could violate a Convention right, it will have to set out what the legitimate aim is it is pursuing and explore the proportionality of its action. As such the courts are going to have to provide more explanation of policy-based decisions in order to justify interference with Convention rights. In all, the introduction of Convention arguments into *Salomon* cases should give new life to the interests of justice case law on veil lifting prevalent in 60s, 70s and early 80s. The restrictive approach evident in *Adams v Cape Industries* is likely to come under strain as the courts are confronted with rights-based arguments as to why the veil should be lifted. Indeed, in cases such as *Connelly v RTZ Corpn plc*[4] and *Schalk Willem Burger Lubbe v Cape plc*[5] rights-based arguments are already having an influence.

4   See n 3 above.
5   See n 3 above.

Chapter ten

Corporations and Article 8: private life

The public have an insatiable curiosity to know everything, except what is worth knowing.[1]

Rights of privacy as they apply to the corporation

Article 8 – Right to private and family life

1) Everyone has the right to respect for his private and family life, his home and his correspondence.

2) There shall be no interference by a public authority with the exercise of this right except such as is in accordance with the law and is necessary in a democratic society in the interests of national security, public safety or the economic well-being of the country, for the prevention of disorder or crime, for the protection of health or morals, or for the protection of the rights and freedoms of others.

1   Oscar Wilde (1891) *The Soul of a Man Under Socialism.*

Privacy generally

Article 8 protects the right to respect for private and family life, the home and correspondence. As all of the protected parts of this right have been interpreted expansively it is almost impossible to distinguish them clearly and to avoid overlaps but, according to the Strasbourg case law, a clear delimitation is not necessary. The Article can therefore be summarised as a right to private life in the sense of a full enjoyment of liberty rather than the narrower sense of privacy as a right to secrecy or to be left alone. As a result of this expansive definition the Strasbourg court has been able to develop the coverage of Article 8 to keep up with social and technological movements. This also makes the development of the case law difficult to predict. The case law on Article 8 covers a huge range of issues, such as sexual privacy,[2] registration,[3] medical examination,[4] wiretapping,[5] the principle of allowing families to be united,[6] the search of one's home[7] and the opening and censoring of letters.[8]

The wording of paragraph 2 is clearly negative in formulation 'no interference by a public authority with the exercise of this right'. There should therefore be no arbitrary interference with Article 8 private life by the state. For example in *Malone v United Kingdom*[9] : an antique dealer had been under police surveillance for several years, this included wire tapping, interceptions and recording of conversations on his telephone. He was eventually arrested and charged with the trafficking of stolen goods. However, the conviction failed and he was acquitted. Following his trial he instigated proceedings against the Metropolitan Police before the national courts, claiming that the surveillance methods had violated his rights, even if done pursuant to a warrant of the Home Secretary. He claimed not to have an effective remedy and that he therefore had to rely on Article 8 of the ECHR. The Vice-Chancellor, Sir Robert Megarry, dismissed the applicant's claim for the reason that the Convention did not confer any direct rights into English law. As a treaty it was in his words not 'justiciable' in the domestic court. The Strasbourg court gave extensive consideration to whether the interference with the applicant's rights were justifiable under paragraph 2 of Article 8 of the Convention. It held that the phrase 'in accordance with the law' relates to the quality of the law, required to be compatible with the rule of law[10] and eventually observed that 'it cannot be said with any reasonable certainty what elements of the powers to intercept are incorporated in legal rules and what elements remain within the discretion of the

---

2   *Dudgeon v United Kingdom* (1981) 4 EHRR 149 concerning homosexuality.
3   *Leander v Sweden* (1987) 9 EHRR 433 concerning secret police registers.
4   *Herczegfalvy v Austria* (1992) 15 EHRR 437 concerning compulsory administering of food in a hospital.
5   *Klass v Germany* (1978) 2 EHRR 214, concerning German legislation authorising wiretapping.
6   *Abdulaziz, Cabales and Balkandali v United Kingdom* (1985) 7 EHRR 471, concerning the denial of permission of spouses living abroad to join their family in the UK.
7   *Niemietz v Germany* (1992) 16 EHRR 97 concerning the search of a lawyer's office.
8   *Golder v United Kingdom* (1975) 1 EHRR 524 concerning censorship of prisoner's correspondence with his lawyer.
9   (1984) 7 EHRR 14.
10   *A-82* § 67.

executive [in England and Wales] … To that extent, the minimum degree of legal protection to which citizens are entitled under the rule of law in a democratic society is lacking.'[11] The Court found that there had been a breach of Article 8.

The wording 'to respect for' in Article 8 creates an additional obligation on the national authorities as they are not only under a duty to refrain from acts that might constitute a violation of Article 8 but also have a positive obligation to secure such 'respect'. An example of the positive element of the rights protected in Article 8 is the case *X and Y v Netherlands*[12] : here the applicants did not claim that the national authorities had violated their right to private and family life but that they had failed to protect their rights from being interfered with by other individuals. Y, a 16-year-old, mentally handicapped girl had been sexually abused while residing in a special institution for mentally ill children. Due to a loophole in the Dutch law, it was impossible to institute criminal proceedings against the perpetrator, as Y did not fall within any of the categories of persons protected by law.[13] The Court considered that the contracting parties have a positive obligation to provide criminal legislation which aims to ensure that private individuals respect the private life of others. As the Netherlands had failed to do so, the Court found a breach of Article 8.

Much of the case law on Article 8 is extremely complex in terms of its context and contains overlaps with other Articles. For example an act by the state aimed at the family, for instance deporting the parents of children lawfully domiciled in the UK, could violate a range of ECHR rights such as Article 8 (privacy), Article 11 (freedom of thought, conscience and religion), Article 6 (fair trial) as 'civil rights' could be affected by the same act and Article 14 (discrimination). Similarly a state act aimed at the home, for example a compulsory purchase order, could affect Article 8 and also Protocol 1, Article 1 (property). This further tends to make it extremely difficult to predict the development of the case law.

Private life

The Strasbourg court has developed the concept of private life expansively. It contains the concept of an 'inner circle' within which individuals can live their private lives as they choose free from state interference excluding the outside world.[14] A state act interfering with this 'inner world', classically the monitoring of communications, runs the risk of violating Article 8.[15] The concept of private life is not confined to the 'inner circle', the court has expanded the concept to include the right to establish and develop relationships with other human beings.[16] As such it includes the rights of prisoners to associate with one another,[17] the development

11   *A- 82* § 79.
12   (1985) 8 EHRR 235.
13   The law at that time only covered offences against minors under the age of sixteen and 'helpless' people, whereby helpless only referred to physical incapacity not mental.
14   *Niemietz v Germany* (1992) 16 EHRR 97.
15   Eg *Klass v Germany* (1978) 2 EHRR 214, concerning German legislation authorising wiretapping.
16   Note 14 above (*Niemitz*).
17   *Mc Feeley v United Kingdom* (1980) 20 DR 44.

of relationships in a business environment[18] and sexual relationships.[19] It also includes the concept of physical integrity in that an act of the state interfering with the physical integrity of an individual will interfere with their private life. Obvious categories here include medical treatment and corporal punishment but the more important and developing category where the state interferes with physical integrity concerns environmental impacts on physical integrity. This is where the state has responsibility for the physical effect of pollution on the person's physical integrity and thus his private life.[20] The environmental case law is examined below.

Family life

The notion of family life as interpreted by the ECtHR is not a static one and has moved in step with general developments in the Council of Europe states. As such it is not necessarily defined by formal legal or blood relationships but rather the 'question on the existence or non-existence of "family life" is essentially a question of fact depending upon the real existence in practice of close personal ties …'[1] As such relationships between parents/children (legitimate, illegitimate, adoptive),[2] grandparents/grandchildren (legitimate, illegitimate, adoptive),[3] married/unmarried hetrosexual[4] couples have all been relationships which the court has deemed could fall within the definition of family life.

Home

The concept of home for the purposes of Article 8 covers generally the place where a person lives on a continuous basis. The rights protected by the concept are generally the right to occupation of the home and to the enjoyment of that home free from interference.[5] In *Buckley v United Kingdom*[6] the court considered that a 'home' was a continuous residence with no intention to establish a home in any other place. Consistent with this the court found in *Barclay v United Kingdom*[7] that 'the mere ownership of property is not sufficient to render it a "home" for the purposes of Article 8'.

The concept of home can extend to re-establishing a home life. In *Gillow v United Kingdom*[8] a couple complained that the refusal of the UK to grant a residence permit to return to their house in Guernsey after they had been absent for 18 years amounted to a violation of Article 8. The husband's job had meant that they

---

18 *Niemietz v Germany* (1992) 16 EHRR 97.
19 *Dudgeon v United Kingdom* (1981) 4 EHRR 149.
20 *Lopez Ostra v Spain* (1994) 20 EHRR 277.
1 *K v United Kingdom* (1986) 50 DR 199 at 207.
2 See *Marckx v Belgium* (1979) 2 EHRR 330 on illegitimate children and *X v France* (1982) 31 DR 241.
3 *Marckx*, n 2 above.
4 On unmarried co-habiting couples see *X v Switzerland* (1978) 13 DR 248. Homosexual relationships are not covered by family life although they may come within the concept of private life. See *S v United Kingdom* (1986) 47 DR 274.
5 As such noise pollution will interfere with the enjoyment of a home. See *Arrondelle v United Kingdom* (1982) 26 DR 5.
6 (1996) 23 EHRR 101.
7 Application No 00035712/97, Judgment date 18 May 1999.
8 (1986) 11 EHRR 335.

had to travel but they had always intended to return to Guernsey. The court found that the couple had a right protected by Article 8 to re-establish a home and that the UK had violated it by refusing them a residence permit. The concept of 'home' for the purposes of Article 8 can also merge into private life and therefore encompass certain places of work. In *Niemietz v Germany*[9] the applicant complained that his Article 8 rights had been violated by a police search of his office. The ECtHR found that there had been a violation of Article 8 because the private life of an individual is not confined to the home and could extend to the office space in which an individual worked. Importantly the wording of the French text of the Convention uses the word 'domicile' which has a wider connotation than the word 'home' and can extend to a professional's office.[10]

Correspondence

The right to respect for a persons correspondence covers generally the ability to conduct uninterrupted and uncensored communication with other persons. It covers a wide range of means of communication such as speech, letters, phone calls, faxes and e-mail. In *Halford v United Kingdom*[11] the applicant complained about the interception of phone calls from her home and work telephones by the police in the course of gathering information to use against her in a sex discrimination case. The court held that the interception of the calls from her office amounted to a violation of Article 8 mainly because there was no regulation either common law or statutory of this area.[12] It is, however, important to realise that the protection is given to the means of correspondence rather than the contents of the correspondence itself. As a result a letter once delivered to the intended recipient is no longer protected by the right to respect for correspondence.[13] The content of the correspondence and the identity of the parties to the correspondence can be important where the correspondence is between a prisoner and lawyer. In such cases the protection accorded to the correspondence is of the highest level.[14]

Interference with Article 8

The state has a particular problem in balancing its obligation to protect private life against the need in a democratic society to allow Article 10 freedom of expression. The Strasbourg court has recognised that this balancing act involves complex policy formulation on the part of the state and so has generally accorded the state a wide margin of appreciation with regard to balancing conflicting rights.[15] Paragraph 2 of Article 8 sets out the legitimate justifications for interference with Article 8. The state should it wish to interfere with Article 8 it must do so as provided by law which is clear, accessible and foreseeable. There must also be a legitimate aim eg 'the

9 (1992) 16 EHRR 97.
10 *Niemietz* (n 9 above) para 30.
11 (1997) 24 EHRR 523.
12 See also *Malone v United Kingdom* (1984) 7 EHRR 14. There was not enough evidence that her home phone was tapped. For a consideration of the employment impact of Article 8 see Chapter 13.
13 *AD v Netherlands* (1994) 76A DR 157.
14 *Golder v United Kingdom* (1975) 1 EHRR 524.
15 Seen for example *Winer v United Kingdom* (1986) 48 DR 154 and *N v Sweden* (1986) 50 DR 173.

interests of national security, public safety or the economic well-being of the country, for the prevention of disorder or crime, for the protection of health or morals, or for the protection of the rights and freedoms of others.' The state's act must also be proportionate to the legitimate aim pursued, that is it must be 'necessary in a democratic society' which in turn must be demonstrated by a 'pressing social need' for the interference with the individual's Article 8 right.[16]

Privacy and the corporation

There is no case law at the Strasbourg level directly on the point of whether the corporation can claim a right to privacy. Such case law as there is on the nature of Article 8 would indicate that it is a right of a personal nature.[17] In Community law the ECJ has considered the applicability of Article 8 with regard to corporations in the course of considering the ECHR as part of the European Community values. In *Hoechst v EC Commission*[18] the ECJ set out its view of the nature of Article 8:

> [i]t should be observed that, although the existence of such a right [home] must be recognised in the Community legal order as a principle common to the laws of the Member States in regard to the private dwellings of natural persons, the same is not true in regard to undertakings …The protective scope of [Article 8] is concerned with the development of man's personal freedom and may not therefore be extended to business premises.[19]

The decision in *Hoechst* was examined by the ECtHR in *Niemietz v Germany*[20] but not followed as the court extended the protection of Article 8 to business premises. In that case the applicant complained of a violation of Article 8 regarding the search of his law office by the state. The government contended that Article 8 did not afford protection against the search of a business premises as the Convention protected private life and home and not business life and premises. The Court disagreed with the government's contention and found that the Article 8 protection of an individual's private life, home and correspondence did extend to the place of work. In coming to this conclusion the court gave an indication of the personal nature of Article 8 by finding that 'to interpret the words 'private life' and 'home' as including certain professional of business activities or premises would be consonant with the essential object and purpose of Article 8 … namely to protect the individual against arbitrary interference by the public authorities …'[1] However while the court in *Niemietz* found that Article 8 operated in the workplace it also considered that the state would retain the entitlement to interfere as set out in paragraph 2 of Article

---

16   See Chapter 3.
17   This is the position in the USA: see Prosser, W L, 'Privacy' (1960) 48 *California Law Review* 383 see also Padfield, F, 'Defamation, Freedom of Speech and Corporations' (1993) *Juridical Review* 294.
18   [1989] ECR 2859.
19   [1989] ECR 2589 at 2924. See also *Dow Benelux v EC Commission* [1989] ECR 3137 at 3157 and *Dow Chemical Ibérica v Commission* [1989] ECR 3165.
20   (1992) 16 EHRR 97.
1   *Niemitz* (n 20 above) *A-251* para 31.

8 'that entitlement might well be more far-reaching where professional or business activities or premises were involved than would otherwise be the case.'[2]

On this basis the scope of Article 8 extends to the individual in the workplace but the state may have a greater ability to interfere with Article 8 in the business context. While cases such as *Niemietz* give some indication that Article 8 is a personal right which may only be applicable to the individual it is important to note that the context of the court's discussion of privacy in that case is on the individual's right to rely on Article 8. It is therefore not surprising that the focus of the court's deliberations on Article 8 is the individual and that the Court uses the word 'individual' consistently in its judgment. The corporation's ability to rely on Article 8 was not at issue nor indeed has it ever been at issue in the Strasbourg case law. Such indications as there are from other Articles of the Convention do not advance or defeat the case of corporate privacy. Cases involving Article 9 (freedom of thought, conscience and religion) have considered that the corporation does not enjoy Article 9 rights.[3] On the other hand, cases involving Article 10 (expression) have allowed the corporation to enjoy the protection of that freedom.[4]

As Boyle et al have commented '[b]ecause so many separate issues may be involved in a single application and the margin of appreciation intrudes into the determination of some of them, the outcome of any particular case may not tell us much beyond its own facts.'[5] Given the difficulty in generally predicting the scope of Article 8 and how it will develop in the future it not possible to say one way or another whether a corporate right of privacy could be encompassed by Article 8 on the basis of the existing case law.

Using Article 8 against corporations: the environmental cases

One of the most significant developments at the Strasbourg level which will directly affect companies in the UK is the environmental case law on Article 8.[6] While the physical integrity aspect of private life contained in Article 8 has given rise to a positive obligation on the part of the state with regard to protecting individuals from

2   *Niemietz* (p 228, n 20) *A-251* para 31. For other cases on privacy in the workplace see *Huvig v France* (1990) 12 EHRR 528 and *Chappell v United Kingdom* (1989) 12 EHRR 1.

3   See *Church of X v United Kingdom* (1969) 12 YB 306, *X and Church of Scientology v Sweden* (1979) 16 DR 68 and *Kontrakt Information Therape v Austria Application No 11921/86*.

4   See for example *Sunday Times v United Kingdom* (1979) 2 EHRR 245, *Observer and Guardian v United Kingdom* (1991) 14 EHRR 153, *Sunday Times v United Kingdom (No 2)* (1991) 14 EHRR 229.

5   Harris, D J, O'Boyle, M, and Warbrick, C, *Law of the European Convention on Human Rights* (1995) Butterworths, p 303.

6   On the way the Court has developed Article 8 see Feldman, David, 'The Developing Scope of Article 8 of the European Convention on Human Rights' (1997) *European Human Rights Law Review*, Issue 3, pp 265-274.

harassment[7] and sexual assault[8] the Strasbourg court has also extended the protection, sometimes combined with protection of home and family life, to serious environmental pollution.[9]

In the 1970s and early 80s a number of applicants attempted to extend the scope of the Convention to cover environmental hazards. The Commission at the time did not consider the ECHR covered environmental issues.[10] In the mid 80s the Commission seemed to accept that there was an arguable case for a breach of Article 8 where excessive noise pollution was present.[11] However on both occasions where Article 8 applications were declared admissable in the environmental context the government settled the cases. By the mid-80s the Commission seemed to accept that Article 8 could be extended to environmental hazards. In *Rayner v United Kingdom*[12] the applicant complained that excessive and continuous aircraft noise was an interference with his right to respect for his private life and home. The Commission in finding a violation of Article 8 found that 'considerable noise nuisance can undoubtedly affect the physical well-being of a person and thus interfere with his private life.'

The 1990s have seen the ECtHR further develop the environmental jurisprudence on Article 8. In *Lopez Ostra v Spain*[13] the case concerned the physical effects of pollution from a factory on the applicants. The applicant lived in the town of Lorca in Spain where there is a heavy concentration of leather industries. A number of the tanneries in Lorca were owned and operated by a limited company called SACURSA. This company also had a plant in Lorca for the treatment of liquid and solid waste which was built with the aid of a State subsidy on municipal land. The plant was 12 metres away from the applicant's home.

The activities of the plant were classified by the state as unhealthy, noxious and dangerous and as such it required a licence to operate. The company did not obtain such a licence but nevertheless started operations in July 1988. As the result of a malfunction during the start up the factory released gas fumes, pestilential smells and contamination, which immediately caused health problems and nuisance to those living nearby. As a result of the pollution caused by the factory the town council evacuated the local residents and re-housed them in the town centre for the months of July, August and September 1988. The applicant and her family did not return to their home until October and lived there until February 1992 when due to combination of frustration at the local authorities and medical advice they moved away. After the initial malfunction the Spanish authorities ordered only a partial shut down of the factory and as a result certain nuisances continued throughout the applicants time living in Lorca. After exhausting the domestic remedies the applicant complained to the ECtHR of a violation of Article 8 and Article 3 (torture,

7   *Whiteside v United Kingdom* (1994) A-76 DR 80.
8   *X and Y v Netherlands* (1985) 8 EHRR 235.
9   Gordon, Richard and Ward, Tim,'Human Rights Act (1) the Environment' (2000) *Solicitors' Journal*, 17 March, pp 240-241.
10   *X and Y v Germany* (1976) 15 DR 161 and *X v Germany* (1981) 26 DR 270.
11   See *Arrondelle v United Kingdom* (1982) 26 DR 5 and *Baggs v United Kingdom* (1985) 44 DR 13.
12   (1986) 47 DR 5.
13   (1994) 20 EHRR 277.

inhuman degrading treatment) caused by the failure of the Spanish state to protect the applicant from the nuisance caused by the treatment plant.

The Spanish government acknowledged that there had been an effect on the applicant and her family's health but not to a sufficient degree that there was an interference with their home and family life. The Court dismissed this contention and found that '[n]aturally, severe environmental pollution may affect individuals' well-being and prevent them from enjoying their homes in such a way as to affect their private and family life adversely without, however, seriously endangering their health.'[14] The Court then went on to examine whether the state had taken the measures necessary to protect the applicant's private and family life and home. It found that even given the margin of appreciation the state has in such matters the state had actively resisted any positive steps to protect the applicant's rights, this had in turn exacerbated the interference with Article 8. As such the Court found a violation of Article 8 but not Article 3.

There are a number of important propositions that arise from the case. First that while a 'public authority' has a wide margin of appreciation with such matters it also has a positive obligation to protect an individual's private and family life and home from environmental hazards. In the *Lopez Ostra* case the state had not just failed to fulfil its positive obligation but had exacerbated the interference with Article 8 by obstructing any positive protection of the applicant's rights. The Court seemed to suggest that once the state could demonstrate that it had taken positive steps to protect the applicant and once those steps were reasonable and appropriate the extent of those steps was up to the state.[15] Second that the concern of the Court was not with establishing a serious danger to health but rather on the extremity and extent of the nuisance caused to private and family life and home. This could occur without any serious health risk being present.[16]

Similarly in *Guerra v Italy*[17] the applicants lived one kilometre away from a factory which made fertiliser and caprolactam. The factory was classified both by the Italian and European Community authorities as high risk. The nature of the production process carried out at the factory involved the emission of large amounts of inflammable gas and toxic materials into the atmosphere continuously. In 1976 there had been an explosion at the factory and as a result 150 people were hospitalised because of the poisonous substances which escaped. The applicants lived near the factory in an area that had been recognised by the local authorities as being at risk from the emissions from the factory. The applicants made two complaints to the court. First that the failure of the state to reduce the risk of accident at the factory amounted to a violation of Article 2 (right to life and physical integrity). Second that the state had failed to provide the applicants with information about the risks posed by the factory and what to do in the event of a major accident in violation of Articles 8 and 10.

14   *Lopez* (p 230, n 13) para 51.
15   See *Lopez* (p 230, n 13) paras 51 and 55.
16   On the general impacts of the case see Sands, Philippe, 'Human Rights, Environment and the *Lopez-Ostra* Case: Context and Consequences' (1996) *European Human Rights Law Review*, Issue 6, pp 597-618.
17   (1998) 26 EHRR 357.

The court, in dismissing the applicant's Article 10 claim, considered '[t]hat freedom [of expression] cannot be construed as imposing on a State, in circumstances such as those of the present case, positive obligations to collect and disseminate information of its own motion.'[18] The court did, however, find a violation of Article 8 by reiterating the position set out in *Lopez Ostra* that severe environmental pollution may interfere with the enjoyment of home and private and family life. The state was aware of the risk of environmental harm to those in the locality. By not providing the applicants with essential information, which would enable them to assess the risks to themselves and their families of continuing to live in a dangerous area, the state had failed to secure the applicant's right to respect for their private and family life in breach of Article 8. The Court having found a violation of Article 8 did not find it necessary to examine the Article 2 claim.

The characteristic in common between *Rayner, Lopez Ostra* and *Guerra* is the seriousness of the environmental hazard. The ECHR is not designed to protect individuals from environmental hazards but the Court has extended the protection of Article 8 in situations where it feels the interference with the individual's Article 8 rights is of a particularly high level. On this basis the Court will only admit an Article 8 environmental claim where the nature of the environmental hazard is or has been extremely serious. In *Glass v United Kingdom*[19] the applicant complained that aircraft noise at his home from planes landing at Heathrow airport amounted to a violation of Article 8. In dismissing the applicant's claim the Commission examined all the previous case law on noise pollution from aircraft and found that the applicant was further away from the airport and suffered lesser noise levels than all the other previous applicants. Specifically they found:

> nothing in the applicant's submissions which would indicate that he suffers a degree of discomfort comparable to that of the applicants in the cases of Arondelle and Baggs. Indeed his position is probably somewhat better than that of the applicants in the cases of Powell and Rayner.[20]

Inconvenience it would seem is not enough to amount to an interference with Article 8. In *Astrid Moe v Norway*[1] the applicant complained that the smell from a waste treatment plant violated her right to respect for private life and home under Article 8. The Court found that the level of nuisance complained of was of a lesser character than in *Lopez Ostra* amounting only to an inconvenience. Further, the state had taken remedial action which brought the nuisance within the limits of tolerable inconvenience.[2]

---

18   *Guerra* (p 231, n 17) para 53.
19   Application No 28485/95 judgment of 16 October 1996.
20   *Glass* (n 19 above) para 1.
1   Application No 30966/96, judgment of 14 December 1999.
2   For a further consideration of the limitations of using the Convention for environmental issues see Jarvis, Francoise and Sherlock, Ann, 'The European Convention on Human Rights and the environment' (1999) 24 *European Law Review Human Rights Survey*, pp HR/15-HR/ 29.

Environmental justifications for state interference with Convention rights

The ECtHR has on occasion accepted environmental protection as a legitimate aim of the state in interfering with an individual's Convention rights. In *Fredin v Sweden*[3] the Court explored the proportionality of the revocation by the state of the applicant's gravel extraction licence which the applicant claimed was a violation of Protocol 1, Article 1 (property). The court found that there had been no violation of the applicant's Protocol 1, Article 1 rights because of the act of revocation was proportionate in the light of the importance of protecting the environment. Similarly in *Pine Valley Developments v Ireland*[4] the court found that the state had interfered with the applicant's rights on the basis of environmental protection which the court considered to be a legitimate aim.

The impact of the environmental cases in domestic law

The environmental case law impacts on domestic law in a number of ways. First the regulatory agencies of the state concerned with environmental supervision are all public authorities under section 6 of the HRA and must act compatibly with the Convention rights. Second local authorities operating environmental hazards such as dumps and incinerators will also be public authorities under section 6 and must act compatibly with the Convention rights. Third certain companies are public authorities under section 6 and must act compatibly with the Convention rights. Fourth the indirect horizontal effect of the HRA affects all companies who carry out activities which might constitute an environmental hazard.[5]

Regulatory agencies and environmental hazard

The regulatory agencies of the state must ensure that any planning and supervisory regimes in which companies who may have environmental impacts operate are compatible with the regulators' positive obligations under the Convention. As a result, any regulatory authority dealing with environmental hazards has a positive obligation to ensure respect for individuals' Convention rights. In particular with regard to environmental hazards the individuals' Article 8 rights must be respected. This responsibility engages even if the environmental hazard is created by a private company. The public authority responsible for planning or licensing must take positive steps to protect individuals' Convention rights.[6] Once the authority can show that those steps were reasonable and appropriate the extent of those steps should

3   (1991) 13 EHRR 784.
4   (1991) 14 EHRR 319.
5   On the impacts see generally Thornton, Justine and Tromans, Stephen, 'Human Rights and Environmental Wrongs- Incorporating the European Convention on Human Rights: Some Thoughts on the Consequences for UK Environmental Law' (1999) *Journal of Environmental Law* Vol 11 No 1, pp 35-57.
6   See Hart, David, 'The Impact of the European Convention on Human Rights on Planning and Environmental Law' (2000) *Journal of Planning and Environmental Law*, February, pp 117-133.

be left to the public authority.[7] Should the regulatory agency either fail to act or obstruct the protection of an individual's rights it will be a breach of Article 8. While the margin of appreciation will not operate at the domestic level some discretion is likely to be left to a public authority on environmental issues which involve a delicate balancing of community against the individual.

The obligation to act compatibly with regard to the Article 8 environmental cases is likely to affect the operation of planning consent and licensing generally where there is an issue of environmental hazard. Planning for waste treatment plants, dumps, incinerators, roads (in particular where it involves compulsory purchase orders and significant noise levels), airports, night clubs and any factories where manufacturing may constitute an environmental hazard, will engage the public authority's obligations under the HRA. As a result the planning or licensing authority will have to give consideration to how it will respect the Convention rights that might be affected by the granting of a licence or planning consent. This might involve not granting the licence or permission or imposing such conditions as the public authority deemed necessary to ensure compatibility with the Convention rights.

The public authority's responsibility does not stop after the initial grant as the continuing operation of the planning or licencing regime will also have to respect the Convention rights. This will mean that even after granting a licence or planning permission the public authority must operate a regime that ensures respect for the Convention rights. For example, a local authority which granted a licence to a private company to operate a waste treatment plant without any way of supervising the continuing operation of the plant would run the risk that in the event of the private company violating an individual's Article 8 rights the state could not ensure respect for the individual's rights because it had no way to supervise the company's activities, either by inspecting and providing risk assessment information to locals, imposing conditions on the company or withdrawing the licence. In such an event, even though the private company is responsible for the interference with the individual's rights, the public authority will have committed an unlawful act under section 6 of the HRA by not ensuring respect for the individual's Convention rights for which the individual affected can claim a remedy. Even where there is a regime in place capable of ensuring respect for the Convention rights of individuals it must actually be operated in a way that ensures respect for the Convention rights. A failure to act or an obstructive act will amount to a violation of an individual's right to respect for their Convention rights.

As a result of the Strasbourg court's decision in *Guerra v Italy*[8] a public authority must as part of its obligation to respect an individual's Article 8 rights provide essential information which would enable individuals to assess the risks to themselves and their families of continuing to live in a dangerous area. At what point this obligation engages is somewhat of a mystery. In *Guerra* the factory had a history of highly dangerous activities and the state was investigating its operation as a result. On this basis, where there is an obvious high risk, the public authority has an obligation to investigate the risks and provide such information to those at risk from

---

7   See *Lopez* (p 230, n 13) para 51 and 55.
8   (1998) 26 EHRR 357 examined above.

living in the area. What is not clear is whether, in order to fulfil, its positive obligations the public authority has a proactive obligation to investigate and report to those who might be at risk on all potential risks, even though there is no history of the risk turning into physical harm to those in the local area. It is likely that if the potential hazard risk to the local population is of an extremely high level the public authority has an obligation to investigate, monitor and report to those potentially at risk in the locality. Where the potential hazard risk is of the character of a tolerable irritation such as a smell or low level noise the public authority would not have such an obligation to investigate, monitor and report although it might do so in the process of making the irritation tolerable.[9]

Local authorities

A local authority will be an obvious public authority under section 6 of the HRA. As such all its functions, including operating for example a dump, waste treatment plant or incinerator, must be compatible with the Convention rights ie operating a waste treatment plant which creates a severe environmental hazard which interferes with an individual's Article 8 rights is an unlawful act. Should the public authority do so the individual affected has a directly enforceable action under the section 6 of the HRA against the public authority. The public authority also has a positive obligation to operate the dump etc in a way which respects the individuals' Article 8 rights. This might involve ceasing to operate the dump at all or more likely operating the dump in a manner which minimises or makes tolerable the effect on the individual's Article 8 rights. If the environmental hazard created by the local authority is of an extremely high level the local authority may as a result of the decision in *Guerra v Italy*,[10] have an obligation to provide risk assessment information to those at risk from the hazard.

Section 6 public authority companies

Certain companies such as British Nuclear Fuels Ltd (BNFL) carry out wholly public functions in which case they are a 'public authority' under section 6 (1) of the HRA 1998. Other companies, such as British Gas and Railtrack, carry out some public functions in which case they are a 'public authority' under section 6 (3) (b) with regard to the carrying out of those functions. All public authorities under Section 6 of the HRA must act compatibly with the Convention rights. If they do not do so it is an unlawful act which gives rise to an action under section 6 of the HRA.[11]

The environmental case law of the Strasbourg court concerning Article 8 rights has a threefold effect on these companies. First they must act compatibly with the Convention rights. For BNFL it will mean that a failure of its safety systems resulting in harm to its employees and/or those living in the locality will result in victims alleging an unlawful act directly, without having to go through the Environmental Agency or the Nuclear Installations Inspectorate. Second it also has a positive obligation to respect the Convention rights of those at risk of harm from a failure

---

9   See *Astrid Moe v Norway* Application No 30966/96, judgment of 14 December 1999.
10   (1998) 26 EHRR 357: see above.
11   See Chapter 6 on section 6.

of its safety systems and so should ensure that all of its safety procedures are designed to fulfill that obligation. Third it may also because of the Strasbourg court's decision in *Guerra v Italy*[12] require BNFL, because of the extremity of the potential harm that could be caused by a breach of its Convention obligations, to inspect, monitor and inform those in the locality about the operation and safety systems at its plants in order to allow them to assess the risk of living in the local area.

For companies such as Railtrack and British Gas their public function most likely to give rise to litigation is safety. For example, Railtrack has a positive obligation to ensure that the Convention rights of those travelling on and living near its lines are respected. If a train crashes as a result of a failure of Railtrack's safety systems, and causes harm to passengers, it will give rise to a claim by those victims that Railtrack committed an unlawful act in breach of its section 6 obligation to act compatibly with their Convention rights. In particular that Railtrack breached their Article 8 rights to respect for private and family life and home. The same is true of British Gas or any of the privatised utilities. Should British Gas be responsible for an explosion which injures individuals and their property the victims can directly claim that British Gas committed an unlawful act by breaching Article 8 violating their right to respect for private and family life and home and additionally allege an interference with Protocol 1, Article 1 (property). Railtrack and British Gas also have to ensure that their safety systems are designed to fulfil their obligations to respect the Convention rights of those at risk from a failure of those systems. This does not mean that they have to choose the best way to respect the Convention rights just that the steps they took were reasonable and appropriate.[13] On this basis the most expensive safety system would not necessarily have to be chosen.

How such section 6 actions would operate in practice is unclear. The individual could claim that a company such as Railtrack had acted unlawfully by violated his Article 8 rights and seek damages under section 6 of the HRA 1998. However rights are not really designed for litigation that is essentially about a wrong. A careless act should attribute liability to a public authority under the HRA just as any other type of act. It does however raise interesting issues. Would the action amount to no-fault liability or would there have to be a process of establishing fault on the part of the public authority? Even where you could show fault could the public authority defend the action with reference to discretion, legitimate aim and proportionality? The applicability of those interpretive tools seems odd where a careless act is at issue. Where is the legitimate aim or the proportionality? In terms of the Article 8 (privacy) case law on environmental hazards it is possible to see a careless act leading to an interference with Article 8 being at least arguably justifiable as pursuing a legitimate aim – BNFL producing electricity for the public grid or Railtrack providing a public rail network. Proportionality may however be more difficult (the escaping radioactivity had to be released in order to stop a larger explosion) or (the failure to improve the safety system was necessary to allow the majority of the rail network to operate). Whatever way the section 6 action plays out when a careless act is at issue it will probably not displace negligence as the main form of action. This is because the damages payable for a section 6 unlawful

12   (1998) 26 EHRR 357: see above.
13   See *Lopez* (p 230, n 13) para 51 and 55.

act are a) not compulsory and b) likely to be low. Section 8 of the HRA does not compel the court to award a remedy and so a public authority breach of a Convention right might not lead the court to award damages. There are essentially two reasons why awards of damages for section 6 unlawful acts are likely to be low. First, the courts have, as we explained in Chapter 6, an obligation to look at the Strasbourg courts[14] principles on compensation. The Strasbourg court has historically been conservative in its awards. Second if the fault criteria is no-fault or a lesser degree of fault than negligence then the amounts payable in damages will correspondingly be lower. For example the damages for successful deceit actions are higher than those available for negligence because of the degree of fault attributable to the wrongdoer.[15]

British Gas's positive obligations under the Convention may also require because of the Strasbourg court's decision in *Guerra v Italy*[16] that where there is a potentially large risk to those living in the locality, for example those living next to a large gas storage tank, British Gas to provide information to those at risk in order to enable them to assess for themselves the risk of living in the area. It is difficult to extrapolate the same obligation in *Guerra* to Railtrack as the potential risk of a safety failure to the travelling population as a whole is minimal but should for example continuous safety failures occur on a particular line or with particular signals there could be an obligation on the part of Railtrack not only to investigate the failure but to inform passengers travelling on that line in order to allow them to assess the possible risk of travelling themselves. For example in the Ladbroke Grove rail disaster, signal SN109 into Paddington had been what is called in the industry 'multi-SPADed' (signal passed at danger). This means that trains had passed while the signal was indicating danger on multiple occasions.[17]

The effect on companies generally

The indirect horizontal effect of the HRA will allow individuals to use Convention rights in litigation against a company that is not a public authority for a physical effect of an environmental hazard caused by the company. An individual could do this alleging a tort (negligence, trespass or nuisance) and also arguing that the court as a public authority under section 6 (3) (a) of the HRA has an obligation to protect the applicant's right to respect for private and family life and home from violation by a private company.[18] Should the court itself not respect the individual's Convention rights this would be an unlawful act for which the individual could seek a remedy under the HRA. It is important to note that a private company has no obligation to respect the Convention rights introduced by the HRA. Rather the HRA has an indirect effect on the company because of the court's obligation to interpret the law compatibly with the Convention rights. As a result, if a private company violates a Convention right, a victim has no directly enforceable right under the

---

14   Section 8 (4) HRA 1998.
15   See the judgment of Lord Steyn in *Smith New Court Securities Ltd v Scrimgeour Vickers (Asset Management) Ltd* [1996] 4 All ER 769 at 790 .
16   (1998) 26 EHRR 357: see above.
17   See the submissions of counsel for the inquiry on the 28 July 2000 at www.lgri.org
18   See Chapter 7 on the horizontal effect of the HRA.

HRA against the company. However in litigation between private parties the court must, under section 6 (3) (a), interpret and develop the law compatibly with the Convention. This would allow the victim of a violation of a Convention right by a private company the ability to raise Convention points in the course of litigation against the company. The company could also raise Convention points in its defence. The parties themselves are therefore not seeking to use Convention rights against each other, because they have no Convention rights exercisable against each other, but rather to ensure that the court as a 'public authority' acts compatibly with such Convention rights as the parties can show are relevant to their case. This will obviously involve the court balancing the competing rights the private parties claim the court should give effect to and a decision for one party will horizontally impact on the Convention rights of the other.

Can companies claim Article 8 rights at the domestic level?

The question of whether corporations could claim a right of privacy arose recently in *R v Broadcasting Standards Commission, ex p BBC*.[19] The case concerned the secret filming by the BBC of Dixons' stores, in the course of an investigation for the television program Watchdog, into misselling of goods. No evidence of misselling was revealed in the course of the investigation and so the item was not broadcast. However Dixons complained to the Broadcasting Standards Commission on the basis that the secret filming was an unwarranted infringement of its privacy. The Commission upheld the complaint, and the BBC applied for judicial review of the decision alleging it was ultra vires and unlawful. Forbes J, sitting in the High Court, quashed the decision of the BSC relying on the Strasbourg case law in finding that a corporation had no right of privacy.[20] He considered that the expression 'privacy' in the Broadcasting Act 1996 was ambiguous 'and that, when properly construed in conformity with the ECHR, it is restricted to human individuals and does not extend to corporations.'[1] On appeal Lord Woolf MR, having considered the ECHR case law, concluded:

> [a]s it happens, I do not regard the position on the issues with which we are concerned on this appeal to have been clearly determined by the [Strasbourg court] in a way which points in either party's favour under Article 8 of the ECHR. Both parties relied on the [Strasbourg court's] decision in *Niemietz v Germany* (1992) 16 EHRR 97. But that case is not decisive as to the approach to Article 8 of the ECHR on the issues with which we are concerned.[2]

He then went on to find, without prejudice to what the position was under Article 8, that a corporation could have a right to privacy. He found that:

---

19 [2000] EMLR 587.

20 He accepted that Article 8 and 9 (religion) are similar in character.

1   *R v Broadcasting Standards Commission* [1999] EMLR 858 at 875.

2   *R v Broadcasting Standards Commission, ex p BBC* [2000] EMLR 587, [2000] All ER 486, para 17.

[w]hile the intrusions into the privacy of an individual which are possible are no doubt more extensive than the infringements of privacy which are possible in the case of a company, a company does have activities of a private nature which need protection from unwarranted intrusion. It would be a departure from proper standards if, for example, the BBC without any justification attempted to listen clandestinely to the activities of a board meeting. The same would be true of secret filming of the board meeting. The individual members of the board would no doubt have grounds for complaint, but so would the board and thus the company as a whole. The company has correspondence which it could justifiably regard as private and the broadcasting of the contents of that correspondence would be an intrusion on its privacy. It could not possibly be said that to hold such actions an intrusion of privacy conflicts with the ECHR.[3]

The BBC has appealed the decision to the House of Lords.[4]

The issue of corporate privacy is a complex one, clearly certain aspects of the general notion of privacy such as the protection of feelings, emotions, fears and sexuality do not sit easily with an artificial entity.[5] However there are aspects of a corporate function which, as Lord Woolf noted, are to some extent private in character. A corporation has correspondence and to a certain extent a home which warrant protection. While the Strasbourg court has excluded the corporation from relying on Article 9 (thought, conscience and religion) on the basis of the personal nature of that right, it has allowed corporations to rely on Article 10 (expression). Article 10 can equally be claimed to be a personal or human personality oriented right. The Strasbourg court has however accorded rights to corporations under that Article but where the expression is commercial in nature the protection accorded is of a lesser degree. [6]

The same logic applies to Article 8. Where the privacy in question is commercial in nature the degree of protection accorded under Article 8 should be of a lesser character than the protection accorded to aspects of privacy emanating from human personality. For example an internal corporate memo may be private but it is not of the same character of privacy as a love poem. Should two e-mails be intercepted by a 'public authority' one containing confidential corporate information the other a love poem, the poem should have a higher degree of protection under Article 8 as both the means of correspondence are protected and the individual's private life ie the ability to form relationships with others.

The corporate memo should also come within the scope of Article 8. The individual who sent the e-mail can clearly claim that his correspondence has been interfered with but the corporation should also be able to assert a violation under Article 8.

---

3   [2000] All ER 486, para 33.
4   The BSC is also determined to fight the case to the last see its annual review http://www.bsc.org.uk/review2k/index.htm
5   However they might be relevant to a one-man company.
6   *Markt Intern Verlag and Klaus Beermann v Germany* (1989) 12 EHRR 161.

The main ground for the corporation's complaint is the interference with its correspondence. Any additional claim that its private life, ie its ability to form relationships, was interfered with would either be inapplicable to the corporation[7] or of a commercial character and thus accorded lesser protection. [8] In essence Article 8 is divided into four parts in that everyone is entitled to respect for his private and family life, his home and his correspondence.[9] Private and family life are the rights that appear least applicable to corporations save that business relationships may be protected under the heading of private life.[10] Home ('domicile' which in the French text of the ECHR has a wider meaning including business premises)[11] and correspondence are however rights that could be accorded to a corporation.[12] A company should be able to claim protection of the right to occupation of its head office and to the enjoyment of that home free from interference. Lord Woolf's example in *R v Broadcasting Standards Commission, ex p BBC,* of the BBC secretly filming a board meeting could amount to a violation of the concept of home or 'domicile'. Correspondence is perhaps the easiest fit for companies. Here again Lord Woolf specifically considered the privacy of corporate correspondence to be worthy of protection.[13]

It is clear from the Strasbourg authorities that individuals within companies have rights of privacy which can be interfered with by the state. As such even though the corporation may not be able to exercise privacy rights against a 'public authority' individuals behind the corporation who have been affected can do so. Employees of a corporation that is a 'public authority' for the purposes of section 6 of the HRA

---

7   Although, as we noted in the introduction to Chapter 7, the courts have on occasion attributed 'feelings' to corporations In *Re Lindsay Bowman Ltd* [1969] 3 All ER 601 at 604 Megarry J stated: 'I must assume that the artificial and impersonal entity that we know as the limited company has been endowed with the capacity not merely of having feelings but also of feeling aggrieved … '.

8   *Niemietz v Germany* (1992) 16 EHRR 97.

9   The use of the word 'his' is common throughout the ECHR and has never precluded a corporation relying on an article. See Article 6 (fair trial) for example.

10   *Niemietz v Germany* (1992) 16 EHRR 97, A251-B, para 29.

11   *Niemietz* (n 10 above) para 30.

12   In the US the work of Prosser, W L, 'Privacy' (1960) 48 *California law Review* 383 has been influential in denying companies a right of privacy but for an alternative working of Prosser's argument which allows companies limited rights of privacy see Schack, David P 'The Right to Privacy for Business Entities' (1984) 24 *Santa Clara Law Review* pp 53-63.

13   This issue is likely to arise fairly quickly in the context of search and freezing orders. In the US and Australia where the documents are corporate in nature the courts have accorded a lower level of protection: see Scherb, Katherine, 'Administrative Subpoenas for Private Financial Records: What Protection for Privacy does the Fourth Amendment Require?' (1996) *Wisconsin Law Review* pp 1075-1099 and Hill, Jennifer, 'Corporate Rights and Accountability – The Privilege against Self-Incrimination and the Implications of *Environment Protection Authority v Caltex Refining Co Pty Ltd*' in: *Corporate and Business Law Journal* (University of Adelaide) Vol 7 No 2, Special Issue – Corporate Theory 1994, pp 127-148. On the other hand, the Canadian courts have protected companies from search and seizure: Tollefson, Chris, 'Constitutional Law – Charter of Rights – Strict Liability Offences – Reverse Onus Clauses – Standing of Corporations – Charter of Rights and Freedoms, ss 1, 7, 11 (1) (d) – Competition Act, RSC 1970, c C-23, ss 6(1) (a), 37.3 (2): *R v Wholesale Travel Group Inc* (1992) 71 Canadian Bar Review pp 369-383.

will have Article 8 rights exercisable against the company.[14] The regulatory bodies of the state will also have to act compatibly with Article 8. This may be particularly difficult where the regulatory body has to balance Article 8 against Article 10 (freedom of expression).[15] As with all the other rights and freedoms it is unclear how the margin of appreciation will operate at the domestic level. The courts are likely to recognise the difficulty the state has in balancing competing rights and so certainly some discretion should be allowable to a 'public authority' with regard to balancing Article 10 against Article 8. The exercise of individual privacy rights in the context of a business may also allow the state to interfere to a greater extent than where the exercise is wholly personal in context.[16] However the big question to be determined at the domestic level is to what extent, if at all, a corporation can rely on Article 8?

Generally speaking the operation of Article 8 at the domestic level is predicted to cause a common law of privacy to develop in the domestic courts probably through the extension of the tort of breach of confidence.[17] Given that there is no case law at the Strasbourg level on corporate reliance on Article 8 there is, as examined above, a question as to whether a corporation can rely on Article 8 and subsequently any privacy law that arises at common law in the domestic courts. Corporations are generally included in any statutory protections of information or communications by virtue of Schedule 1 to the Interpretation Act 1978 which states that '"Person" includes a body of persons corporate or incorporate'. Common law protection of confidentiality is also accorded to corporations.[18] The concept of privacy for an artificial entity seems to raise special difficulties which will have to be resolved quickly. The appeal of the BBC to the House of Lords against the decision in *R v Broadcasting Standards Commission, ex p BBC* should provide such an opportunity.

14   We consider the employment aspects of the HRA in Chapter 13.
15   See the discussion of this balance in Chapter 11.
16   *Niemietz v Germany* (1992) 16 EHRR 97.
17   See Singh, Rabinder, 'Privacy and the Media after the Human Rights Act'(1998) *European Human Rights Law Review*, Issue 6, pp 712-729. See also *Hellewell v Chief Constable of Derbyshire* [1995] 1 WLR 804. On Article 8 and its use in conjunction with other actions see the Home Office Minister Mike O'Brien HC Debates, 2 July 1998: Column 561.
18   See *Camelot Group plc v Centaur Communications* [1998] 1 All ER 251 and *Goodwin v United Kingdom* (1996) 22 EHRR 123.

Commercial expression

Instead of being arrested, as we stated, for kicking his wife down a flight of stairs and hurling a lighted kerosene lamp after her, the Rev James P Welleman died unmarried four years ago.[1]

Freedom of commercial expression

Article 10- Freedom of expression

1) Everyone has the right to freedom of expression. This right shall include freedom to hold opinions and to receive and impart information and ideas without interference by public authority and regardless of frontiers. This article shall not prevent States from requiring the licencing of broadcasting, television or cinema enterprises.

2) The exercise of these freedoms, since it carries with it duties and

1   Apology in a US newspaper, cited by Sir Edward Burne-Jones.

responsibilities, may be subject to such formalities, conditions, restrictions or penalties as are prescribed by law and are necessary in a democratic society, in the interests of national security, territorial integrity or public safety, for the prevention of disorder or crime, for the protection of health or morals, for the protection of the reputation or rights of others, for preventing the disclosure of information received in confidence, or for maintaining the authority and impartiality of the judiciary.

Freedom of expression as contained in Article 10 of the ECHR is one of the most rigorously policed freedoms in the Convention. It can be invoked by both natural and legal persons.[2] While Article 10 has at its core political expression[3] it also includes generally the right to hold opinions and receive and impart information, it also covers artistic expression.[4] Expression is not exhaustively defined and covers words both written and spoken, pictures,[5] images[6] and acts such as dress which convey information or ideas.[7]

The reason the Court has placed great weight on the importance of Article 10 is that it constitutes 'one of the essential foundations of a democratic society and is one of the basic conditions for its progress'.[8] As a result it is very difficult for a state to justify interference with Article 10 rights once the expression concerned is considered necessary to allow the promotion of democracy. Commercial expression will not necessarily fall into this category.

Protecting commercial expression

There are two tiers of protection offered by the Strasbourg court where commercial expression is concerned. The first tier offers a high level of protection where the commercial expression concerned is part of the role of the free press in promoting a democratic society. As a result media companies generally will have a greater claim to protection where the expression even though for profit is part of their role as a free press. Where the commercial expression concerned is a television/radio broadcast or newspaper article the Strasbourg court has always scrutinised very closely whether restrictions imposed on the publication of information amounted to censorship.[9] If the Court finds that the restriction on this form of commercial expression amounts to censorship the Court will find that a violation of Article 10 has occurred. This is because the Court sees its supervisory role as supporting the press in playing 'its vital role as a watchdog'.[10]

2   *Autronic AG v Switzerland* (1990) 12 EHRR 485, judgment of 22 May 1990, A- *178* § 47.
3   *Lingens v Austria* (1986) 8 EHRR 407 and *Handyside v United Kingdom* (1976) 1 EHRR 737.
4   See *Muller v Switzerland* (1988) 13 EHRR 212.
5   *Muller* (n 4 above).
6   *Chorherr v Austria* (1993) 17 EHRR 358.
7   *Stephens v United Kingdom* (1986) 46 DR 245.
8   *Handyside v United Kingdom* (1976) 1 EHRR 737; *Lingens v Austria* (1986) 8 EHRR 407; *Jersild v Denmark* (1994) 19 EHRR 1.
9   See for example *Sunday Times v United Kingdom* (1979) 2 EHRR 245, *Observer and Guardian v United Kingdom* (1991) 14 EHRR 153, *Sunday Times v United Kingdom (No 2)* (1991) 14 EHRR 229.
10   *Observer and Guardian v United Kingdom* (1991) 14 EHRR 153.

Article 10 (1) specifically allows the state to impose controls on broadcasting through licensing regimes. However Article 10 (1) has been interpreted by the ECtHR as only allowing licensing controls with regard to the technical process of broadcasting.[11] If the state wished to impose restrictions as to the content of the broadcast or the aims of the broadcasting company itself it would run the risk of breaching the company's Article 10 rights.[12] In *Informationsverein Lentia v Austria*[13] the Austrian state refused to grant any licences to any private companies on the basis that a state monopoly on broadcasting was the only way to ensure proper standards of objectivity, independence, diversity and balance. The Strasbourg court found that such a justification was untenable as a state monopoly imposed the greatest restriction on Article 10 rights.[14] Even restricting private companies to limited radio frequencies has been held by the Strasbourg court to amount to a violation of Article 10.[15] The ECtHR has allowed restriction of licences which concern the content of broadcasting where the restrictions are imposed on expression which might impact on national security.[16]

The second tier of protection for commercial expression is of a much less protective character. This is where the commercial expression falls outside that form of expression which is considered necessary to promote a democratic society. Second tier commercial expression is where the expression itself is aimed at protecting or advancing the business interests of a commercial enterprise. This might be positively through advertising or other means of consumer communication or negatively through addressing defects in their rivals' products. Where this is the case the national authorities enjoy a wide margin of appreciation. Importantly here the fact the expression is true may not be enough to override the state's margin of appreciation.

Early case law on this type of commercial expression left open the question of whether it came within the ambit of Article 10.[17] Since then the ECtHR has confirmed that such expression does come within Article 10. In the case *Markt Intern Verlag and Klaus Beermann v Germany*[18] a publishing company and its editor continuously reported on the status of dissatisfied clients of mail-order firms in their information bulletin. Markt Intern, which had been founded and run by journalists, sought to defend the interests of small- and medium-sized retail businesses against the competition of large-scale distribution companies, such as supermarkets and mail-order firms. It also provided the less powerful members of the retail trade with financial assistance in test cases, lobbying public authorities, political parties and trade associations on their behalf and on occasion making proposals for legislation to Parliament.

11   *Groppera Radio AG v Switzerland* (1990) 12 EHRR 321.
12   The ITC in imposing conditions on a licence would have to ensure that those restrictions were proportionate. For example the Independent Television Commission's attempt in a order dated 20 July 2000 to make ITV move its news programme to an earlier time is a possible violation of Article 10.
13   (1993) 17 EHRR 93.
14   *Lentia* (n 13 above) para 39.
15   See *Radio ABC v Austria* (1997) 25 EHRR 185.
16   See *Purcell v Ireland* (1991) 70 DR 262.
17   *Barthold v Germany* (1985) 7 EHRR 383.
18   (1989) 12 EHRR 161.

On several occasions undertakings which had suffered from the applicants' criticism or their calls for boycotts, instituted proceedings against them for infringement of the German Unfair Competition Act of 7 June 1909. On one such occasion the German courts ordered an injunction on behalf of a mail-order firm selling beauty products prohibiting Markt Intern from publishing critical statements.

The case is of importance for two reasons. First the German government argued that the expression in question was primarily commercial in nature and as such, because it was not targeted at public opinion generally but rather at furthering the interests of a group of small businesses, it did not warrant protection under Article 10. The ECtHR rejected the German government's argument on this point and found that this type of commercial expression was protected by Article 10.[19]

Second the Strasbourg court found the national authorities had a wide margin of appreciation with regard to such commercial matters as they were in a better position to determine the right balance between the various interests concerned. This type of commercial expression was not deemed essential to promote democracy and so a wide discretion would be left to the national authority. The ECtHR found that 'such a margin is essential in commercial matters and, in particular, in an area as complex and fluctuating as that of unfair competition'.[20] In this case the qualification in the second paragraph of Article 10 regarding 'the rights of others' ie the large mail-order firms, justified the restriction imposed therefore no violation was found.[1]

The vote of the court was finely balanced at nine votes for a violation to nine votes against with the president providing the casting vote against a violation. As such the dissenting judgments have attracted some attention. The reason why the case was so finely balanced seems to relate to the fact the German government did not in fact advance convincing evidence that there was a 'pressing social need' for the restriction. Judge Pettiti, dissenting, considered that even where the matter concerned commercial expression, censorship or a ban on publication should only be allowable in rare cases. He considered that the 'protection of the interests of users and consumers in the face of dominant positions depends on the freedom to publish even the harshest criticisms of products'.

In *Groppera Radio AG v Switzerland*[2] the applicant was an company broadcasting music and advertising from a base in Italy for reception in Switzerland. In Switzerland the broadcasts were either received directly or redistributed by Swiss cable companies. In 1983, and again in 1984, the Swiss authorities banned any broadcasts by cable operators which did not comply with international radio and telecommunications standards. As a result the Swiss redistribution of the broadcasts ceased. *Groppera* challenged the ban in the Swiss courts but to no avail and so,

---

19   This is similar to the position in the US where the First Amendment applies to commercial speech see *Virginia State Board of Pharmacy v Virginia Citizens Consumer Council* 425 US 748 (1976).
20   *A-165* § 33.
1   See also *Jacubowski v Germany* (1994) 19 EHRR 64, *Casado Coca v Spain* (1994) 18 EHRR 1 and *Hertel v Switzerland* [1999] EHRLR 116.
2   (1990) 12 EHRR 321.

eventually, the company applied to the Strasbourg court claiming the Swiss ban amounted to a violation of *Groppera's* Article 10 freedom of expression.

The court found that the expression in question – the music and advertising – although commercial in nature, did come within the scope of Article 10. However the court also found that the Swiss authorities had a wide margin of appreciation with regard to such matters. The court seemed to place great emphasis on the fact that the act of the Swiss authorities was not aimed at censorship of the broadcasting content but at ensuring proper recognised international standards of broadcasting within the Swiss jurisdiction.[3]

In *Casado Coca v Spain*[4] the applicant was a barrister who had been disciplined for circulating advertising materials.[5] The Strasbourg court found that the disciplinary proceeding had interfered with the applicant's Article 10 rights but that the interference was justified because regulation of barristers' advertising was a legitimate aim. The court affirmed that on matters such as the regulation of commercial expression the state had a wide margin of appreciation. The court outlined its thinking on advertising as follows:

> [f]or the citizen, advertising is a means of discovering the characteristics of services and goods offered to him. Nevertheless, it may sometimes be restricted, especially to prevent unfair competition and untruthful or misleading advertising. In some contexts, the publication of even objective, truthful advertisements might be restricted in order to ensure respect for the rights of others or owing to the special circumstances of particular business activities and professions. Any such restrictions must, however, be closely scrutinised by the Court, which must weigh the requirements of those particular features against the advertising in question.[6]

A factor in the court's decision was that it could not find any European standard to refer to for guidance as to what level of regulation was acceptable. As the court explained:

> [t]he wide range of regulations and the different rates of change in the Council of Europe's member States indicate the complexity of the issue. Because of their direct, continuous contact with their members, the Bar authorities and the country's courts are in a better position than an international court to determine how, at a given time, the right balance can be struck between the various interests involved, namely the requirements of the proper administration of justice, the dignity of the profession, the right of everyone

---

3   See *Groppera* (p 246, n 2) para 73. The case makes an interesting contrast to the
    Informationsverein Lentia v Austria (1993) 17 EHRR 93 in illustrating the extent of the margin
    of appreciation. The discretion will encompass conditions and even a ban in order to ensure
    recognised standards but not a total ban on all bradcasting by private companies in order to
    ensure an individual state's standards.
4   (1994) 18 EHRR 1.
5   The material in question contained only his name, address and contact number.
6   *Casado* (n 4 above) para 51.

to receive information about legal assistance and affording members of the Bar the possibility of advertising their practices.[7]

In coming to this decision the court here was again finely balanced, with the president providing the casting vote in finding no violation.

In *Jacubowski v Germany*[8] the applicant was a newspaper editor who had been dismissed by his employer, a news agency. When the agency dismissed him they also produced a press release outlining the reasons for his dismissal and questioning his professional abilities. In response the applicant produced a circular which he sent to the agency's clients addressing the agency's criticism of him and containing critical newspaper articles about the agency. The German courts had imposed an injunction on the applicant from circulating any more of the documents. The basis of the German court's decision was that the applicant was attempting to advance his own economic interests to the disadvantage of the agency. As they were likely to be competitors in the future the German court found the distribution of the document to be unfairly competitive. The Strasbourg court relied heavily on the German court's view of the matter and found the interference with Article 10 to be within the state's wide margin of appreciation.

In what appears to have been a fractious judgment the minority criticised the majority judgment for not requiring the German state to show a 'pressing social need' for its action. Judges Walsh, Macdonald and Wildhaber in their joint dissenting opinion considered that:

> [t]his is an important case in which admittedly the requirements of protecting the reputation and rights of others (of potential commercial competitors) must be weighed against the applicant's freedom to distribute his circular of 25 September 1984 along with the appended thirteen newspaper articles.
>
> In our opinion, the majority judgment makes it appear as though this case involves simply a choice between two conflicting principles of equal weight. It relies too heavily on the findings of fact by the national courts. In so doing, it gives an excessive significance to the doctrine of the margin of appreciation.

Proportionality and commercial expression

While the state enjoys a wide margin of appreciation with regard to commercial expression the court will still assess the proportionality of the state action. This will involve the court assessing the basis in law for the state action, the legitimate aim the state is attempting to achieve and whether the action is necessary in a democratic society.[9] While the cases in the section above indicate that because the state has a wide margin of appreciation the Strasbourg court is also less than rigorous when

---

7   *Casado* (p 247, n 4) para 55.
8   (1994) 19 EHRR 64.
9   For a full explanation of proportionality see Chapters 3 and 7.

requiring the state to justify its action as evincing a 'pressing social need',[10] the court has drawn the line in certain circumstances.

In *Barthold v Germany*[11] the applicant was a vet who had given a newspaper interview in which he had highlighted the deficiencies of his competitors practices and the merits of his own practice. His conduct in giving such an interview had breached his professional conduct rules prohibiting advertising and unfair competition. As a result of this he had an injunction imposed on him by the German courts. The injunction prohibited him from repeating the original or any new remarks of the same character. The Strasbourg court decided the matter with regard to the proportionality of the state's action. It found that while there was a legitimate aim being pursued in that the state was aiming at 'the protection of the rights of others' ie his competitors, the action was not proportionate because it was more than was necessary to achieve the legitimate aim. The court emphasized the concern that the professional conduct rules might result in:

> discouraging members of the liberal professions from contributing to public debate on topics affecting the life of the community if even there is the slightest likelihood of their utterances being treated as entailing, to some degree, an advertising effect. By the same token, application of a criterion such as this is liable to hamper the press in the performance of its task of purveyor of information and public watchdog.[12]

The case is important to demonstrate the application of proportionality with regard to commercial expression but also to show the sensitivity of the Strasbourg court to matters which, although primarily commercial in nature, might spill over into prohibiting expression which was necessary to promote a democratic society. Therefore professional conduct rules, although aimed at promoting certain commercial standards, must not be so onerous as to run the risk of smothering legitimate expression.

The more important the profession is in terms of its influence on the general public the more carefully a professional standard affecting freedom of expression would have to be. For example, protecting freedom of expression with regard to the medical profession is of a higher level of importance than protecting freedom of expression where it concerns a member of the Professional Footballers Association. In *Colman v United Kingdom*[13] a similar ban on the medical profession to that imposed in *Barthold* was challenged. The GMC changed its rules before the case went to a full hearing and the UK agreed to pay compensation. Similarly in *Hertel v Switzerland*[14] the Strasbourg court found that an injunction banning a scientist from expressing the view that microwave ovens were unsafe was not proportionate to the legitimate aim of protecting the 'rights of others' ie the manufacturers.

10 On this point see Harris, D J, O'Boyle, M, and Warbrick, C, *Law of the European Convention on Human Rights*, (1995) Butterworths, p 406.
11 (1985) 7 EHRR 383.
12 (1985) 7 EHRR 383 at para 58.
13 (1993) 18 EHRR 119.
14 Judgment 25 August 1998.

In *Informationsverein Lentia v Austria*[15] the Strasbourg court recognised the ability of the state to impose restrictions on broadcasting in order to achieve certain legitimate broadcasting standards. The proportionality of the measures taken to ensure such standards would, however, be closely scrutinised by the court. If such standards could be achieved by imposing restrictions on the licences of broadcasters rather than a total ban on broadcasting to achieve these standards, a ban would amount to a violation of Article 10.[16]

In *Autronic AG v Switzerland*[17] the applicant was an electronics company that had been refused permission to receive television programmes from a Soviet satellite. The reason the company wished to receive the broadcasts was to test the capabilities of its equipment which would in turn increase sales. The Swiss authorities refused permission because there had been no consent from the Soviet broadcaster. The company applied to the Strasbourg court claiming the refusal to let it receive the broadcast amounted to an interference with its Article 10 freedom.

The Swiss government argued that because the content of the broadcast was immaterial to the company's aim in receiving the broadcast ie to sell more satellite dishes, the applicants were seeking to protect an economic right and not a right protected by Article 10. The court rejected this submission and held that Article 10 protection covered both the means of transmission or reception as well as its content. The court further considered that the legal status of the applicant (a company) made no difference to its ability to rely on Article 10. It also held that even though the nature of its activities were commercial they still came within the scope of the protection accorded by Article 10.[18] The court then went on to recognise the wide margin of appreciation allowable to the state on commercial matters but found that the restriction on Article 10 imposed by the Swiss state was not 'necessary in a democratic society'. The key factor in the case seems to have been that the Swiss state failed to explain the necessity for the restriction to the satisfaction of the court.[19] As a result of the case it is clear that the means of receiving or transmitting information is also protected by Article 10. Therefore the means of conveying or receiving speech, radio, television, print, art, film and information in electronic form will be protected by Article 10.

The domestic application of Article 10

First tier commercial expression

For first tier commercial expression the incorporation of Article 10 should provide media companies with high levels of protection from state interference. A good example of the difference in approach is found in *Goodwin v United Kingdom*.[20]

---

15   (1993) 17 EHRR 93.
16   *Lentia* (n 15 above) para 39.
17   (1990) 12 EHRR 485.
18   *Autronic* (n 17 above) para 47.
19   *Autronic* (n 17 above) para 61.
20   (1996) 22 EHRR 123.

A journalist received information about the financial problems of a British company from an employee on the basis that the information should not be attributed to the employee. The journalist believed that the information had derived from a genuine source and had no idea that it might have been stolen or was a confidential document. Before publishing his findings, he contacted the company in question to verify the alleged financial difficulties. At this point it became clear, that the information had been derived from a confidential draft corporate plan. The domestic courts then granted an interim injunction to the company restraining the journalist from publishing any of the information he had received. Additionally, the court ordered the journalist to disclose the identity of the source. The applicant refused to do so and the domestic court imposed a fine upon him.

The journalist applied to Strasbourg claiming the actions of the court amounted to a violation of his Article 10 rights. The Strasbourg court took the view that 'limitations on the confidentiality of journalistic sources call for the most careful scrutiny by the court'.[1] Notwithstanding the margin of appreciation available to the national authorities, the Court did not regard the restrictions imposed on the applicant as having been 'necessary in a democratic society'. When balancing the company's interest in unmasking a disloyal employee against the interest of a democratic society in securing a free press,[2] the Court found in favour of the applicant.[3] The protections accorded to the journalistic endeavours protects not just the expression itself, the means of expression but also extends to the gathering of information.

The high level of protection accorded to media companies by the Strasbourg court should be further enhanced by section 12 of the HRA 1998.[4] Section 12 has been formulated to curb interference with freedom of expression by emphasizing the importance of Article 10 in any hierarchy of rights the court may have to consider.[5] Section 12 (2) further provides that if the respondent is not present nor represented the court should not grant relief unless it is satisfied that the applicant has taken all practicable steps to notify the respondent or there are compelling reasons[6] why the respondent should not be notified. Therefore under the HRA a presumption exists that ex parte injunctions will not be granted unless the above criteria are filled.[7] Relief is not to be granted to restrain publication before trial unless 'the court is satisfied that the applicant is likely to establish that publication should not be allowed.'[8] Therefore there must be an assessment of the applicant's case before a grant can be made.[9]

1   See p 250, n 20, Reports 1996- II, § 40.
2   See p 250, n 20, Reports 1996- II§ 45.
3   See also *Camelot Group plc v Centaur Communications* [1998] 1 All ER 251 and *Fressoz and Roire v France* [1999] EHRLR 339.
4   See for example *Sunday Times v United Kingdom* (1979) 2 EHRR 245, *Observer and Guardian v United Kingdom* (1991) 14 EHRR 153, *Sunday Times v United Kingdom (No 2)* (1991) 14 EHRR 229.
5   See Chapter 6 on section 12.
6   The Home Secretary gave the example of an issue of national security and considered that it would be rarely used. See HC Debates, 2 July 1998: Column 536.
7   See the Home Secretary at HC Debates, 2 July 1998: Column 537.
8   Section 12 (3), HRA 1998.
9   This is in line with the Convention case law see *Observer and Guardian v United Kingdom* (1991) 14 EHRR 153.

Second tier expression

Second tier expression has at least the potential to operate in a different way at the domestic level. The main reason for the low level of protection accorded to second tier commercial expression by the Strasbourg court is the fact the court accords a large margin of appreciation to the state where this type of commercial expression is concerned. The margin of appreciation is an international law concept aimed at maintaining a respect for the contracting states' social, economic, cultural and political traditions.[10] It accords a measure of discretion to national authorities when interfering with Convention rights. As such it has no application in the domestic courts.[11] The domestic courts are however likely to accord some measure of discretion to the state on such matters where the aim is economic regulation but it remains to be seen how wide or narrow that discretion will be.[12] It also remains to be seen to what extent the domestic courts would follow the Strasbourg court's approach to proportionality with second tier commercial expression. It would seem that the ECtHR has taken a very lax approach to proportionality because of the state's wide margin of appreciation. At times the Strasbourg court has appeared to apply a 'reasonable' test rather than the more difficult 'pressing social need' test for proportionality.[13]

Again, with second tier commercial expression the emphasis on freedom of expression in section 12 of the HRA could mean a higher level of protection for this type of commercial expression. Section 12 (4) (the court must have regard to the importance of the right to freedom of expression) is worded in broad terms applying to all matters where Article 10 could be affected. In taking account of the Strasbourg jurisprudence under section 2 the courts must also have regard to the special place accorded to Article 10 in section 12 (4), which may lead to a higher level of protection for commercial expression. The domestic courts must work out their own order of primacy. It is almost certain though that a two tier protection for commercial expression at the domestic lever similar to the Strasbourg case law will arise, it is just the extent to which the second tier will be protected that is in question.[14]

Tobacco advertising and Article 10

Certain industries present a higher level of difficulty where advertising restrictions have been imposed. For example, the tobacco industry has traditionally had high

10   See Chapters 3 and 7 on the margin and its application in domestic law.
11   On this see Pannick, D, 'Principles of Interpretation of Convention Rights under the Human Rights Act and the Discretionary Area of Judgment' (1998) *Public Law* p 545, Singh, R, Hunt, M and Demetriou, M, 'Is there a Role for the Margin of Appreciation in National Law after the Human Rights Act?' (1999) *European Human Rights Law Review* 14 and Lord Lester and Pannick, D, *Human Rights Law and Practice* (1999) Butterworths, p 74.
12   See Chapter 7 on the margin of appreciation at the domestic level.
13   *Jacubowski v Germany* (1994) 19 EHRR 64.
14   For a consideration of how the German courts have accommodated Article 10 in the context of competition law see De Merieux, Margaret, 'The German Competition Law and Article 10 of the Convention' in (1995) *European Law Review* pp 388-399.

levels of restrictions placed on their ability to advertise and sell products.[15] Fears obviously exist that the availability of human rights such as Article 10 will allow tobacco companies, in particular, to challenge the restrictions placed on their ability to advertise.[16] Less obviously, such challenges could include a challenge to the requirement that tobacco companies place a health warning on their cigarette packets on the basis that Article 10 protects not only the expression itself but the means of expression.[17] The state, by imposing such a requirement on the means of commercial expression, is therefore interfering with the companies Article 10 freedom of commercial expression.[18] As Gearty stated:

> [a] Canadian court has recently struck down a ban on cigarette advertising on account of the tobacco companies' freedom of expression. The Convention presents a temptation for similar litigation … As things stand at present, it would be possible but surely odd if advertisers could win for themselves a human right to lie; and bitterly ironical if tobacco companies were found to have a human right to persuade us and our children to smoke nicotine. But can we honestly say that restrictions on either group would be "necessary in a democratic society"?[19]

As Gearty has noted the Canadian courts have found that the Tobacco Products Control Act 1988 constituted a violation of the Canadian Charter right of freedom.[20]

Similarly in the United States companies have established a high level of protection for commercial speech under the First amendment, described by the US courts as 'indispensable'.[1] There are however a number of reasons why a similar outcome is unlikely in the UK.

15   See for example the Children and Young Persons Act 1933 s 7. See also John Willman 'The industry that fears brand loyalty going up in smoke' *Financial Times* 23 September 1998, p 3.
16   The tobacco companies have already challenged the EU advertising restrictions see *R v Secretary of State for Health, ex p Imperial Tobacco Ltd* [2000] 1 All ER 572, [2000] 2 WLR 834 .
17   See *Autronic AG v Switzerland* (1990) 12 EHRR 485. For the German experience of this see Nolte, Georg and Raedler, Peter.' German Public Law Case 1996/97' (1997) *European Public Law* vol 3, Issue 4, pp 489-497.
18   On the use of human rights against US tobacco companies in Asia see Wike, Jonathan, 'The Marlboro Man in Asia: US Tobacco and Human Rights' (1996) 29 *Vanderbilt Journal of Transnational Law*, pp 329- 361.
19   Gearty, C A, 'The European Court of Human Rights and the protection of Civil Liberties: an overview' (1993) *Cambridge Law Journal* 1993, p 125.
20   See *RJR-MacDonald Inc v A-G* (1995) 127 DLR (4th) 1. See also NLJ 1996, 146(6757), 1232,1234-1235, Dubick, Keith, 'Commercial Expression: A 'Second-Class' Freedom?' (1996) 60 *Saskatchewan Law Review*, pp 91-130 and Mize, Selene, 'The Word 'Dog' Never Bit Anyone – the Tobacco Advertising Ban and Freedom of Expression' (1995) *Otago Law Review* vol 8, No 3, pp 425-439.
1   See *Virginia State Board of Pharmacy v Virginia Citizens Consumer Council Inc* 425 US 748, 765 (1976). On the use of the First Amendment by companies in the US see Garrison, Michael J, 'Corporate Political Speech, Campaign Spending, and First Amendment Doctrine' (1989) 27 *American Business Law Journal*, pp 163- 213 and Redish, Martin H and Wassermann, Howard M, 'What's Good for General Motors: Corporate Speech and the Theory of Free Expression?' (1998) 66 *The George Washington Law Review*, pp 235-297, Schofield, Michael, 'Muzzling Corporations: The Court Giveth and the Court Taketh Away a Corporation's 'Fundamental Right' to Free Political Speech in *Austin v Michigan Chamber of Commerce*'

First the formulation of the HRA preserves the ability of Parliament to legislate contrary to the Convention rights. Should the tobacco companies challenge the legislation restricting their ability to advertise, the only remedy they could get would be a declaration of incompatibility under section 4 of the HRA. Even if they could succeed in getting such a declaration the state could still decide to leave the provisions untouched. Obtaining a declaration of incompatibility in itself is unlikely as advertising falls into the second tier of commercial expression explained above and as such does not warrant a high level of protection under the Convention.[2] Further, any restriction, even a total ban on tobacco advertising, is likely to be proportionate to the legitimate aim pursued by the state.[3] In particular Article 10 is subject to the qualifications in paragraph 2 which states that freedom of expression 'may be subject to such formalities, conditions, restrictions or penalties as are prescribed by law and are necessary in a democratic society ... for the protection of health ...' The health justification should prove adequate to demonstrate 'a pressing social need' at least from the non-smoker's point of view.

Public authorities and commercial expression

Section 6 of the HRA 1998 makes it unlawful for a 'public authority' to act incompatibly with a Convention right unless they are compelled to do so by primary legislation or provisions made under primary legislation. The types of public authorities that must act compatibly with Article 10 range from obvious public authorities such as the Press Complaints Commission (PCC), the Broadcasting Standards Commission (BSC), the Independent Television Commission (ITC) and the Advertising Standards Authority (ASA), to the courts themselves as a 'public authority' under section 6 (3). All these bodies must, in the exercise of their function, act compatibly with the Convention rights. This includes a positive obligation to protect Convention rights, for example in controlling the award of compensation eg damages for libel. The award must not be of such a quantum that it amounts to a smothering of Article 10.[4] If they do not act compatibly it gives rise to a cause of action alleging a section 6 HRA 1998 unlawful act.[5]

This obligation for these bodies will inherently involve them reviewing whether the standards they presently apply are compatible with the Convention rights.[6] Where these 'public authorities' exercise an adjudicatory function their role will be more

---

(1991) 52 *Louisiana Law Review* 1991, pp 253- 271 and on the Clinton administration's attempts to get round those First Amendment protections see Murphy, Kathryn, 'Can The Budweiser Frog be Forced to Sing a New Tune?: Compelled Commercial Counter-Speech and the First Amendment' (1998) *Virginia Law Review*, pp 1195-1224.

2   *Markt Intern Verlag and Klaus Beermann v Germany* (1989) 12 EHRR 161.

3   The proportionality argument has already been advanced and lost see *R v Secretary of State for Health, ex p Imperial Tobacco Ltd* [2000] 1 All ER 572, [2000] 2 WLR 834.

4   See *Times Newspapers v United Kingdom* (1990) 65 DR 307 and *Tolstoy v United Kingdom* (1995) 20 EHRR 442. See also *Costello – Roberts v United Kingdom* (1993) 19 EHRR 112 and *A v United Kingdom* [1998] 5 BHRC 137.

5   See Chapter 6 on section 6.

6   The BSC has already reviewed its standards see http://www.bsc.org.uk/review2k/index.htm

complex. In particular, the PCC and the BSC will inherently, in the nature of many of the complaints they receive, have to decide whether to interfere with Article 10 or protect Article 8 rights to privacy. A finding for one side will necessarily involve an interference with the other side's Convention rights. In making such a decision these bodies will have to explore the proportionality of their action setting out the aim they are attempting to achieve and explaining why it is necessary in a democratic society.

This balancing act between Article 10 and Article 8 is likely to see numerous challenges to the decisions of these types of 'public authority' in the initial stages of the HRA coming into force. In particular, the German experience of balancing these competing rights will be extremely helpful to both the regulatory bodies and the courts should there be a challenge to a decision of one of these bodies under Section 6.[7] As Professor Markesinis explained:

> in cases where speech clashes with privacy we finds German courts weighing such factors as: (a) the motives of the publisher which, in the context of privacy protection, has been taken to mean if the invasion was motivated by a wish to make money at the expense of the plaintiff damages should be assessed in a way which would deprive the tortfeasor of his ill gotten gains; (b) the importance of the speech, eg does it advance knowledge and public debate or merely benefit the speaker financially? (c) the way in which the information about the plaintiff was obtained: illegal means, telephoto lens (indicating to the 'intruder' that the plaintiff wished to be left alone); (d) the extent of the dissemination of the information; (e) the accuracy of the statement or whether it was fabricated by a news medium; (f) the breath of the restriction which the plaintiff wishes to place on the defendant's speech rights; (g) other, wider societal objectives which may be involved in the dispute and so on. The courts also take the view that a severe attack may justify an otherwise excessive counter-attack …[8]

As with all the other rights and freedoms it is unclear how the margin of appreciation will operate at the domestic level. The courts are likely to recognise the difficulty the broadcasting, press and advertising authorities have in balancing competing rights and so certainly some discretion should be allowable to them with regard to balancing Article 10 against Article 8. While context will be everything in such balancing acts, in general a public authority has had a greater margin of appreciation at the Strasbourg level with regard to privacy than with expression. This is likely to be reflected at the domestic level and so expression will generally be protected to a greater extent than privacy.

7   The US experience of this does not offer much assistance because freedom of speech is expressed in unequivocal terms: see the judgment of Justlice Black in *Konigsberg v State Bar* 366 US 36 (1966).
8   Markesinis, B, 'Privacy, Freedom of Expression, and the Horizontal Effect of the Human Rights Bill: Lessons from Germany` (1999) 115 LQR 62-63 see also Craig, John and Nolte, Nico, 'Privacy and Free Speech in Germany and Canada: Lessons for an English Privacy Tort' (1998) *European Human rights Law Review*, Issue 2, pp 162-180 and Youngs, Raimond, 'Freedom of speech and the protection of democracy: The German approach' (1996) *Public Law* Summer, pp 225-234.

Chapter 11   Commercial expression

Where the balance between Article 10 and Article 8 concerns intrusion into the private lives of members of the board or the managing director of a large corporation the Strasbourg court has taken the view that the ability to express criticism is particularly important. In *Fayed v United Kingdom*[9] the applicant complained about a DTI investigation into the take-over of the House of Fraser which claimed that the Fayed brothers had lied about their origins. The court held that the limits of acceptable criticism for businessmen conducting the affairs of large companies were wider than those applicable to private individuals. Similarly in *Fressoz and Roire v France*[10] the court found a violation of Article 10 where the French courts had punished journalists for publishing details of the salary increases of Jacques Calvet the managing director and Chairman of the Peugot company during an industrial dispute at the company. The court placed great importance on the freedom of the press to contribute to a debate about a company which was a major French car manufacturer and as such its affairs were a matter of public interest. Large corporations may also have to accept a much higher level of criticism of their business activities than would apply to individuals.[11]

The Advertising Standards Authority is to some extent in a more secure position with regard to its maintenance of standards and its adjudication of complaints. Advertising clearly comes within the second tier of commercial expression protected by Article 10 and as such is accorded a lesser protection that other forms of expression. This should remain the case at the domestic level unless the courts decide that the state has a narrow discretion with regard to second-tier commercial expression perhaps relying on the importance of Article 10 as emphasised in section 12 of the HRA. It is, however, likely that this type of expression (advertising) will remain of a lesser order of importance than expression normally categorised as free speech.

The operation of the UK's system of media regulation has recently been challenged in the Strasbourg court. In *Barclay v United Kingdom*[12] the applicants complained about an invasion of privacy by the BBC (a reporter landed on their island) to the Broadcasting Complaints Commission (now part of the BSC). The BCC denied jurisdiction unless and until the relevant broadcast took place. The applicants had brought domestic proceedings challenging the decision of the BCC. In his judgment on the application for judicial review, Mr Justice Sedley agreed that on a proper construction of Section 143 of the Broadcasting Act 1990, the BCC had no role to play until a broadcast had occurred. He concluded in refusing leave to appeal:

> [t]he law of England and Wales at present places no general constraints upon invasions of privacy as such. Section 143 of the Broadcasting Act 1990 unambiguously limits the power of the [BCC] to adjudication upon complaints of infringement of privacy against the BBC arising out of programmes which have been broadcast. If an unwarranted infringement of privacy has been committed by the BBC otherwise that in connection with the obtaining of

9   (1994) 18 EHRR 393.
10   [1999] EHRLR 339.
11   See Padfield, F, 'Defamation, Freedom of Speech and Corporations' (1993) *Juridical Review* 294.
12   Application No 00035712/97, judgment date 18 May 1999.

material included in a broadcast programme – whether because the nexus is insufficient or because no programme has been broadcast - the Commission is without adjudicative power. It cannot therefore entertain an anticipatory complaint even where, once the programme is broadcast, the complaint is bound to succeed. It follows that in this field and to this extent, as elsewhere in English law, the individual is without an effective remedy before a national authority if the right to respect for his or her private and family life is violated.

After the broadcast the BCC delivered its adjudication on the applicants' complaint. It found that 'in landing on the Barclays' private island and in broadcasting footage obtained, the BBC unwarrantably infringed the Barclays' privacy.'[13] The applicants then applied to the Strasbourg court alleging violations of Articles 8 and 13 of the Convention. The substance of the complaint was that the absence of adequate protection of their privacy against the public broadcast of a BBC television programme filmed on their private island denied them the protection required under the Convention. Specifically the scope of the BCC jurisdiction was too narrow as they could not prevent a programme from being shown, they could only deal with programmes that had already been broadcast, and they had no power to award damages where they did find that an unwarranted breach of privacy has occurred.

In dealing with the complaint the ECtHR considered that the behaviour of the BBC had not in fact breached the applicants Article 8 rights. The ECtHR considered:

that an interference with an applicant's private life could result from an unauthorised entry into and filming on premises where the applicant had established his home life. However, the mere ownership of property is not sufficient to render it a 'home' for the purposes of Article 8; nor does unauthorised entry onto property owned by another, without more, necessarily entail any interference with respect for private life. The Court notes that, at the relevant time, the applicants did not have a private or family life or home on Brecqhou. They were in the process of having a house built so they were not living on the island and there was only a construction site with builders working there. The applicants were not on the island when the film was taken. The film shows the island where the reporter landed, and the building site. The Court thus considers that the presence of the reporter on the island cannot, itself, therefore have interfered with the applicants' right to respect for their private and family life, or their home.

The judgement itself is a strange one as the substance of the applicants complaint was about the BCC not protecting their privacy and not the BBC's actions. As a result the question remains open as to whether if there had of been an infringement of the applicants Article 8 rights by the BBC the inadequacies of the BCC would have been held to amount to a violation of Article 8 and 13.

The PCC, BSC, ITC and the ASA are also vulnerable to a claim that they are insufficiently independent for the purposes of Article 6 (fair trial) of the ECHR. The right to a fair trial contained in Article 6 includes the right to a hearing before an

13   See the decision of 16 December 1996.

independent and impartial tribunal. The Strasbourg court has applied very high standards with regard to this requirement.[14] As a result, the fact that the Secretary of State appoints and pays lay members of employment tribunals has been held to be insufficiently impartial for the purposes of Article 6 of the ECHR.[15] The ECtHR has similarly found that the Bailiff of Guernsey is in breach of Article 6 because of his combined role as the executive, administrative and judicial function on the island.[16] The claim that a body is insufficiently independent and impartial is often combined with a claim that Article 13 (right to an effective remedy) has also been breached. In *Govell v United Kingdom*[17] the Commission took the view that a complaint to the Police Complaints Authority (PCA) was an insufficiently effective remedy because the PCA did not have the requisite level of independence.

To take the PCC as an example, its independence and impartiality can be questioned because of its reliance on the publishing industry. First it is entirely funded by the publishing industry. Second its Chairman (currently Lord Wakeham) is appointed by the newspaper and magazine publishing industry. Third approximately one third of the Commission members are senior members of the publishing industry. Fourth the public members (the majority) are appointed by a body called the 'independent appointments commission'. This commission contains five people including the Chairman of Press Standards Board of Finance and is chaired by the Chairman of the PCC who also chooses the three other members of the 'independent appointments commission'. Because of these factors there is some doubt as to whether the PCC is sufficiently impartial and independent for the purposes of Article 6 and 13.[18] The ITC is certainly open to challenge on Article 6 grounds as the Secretary of State for Culture, Media and Sport appoints the Chairman, Deputy Chairman and (usually eight) Members of the Commission. The ASA is organised in a similar way to the PCC and so is open to similar claims about its impartiality and independence.

The BBC and C4 as public authorities under section 6 HRA 1998

Certain implications of 'public authority' status under the HRA remain unclear. Both the BBC and Channel 4 are likely to be considered to be public authorities under either section 6 (1) (obvious public authorities) or section 6 (3) (any person certain of whose functions are functions of a public nature) in which case they must act compatibly with the Convention rights.

14   See van Dijk, P and van Hoof, G J H, *Theory and Practice of the European Court of Human Rights*, p 452.
15   *Smith v Secretary of State for Trade and Industry* [2000] ICR 69, [2000] IRLR 6. In Scotland temporary sheriffs have been held to be insufficiently impartial on the same basis which in turn casts doubt on the operation of part-time recorders in the English courts.
16   *McGonnell v United Kingdom* (2000) Application No 00028488/95, (2000) Times, 22 February.
17   Appl 27237/95 Commission 14 January 1998: [1999] EHRLR 121.
18   Requirements of impartiality have been set down recently by the House of Lords in *Re Pinochet Ugarte* [1999] 1 All ER 577, [1999] 2 WLR 272, and guideleines on bias can be found in *Locabail (United Kingdom) Ltd v Bayfield Properties Ltd* (1999) [2000] 1 All ER 65, [2000] 2 WLR 870. See also Chapter 4 (Articles 6 and 13) and Chapter 9.

The BBC, for example, has the following characteristics which would make it a 'public authority'. The BBC was incorporated by Royal Charter granted in exercise of the Royal Prerogative on 20 December 1926. It is funded almost entirely by the state. The objects of the BBC are primarily the provision of public radio and television broadcasting services (Article 3(a)) and, for this purpose, the BBC is empowered to acquire from the Secretary of State a licence for such period subject to such terms as he might set out. The conduct of the Corporation's affairs is the responsibility of the Governors who are, by Article 1 of the Charter, expressed to be members of the Corporation. The Governors are appointed by the state.

However the status of the BBC as a state body was considered in *BBC v Johns*.[19] The Court considered whether the BBC was an instrument of government which was entitled to the immunities and privileges of the Crown in relation to taxation. The Court concluded that the BBC was not a servant or agent of the Crown for those particular purposes. The Court of Appeal provided the following reasons for its decision: there was no evidence that Parliament intended broadcasting to be a function of government; the BBC had been created by Charter and had been given an independent legal personality which was licensed to carry out a broadcasting service because this was in the public interest; the fact there was a charter did not make it an agent of the Crown; the licence agreement emphasised the independent contractor status of the BBC; while the government could maintain control over technical aspects of the BBC's broadcasting function its general function was free of state control.[20]

Nevertheless the government has accepted that the BBC, and possibly C4, are a 'public authority' for the purposes of section 6 of the HRA. Responding to the concerns raised on this matter on Second Reading of the HRA 1998 in the House of Lords the Home Office Minister, Lord Williams of Mostyn, stated:

> Lord Simon of Glaisdale, asked what would or would not be a public body. He rightly conjectured that we would anticipate the BBC being a public authority and that Channel 4 might well be a public authority, but that other commercial organisations, such as private television stations, might well not be public authorities. I stress that that is a matter for the courts to decide as the jurisprudence develops. Some authorities plainly exercise wholly public functions; others do not. There is no difficulty here.[1]

It is most likely that, because their primary function is public in nature, both the BBC and C4 will be considered to be obvious public authorities under section 6 (1), all of whose functions both private and public must be compatible with the Convention rights.[2] However, even if they were considered quasi-public bodies under section 6 (3), should make no difference if the substance of a Convention complaint concerns an aspect of their public function, ie a broadcast has interfered

---

19   [1965] Ch 32.
20   This did not mean the BBC was free from judicial review.
1   HL Debates 3 November 1997: Column 1309, Channel 4 is a public service broadcaster for information, education and entertainment governed by the Broadcasting Act 1990.
2   See Chapter 6 on section 6.

with a person's Article 8 rights. Should either the BBC or C4 interfere with a Convention right this gives rise to a claim under section 6 of the HRA that the 'public authority' acted unlawfully. These bodies are therefore under a more onerous obligation when it comes to Convention rights than their private competitors, although should a law of privacy develop as a result of the HRA this would affect all broadcasters equally.

There is another potentially more serious impact for the BBC and C4 with regard to claims that their own Convention rights have been infringed. As they are a 'public authority' they may as such not be able to rely on the HRA. This is because a 'public authority' at the Strasbourg level cannot bring proceedings under the Convention as it is incapable of fulfilling 'victim' status.[3] The HRA similarly requires the Strasbourg test of 'victim' status to be fulfilled in order to claim a violation of a Convention right. At the Strasbourg level the court has been very careful to leave open the question of whether or not the BBC is part of the state.[4] As such the BBC and C4 have been able to fulfil the criteria for 'victim' status at the Strasbourg level.[5] The HRA, however, disturbs this delicate balance as prima facie both the BBC and C4 are public authorities for the purposes of the HRA and as such there is a question as to the extent they can rely on the Convention rights contained in the HRA.[6] Whether they are an obvious public authority under section 6 (1) or a quasi-public body under section 6 (3) should make no difference if the substance of their Convention complaint concerns an aspect of their public function eg a broadcast has been interfered with by the state. They will still be unable to fulfil 'victim' status as the interference concerns their public function and as such they are acting as a 'public authority'.[7]

There are two impacts for the BBC in terms of its inability to fulfill victim status. First should the state interfere with its Convention rights it cannot claim to be a 'victim' and therefore cannot challenge the state action under the HRA. Second and less obviously should the BBC be subject to a claim that it has acted unlawfully in breach of its Section 6 obligation with regard to a member of the public's privacy rights it cannot defend its action by reference to a competing claim to Article 10 as only a 'victim' has rights enforceable against the court. It would be an odd state of affairs if the result of the BBC and C4 having 'public authority' status conferred upon them means they are denied the ability to rely on the HRA in challenging state interference with their activities even though they could challenge that act in Strasbourg.[8] It would also place the BBC at a significant disadvantage if it could not rely on the HRA but ITV could because it is private in nature.

The courts may have to find a way to broaden 'victim' status or somehow differentiate the BBC and C4's public authority status for HRA purposes from victim test purposes

3   See *Ayuntamiento de M v Spain* (1990) 68 DR 209.
4   See *Hilton v United Kingdom* (1988) 57 DR 108.
5   See *BBC v United Kingdom* (1996) *A-84* DR 129 and *Channel Four v United Kingdom* (1989) 61 DR 285.
6   See Chapter 6 on section 6.
7   This does not seem to have hampered the BBC in Scotland claiming, unsuccessfully, Convention rights: BBC, (2000) Petitioners Times, 11 April.
8   Although if the BBC is a public authority for the purposes of the HRA the Strasbourg court may have to re-examine its status.

to deal with this particular situation. Alternatively, the court's free standing obligation in section 6 to act compatibly with the Convention rights should allow the courts to consider the BBC's Convention rights even though the BBC itself is incapable of fulfilling victim status. On this basis, if the matter before the court concerned an alleged violation of Article 8 committed by the BBC in its role as a 'public authority', the court could independently weigh up the competing rights of Article 10 and Article 8 even though the BBC could not claim to be a victim. Additionally, as section 11 of the HRA preserves pre-existing claims, both the BBC and C4 should still be able to challenge actions of the state which interfere with their function relying on those forms of action available before the HRA.[9]

9   See for example *A-G v BBC* [1980] 3 All ER 161.

Chapter twelve

Protocol 1, Article 1: Shareholders and protection of property

The meek may inherit the earth – but not its mineral rights.[1]

Protocol 1, Article 1 appears in Schedule 1 of the HRA as follows:

[e]very natural or legal person is entitled to the peaceful enjoyment of his possessions except in the public interest and subject to the conditions provided for by law and the general principles of international law.

The preceding provisions shall not, however, in any way impair the right of the state to enforce such laws it deems necessary to control the use of property in accordance with general interest or to secure the payment of taxes or other contributions or penalties.

1   J Paul Getty.

Companies as will be observed below have no difficulty relying on Protocol 1, Article 1, where an act of a public authority interferes with its property rights. [2] However, one of the more persistent myths about the HRA in the media and the practitioner journals is that the HRA will lead to a multitude of frivolous actions brought by shareholders alleging rights violations. On the surface such a myth has a veneer of truth: shares are property, property is protected by Protocol 1, Article 1 therefore shareholders can sue if something affects their shares. Our main purpose in this particular Chapter, after setting out the general application of Protocol 1, Article 1, is to dispel that myth. As we have already observed in terms of victim status the shareholder cannot fulfil victim status where the violating act of a public authority relates to Protocol 1, Article 1 and is aimed at the property of the company. [3] During the life of the company this would preclude most HRA litigation by shareholders for acts aimed at the company. However, it is the case that shareholders can fulfil victim status where the violation aimed at the company concerns other articles such as Article 6 and Article 10. [4] As a result should the government attempt to remove the broadcasting licence of a commercial radio company the company, shareholders, employees and possibly creditors could all be potential victims of a rights violation. These cases tend however to be extremely rare and serious and not at all frivolous litigation. Similarly where the company is in liquidation, administration, receivership or subject to a court order the shareholders may fulfil the criteria necessary to be the victim of a rights violation with regard to Protocol 1, Article 1. Again these situations are extreme and while this may make the life of the receiver somewhat more difficult, a court will have already had to consider the Convention in making any order, an administrator or liquidator is also likely to fulfil public authority status under the HRA because of the public nature of their functions and so respect Convention rights. [5]

As will be observed below companies are in general not public authorities and so have no obligation to act compatibly with the Convention rights. Even where they are quasi-public bodies they will not have any obligations under the HRA where the company is acting in its private capacity. Actions of the company which affect the shareholders' Protocol 1, Article 1 rights such as compulsory purchase of shares, allotment and issue of shares and variation of class rights are essentially private in nature and do not give rise to any directly enforceable rights under the HRA. Rather, should a shareholder wish to allege that an act of the company violated a shareholder's Protocol 1, Article 1 rights they would have to rely on the horizontal effect of the HRA by relying on the appeal mechanism for compulsory purchase in the Companies Act 1985 or alleging 'unfairly prejudicial conduct' under section 459 and arguing that the court as a public authority under the HRA should protect their Convention rights. The ability of shareholders to succeed in such actions will not be very different from those prior to the HRA because Protocol 1, Article 1 as interpreted by the Strasbourg court is a very weak right. It may however help where the compensation for a violation of Protocol 1, Article 1 is very low.

2 See *Pine Valley Developments v Ireland* (1991) 14 EHRR 319.
3 See Chapter 8.
4 See Chapter 8.
5 See below.

How has the Strasbourg Court interpreted Protocol 1, Article 1?

The Strasbourg authorities demonstrate that Protocol 1, Article 1 of the ECtHR offers to deliver more from an initial reading, than it has ever delivered in practice. While Article 1 of Protocol 1 is one of the guaranteed rights contained in the ECHR, it is heavily qualified.[6] The decision to include Protocol 1, Article 1 in the ECHR was a controversial one. It was not included in the original Convention rights because its inclusion could have endangered agreement on the Convention in 1950. Even when it was added in 1952 it was not without difficulty. The decision to include Article 1 of Protocol 1 in the ECHR revealed fundamental differences between member states in the 1950s as to whether such provisions should be included within the Convention. Specifically, the governments of Sweden and the United Kingdom were concerned that the addition of a property right would interfere with their programmes of nationalisation. They made it clear that they did not want a Convention which would prevent them from forcibly acquiring property as part of a bona fide socio-economic programme. They wanted to ensure that their right to acquire property under compulsion as part of a policy of nationalisation would remain.[7] There were other fundamental objections too: it was argued, for example, that the right to possess property and protect property ownership was an *economic* right rather than a civil right, and that a convention concerned with the protection of human rights was an inappropriate vehicle within which to formulate and by which to protect such rights.[8] As a consequence of these objections, the right to the protection of property conferred by Article 1 of Protocol 1, both in the express wording and its interpretation by the ECtHR, is highly qualified to the detriment of the individual or company in whom those rights are vested.[9]

The case law of the ECtHR reveals common themes in the interpretation and construction of Article 1 of Protocol 1. The ECtHR has tended to ask two questions in determining whether the Article has been violated on the facts of any one given case. First, have the claimant's possessions been interfered with and, if so, is there nevertheless a 'fair balance' between the interests of the public and those of the individual claimant, ie is the act proportionate to the legitimate aim pursued?[10]

6   ECHR Article 1 of Protocol 1 was signed by the United Kingdom on 20 March 1952, ratified on 3 November 1952 and came into force with non-material reservations on 18 May 1954.
7   See Chapter 2 on the background to the Convention.
8   See J Kingston, 'Rich People Have Rights Too? The Status of property as a fundamental right' in L Heffernan (ed), *Human Rights: A European Perspective*, (1994) Round Hall Press Dublin.
9   See generally Reid *A Practitioner's Guide to the European Convention on Human Rights* (1998) Sweet & Maxwell, pp 335-340 and for a consideration of the Fifth Amendment in the US which operates in a similar way see Vickory, Frank A and Diskin, Barry A, 'Advances in Private Property Protection Rights: The States in the Vanguard' (1997) 34 *American Business Law Journal*, pp 561-605.
10 Although an analysis of the authorities reveals that the court's time is largely taken up with a consideration of the 'fair balance' test on the facts, including a consideration of the concept of proportionality, it is clear that the test under Protocol 1, Article 1 is a two-stage one. When commentators state that under Article 1 of Protocol 1 there is a '*single principle of fair balance*' (Sir Nicholas Bratza, 'The Implications of the Human Rights Act 1998 for Commercial Practice

Interference with possessions

The word 'property' does not actually appear in the first part of Protocol 1, Article 1. Instead the word 'possessions' is used. The word 'possessions' has been defined very widely by the ECHR.[11] The word includes, but is not limited to, movable and immovable property, incorporeal interests such as shares,[12] patents,[13] contractual rights including rights in leases,[14] the right to exercise a profession,[15] judgment debts,[16] and unestablished legal claims.[17]

Have an individual's possessions been interfered with?

Having established whether or not the item affected is a 'possession', the act complained of must interfere with that 'possession'. The leading case of *Sporrong and Lönnroth v Sweden*[18] sets out the criteria for deciding whether a person's or company's possessions have been interfered with. The ECtHR produced guidelines to determine whether an individual's possessions have been interfered with at paragraph 61 of the judgment, which has been applied and followed in subsequent cases. The *Sporrong* ratio provides that an individual's possessions will have been 'interfered with', within the meaning of Article 1 of Protocol 1 on the facts of any given case if:

(1) an individual's possessions has been interfered with by the state; this is where the interference is not the actual taking of possessions. Examples have been the provisional transfer of land[19] and the voiding of an order in favour of the applicant;[20] or

(2) an individual has been deprived of his possessions by the state; this rule applies to obvious taking of possessions and to de facto deprivations. For example the loss of use but not title to land was deemed 'interfered with' in *Papamichalopoulos v Greece*;[1] or

(3) an individual's possessions have been subjected to control by the state. Here again this is not a taking of property but the interference through control such as planning[2] and rent controls.[3]

(2000) *European Human Rights Law Review*, Issue 1, p 6, they are referring to the single principle of the second stage.

11 'Beins' in the French text of the Convention, which is wider than the English concept of possessions.

12 *Bramelid and Malmstrom v Sweden* (1982) 29 DR 64.

13 *Smith Kline and French Laboratories v Netherlands* (1990) 66 DR 20.

14 *A, B and Co AS v Germany* (1978) 14 DR 146; *Mellacher v Austria*, Series A, No 169; (1989) 12 EHRR 391.

15 *Van Marle v Netherlands* (1986) 8 EHRR 483.

16 *Stran Greek Refineries and Stratis Andreadis v Greece* (1994) 19 EHRR 293.

17 *Pressos Compania Naviera SA v Belgium* Series A, No 332; (1995) 21 EHRR 301.

18 Case (1982) 5 EHRR 35.

19 *Erkner and Hofauer v Austria* (1987) 9 EHRR 464.

20 *Stran Greek Refineries v Greece* (1994) 19 EHRR 293.

1 (1993) 16 EHRR 440.

2 See *Pine Valley Developments v Ireland* (1991) 14 EHRR 319.

3 *Mellacher v Austria* (1989) 12 EHRR 391.

Fair balance test

If a court concludes, on the facts, that there has been interference, deprivation or control by the state, it will move to decide whether such interference was justified by the second paragraph of Protocol 1, Article 1 in that it was done 'in the public interest' or 'to enforce such laws ... [as the state] ... deems necessary to control the use of property in accordance with general interest.' When determining whether the public or general interest has been satisfied, the ECtHR will consider whether the interference results in a 'fair balance' between the interests of the wider community and those of the applicant. The court, in considering fair balance, will have regard to the reasons for the interference (the legitimate aim) and the proportionality of the interference itself.[4] The availability of an effective remedy and compensation for the applicant is highly relevant when assessing whether there is a 'fair balance' justifying the state interference.[5]

In *Sporrong v Sweden*, the applicants were property owners in Stockholm who objected to the length of expropriation permits and prohibitions on construction which they claimed wrongfully interfered with the peaceful enjoyment of their possessions. They claimed and the ECtHR found that their property ownership had been rendered 'precarious and defeasible' by the permits and prohibitions.[6] The construction controls were found to have been an interference with possessions in that the applicant's possessions had been subjected to state control, whilst the expropriation permits were found to be an interference by the state within the first part of the *Sporrong* ratio. The fair balance between the rights of the individuals in their private property and the requirements of the general interest had been upset by the prolonged extension of the permits and prohibitions. Swedish domestic law did not provide a means for the applicants to challenge or reduce the time limits for expropriation or to claim compensation. The court found that the applicants had unnecessarily borne excessive burdens and Article 1 of Protocol 1 was found to have been violated.

Similarly, in *Holy Monasteries v Greece*,[7] the government of Greece passed laws that created a presumption of state ownership in cases of disputed ownership of monastic lands. When applying and considering the 'fair balance' test, the court considered evidence as to the compensation available to the monasteries following the deprivation of disputed land, and the level of compensation. The ECtHR held at paragraph 61 of the judgment:

> [i]n this connection, the taking of property without payment of an amount reasonably related to its value will normally constitute a disproportionate interference and a total lack of compensation can be considered justifiable under Protocol 1, Article 1 only in exceptional circumstances. Article 1 does

4   Proportionality is, since the introduction of the Civil Procedure Rules 1998, a concept formally known to English lawyers: see CPR Parts 1, 3, 5 (overriding objective); 1.4.10 (duty to the Court); 31.02 (disclosure) and 44.4.1 (costs).
5   On compulsory purchase and compensation at the domestic level see Redman, Michael, 'Compulsory Purchase, Compensation and Human Rights' (1999) *Journal of Planning and Environmental Law*, April, pp 315- 326.
6   *Sporrong and Lönnroth v Sweden* (see p 266, n 18) at page 50, para 60.
7   *Holy Monasteries v Greece* (1994) 20 EHRR 1.

not however guarantee full compensation in all circumstances, since the legitimate objectives of a 'public interest' may call for reimbursement of less than the full market value.

The ECtHR found that the lack of compensation provided by the Greek government meant that the Greek legislation violated ECHR Article 1 of Protocol 1.

By contrast, in *Lithgow v United Kingdom*[8] the government compulsorily took possession of land and properties belonging to companies as part of a nationalisation scheme empowered by the Aircraft and Shipbuilding Industries Act 1977. The applicants accepted the validity of compulsory acquisition as part of a programme of nationalisation, but complained that the compensation afforded to them, once the property had been compulsorily purchased, was too low and improperly calculated, as it was based on a hypothetical assessment of the individual share value of the companies immediately prior to the decision to nationalise was announced. It was not based on the asset value of the companies and so the shareholders would have recovered more in a liquidation of the companies involving a sale of assets than they received from the government as compensation. The ECtHR rejected the claims and held at paragraph 122 of their judgment:

> [c]ompensation must normally be reasonably related to the value of the property taken, but Protocol 1, Article 1 does not guarantee full compensation in all cases. Legitimate objectives of public interest may justify reimbursement at less than the full market value; the nature of the property taken and the circumstances of the taking may be taken into account in holding the balance between the public and private interests. The standard of compensation for a whole industry may therefore differ from the standard required in other cases. The Court will respect the national legislature's judgment in this respect unless manifestly without reasonable foundation.

These dicta serves to demonstrates how toothless Protocol 1, Article 1 has been and is in practice. The ECtHR has allowed a huge margin of appreciation to the individual states in interfering with possessions. It is only if the state acts 'manifestly without reasonable foundation' that the court will intervene. The applicant's task is made more difficult by the fact that the Strasbourg court has no mechanism for determining factual matters. This, it has been argued, results in the ECtHR being excessively deferential to the factual assertions of the contracting states.[9]

A further example of this can be found in *James v United Kingdom*;[10] the application centred around the Leasehold Reform Act 1967 which was designed to protect a right of long-term tenants to buy the leased properties at the end of the term of the lease. The property owners complained that the compulsory transfers and calculation of compensation paid violated Protocol 1, Article 1 of the ECHR. However, the Court was unanimous in holding that a compulsory transfer from

8   *Lithgow v United Kingdom* (1986) 8 EHRR 329.
9   See Jordan Nicholas, 'The Implications for Commercial Lawyers in Practice' in *The Impact of Human Rights Bill on English Law* Basil S Markesinis (ed) (1998).
10   *James v United Kingdom* (1986) 8 EHRR 123.

one individual to another may be a legitimate means of promoting the public interest, even though the public at large has no direct benefit from the transfer. Regulating private ownership as part of a socio-economic programme is within the State's margin of appreciation in the context of Protocol 1, Article 1. The compensation payable under the Act to the property owners was less than full market value but the Act was not found to contravene Protocol 1, Article 1 by reason of this undervaluation of compensation in market terms.

In conclusion, the ECHR will allow an interference with an individual's property, provided a 'fair balance' is struck between the interfering party and the property owner. Central to the question of whether a 'fair balance' has been struck, is a consideration of the level of compensation (if any) paid by the interfering party to the property owner. It should be noted that it is clear from the authorities that the ECtHR will not, for example, guarantee the payment of compensation at any given rate, let alone fair market rate. It is also clear that the state has a wide margin of appreciation for determining what property to take and what compensation to pay.

Will Protocol 1, Article 1 operate in the same way at the domestic level?

There are two significant differences between the way Protocol 1, Article 1 has operated in the Strasbourg court and the way it will operate at the domestic level. First, the case law at the Strasbourg level accords a large margin of appreciation to the contracting state when dealing with Protocol 1, Article 1. Second the domestic courts are likely to be more protective of property rights than the Strasbourg court. The margin of appreciation will not operate at the domestic level in its Strasbourg form. There is, however, likely to be some discretion accorded to the state at the domestic level but that is unlikely to be as wide as the Strasbourg court would accord. In particular that discretion in the context of Protocol 1, Article 1 is more likely to be limited because of the value English courts have traditionally placed on property rights. A possible justification for the English courts in departing from the Strasbourg jurisprudence is the evolutionary character of the Convention.

As noted above it has been argued that the ECtHR, because it has no mechanism for determining factual matters, is excessively deferential to the factual assertions of the contracting states.[11] The domestic courts are unlikely to be as deferential to the factual assertions of the state as to the respective merits of balancing private and public interests. Should the domestic courts wish to go further and restrict the state's wide discretion to interfere with 'possessions' they could depart from the Strasbourg case law by utilising the dynamic character of the Convention.[12] Treating the Convention as an evolving dynamic document which reflects the values of the member states would certainly restrict the state's ability to interfere with individual possessions. While with other qualified rights the Strasbourg court has interpreted

11   See Jordan Nicholas, 'The Implications for Commercial Lawyers in Practice' in *The Impact of Human Rights Bill on English Law* Basil S Markesinis (ed) (1998).
12   On the dynamic character of the Convention see Chapter 3.

the qualifications restrictively[13] the ECtHR has always given full rein to the qualifications in Protocol 1, Article 1. As appears from the authorities set out above, the ECtHR will even permit compensation at less than market level in certain circumstances. This interpretation of Protocol 1, Article 1 reflects a concern by the original framers of the ECHR to ensure that the ECHR does not act as a de facto bar to policies such as nationalisation. There is a sub-text in these and related judgements[14] that the ECHR assumes that nationalisation policies are sufficiently in the public interest to justify an individual's private compensation at less than market value, ex hypothesi disturbing market equilibrium and compensating at a loss making level.[15] In this regard, the ECtHR has reflected the intentions of the framers in the 1950s in promoting socialist policies and doctrines in preference to the economic 'rights' of individuals.

This indicates that the ECtHR has placed the rights contained in Protocol 1, Article 1 at the bottom of the hierarchy of rights contained in the ECHR. It is after all a document primarily aimed at protecting civil and political rights. There is however the possibility that the domestic courts could begin to move Protocol 1, Article 1 up the hierarchy. The ECtHR has in the past looked at the intentions of the framers in qualifying Protocol 1, Article 1 when deciding on an alleged violation. The dynamic interpretation of the Convention has had little role to play in the case law thus far. There is a strong argument to the effect that the ECtHR's approach to Protocol 1, Article 1 is out of step with the values of the member states of the Council of Europe. The collapse of communism in 1989 and the development of capitalist systems in most European states has placed a great deal of emphasis on the creation of individual wealth. In turn the importance placed on individual 'possessions' by the member states at the start of the 21st century is of a significantly higher order than that accorded to property by the framers of the ECHR in the 1950s. The ECtHR in maintaining a highly qualified right to property is sustaining an outmoded concept of the state's right to interfere with individual possessions. Not only are nationalisation programmes relatively uncommon but most members of the Council of Europe are engaged in privatisation programmes. The only reason for the qualifications in paragraph two of Protocol 1, Article 1 is the need to pursue nationalisation programmes and so they become more difficult to sustain.

In general, whether utilising the evolutionary character of the Convention or not, the domestic courts are more likely to offer a higher level of protection to property than the Strasbourg court has. At the very least this should mean that the levels of compensation provided for compulsory purchase should be at market rate. There is some authority for this in the case law. In *Lithgow v United Kingdom*,[16] the Court distinguished compensation for whole industries from other cases. This distinction, coupled with the Court's preamble that '. . . compensation must normally be

13   See Chapter 11 on Article 10.
14   *Mellacher v Austria* (1989) 12 EHRR 391; *Scollo v Italy* (1995) 22 EHRR 514; and *Handyside v United Kingdom* (1976) 1 EHRR 737.
15   Whether an individual suffers a 'loss' at a prescribed level of compensation is a question of fact in any given circumstance; but it is suggested that in other contexts, an individual would expect to receive a market rate for the forcible disposal of a chattel (eg damages at common law).
16   See p 268, n 8 at para 122.

reasonably related to the value of the property taken'[17] leads to a fair conclusion that corporations and individuals should under ECHR Protocol 1, Article 1 be compensated at no less than market value, if their property is compulsorily interfered with.

Will Protocol 1, Article 1 protect dissenting minority shareholders?

Where shareholders are subject to an act authorised by the general meeting or by the articles of association there may be an interference with Protocol 1, Article 1. Compulsory purchase, alteration of share capital, variation of class rights all have a potentially detrimental effect on the shareholders' property rights. However in almost all cases the act of compulsion, alteration or variation will have been taken by a company that is not a 'public authority' for the purposes of the HRA. Even quasi-public bodies under section 6 (3) (b) of the HRA such as British Gas and British Telecom are unlikely to be acting in their public capacity when dealing with the shares of the company. As such a dissenting shareholder has no vertical cause of action under the HRA. There is, however, a horizontal effect of the HRA which could aid a dissenting minority shareholder. Either utilising the appeal mechanism in Part XIIIA of the Companies Act 1985 where compulsory purchase is at issue under the Companies Act 1985, or using section 459 and in both cases arguing that the court as a 'public authority' has an obligation to act compatibly with the Convention rights, the shareholder can introduce the fact that the compulsion, alteration or variation is an interference with Article 1 of Protocol 1.

Using section 459 and the HRA

Section 459 of the Companies Act 1985 contains the concept of 'unfairly prejudicial conduct'. The court have interpreted this section broadly to cover not just strict legal rights but also expectations and at times have allowed the shareholders to bring an action even though the corporate property is at issue. The operation of this section may allow shareholders to utilise Protocol 1, Article 1 to a greater extent than would normally be the case.

The 'exceptions' to *Foss v Harbottle*[18] proved extremely difficult for members to use in practice and so in 1962 the Jenkins Committee recommended the creation of a statutory unfair prejudice remedy.[19] The remedy would allow easier access to the courts should an unfairly prejudicial act occur. It was not until 1980 that the remedy was introduced in its modern form and it now lies in section 459 of the Companies Act 1985. A member of the company can bring an action where unfairly prejudicial conduct has occurred. This statutory provision moved the courts away from their traditional role of maintaining the corporate nature of the company and towards the evaluation of individual expectations within the company.

17 See p 268, n 8 at para 122.
18 (1843) 2 Hare 461.
19 Report of the Company Law Committee (1962) Cmnd 1749 para 206.

Section 459 has been an extremely successful statutory exception to the rule in *Foss v Harbottle* but has led to some disquiet about the number of shareholder actions under Section 459 and the amount of court time they take up. Addressing these concerns Lord Hoffman in *O'Neill v Phillips* [1999] 2 BCLC 1, the first section 459 case to reach the House of Lords, indicated that the courts would move to restrict the concept of unfairness to breach of the articles or using the articles in a manner which equity would regard as contrary to good faith. This would move the courts back to the maintenance of the corporate structure. Addressing the Law Commission's[20] concern that defining the unfairness concept in this way would unduly restrict the availability of the remedy he stated:

> [i]n my view, a balance has to be struck between breath of the discretion given to the court and the principle of legal certainty. Petitions under s 459 are often lengthy and expensive. It is highly desirable that lawyers should be able to advise their clients whether or not a petition is likely to succeed.[1]

The principle of legal certainty in the context of section 459 may come under strain when the courts are faced with interpreting it compatibly with the Convention rights. The courts have maintained throughout their interpretation of the concept of unfairly prejudicial conduct that, while mismanagement of the company may theoretically lead to conduct which is unfairly prejudicial within the meaning of Companies Act 1985, section 459, they are usually reluctant to accept that legitimate management decisions fall within the ambit of that section. In *Re Elgindata Ltd* [1991] BCLC 969 Warner J at 993 stated:

> I was referred, on this point also, to the judgment of Peter Gibson J in *Re Sam Weller & Sons Ltd* (1990) Ch 682 at the end of which ... he said that he had no doubt that the court would ordinarily be very reluctant to accept that managerial decisions could amount to unfairly prejudicial conduct ... I do not doubt that in an appropriate case it is open to the court to find that serious mismanagement of the company's business constitutes conduct that is unfairly prejudicial to the interests of minority shareholders. But I share Peter Gibson J's view that the court will normally be very reluctant to accept that managerial decisions can amount to unfairly prejudicial conduct.[2]

The HRA may have an effect on this position where legitimate management decisions have been made which have a drastic effect on a particular shareholder. For example, in *Re A Company* [1986] BCLC 362 a minority shareholder alleged unfairly prejudicial conduct regarding a rights issue which would reduce his shareholding. The company proposed to make a rights issue, and the shares not taken up according to the offer were to be offered to other shareholders. The minority shareholder claimed that he had neither the resources nor the inclination to take up his share entitlement. The effect of his not taking up his entitlement was drastic as his interest in the company would be reduced from 25% to 0.125%. The other shareholder offered to buy him out but he rejected the offer as he considered the price offered was too low. The minority shareholder claimed that

---

20   Shareholders Remedies, Law Commission Report No 246 (1997), para 4.11, p 43.
1   *O'Neill v Phillips* [1999] 2 BCLC 1 at 8.
2   See also *Re A Company* [1986] BCLC 362.

his exclusion from the company and the proposed rights issue constituted unfairly prejudicial conduct. The court dismissed the petition finding that the minority shareholder had in fact been treated well and that in particular the rights issue was motivated by a bona fide desire to raise needed capital and was not aimed at prejudicing the petitioner, even though its effect was to do so. Accordingly, there was no basis on which the court had jurisdiction to make an order.

In section 459 cases such as this, where there is a delicate balance to be maintained between allowing the company to function according to its internal rules and the need to protect the minority shareholder's interest, the Convention rights may have some impact in tipping the balance. The court has a duty to act compatibly with the Convention rights and also an obligation under section 3 of the HRA to give effect to legislation wherever possible in a manner which is compatible with the Convention rights. In *Re Saul D Harrison & Sons*[3] Lord Hoffman described section 459 as protecting the legitimate expectations of the shareholders. These expectations were not confined to an expectation of compliance with the Companies Acts and the articles of association but extended to such other expectations as can be shown to have existed between the shareholders. On this basis an expectation to manage although never formally agreed, can come within the shareholders' interests protected by section 459. Clearly on this formulation a shareholder's Convention rights form part of his interests. As such the Court would have to consider whether the interference with the shareholders property could amount to a violation of Protocol 1, Article 1 and whether the violation was proportionate to the legitimate aim pursued by the court. In cases where the compensation for the violation is deemed to be adequate this may not be a problem but in cases where the shareholder has received no compensation the violation of the property right may be more difficult to justify.[4]

Section 459 protects the members 'interests' rather than their strict legal rights. As such the members' interests can be affected by an action which is strictly speaking aimed at the corporation's property. On this basis the domestic courts have allowed shareholders to petition on the basis of a wrong done to the company which affected their interests.[5] An act affecting the corporation's Convention rights could similarly give rise to a petition under Section 459. Therefore while shareholders may not be able to fulfil 'victim' status generally for the purposes of Protocol 1, Article 1 under the *Agrotexim* test,[6] they may be able to utilise section 459 to indirectly claim 'victim' status with regard to their 'interests'.[7]

Will Protocol 1, Article 1 protect shareholders from compulsory expropriation by statute?

In addition to expropriation of shares permitted by the articles of association, there is a statutory mechanism whereby a shareholder may be forced to sell his shares

3   [1995] 1 BCLC 14 at 19.
4   See Chapter 8 on Protocol 1, Article 1.
5   See *Re London School of Electronics* [1986] Ch 211 and *Re Cumana Ltd* [1986] BCLC 430 where the issues involved a misappropriation of corporate property by the majority.
6   See above.
7   See Chapter 8.

to a take-over bidder who has obtained a 90% or higher shareholding in a company. The provisions requiring a shareholder to sell are found in sections 428-430F of the Companies Act 1985 (Part XIIIA).

The scheme under these sections of the Companies Act is straightforward and operates as follows. First, the offeror company must make a take-over offer for all of the shares, or the whole of any class of shares to the offeree company other than those already held at the date of the offer by the offeror or its associates.[8] The offer must be on the same terms for all of the shares of the same class. If the offer is accepted within four months of its being made by the holders of 90% or more in the value of the shares to which the offer relates, the offeror may within two months, serve a notice to acquire the remaining shares. The recipients of the notice then have six weeks in which to apply to the court, which may allow or disallow the final acquisition on such terms as it sees fit. If the recipients do not apply to the court, then the offeror is entitled and bound to acquire the shares on the same terms as the offer accepted by no less than 90% of the shareholding.

Compatibility with ECHR Protocol 1, Article 1

All companies concerned with a take over of another company should be concerned to know whether their strategy might offend ECHR Protocol 1, Article 1, especially if the strategy does or might involve the offeror *requiring* the shareholders of a minority of 10% or less of the value of the offeree company selling their shares to the offeror under the authority of sections 428-430F of the Companies Act.

Interference with an individual's possessions

It is clear from the Strasbourg case law[9] that shares fall within the definition of property in Protocol 1, Article 1. The statutory scheme provides for the compulsory acquisition of shares owned by a minority shareholder by a majority shareholder. Prima facie therefore, the scheme offends Protocol 1, Article 1 because if a compulsory purchase proceeded pursuant to sections 428-430F, there would be a deprivation of the minority shareholder's possessions according to the criteria laid down in *Sporrong*.

The fact that the scheme allows for contingent acquisition, in the sense that a minority shareholder can appeal to the Court, and the Court can disallow the purchase, may well be relevant to considerations of 'fair balance' and any Article 6 (fair trial) impacts, however that does not derogate from the proposition that sections 428-430F of the Companies Act provide for the deprivation of individuals' private property against their will.

What is the fair balance?

In the case of compulsory purchase of shares pursuant to sections 428-430F, there are no apparent public purposes, such as the perceived need to acquire property

---

8   For a definition of 'associate', see section 430E(4) Companies Act 1985.
9   See *Bramelid and Malmstrom v Sweden* (1982) 29 DR 64 and R*uiz-Mateos v Spain* (1993) 16 EHRR 505.

to nationalise an industry. In so far as there are any public policy considerations, these are overshadowed by the particular purposes of the offeror bidder, which is usually to take the company private. It would seem therefore, from an analysis of first principles, that a sections 428-430F compulsory purchase would offend Protocol 1, Article 1.

However, similar provisions were considered by the European Commission in *Bramelid and Malmstrom v Sweden*[10] and found to satisfy the provisions of Protocol 1, Article 1. Swedish law provides that when a company owns directly or through a subsidiary, more than 90% of the shares and votes in another company, it has the right to purchase the remainder of the shares in the other company. In so far as the owner of the majority of the shares acquired them via a takeover bid, the Swedish legislation required that the price for compulsory purchase should be the offer price, unless there were special reasons justifying a different price. On the facts of the case in *Bramelid*, the minority complained about the intended compulsory purchase claiming, as the arbitrator appeared to accept, that the offer price was lower than the true value of the shares.

However, whilst accepting that the applicants' shares came within the confines of Protocol 1, Article 1, the Commission did not find that the legislation or the intended acquisition offended the Article. The Commission commented on the fact that the compulsory transfer of property between individuals was a feature of the laws in all states of the Human Rights Convention. Examples appearing in the report include the division of property upon succession, particularly in the case of agricultural property, the winding up of matrimonial settlements, and the seizure and sale of goods in the course of execution proceedings. Although the Commission emphasised the need to maintain a balance between individuals, and that a state must not create an imbalance between individuals which would result in one person arbitrarily and unjustly being deprived of his goods for the benefit of another, it found that the price to be paid for the applicants' shares in the compulsory purchase scheme was fixed by qualified arbitrators in a carefully reasoned decision and following criteria which did not appear either arbitrary or unreasonable[11].

The UK statutory scheme was introduced by the legislature to resolve a conflict of interest between the owners or contingent owners of a newly acquired majority shareholding in a company and the minority shareholders in the same company. The legislation provides a contingent right of the majority shareholder to purchase compulsorily the shares of the minority shareholders. In many cases, a company acquiring shares in another company is content with a controlling interest, so that it can take corporate decisions as it sees fit. However, there are good commercial reasons why, in certain circumstances, a majority shareholder will want to have complete control of a company and will not be satisfied with a mere controlling interest. For example, the offeror might want to invest large sums of money into the company, but could not realistically expect the existing minority shareholders to invest a proportionate amount. The benefits of such investment would be expected to be felt by all of the shareholders equally, and the offeror may well consider it

10 *Bramelid and Malmstrom v Sweden* (1982) 29 DR 64.
11 *Bramelid* (note 10 above) at 257.

unfair if the minority shareholders benefited from an investment in respect of which they did not themselves contribute in proportion. In such circumstances, the competing interests of the majority and minority shareholders might be balanced more fairly if the majority shareholder could buy out the minority shareholder, prior to the investment being made.

A further example is that of a holding company which may legitimately wish to operate its subsidiaries in the interest of the enterprise or group as a whole. It will clearly be able to do this more easily if the subsidiaries are wholly owned, so that the interests of the minority shareholders do not need to be considered.

By contrast, prior to the Companies Act 1929, the rights of the individual minority shareholder were protected absolutely, so that the majority shareholder had no right to acquire minority shares compulsorily.[12] In *Brown v British Abrasive Wheel*, Astbury J, considered a case where a group holding 98% of a company's shares wanted to force the remaining 2% of the shareholders to sell their shareholding to the majority prior to a major reinvestment in the company by the majority shareholder. The minority shareholders did not want to sell their shares, presumably because they wanted to benefit from an investment which was about to be made by the majority shareholder. The reaction of the majority shareholder was to attempt to change the articles of the company to force the minority shareholders to deliver up their share certificates in return for a 'fair price'. Astbury J said 'I find it very difficult to follow how it can be just and equitable that a majority, on failing to purchase the shares of a minority by agreement, can take power to do so compulsorily'.[13] The judge proceeded to decline compulsory purchase on the grounds that it contravened natural justice.

Part XIIIA was inserted into the Companies Act 1985 by section 172 and Schedule 12 of the Financial Services Act 1986, superseding earlier less sophisticated provisions to the same effect. It is possible that the provisions were initially inserted by the Companies Act 1929 with the intention of reversing *Brown v British Abrasive Wheel Co Ltd*[14] and following cases such as *Dafern Tinplate Co Ltd v Llanlelly Steel Co (1907) Ltd*,[15] but there are no specific discussions of policy considerations in Hansard.[16] The only indication of the policy being pursued is found in the report of the Greene Committee.[17] The Committee was of the view that the provisions had worth in assuming that the offeree company remained as a going concern,

---

12   Cf *Sidebottom v Kershaw Leese & Co Ltd* [1920] 1 Ch 154 CA.
13   [1919] 1 Ch 290 at 295 to 296.
14   [1991] 1 Ch 290.
15   [1920] 2 Ch 124 cf *Sidebottom v Kershaw Lease & Co Ltd* [1920] 1 Ch 154, CA.
16   See Hansard 5th Series, vol 213, page 1442 (February 1928) (Commons); vol 67, page 15 (May 1927) (Lords).
17   *Company Law Amendment Committee Report 1925 to 1926* 'The Greene Report' (Cmd 2657) at p 43. The predecessors to the present day sections 428 to 430F were section 209 of the 1948 Act, section 155 of the 1929 Act (the consolidating statute) and section 50 of the 1928 Act (which did not enter into force until the entry into force of the 1929 Act). There is no specific discussion of the policy surrounding the emergence of these provisions in Hansard (*Hansard* 5th series, vol 213, p 1442 (Feb 1928) (Commons); vol 67, p 15 (May 1927) (Lords). *Palmer's Company Law* (13th edn 1929) does not contain any discussion of the policy considerations.

for commercial reasons. The Committee's relevant opinions are stated at paragraph 84:

> [t]he acquiring company generally desires to obtain the whole of the share capital of the company which is being taken over and in some cases will not entertain the business except on that basis. It has been represented to us that holders of a small number of shares of the company which is being taken over (either from a desire to exact better terms than their fellow shareholders are content to accept or from lack of real interest in the matter) frequently fail to come into an arrangement which commends itself to the vast majority of their fellow shareholders with the result that the transaction fails to materialise. In our opinion this position – which is in effect an oppression of the majority by the minority – should be met.

It seems therefore, that the objective of the statutory interference in the form of what are now sections 428 to 430F Companies Act 1985 was to remove the impasse between the predator company which wanted to acquire a company, and the minority which wanted to obstruct the sale. The general interests of commerce were preferred to the rights of the individual previously protected *by Brown v British Abrasive Wheel.*

Whether there is a fair balance in the legislation, resulting in proportionality, will however depend on a number of factors. In particular, it will depend on the provisions for the compensation of the minority shareholders: 'the level of compensation provided is central to the assessment of whether or not the "fair balance" has been struck'.[18]

Proportionality and compensation

Under sections 428 to 430F of the Companies Act 1985, if dissenting shareholders wish to object to the compulsory acquisition of their shares, the onus is on them to convince a court that the compulsory acquisition would be unfair.[19] This would include the court where possible interpreting the compulsory purchase legislation compatibly with the Convention rights under section 3 of the HRA and the court itself acting compatibly with regard to the applicants' Convention rights.

However, the test applied so far by the courts is whether the offer is fair to the shareholders as a body, without reference to the particular circumstances of the applicants. It is here that the HRA will impact as the court will have to consider the applicants' individual rights. It was irrelevant as a matter of English law prior to the HRA whether the individual shareholders would have to transfer ownership of their shares at a loss (even a substantial loss). If an investor purchased shares at a high price, and then saw the share price fall, but maintained his holding in the hope that a 'buy-out' would revive his fortunes, he may well have had his hopes dashed if the buyer wants complete control. Indeed, it is probably these very shareholders

18   Duffy Peter, 'The Protection of Commercial Interests Under the European Convention of Human Rights in Making Commercial Law' in *Essays in Honour of Roy Goode* (R Cranston ed) (1997).
19   See *Re Lifecare International plc* [1990] BCLC 222.

who will be holding out against a compulsory purchase, on the grounds that they will suffer a loss when the purchase price is subtracted from the sale price.

It should be remembered that the statutory scheme does not provide for compensation to the minority shareholder at any level; it is the offeror who sets the de facto level of compensation by the form and content of the offer, which, ex hypothesi, has been accepted by at least 90% of the shareholders. The Court either endorses the offer in the face of objection, or it does not. It is submitted that sections 428 to 430F of the Companies Act 1985 do not violate Article 1 of Protocol 1 inter se, merely because the legislation does not expressly specify a particular level of compensation. Indeed, neither Protocol 1, Article 1 nor the case law surrounding it provides for a particular level of compensation, and that in itself, it is submitted, would be a bar to a finding of violation on this basis. However, the legislative scheme does allow for an objection to an offer by a minority shareholder if he considers that the compensation offered by the offeror is unfairly low.

Given that 90% of the shareholders accepted the offer, there must be a prima facie presumption that the 'compensation' offered for the share acquisition was fair. But this will not always be the case. It might be that the 90% majority belongs to or is controlled by the offeror. In these circumstances, the courts could consider the market value of shares when considering whether the offer was fair or not. The court will look at the exchange price immediately before the offer was made for a listed company, to see whether the offer made was prima facie fair.[20] In the case of private companies (which account for the vast majority of registered companies), there is neither a list price nor any recognised market *per se*, but the Courts could determine whether the price offered was a market price by reference to expert accountancy evidence.

If the offer made results in the minority receiving compensation at market rate, it is highly unlikely that the scheme or a decision by a court would contravene Protocol 1, Article 1. Nevertheless, the absence of a *requirement* in the statute for minority shares to be purchased at no less than market price means that it is within the Court's discretion to approve of schemes which are at less than market value.[1] In such circumstances, the courts run the risk of violating Protocol 1, Article 1 by approving such a scheme. Whilst compensation at less than market value might be justifiable as part of a socio-economic programme, as in the *Lithgow* case for example, it is difficult to imagine a well founded submission in support of compensation at less than market price in the context of a take-over, a fortiori when there is an established market (at least for listed companies).

For these reasons any judgment approving a scheme in which the minority shareholder is compensated at less than market value will have to be well reasoned in order to avoid violating Protocol 1, Article 1. It is submitted that there should be a strong presumption that any compensation at less than market value does not satisfy the 'fair balance' test in the context of a take-over.

---

20   *Re Grierson, Oldham and Adams Ltd* [1968] Ch 17; *Re Press Caps Ltd* [1949] Ch 434.
1   It is common for offers to be advanced at less than market value.

There is precedent for compensating a shareholder following the compulsory acquisition of his shares, at market value. In *Short v Treasury Comrs*,[2] the Court considered an order by the Minister for Aircraft Production transferring all shares in Short Brothers to nominees under the provisions of Defence Regulation 78(5) which provided:

> [t]he price to be paid by a competent authority in respect of any shares transferred by virtue of such an order as aforesaid shall be such price as may be specified in an order given by the Treasury, being a price which, in the opinion of the Treasury, is not less than the value of the shares as between willing buyer and a willing seller on the date of the order made under authority ...

Other jurisdictions have refrained from incorporating such a provision in equivalent statutes, requiring compensation at market level. For example, the New Zealand Companies Act 1993, sections 110 to 115 and 118, permit minority 'squeeze-outs' if a 'fair and reasonable' price is paid for the shares. Following Canadian authorities,[3] the New Zealand legislature refrained from fixing the price at market level, to allow for discount or premium to reflect the facts of any given case.[4] Whilst it is envisaged that the courts might want to give a premium to the minority shareholder, it is difficult to envisage circumstances where the courts would want to discount the market price.[5]

As the shareholders under the statutory scheme get the same price as the majority shareholders it is difficult to perceive of a take-over bidder falling foul of Protocol 1, Article 1 when acquiring a minority's shares through the Sections 428-430F Companies Act mechanism, unless there is a deliberate sale by the majority at an undervalue. Market value for a minority stake is likely to be less than the price offered for a majority stake. The statutory scheme provides for the minority being offered the same as the majority price and as such the price offered will normally be more than the market price. There might even be an arguable case for the majority that the statutory scheme interferes with their Protocol 1, Article 1 rights by requiring them to purchase a minority holding at the same value as a majority holding when clearly a minority holding is less valuable as it does not confer voting control.

Will Protocol 1, Article 1 protect shareholders from a compulsory purchase under the articles of association?

English company law allows the compulsory expropriation of shares to be provided for in the articles of association. If the constitution of the company allows for it,

2   *Short v Treasury Comrs* [1948] AC 534.
3   For example, *Domglas Inc v Jarislowsky, Fraser & Co Ltd* (1982) 138 DLR (3d) 521; *Brant Investments Ltd v KeepRites Inc* (1991) 3 OR (3d) 289.
4   See *Morison's Company and Securities Law*, Butterworths New Zealand Ltd, para 16.24.
5   There are no reported New Zealand authorities where a court had discounted in the way contemplated by the New Zealand legislature.

then a shareholder may be obliged to sell shares against his wishes at the particular time of sale. The only way the shareholder could use the Convention rights in such a situation would be to utilise section 459, alleging unfairly prejudicial conduct and arguing that the courts discretion should be exercised compatibly with the Convention ie not to interfere with the petitioners Protocol 1, Article 1 rights.

Expropriation of shares by the articles of association

Provisions which require shareholders to sell their shares in any given situation, including that of a takeover bid, may exist from the incorporation of a company in the articles of association or may by special resolution be incorporated in the articles of association by amendment.

On one view, it may be said that the expropriation of shares relying upon the Articles of Association which allow for such expropriation cannot be said to be a compulsory expropriation, or the individual shareholder has agreed to such expropriation, either tacitly or otherwise. There is no compulsion obliging any individual to purchase shares in a company, either at formation or subsequently. Any would-be shareholder knows that he will be bound by the provisions of the articles of association in that section 14 of the Companies Act invests the memorandum and articles of association with contractual status. Section 14 provides that the memorandum and Articles 'shall, when registered, bind the company and its members to the same extent as if they respectively had been signed and sealed by each member, and contained covenants on the part of each member ...'.

The precise nature and scope of section 14 of the Companies Act is beyond the ambit of this book but it is clear that the section creates a contract between members and other members, and also between individual members and the company.[6] Moreover, section 9 of the Companies Act 1985 provides for the articles to be amended by special resolution and so the contract in the articles can be amended at any time post-formation once three-quarters of the shareholders agree.

A would-be shareholder has free choice not to purchase shares in a company which the articles of association permits compulsory expropriation of shares in certain situations and if possible can sell shares if a company without expropriation provisions in its articles subsequently amends the articles to permit expropriation. As such the exercise of a power to compulsorily purchase is an act which has been agreed between the shareholders and the company. It prima facie does not give rise to an action under the HRA as there is no 'public authority' violating a Convention right. There is the possibility that the company itself might be a 'public authority' if some of its actions are public in nature. Should this be the case the exercise of a power agreed in the articles is unlikely to be a public act. However this still leaves the possibility of a dissenting minority trapped within a company where the majority have changed the articles of association by special resolution or where the exercise of the power to expropriate property is part of an intra-shareholder dispute. If the articles provide for the purchase at full market value then, on a present reading of

---

6   *Hickman v Romney Marsh Sheep-Breeders Association* [1915] 1 Ch 881, See Astbury J at 897.

the Strasbourg case law, there will be no violation of Protocol 1, Article 1. If the compensation is significantly below the market price then the case law would indicate there may be a violation.[7]

In such circumstances, a shareholder could claim that the operation of a provision of the articles has resulted in unfairly prejudicial conduct, perhaps because the circumstances of the operation had not been contemplated at the time at which the shares had been purchased, or the articles amended, and redress could be sought by the shareholder bringing an action relying upon the provisions of Section 459 of the Companies Act 1985. The shareholder could as part of this action argue that the court must where possible under Section 3 of the HRA interpret legislation compatibly with the Convention rights and must as a 'public authority' under Section 6 of the HRA act compatibly with the Convention rights. Even though the company is empowered to purchase members shares against their will the courts have already held in the context of Section 459 that strict legal rights contained in the Articles and the Companies Act can be restricted by equitable considerations.[8]

The main remedy utilised by the courts when unfairly prejudicial conduct has occurred is to buy out the minority shareholder. It will therefore only be useful for a shareholder to utilise a combined Section 459 and HRA action where the compulsory purchase price is significantly below market rate. The flexibility afforded to the Courts under Section 459 might well be sufficient to provide a remedy to an offended shareholder making recourse to Convention arguments an additional extra to strengthen a Section 459 action.

Will Protocol 1, Article 1 protect shareholders from a variation of class rights?

The Companies Act regulates the way in which class rights can be varied and abrogated. Variation presupposes a continuation of rights in a varied form, whereas abrogation contemplates the termination of rights without fulfilment.[9] In circumstances where variation or abrogation is proposed, the Companies Act, section 125 requires adherence to the scheme set out within it, which requires the consent in writing of 75% of the shareholders of that class. Should a holder of 15% of the shares in that class object to the variation they can apply to the court under section 127 to have the variation cancelled. There is little case law on this section which may indicate that actions concerning variations of class rights are more commonly litigated under section 459.

Statutory protection under section 125 of the Companies Act 1985 only applies if what has occurred does amount to a variation or abrogation of class rights, but the courts have interpreted 'variation' and 'abrogation' restrictively. In approaching the question of whether a variation or abrogation has occurred, the courts have drawn an artificial distinction between matters affecting the rights attaching to a

---

7   See above.
8   *Ebrahimi v Westbourne Galleries Ltd* [1973] AC 360, HL.
9   *Re House of Fraser plc* [1987] BCLC 293 at 301.

share, and matters affecting the enjoyment of those rights. Where only the enjoyment of the right is affected then the shares may be commercially less valuable, but their rights remain always what they were.

In *Greenhalgh v Arderne Cinemas Ltd*[10] a subdivision of a class of ten shilling ordinary shares into two shilling shares was held not to vary the rights of Mr Greenhalgh, a holder of the existing two shilling ordinary shares, although the result of the sub-division was to alter control of the company. Lord Greene noted:

> ... I agree, the effect of this resolution is, of course, to alter the position of the two shilling shareholders. Instead of Greenhalgh finding himself in a position of control, he finds himself in a position where control has gone, and to that extent the rights of the two shilling shareholders are effected, as a matter of business. As a matter of law, I am quite unable to hold that, as a result of the transaction, the rights are varied; they remain what they always were – a right to have one vote per share pari passu with the ordinary shares for the time being issued which include the new two shilling shares resulting from the subdivisions.[11]

On the facts of this case, there could be no complaint as a matter English law prior to the HRA, but Mr Greenhalgh could justifiably say that his property rights had been affected (described by Lord Greene as 'business' rights), without the law providing for any compensation. The court's traditional approach to variation of class rights has been extremely restrictive in terms of allowing shareholders to object to an onerous variation. Utilising the HRA the court would be faced with an extra argument. A petitioner under section 459 or section 127 in the position of Mr Greenhalgh could plead and rely upon Protocol 1, Article 1, claiming either a) that the Companies Act should be interpreted so that it does not permit his 'business' rights which constitute 'possessions' as interpreted by the Strasbourg court[12] to be interfered with, or b) that if the Companies Act does interfere with his 'possessions' then the law must also provide a fair balance by providing adequate compensation.

Will Protocol 1, Article 1 protect shareholders from the detrimental effects of an allotment and issue of shares?

The ability of the board of directors to allot and issue shares of the company to the potential detriment of some or all of the shareholders is an area governed by minimal statutory protection. Essentially the statutory scheme in Part IV 'Allotment of Shares and Debentures' of the Companies Act 1985, sections 80-116 provides that directors do not have authority to allot shares unless they have been authorised to do so by the shareholders or by the company's articles and that rights of pre-

---

10   *Greenhalgh v Arderne Cinemas Ltd* [1946] 1 All ER 512.
11   See also *Adelaide Electric Co v Prudential Assurance* [1934] AC 122, HL.
12   An established economic interest by an applicant may be sufficient to establish a right protected by the Convention see *Gasus Dosier-und Fördertechnik GmbH v Netherlands*, (1995) 20 EHRR 403.

emption be given to existing shareholders.[13] However such authority is easily given and pre-emption rights easily disapplied. Such authority, including one given in the articles, may be revoked or varied by the general meeting at any time (s 80(4)). The authority of the directors to issue relevant securities is limited to five years unless it is a private company, which can by elective resolution give indefinite authority.[14] If the company has different classes of shares and the issue of new shares affects the rights attached to a particular class then the approval of a three-quarters majority of that class is needed for the new issue (s125(3)).

The shareholders' pre-emption rights are governed by sections 89-96 of the 1985 Act. These sections provide that the company must offer the new shares to all the existing holders of its equity shares on the same or more favourable terms, in equal proportion to the nominal value of their shares. They are also allowed a period of at least 21 days to accept the offer before the company can allot the shares elsewhere. Such an allotment elsewhere cannot be on more favourable terms than the original offer to the shareholders. If the new issue of shares is made for a consideration other than cash the statutory pre-emption rights do not apply (s 89(4)).

Private companies can exclude the statutory pre-emption regime (s 91(1)). A board of a private or public company can, when it is seeking a power from the shareholders to allot shares under section 80, also be given a power to disapply or modify the statutory pre-emption regime.[15]

For listed companies the Act and Listing rules combine to create slightly better situation for the shareholder. The Listing Rules provide for more shareholder votes than the Act but the basic ethos is the same. That is a presumption of protections both in the authority needed to allot and the pre-emption provisions, which can be removed by the shareholders. The growth of institutional ownership of listed companies has had a significant impact on this area. Institutions are extremely wary of any dilution in their shareholdings, both in terms of voting and share watering. Thus the institutions have created informal guidelines where they will only vote in favour of the disapplication regime if the company limits the number of shares to be issued on a non-pre-emptive basis to 5% of the issued capital of the company in any one year and to 7.5% over three years. The discount must also be restricted to 5% of the market price. Note that these guidelines cover vendor placings also.[16] The guidelines are very unpopular with companies although this unhappiness seems to revolve around the cost of fees payable when they have to comply with the pre-emption provisions.[17]

The statutory presumption of protection for shareholders is very basic in that it provides that directors should seek authority to allot and that existing shareholders should have pre-emptive rights. However these provisions do not in reality provide much

13 Section 80.
14 Section 379A.
15 Section 95.
16 See 'Pre-emption Rights' (1987) 27 *Bank of England Quarterly Bulletin* 545.
17 See Underwriting of Equity Issues: Second Report by the Director General of Fair Trading 1996.

protection for shareholders as they can easily be disapplied. In terms of the HRA the lack of effective statutory protection can have a detrimental effect on the shareholders' Protocol 1, Article 1 property rights. The ease with which the statutory regime can be disapplied leaves shareholders at risk of directors using their power to allot to, resist take-overs, entrench their own internal voting position at the general meeting, share watering and vote watering with the consequential detrimental effect on the shareholders' property.

While the first two may be obvious abuses the second two are not so obvious. Vote watering is where the ratio of shares to votes is reduced, thus diluting existing voting strength to the point where elements of the balance of control may be affected ie special resolution and ordinary resolution power may be lost. Or just quite simply a shareholder may be unhappy because they no longer control the same number of votes. In listed companies this really only impacts on large institutional shareholders. In private companies it may be of greater concern and has given rise to section 459 actions and actions for breach of duty.[18]

Share watering is possibly of more concern given that it occurs even where the shares allotted are non-voting. This means that the ratio of shares to dividends reduces, ie if there are more shareholders there will be more shareholders between which to divide the existing and future earnings of the company. Even though the company will have raised more money it usually takes some years for the earnings per share ratio to return to its previous level. The effect of this on the value of the shares in the market place is obvious. In a large issue of new shares there is likely to be an incentive to take up the new shares, ie a discount on the market value. After the shares have been allocated all the shares new and old will trade at a price somewhere between the discount price and the previous price. Where the price falls in that range will depend on the size of the discount and the market's confidence in the directors' plans for the new funds. If a shareholder does not take up the shares then, unless the market is hugely confident in the company's plans, that shareholder would suffer a large loss.

The fact that the pre-emption regime does not apply to non-cash transactions can also have a detrimental effect on the shareholders' position. While it is advantageous for a company to be able to provide shares as consideration for property transactions, obviously the company could not offer the same terms to existing shareholders. It does, however, greatly diminish shareholder protection. From the point of view of share watering, where an inflated value might be placed on the non-cash consideration, some protection is provided for public companies by s103 which requires an independent valuation report in the case of share issues by public companies for non-cash consideration.

Section 103 does not apply to private companies or to share issues by public companies in connection with a take-over or merger (s103 (3) and (5)) which is odd given the level of risk of share watering. Listed companies do have more protection. Where a listed company intends to enter a transaction involving the issue of equity shares for a consideration in cash or other form equivalent to 25% or more of the existing market value of its equity shares the shareholders' approval

18   *Re A Company* [1986] BCLC 362.

is needed – Listing Rules, paras 10.4, 10.5, and 10.37. Despite the lack of any real protection for shareholders in these sections the DTI in its consultation document 'Modern Company Law: Developing the Framework (March 2000)' recommends the statutory protections should be removed and directors should have the facility to allot shares without shareholder authorisation.

The directors' abuse of their power to allot shares has already been the subject of successful minority actions where the directors have used their powers not for the purpose of capital raising, which is the purpose for which it was given, but to gain voting control for themselves at the general meeting,[19] or to deprive others of their present control,[20] or to defeat a take-over bid[1] and unsuccessful ones where it was a legitimate management decision which had a detrimental effect of a minority shareholding. The HRA's impact in terms of allowing minority shareholders to challenge a board's decision to allot will not be enormous. A company is a private actor not bound to act compatibly with the Convention rights. Even where a company is a 'public authority' the exercise of a power to allot shares would be a private act. Should shareholders wish to challenge an act of the board they would have to allege unfairly prejudicial conduct and argue that additionally the court must interpret the Companies Act compatibly with the Convention rights. In all it adds an additional factor to be considered by the court when assessing the interests of the shareholders that may have been unfairly prejudiced.

What will the effect of the HRA be on company reconstruction, administration and liquidation?

The HRA has a twofold effect on the operation of companies in crisis. First the court, in making any order concerning the affairs of the company, must act compatibly with the Convention rights. Primarily the rights of the creditors will need to be considered but also the employees' and the shareholders' rights. Second the officials appointed by the court will have to act compatibly with the Convention rights. reduction of capital under Parts IV and V of the Companies Act 1985, reorganisations under sections 110 and 111 of the Insolvency Act, schemes of arrangements under sections 425-427A of the Companies Act 1985, administrations under sections 8-27 of the Insolvency Act 1986, and winding-up by the court in Chapter VI of the Insolvency Act 1986 all require the court either purely to make orders or to appoint officers such as administrators and liquidators. In the course of such activities the court, as we have noted, has an obligation under section 6 of the HRA to act consistently with the Convention rights. So too will the officers appointed by the court as they are likely to be considered a 'public authority' under the HRA. Should they fail to do so and interfere with a Convention right it is directly actionable under the HRA.[2]

19   *Re Jermyn St Turkish Baths Ltd* [1970] 3 All ER 57, [1970] 1 WLR 1194.
20   *Howard Smith Ltd v Ampol Petroleum Ltd* [1974] AC 821.
1   *Bamford v Bamford* [1969] 1 All ER 969.
2   See Chapter 6 on section 6.

The Convention rights likely to be at issue in a company reconstruction, administration and liquidation are Protocol 1, Article 1 (property) and Article 6 (fair trial). As we have explained above the Strasbourg court has allowed a high level of interference with Protocol 1, Article 1 as long as there is a legitimate aim being pursued and the act is proportionate. It is unlikely then, in the context of a company in trauma, that a creditor would be able to succeed in maintaining a violation of Protocol 1, Article 1 against a court or officer of the court in the course of a company reconstruction, administration and liquidation because of the importance of the public function they carry out.

However Article 6 (fair trial) does have a significant effect. Any scheme or reconstruction where there is no appeal to a court on the facts of the matter runs the risk of breaching Article 6 (1). Generally an individual can waive their right of access to the court through a voluntary submission to arbitration. However, should there be any element of compulsion present (for example a court order) the arbitrator must comply fully with Article 6 or else there will be a violation of Article 6.[3] The High Court recently considered a scheme of arrangement for an insurance company in provisional liquidation. The scheme provided for the appointment of an independent adjudicator to resolve disputes between the creditors and the administrators of the scheme. While the High Court initially refused to sanction the scheme, because it involved the creditors' having to waive any right to appeal, it allowed it when after further argument the court accepted that the ability to sue the adjudicator for negligence, breach of trust or fraud was sufficient to provide access to the courts under the scheme.[4] It is doubtful whether this decision is sufficient for the purposes of Article 6 (1). Should the arbitrator fail to comply with Article 6 in the determination of any dispute it will most likely be a breach of Article 6, regardless of the ability of the parties to sue in negligence, breach of trust or fraud.

3   *Malmstrom v Sweden* (1983) 38 DR 18.
4   *Re Hawk Insurance Co Ltd* Ch D (13 January 1999, unreported).

Chapter thirteen

Companies, labour law and the HRA

I don't want any yes-men around me. I want everybody to tell me the truth even if it cost them their jobs.[1]

Companies as employers

Companies are invariably employers. It is difficult to imagine how a company could conduct business, its life blood, without the benefit of its human employees. As employers, companies are already subject to a great deal of what can be described as labour law. To this will be added the Human Rights Act 1998. As already discussed, when interpreting domestic labour provisions the courts and tribunals must take the Strasbourg case law into account. It is important therefore for officers of companies to understand the implications of the HRA on their company as an employer. Whilst it is not the purpose of this section to set out in full detail all of the Strasbourg cases which will or could affect employment law, it is important to outline what articles of the ECHR should be considered in this context. The impacts may not, as Professor Ewing has considered, be enormous:

> [w]ithout wishing too forcefully to question the hyperpole of a least some labour lawyers who have warmly received the 1998 Act, there may be three reasons to think that in terms of the big picture – that being the one which focuses on extending the rights of citizens at work – its impact will be quite limited, though

---

1   Samuel Goldwyn.

not altogether negligible. The first relates to the range of matters covered by the Convention, which are important but limited, and sometimes peripheral. Secondly, the potential for effective application in a number of hugely significant areas is at best uncertain and highly speculative ... And thirdly, it remains an incontrovertible fact that in the interpretation of Convention protected rights, both the Strasbourg authorities and the English courts have been deaf to the calls of workers and trade unions.[2]

Does the HRA affect public and private employers equally?

If an employer is an obvious 'public authority' under section 6 (1) of the HRA then it must act compatibly with the Convention rights and freedoms. An employee would then be able to bring an action directly against a 'public authority' employer under section 6 of the HRA alleging an unlawful act.[3] Section 8 (1) of the HRA provides that a court can award a remedy which may include damages for an unlawful act. There are, however, difficulties with regard to such claims where the employer is acting under primary and certain subordinate legislation.[4] Section 6 (2) provides that if the employer as the result of one or more provisions of primary legislation or certain subordinate legislation could not have acted differently it will not be an unlawful act. The only remedy available then would be for the court to issue a declaration of incompatibility under section 4 (2) but only a higher court can make such a declaration.

If the employer is a quasi-public body under section 6 (3) (b) then the issue of employment law becomes more complex. A quasi-public body such as British Gas or British Telecom must act compatibly with the Convention rights with regard to its public function but not where it is acting in its private capacity.[5] If the company is acting in its private capacity then an employee has no free-standing action alleging an unlawful act under section 6. However, as we discussed in Chapter 7, the issue of where the public/private divide is within such a company is a complex one.[6] Railtrack and British Gas are quasi-public bodies whose safety function is certainly a public one. The question arises for employment matters as to whether an employee whose function is rail or gas safety can bring a free-standing claim against his quasi-public employer alleging an unlawful act under section 6. Arguably they could as they are employed to carry out a public function for their employer. Whether the

---

2   Ewing, K D, 'The Human Rights Act and Labour Law' (1998) *Industrial Law Journal* (1998) Vol 27, No 4, p 292. For an argument that it does have broad implications see Palmer, Stephanie, 'Human rights: Implications For Labour Law' (2000) *Cambridge Law Journal*, Vol 59, Issue 1, March, pp 168- 200.
3   See Chapter 6.
4   Ibid Chapter 6.
5   Section 6 (5).
6   On the impact in the employment sphere see Morris, Gillian S, 'The Human Rights Act and the Public/ Private Divide in Employment Law' (1998) *Industrial Law Journal*, Vol 27, No 4) pp 293-308.

act of employment is private or part of the public function is open to question. Other questions arise where quasi-public bodies are at issue in employment law. What is the status of an employee who carries out some private functions for Railtrack but also deals with aspects of safety as a secretary might who files safety reports? Issues such as these will take some working out but it is at least arguable that such employees are able to allege section 6 unlawfulness. A real difficulty for quasi-public bodies is that they may have employees who are covered by the Convention and others who are not. In terms of the company's employment policy and disciplinary procedures this causes a problem. Should they have two policies and procedures applicable depending on the status of the employee or just one extending the Convention rights to all? We would suggest that extending the Convention rights to all is perhaps the best approach as even for private companies the Convention has a trickle down effect.

However, prima facie private employers have no obligation under the HRA to act compatibly with the Convention rights and freedoms. This does not mean however that the HRA has no effect on a private employer. An employment tribunal has an obligation as a public authority under section 6 (3) (a) to interpret legislation compatibly and to act compatibly with the Convention rights. If it does not apply those standards the tribunal itself will have acted unlawfully, which gives rise to a claim under section 6. For example, if a private employer in breach of Article 8 (privacy) and 14 (discrimination) dismisses someone because he is gay a tribunal could not find that that was a 'substantial reason' which would justify a dismissal under section 98 (1) (b) of the Employment Rights Act 1996 (ERA). Additionally a tribunal exercising its discretion under section 98 (4) of the ERA as to whether an employer acted 'reasonably or unreasonably' could not find such an act to be reasonable as it is bound to act compatibly with the Convention in the exercise of its discretion. This will necessarily mean that previous case law on such subjects will not be a reliable precedent.[7] As such the standards that will be applied by such tribunals with regard to fair trial, privacy, expression will be those of the Convention and its case law. If an employer wishes to ensure that it does not fall foul of an employment tribunal applying such standards it would be best to incorporate those standards into the company's employment procedures.[8] However the employee of a private employer has no free-standing cause of action to rely on and must therefore identify an existing cause of action for the court to consider compatibly with the Convention. If that cause of action is legislation and it is incapable of being applied compatibly the tribunal will have no way of applying the Convention.[9] As an employment tribunal is not a higher court under the HRA it cannot even issue a declaration of incompatibility. Common law causes of action are not restricted in this way and are always capable of being interpreted compatibly with the Convention rights.

7   See for example *R v Ministry of Defence, ex p Smith* [1996] 1 All ER 257 (gays in the military).
8   An employer would also need to review procedures generally with regard to proportionality. See Chapter 7.
9   Section 3.

Which ECHR articles are relevant to companies as employers?

The main ECHR Articles of relevance to employment are

Article 6:   Right to a fair trial

Article 8:   Right to respect for private and family life

Article 9:   Freedom of thought, conscience and religion

Article 10:   Freedom of expression

Article 11:   Freedom of assembly and association

Article 14:   Freedom from discrimination

How these Articles will be relevant to employer companies is set out below.

Article 6 - Right to a fair trial

As we have already examined in Chapter 9, Article 6 provides that 'everyone is entitled to a fair and public hearing within a reasonable time by an independent and impartial tribunal established by law.' This right is considered by the Strasbourg court to be of fundamental importance.[10] The right involves practical and effective access to a court in order to determine civil rights and obligations. It cannot be restricted. The standard applicable to courts and tribunals under Article 6 will be applicable to employment tribunals as they determine civil rights and obligations.[11]

In the context of company employers, Article 6 will be important because companies often have written procedures in their contracts with their employees to appear at inter company disciplinary hearings to answer disciplinary charges. The ultimate sanction is often dismissal. There is, however, some doubt as to whether the right to be appointed and retained in civil service employment is a 'civil right'.[12] Because of this an obvious public authority under section 6 (1) may not have to comply with Article 6. However, bodies such as the professional associations when considering a right to practice or disciplinary proceedings, must comply with the Article 6 standards as to fair trial.[13]

For private companies the standards of fairness applied to their procedures by an employment tribunal will be those of Article 6. In this sense companies do have to have regard to the provisions of Article 6 to ensure that their internal hearings are fair, as the tribunal will or may determine the employee's civil rights (in particular with regard to the disciplinary provisions of the employees's contract of employment) with reference to Article 6. In terms of the compatibility of procedures Article 6(1)

10   *Delcourt v Belgium* (1970) 1 EHRR 355.
11   *Stedman v United Kingdom* [1997] EHRLR 545.
12   See *Balfour v United Kingdom* (2 July 1997, unreported) noted in [1997] EHRLR 665 and for a contrary view in the context of Article 10 see *Vogt v Germany* (1995) 21 EHRR 205.
13   *König v Germany* (1978) 2 EHRR 170; see also *Wickramsinghe v United Kingdom* [1988] EHRLR 338.

requires an independent tribunal. This will be difficult to achieve given that the tribunal is likely to consist of representatives of the company. In small companies, the problems of achieving an independent tribunal are particularly difficult. A number of options are available to the company however. At the very least, the company should ensure that the tribunal does not consist of personnel intimately involved in a complaint against the employee. So for example, if the complaint is that an employee has abused a director of the company or stolen from one of them, it would not be wise for that director to be on the tribunal. A company would be well advised to have within the contract of employment the right to appeal any decision to a truly independent third party, perhaps a local solicitor or other arbitrator. Alternatively, it might be better for the internal tribunal to include independent third parties, perhaps even an independent chairman. Although this will probably be more expensive than having the directors of the company act in the first instance as the disciplinary tribunal it would supply a measure of independence.

There is a general requirement in Article 6 to ensure that hearings are conducted in public, and this has been held to apply, for example, to medical disciplinary hearings.[14] However, it is possible for an employee to waive the public trial part of Article 6 in their employment contract.[15] This will stand as long as it does not contravene an important public interest. Indeed, it is foreseeable that companies might well want to keep such hearings private for a number of legitimate reasons. If the employee is not disciplined, or is not found to have contravened any rule, the employer will almost certainly want the employee to return to work with as little stigma attached to him as possible. The dispute could also concern confidential information the employee had access to and the company would legitimately wish confidential matters to remain so.

There is also a general requirement for a trial to take place within a reasonable time. In the case of company employers, the timing of a hearing will often depend on how quickly evidence can be gathered and marshalled. Nevertheless, it would be prudent for an employer company to prescribe a timetable leading to a hearing either in its contracts of employment, or upon the discovery of a suspected offence. The timetable should ensure that a hearing take places as expeditiously and as prudently possible. Although it is not clear in the employment context there may also in certain circumstances be a requirement to allow the employee to be represented at the disciplinary proceedings.[16]

Article 8 - Right to respect for private and family life

Article 8 provides that everyone has the right to respect for his private and family life, his home and his correspondence. The right, however, is not absolutely guaranteed. Article 8 (2) provides that it can properly and lawfully be interfered with: if the interference is in accordance with the law and is necessary in a democratic society in the interests of national security, public safety or the economic well-being

14   See *Diennet v France* (1995) 21 EHRR 554.
15   *Schuler-Zgraggen v Switerland* (1993) 16 EHRR 405 para 58.
16   *Airey v Ireland* (1979) 2 EHRR 305.

of the country, for the prevention of disorder or crime, for the protection of health or morals, or the protection of the rights and freedoms of others.

The Article is relevant where the actions of an employer relate to a part of an employee's private, family life, home and correspondence. This is because the concept of privacy as interpreted by the ECtHR extends into the workplace.[17] In *Halford v United Kingdom*,[18] the applicant, a former Assistant Chief Constable in an English police force, successfully complained that her employer had breached Article 8 when monitoring her private telephone calls which she made whilst she was at work. Two factors compounded the applicant's complaint, first she had been provided with a telephone on which she was permitted to make private calls, second, she was specifically told that she could use her workplace telephone to make calls in connection with a claim brought by her against her employer. For these reasons, she had a clear expectation for privacy in the work place, which was denied her. Moreover, the monitoring of her private telephone calls by her employer was not contemplated or prescribed by the Interception of Communications Act 1985 and was therefore not in accordance with the law, which is a necessary requirement before 'interference' can be justified.

In *Malone v United Kingdom*[19] the court as part of its judgment took the view that, unlike telephone tapping, recording telephone numbers was a legitimate and normal business activity. The conceptual difference between monitoring numbers dialled and received and recorded conversations might become difficult to apply to other practical monitoring situations. Recording the number of key taps made by an employee on a computer keyboard in order to monitor productivity (a practice already undertaken by some companies) might fall into the *Malone* category of legitimate business activity; but what if the company employer views the screen history of an employee for any particular day to monitor the productivity and quality of the employee's work rather than merely viewing a log of key taps: in other words, what if the employer knows not just that a certain number were tapped but which keys were tapped? It is difficult to know on the state of the present case law whether the courts would view this as a legitimate *Malone* business activity or an illegitimate *Halford* activity.

The monitoring of employees in the workplace is increasingly a feature of the modern employment experience. Although the applicant in the *Halford* case had good cause to complain on the facts of her case, it is entirely understandable that an employer might want to monitor the telephone calls of its employees. The company may, for example, want to safeguard against fraud or other unlawful activities, for purposes of clarity where orders are taken over the phone, it might want to monitor the quality of the calls being made by its employees to third parties (subcontractors, suppliers, customers etc) and it may want to monitor productivity. OFTEL the telecommunications regulator has already issued guidance to companies regarding the recording of employee's private telephone calls. OFTEL has taken

---

17   *Niemietz v Germany* (1992) 16 EHRR 97.
18   *Halford v United Kingdom* (1997) 24 EHRR 523.
19   *Malone v United Kingdom* (1984) 7 EHRR 14.

the view that any recording of employees' private telephone calls could run the risk of breaching the employees' Article 8 (privacy) rights.[20] As a result it has recommended that companies which routinely record telephone calls must provide a facility for the employees to make private calls that are not monitored.[1] The guidance is aimed at all companies and not just 'public authorities'.

Article 9 - Freedom of thought, conscience and religion

Article 9 protects the rights of individuals to freedom of thought, conscience and religion. In addition, the Article provides the right to manifest the religion or beliefs in public or private in worship, teaching, practice and observance. The right to hold such beliefs is absolute but the right to manifest them may be restricted. Article 9 (2) provides that the right can be limited by such:

> limitations as are prescribed by law and are necessary in a democratic society in the interests of, public safety for the protection of public order, health or morals, or for the protection of the rights and freedoms of others.

For a private employer Article 9 should not make much difference in terms of dismissal on the basis of religious belief. Prior to the HRA such an act would be likely to be unfair. Under the HRA the tribunal could not find such an action of an employer to be within the statutory grounds for dismissal or that it was reasonable. However, because of the extremely limited protection given by the Strasbourg court to manifesting belief, a dismissal on the grounds of the religious practice interfering with the employee's ability to work is likely to be justifiable. It might be possible for an employee dismissed for such activities to claim discrimination under the Race Relations Act 1976 if they can show that the discrimination is against their ethnic group rather than just a religious group.

Employer companies are most likely to have to consider Article 9 in the context of employees who wish to manifest their religion in the workplace or leave the work place to manifest their religion. It might be, for example, that a Sikh finds it difficult to wear protective headgear prescribed by the employer, that a Muslim requires a place for prayer and to leave his or her workstation during the Western working day, a Jew wishes to leave work prior to sundown on Friday, a Christian does not wish to work on a Sunday.

Whilst each case must be considered on its own merits following an analysis of the facts, the Strasbourg case law has appeared to recognise the rights of employers in construing the breadth of Article 9(2) in preference to those of the individual employees.

In *X v United Kingdom*,[2] the Commission did not find a breach of Article 9 when the applicant complained about a refusal by his employer to release him from the workplace to attend mosque on Friday afternoons. Of particular significance to the Commission, on the facts of the case, was the fact that the applicant had not

20 The guidance is available at http://www.oftel.co.uk/
1   Singleton, Susan, 'Business Recording Telephone Calls: New Oftel Guidance' (1999) *Justice of the Peace,* Vol 163, October, pp 833- 834.
2   *X v United Kingdom* (1981) 22 DR 27.

mentioned when interviewed of his requirement to attend the mosque on Friday afternoons. It was therefore the case that the employer had a legitimate expectation when entering into the contract of employment following and on the basis of the interview, that the employee would work the allotted hours. In addition, the Commission took note of the fact that the applicant had not requested to attend mosque on Friday afternoons for the previous six years of employment. This gave the employer continuing reassurance of its initial expectation.[3]

In *Stedman v United Kingdom*,[4] a similar case produced a similar result with the application against the employer failing. The applicant employee, a Christian, complained that her Article 9 rights were being infringed when she was required to work on a Sunday. Whilst recognising that the United Kingdom could be required to protect the applicant from the actions of a private company, it did not find that the applicant's Article 9 rights had been violated as the applicant had been dismissed for failing to work the hours required of her by her employer. The positive obligation of the state to respect Article 9 is likely to be fulfilled by the provisions of the Sunday Trading Act 1994 which allows workers to opt out of Sunday working.

The impact of Article 9 at the Strasbourg level has been minimal in the employment context and should well continue so at the domestic level. There is however one potentially significant difference between the Strasbourg interpretation and the way it may be interpreted domestically. Section 13 of the HRA provides that a court or tribunal must have particular regard to the importance of Article 9 in determining any issue affecting a religious organisation. This may mean that employees of religious organisations may be subject to discrimination on the basis of their religious belief eg the Church of England could discriminate on grounds of religious belief in choosing an employee.

Article 10 - Freedom of expression

Article 10 guarantees the right to the 'freedom to hold opinions and to receive and impart information and ideas without interference by public authority and regardless of frontiers'. The nature and forms of expression protected by Article 10 are extensive, reflecting that the freedom of expression is one of the foundations of a democratic society[5]. Article 10 (2) provides for the usual exceptions but also emphasises duties and responsibilities in that:

> [t]he exercise of these freedoms, since it carries with it duties and responsibilities, may be subject to such formalities, conditions, restrictions or penalties as are prescribed by law and are necessary in a democratic society, in the interests of national security, territorial integrity or public safety, for the prevention of disorder or crime, for the protection of health or morals, for the protection of the reputation or rights of others, for preventing the disclosure of information received in confidence, or for maintaining the authority and impartiality of the judiciary.

3   The effect of this case is that whilst an employee has an absolute right to change religion, there is no absolute right to carry the change over in the manifestation of the new religion.
4   *Stedman v United Kingdom* [1997] EHRLR 545.
5   See *Handyside v United Kingdom* (1976) 1 EHRR 737.

The Court has emphasised on several occasions that Article 10 constitutes 'one of the essential foundations of a democratic society and is one of the basic conditions for its progress',[6] and has, thus, adopted a broad interpretation. The restrictions on Article 10 have consequently been interpreted narrowly by the Strasbourg court.[7]

How then will the company employer be affected by Article 10? In essence, the rights prescribed by the Article might mean, that an employee could dress in a way contrary to company policy or that a company is unable to discover from a third party by injunction the identity of an employee who, in breach of confidence, disclosed information belonging to the company to the third party as a 'whistleblowing' protest.

Employees' dress

It is a matter of common observation that individuals express themselves not only in what they say, but also, in what they wear. It is clear that the rights of Article 10 extend to protect not only the ideas expressed themselves, but the way in which they are expressed, including in the form of dress.[8]

Employers often want to project their own image and individual expression through the dress of their employees. A uniform gives the impression of order, a badge of authority and unity, an open-necked shirt an air of relaxation, a jacket and tie of austerity and so on. Domestic law has previously protected the employer when it has imposed its view as to dress on its employees, extending to hair length, beards and body piercing. This has applied even when there has been admitted discrimination between the dress requirements for men and women.[9] Under the HRA a court or tribunal must exercise its discretion compatibly with Article 10. Company employers might therefore face renewed action by employees dissatisfied that they are not able to express themselves by adopting dress of their own choosing whilst working for their employer, or because the company dress code for men and women is different. The Strasbourg court has been particularly aware of the practicalities involved in such issues and has allowed restrictions to dress in the context of employment. Article 10 (2) in particular allows restrictions on the grounds of the reputation of others. In *Kara v United Kingdom*[10] the applicant was a transvestite who wore female clothes at work. The court considered that the employer was justified in requiring the applicant to wear appropriate clothing (male) in order to prevent the council being brought into disrepute.

The standard required by Article 10 in order to justify rules as to clothing will be proportionality and not just that the requirement is reasonable.[11] On this basis the employer's present ability to require women to wear skirts and men to have short hair will have to be justifiable as pursuing a legitimate aim and proportionate to that aim, not just that it is reasonable. This will be an even stricter justification where

6   *Handyside v United Kingdom* (1976) 1 EHRR 737; *Lingens v Austria* (1986) 8 EHRR 407; *Jersild v Denmark* (1994) 19 EHRR 1.
7   See Chapter 11 for a fuller consideration of Article 10.
8   *Stephens v United Kingdom* Application 11674/85, 46 DR 245.
9   For example, see *Smith v Safeway plc* [1996] ICR 868.
10   [1999] EHRLR 232.
11   See Chapter 7.

the requirement is discriminatory eg men can wear trousers but not women and women can have long hair but not men.[12] It is likely that justifications for dress code based on customer preference for short skirts or dislike of beards will not be a sufficient justification.[13] Rather the employer would have to show that it is designed to aid the functioning of the business.

Whistleblowing

There is an increasing tendency for employees to protest against the actions of their employer company which the employee finds offensive by telling third parties of the offensive actions. This is commonly known as whistleblowing. Often, whistleblowing will involve the employee advising the third party, often a newspaper or other media group, of facts in breach of confidence or otherwise in breach of the employee's contract of employment. Where the employer is a public authority an employee if they suffer any detriment as a result of whistleblowing could allege an unlawful act on the part of the public authority under section 6 of the HRA. The employer will however be able to draw on the Strasbourg case law in order to defend itself, as the Court has in the past accepted that public sector employment may entail certain restrictions on the employees Article 10 rights.[14] However recently in *Fuentes Bobo v Spain*[15] the ECtHR found a breach of Article 10 where the applicant had been dismissed for criticising the management of the Spanish state television company for which he worked. While it was the state television company at issue the Court found that Article 10 applied even where relations between an employer and an employee were governed by private law.

Article 10 impacts on this situation in a number of ways. If the employer is a private sector company then there is no right of action under the HRA but if the employee is dismissed for the whistleblowing the tribunal would have to consider whether the action breached Article 10. Where the information has not been published and the company wishes to get an injunction to restrain publication this may be difficult even where the information is confidential. The court will have an obligation to consider the Article 10 right of the publisher which depending on the nature of the information will be particularly strong in view of section 12 of the HRA which emphasises the importance of Article 10. However when the company becomes aware of the disclosure of privileged information, the immediate damage has usually been done, and the confidential information published. The company, however, will probably want to ensure that the guilty employee is caught and punished (perhaps dismissed) or that further leaks of confidential information do not emanate from the same source. Usually the only way for the company to discover the identity of the employee is from the third party newspaper organisation, who are generally unwilling to reveal their sources.

12   *Schmidt v Germany* (1994) 18 EHRR 513.
13   The US case law on this indicates that such justifications are not acceptable. See *Diaz v Pan American World Airways Inc* 442 Fd 385, 404 US 950 (5th Cir 1971).
14   See *Morissens v Belgium* (1998) 56 DR 127.
15   29 February 2000, unreported.

The common law action available to the injured company is to injunct the third party to disclose the identity of the disloyal employee. The question uppermost on the mind of a company will be whether Article 10 of the ECHR will prevent the company from discovering the identity of the whistleblower. Under the HRA the courts must have regard *to Goodwin v United Kingdom*,[16] in which case the European Court held that a court order requiring a journalist to disclose his sources was not necessary in a democratic society, especially given that the disclosure was for the company to identify the guilty employee. The rights of the company were outweighed by what was perceived as the public interest in allowing the journalist to protect his sources (and presumably the right of the journalist to practice his trade which relies on informants being assured of their anonymity). However in *Camelot Group plc v Centaur Communications Ltd*[17] the court prior to the HRA considered the Article 10 implications in a whistleblowing case and found that the Contempt of Court Act 1981 was enough to protect Article 10 rights. In this particular case revealing the identity of a whistleblower did not breach Article 10. Whether this could be maintained under the HRA is questionable.

It follows that an inability of an injured company to discover the identity of a whistleblower employee, as a consequence of the rights embodied in Article 10, might well leave the company without a common law remedy for the damage it suffers flowing from the breach of confidence. There is now statutory legislation governing whistleblowing in the form of the Public Interest Disclosure Act 1998, which safeguards the interests of the employee, providing that certain procedures are followed. Employees who whistleblow without following the procedures prescribed by the Act lose the protection of it.

Article 11 - Freedom of assembly and association

Article 11 protects the right to freedom of peaceful assembly and the freedom of association with others. It provides in Article 11(1) the right to form and join trade unions for the protection of his interests. Article 8 (2) provides a number of qualifications in that:

> [n]o restrictions shall be placed on the exercise of these rights other than such as are prescribed by law and are necessary in a democratic society in the interests of national security or public safety, for the prevention of disorder or crime, for the protection of health or morals or for the protection of the rights and freedoms of others. This article shall not prevent the imposition of lawful restrictions on the exercise of these rights by members of the armed forces, of the police or of the administration of the State.

On a number of occasions the Strasbourg court has interpreted this Article as requiring the state to take positive steps to protect individuals. For example in the case of *Plattform Ärzte für das Leben v Austria*[18] the applicants, an association against legalised abortion, did not claim that the national authorities had interfered

16   *Goodwin v United Kingdom* (1996) 22 EHRR 123.
17   [1998] 1 All ER 251.
18   *Plattform Ärzte für das Leben v Austria* (1988) 13 EHRR 204.

actively in a demonstration held by Plattform, but that the police had failed to protect the peaceful demonstrators against disruptions by counter-demonstrators. Not only did the Court confirm its case law with respect to positive obligations[19] and accept for the first time that such obligations can arise under Article 11 as well, but it held that national authorities can additionally be under a duty to intervene in relations between private individuals. However, in the context of horizontal effect, in the words of the Court, the national authorities enjoy a 'wide discretion in the choice of means to be used'.[20]

In the context of picketing it is important to note that Article 11 protects 'peaceful' assembly not an assembly designed to cause disturbance. The fact that the assembly does in fact cause disruption and inconvenience to others does not mean it is not 'peaceful'. The domestic provisions on picketing contained in section 220 of the Trade Union and Labour Relations (Consolidation) Act 1992 and the Code of Practice on Picketing are probably justifiable as proportionate to the legitimate aim pursued by the state. The law of trespass in so far as it is used to keep pickets away from company premises could possibly be a breach of Article 11.

It should be noted that Article 11 does not give an employee the right to join a trade union or not to be expelled from a trade union. A union itself can choose to associate with whomsoever it pleases.[1] However, should an employer dismiss an employee for failing to join a prescribed union, then the company would be found to have violated Article 11, because of the seriousness with which the courts would view sanctions leading to the loss of livelihood: see *Young v United Kingdom*.[2] This does not follow simply because there is a closed shop operating within a company; the real complaint in the *Young* case was not the concept of the closed shop, but the sanction of dismissal which offended Article 11. In *Sibson v United Kingdom*,[3] there was no violation of Article 11, when the employer removed an employee from the workplace when he had left union 'A' to join union 'B', and his fellow employees declined to work with him or speak with him. The key point was that the applicant was not in danger of losing his job as a consequence of the closed shop arrangement. Of course, greater difficulties would face the employer who did not have the luxury of being able to move the employee to another location. One of the difficulties that may face employers under Article 11 is whether a policy of refusing to allow employees representation by their trade union would infringe Article 11. At present the position is unclear at the Strasbourg level but there is certainly the risk that such a policy might infringe Article 11.[4] The same is true as to whether there is a right to strike protected by Article 11.[5]

---

19   See *Marckx v Belgium* (1979) 2 EHRR 298 with regard to Article 8.
20   *A- 139* § 32 .
1   See *Cheall v United Kingdom* (1985) 42 DR 178.
2   See *Young v United Kingdom* (1981) 4 EHRR 38.
3   *Sibson v United Kingdom* (1993) 17 EHRR 193.
4   See *Wilson, Palmer and Doolan v United Kingdom* (1996) Application 30668/96.
5   See *Schmidt and Dahlstrom v Sweden* (1976) 1 EHRR 632.

Article 14 – Freedom from discrimination

Article 14 contains the prohibition of discrimination on a number of non-exhaustively enumerated grounds such as 'sex, race, colour, language, religion, political or other opinion, national or social origin, association with a national minority, property, birth or other status.' By definition, Article 14 can have no independent meaning, as its applicability is limited to the exercise of other Convention rights or freedoms.[6] However, this linkage-principle does not necessarily presuppose a breach of that other provision. In the *Belgian Linguistic Case*,[7] the Court held that 'a measure which in itself is in conformity with the requirements of the Article enshrining the right or freedom in question may however infringe this Article when read in conjunction with Article 14 for the reason that it is of a discriminatory nature'.[8] The only requirement is that the facts at issue 'fall within the ambit of one or more' of the substantive rights.[9] Article 14 is often used in conjunction with other rights and freedoms in the employment context.[10]

An additional factor in the area of discrimination is the interplay of EC law and the Convention. As we have outlined in Chapters 5 and 6 the Convention rights form part of the European Community influences and as such play a part in interpreting Community legislation. Equal treatment is one of the values that the ECJ has considered to be extremely important when interpreting the Equal Treatment Directive.[11] On this basis domestic legislation has been interpreted to protect transsexuals from sex discrimination.[12]

6   Confirmed in *Airey v Ireland* (1979) 2 EHRR 305; *Abdulaziz, Cabales and Balkandali v United Kingdom* (1985) 7 EHRR 471; *Rasmussen v Denmark* (1984) 7 EHRR 371, *Karlheinz Schmidt v Germany* (1994) 18 EHRR 513.
7   *Belgian Linguistics v Belgium (No 2)* (1968) 1 EHRR 252.
8   See n 7 above, A-6 p 33.
9   *Abdulaziz v United Kingdom* (1985) 7 EHRR 471.
10 On the way the German courts deal with Article 14 see Kischel, U,' Zur Dogmatik des Gleichheitssatzes in der Europäischen Union' (1997) *Europäische Grundrechtszeitschrift*, p1; Störmer, R.: 'Gemeinschaftsrechtliche Diskriminierungsverbote versus nationale Grundrechte?' (1998) *Archiv des öffentlichen Rechts (AöR)* 123, p 541.
11 See *P v S & Cornwall County Council* [1996] 2 CMLR 247.
12 *Chessington World of Adventures Ltd v Reed* [1998] ICR 97.

Chapter fourteen

Researching human rights

In England we have come to rely on a comfortable time-lag of 50 years or a century intervening between the perception that something ought to be done and a serious attempt to do it.[1]

Comparative research under the HRA will be of greater importance than ever before because of the need to seek out differing ways in which either ECHR rights and freedoms or similar rights have been interpreted by other jurisdictions. Where possible during the course of this book we have drawn on comparative materials from other jurisdictions with a longer tradition of interpreting rights. These included US, Canadian, Hong Kong, New Zealand, South African, Irish and German sources offering comparative interpretative examples on which the English courts might draw in interpreting Convention rights. However, the ECHR is, as its name suggests, primarily a European document which most of the continental European states have a long history of interpreting. Any consideration of the Strasbourg case law necessarily brings the reader into contact with the domestic provision that interfered with the Article or Articles in question. For example in *Markt Intern Verlag and Klaus Beerman v Germany*[2] the operation of the German Competition regime was in question and offers a useful guide to the extent to which competition grounds can justify interference with Convention rights. As such researching both the case law of the ECHR and the case law of the other European jurisdictions that have incorporated the ECHR rights and freedoms will be a necessary part of determining how the ECHR will operate in the UK. The following sources are intended to aid the researcher in accessing material both in the UK and in other jurisdictions to aid that task.

1   HG, Wells, *The Work, Wealth and Happiness of Mankind* (1931).
2   (1989) 12 EHRR 161.

ECHR

Reading

There are numerous books on the subject of the ECHR but these three are the best, in our opinion, combining excellent coverage with an explanatory style. Harris et al is looking a bit old now but there is a new edition due out in October 2000.

Harris, DJ, O'Boyle, M, and Warbrick, C *Law of the European Convention on Human Rights* (1995) Butterworths.

Reid, K *A Practioner's Guide to the European Convention on Human Rights* (1998) Sweet & Maxwell

Van Dijk, P and Van Hoof G J H *Theory and Practice of the European Convention on Human Rights* (3rd edn, 1998) Kluwer Law

Websites Relevant to the ECHR

European Court of Human Rights

http://www.echr.coe.int/

Search for case law of the European Court of Human Rights from mid-Eighties to present day:
http://www.dhcour.coe.fr/hudoc/default.asp?Language=en&Advanced=1

European Commission on Human Rights

http://www.dhcommhr.coe.fr/

Council of Europe's human rights website

http://www.humanrights.coe.int/

Council of Europe main website

http://www.*coe.int/portal.asp?L=E&M=$t/1-1-1-1/EMB1.asp*

(click on human rights links on the right)

Council of Europe's Committee of Ministers' Human Rights Resolutions

http://www.*coe.fr/cm/site2/ref/dynamic/resolutions_hr.asp*

Council of Europe's Parliamentary Assembly

http://stars.*coe.fr/index_e.htm*

The Human Rights Act 1998

Reading

While the material on the HRA is beginning to expand rapidly, the three books below offer something above the rest. Waham and Mountfield offer without doubt the most easily accessible, explanatory guide to the HRA. Lester and Pannick offer a much more in-depth analysis of the implications of the HRA for English law generally. Kier Starmer offers a thematic approach to the HRA which is extremely useful to get an idea of the impacts of the HRA in a specific area of law.

Wadham, J and Mountfield, H *Blackstones Guide to the Human Rights Act 1998* (1999) Blackstones

Lord Lester and Pannick, D *Human Rights Law and Practice* (1999) Butterworths

Kier Starmer *European Human Rights Law: The Human Rights Act 1998 and the European Convention on Human Rights* (1999) LAG

Websites on the HRA 1998

Lord Chancellor's Department Human Rights website

http://www.open.gov.uk/lcd/humanrights/humanrfr.htm

Two websites from Beagle on the HRA and human rights in general

http://www.beagle.org.uk/hra/

http://www.beagle.org.uk/hra/indexold.htm

Northern Ireland Human Rights Commission

http://www.nihrc.org/

Law Society's Human Rights page (click on the human rights link on the menu)

http://www.lawsoc.org.uk/index.html

Home Office's Human Rights Unit

http://www.homeoffice.gov.uk/hract/hramenu.htm

Home Office's Human Rights Task Force

http://www.homeoffice.gov.uk/hract/tasklist.htm

Home office specifically on the Parliamentary debates on the HRA

http://www.homeoffice.gov.uk/hract/lawlist2.htm

Liberty

http://www.liberty-human-rights.org.uk/

(for specific info on HRA click on the Policy link and then select HRA)

Doughty Street Chambers

http://www.doughtystreet.co.uk/

(click on human rights link and then select HRA)

Scottish Human Rights Trust

http://www.scotrights.org/shrt.htm

(click on link to HRA)

Legal Resources in the UK and Ireland by Delia Venables

(Good general source of information)

http://www.venables.co.uk/

Commons and House of Lords debates

http://www.parliament.uk/hophome.htm

Stationary Office:

http://www.hmso.gov.uk/

Lexicon-legal information for the courts online:

http://www.courtservice.gov.uk/lexicon/index.htm

UK government Acts:

http://www.legislation.hmso.gov.uk/acts.htm#acts

Comparative sources of case law and materials

Human rights in general

University of Minnesota Human Rights Library

http://www1.umn.edu/humanrts/index.html

(This site is one of the best with materials, case law and links on every jurisdiction)

Huge links page (2000+ sites) from University of Minnesota

http://www1.umn.edu/humanrts/links/links.htm

UN High Commissioner for Human Rights

http://www.unhchr.ch/hchr_un.htm

Human Rights Watch

http://www.hrw.org/home.html

Amnesty International

http://www.amnesty.org/

Human Rights Internet

http://www.hri.ca/

Interights

http://www.interights.org/

International Labour Organisation:

http://www.ilo.org/

International Commission of the Red Cross:

http://www.wwlia.org/ca-hr.htm

Human rights/constitutional rights in other jurisdictions

A. INDIA

South Asia Human Rights Resource Centre

(India has a very advanced rights-based system of litigation especially on environmental hazard)

http://www.hri.ca/partners/sahrdc/

B. SOUTH AFRICA

Truth and Reconciliation Commission

http://www.truth.org.za/

C. NEW ZEALAND

NZ Human Rights Commission

http://www.hrc.co.nz/

D. HONG KONG

Hong Kong Human Rights Commission

http://is7.pacific.net.hk/~hkhrc/

E. AUSTRALIA

Australian Human Rights and Equal Opportunities Commission

http://www.hreoc.gov.au/index.html

Human Rights Council of Australia

http://www.ozemail.com.au/~hrca/

F. USA

American Civil Liberties Union

http://www.aclu.org/index.html

The US State Department Annual Reports on Human Rights Practices in countries throughout the world can be found at:

http://www.usis.usemb.se/human/index.html

G. CANADA

Candian Human Rights Commission

http://www.chrc-ccdp.ca/menu.asp?l=e

Canadian Human Rights Foundation

http://www.chrf.ca/english/general/files/master_eng.htm

Canadian Human Rights Tribunal

http://www.chrt-tcdp.gc.ca/english/index.htm

H. GERMANY

University of Wuerzburg's Collection of International Constitutional Law:

http://www.uni-wuerzburg.de/law/index.html *(English & German)*

Max Planck Institute for Comparative Public Law and International Law

http://www.virtual-institute.de/eindex.cfm *(English and German)*

Mainz University

http://radbruch.jura.uni-mainz.de/

(German)

Humboldt-University (Berlin)

http://www.rewi.hu-berlin.de/

(English and German)

Bayreuth Universtity

http://www.uni-bayreuth.de/students/elsa/elsa-home-english.html#jurweb

http://www.uni-bayreuth.de/students/elsa/jura/jurweb-home-english.html

(German and English)

Sarrburuken University

http://www.jura.uni-sb.de/ (German and English)

Beck Verlag (publisher)

http://www.beck.de/

(German)

The German Constitution

http://www.jura.uni-sb.de/english/

(English and German)

German case law

http://www.jura.uni-sb.de/Entscheidungen/

(German)

I. FRANCE

General government sites

Assemblée

http://www.assemblee-nat.fr

(English and French)

Senat

http://www.senat.fr

(English and French)

Ministre de justice

http://www.justice.gouv.fr/

(English and French)

Le Ministère de la culture

http://web.culture.fr/

(French)

Ministry of Justice and Human Rights

http://www.justice.gouv.fr/textfond/textfond.htm

(French)

J.   EUROPEAN UNION

General

http://europa.eu.int/index-en.htm

http://db.consilium.eu.int/df/default.asp?lang=en

On the Presidency's proposals for a Charter of Fundamental Rights

http://db.consilium.eu.int/DF/
listdate.asp?bd=28&bm=07&by=2000&ed=28&em=07&ey=2000

http://db.consilium.eu.int/dfdocs/EN/04422en.pdf

On civil liberties in the EU

http://www.statewatch.org/

K. OTHER REGIONAL/COUNTRY HR PAGES

To investigate more regional/country HR pages try this page at Essex University:

http://libwww.essex.ac.uk/Human_Rights/bycountry.htm

For links to official government sites worldwide try this other page of links at

Essex Universtiy

http://libwww.essex.ac.uk/Officialinformation.htm

Appendix 1

Human Rights Act 1998
(c 42)

An Act to give further effect to rights and freedoms guaranteed under the European Convention on Human Rights; to make provision with respect to holders of certain judicial offices who become judges of the European Court of Human Rights; and for connected purposes.

[9th November 1998]

BE IT ENACTED by the Queen's most Excellent Majesty, by and with the advice and consent of the Lords Spiritual and Temporal, and Commons, in this present Parliament assembled, and by the authority of the same, as follows:—

Introduction

1 The Convention Rights

(1)   In this Act 'the Convention rights' means the rights and fundamental freedoms set out in—
- (a) Articles 2 to 12 and 14 of the Convention,
- (b) Articles 1 to 3 of the First Protocol, and
- (c) Articles 1 and 2 of the Sixth Protocol,

as read with Articles 16 to 18 of the Convention.

(2)   Those Articles are to have effect for the purposes of this Act subject to any designated derogation or reservation (as to which see sections 14 and 15).

(3)   The Articles are set out in Schedule 1.

(4)   The Secretary of State may by order make such amendments to this Act as he considers appropriate to reflect the effect, in relation to the United Kingdom, of a protocol.

(5)   In subsection (4) 'protocol' means a protocol to the Convention—
   (a)   which the United Kingdom has ratified; or
   (b)   which the United Kingdom has signed with a view to ratification.

(6)   No amendment may be made by an order under subsection (4) so as to come into force before the protocol concerned is in force in relation to the United Kingdom.

2   Interpretation of Convention rights

(1)   A court or tribunal determining a question which has arisen in connection with a Convention right must take into account any—
   (a)   judgment, decision, declaration or advisory opinion of the European Court of Human Rights,
   (b)   opinion of the Commission given in a report adopted under Article 31 of the Convention,
   (c)   decision of the Commission in connection with Article 26 or 27(2) of the Convention, or
   (d)   decision of the Committee of Ministers taken under Article 46 of the Convention,

whenever made or given, so far as, in the opinion of the court or tribunal, it is relevant to the proceedings in which that question has arisen.

(2)   Evidence of any judgment, decision, declaration or opinion of which account may have to be taken under this section is to be given in proceedings before any court or tribunal in such manner as may be provided by rules.

(3)   In this section 'rules' means rules of court or, in the case of proceedings before a tribunal, rules made for the purposes of this section—
   (a)   by the Lord Chancellor or the Secretary of State, in relation to any proceedings outside Scotland;
   (b)   by the Secretary of State, in relation to proceedings in Scotland; or
   (c)   by a Northern Ireland department, in relation to proceedings before a tribunal in Northern Ireland—
      (i)   which deals with transferred matters; and
      (ii)   for which no rules made under paragraph (a) are in force.

Legislation

3   Interpretation of legislation

(1)   So far as it is possible to do so, primary legislation and subordinate legislation must be read and given effect in a way which is compatible with the Convention rights.

(2)   This section—
   (a)   applies to primary legislation and subordinate legislation whenever enacted;

(b) does not affect the validity, continuing operation or enforcement of any incompatible primary legislation; and

(c) does not affect the validity, continuing operation or enforcement of any incompatible subordinate legislation if (disregarding any possibility of revocation) primary legislation prevents removal of the incompatibility.

4 Declaration of incompatibility

(1) Subsection (2) applies in any proceedings in which a court determines whether a provision of primary legislation is compatible with a Convention right.

(2) If the court is satisfied that the provision is incompatible with a Convention right, it may make a declaration of that incompatibility.

(3) Subsection (4) applies in any proceedings in which a court determines whether a provision of subordinate legislation, made in the exercise of a power conferred by primary legislation, is compatible with a Convention right.

(4) If the court is satisfied—
    (a) that the provision is incompatible with a Convention right, and
    (b) that (disregarding any possibility of revocation) the primary legislation concerned prevents removal of the incompatibility,

it may make a declaration of that incompatibility.

(5) In this section 'court' means—
    (a) the House of Lords;
    (b) the Judicial Committee of the Privy Council;
    (c) the Courts-Martial Appeal Court;
    (d) in Scotland, the High Court of Justiciary sitting otherwise than as a trial court or the Court of Session;
    (e) in England and Wales or Northern Ireland, the High Court or the Court of Appeal.

(6) A declaration under this section ('a declaration of incompatibility')—
    (a) does not affect the validity, continuing operation or enforcement of the provision in respect of which it is given; and
    (b) is not binding on the parties to the proceedings in which it is made.

5 Right of Crown to intervene

(1) Where a court is considering whether to make a declaration of incompatibility, the Crown is entitled to notice in accordance with rules of court.

(2) In any case to which subsection (1) applies—
    (a) a Minister of the Crown (or a person nominated by him),
    (b) a member of the Scottish Executive,
    (c) a Northern Ireland Minister,
    (d) a Northern Ireland department,

is entitled, on giving notice in accordance with rules of court, to be joined as a party to the proceedings.

(3) Notice under subsection (2) may be given at any time during the proceedings.

(4) A person who has been made a party to criminal proceedings (other than in Scotland) as the result of a notice under subsection (2) may, with leave, appeal to the House of Lords against any declaration of incompatibility made in the proceedings.

(5) In subsection (4)—
'criminal proceedings' includes all proceedings before the Courts-Martial Appeal Court; and
'leave' means leave granted by the court making the declaration of incompatibility or by the House of Lords.

Public authorities

6 Acts of public authorities

(1) It is unlawful for a public authority to act in a way which is incompatible with a Convention right.

(2) Subsection (1) does not apply to an act if—
(a) as the result of one or more provisions of primary legislation, the authority could not have acted differently; or
(b) in the case of one or more provisions of, or made under, primary legislation which cannot be read or given effect in a way which is compatible with the Convention rights, the authority was acting so as to give effect to or enforce those provisions.

(3) In this section 'public authority' includes—
(a) a court or tribunal, and
(b) any person certain of whose functions are functions of a public nature,

but does not include either House of Parliament or a person exercising functions in connection with proceedings in Parliament.

(4) In subsection (3) 'Parliament' does not include the House of Lords in its judicial capacity.

(5) In relation to a particular act, a person is not a public authority by virtue only of subsection (3)(b) if the nature of the act is private.

(6) 'An act' includes a failure to act but does not include a failure to—
(a) introduce in, or lay before, Parliament a proposal for legislation; or
(b) make any primary legislation or remedial order.

7 Proceedings

(1) A person who claims that a public authority has acted (or proposes to act) in a way which is made unlawful by section 6(1) may—
(a) bring proceedings against the authority under this Act in the appropriate court or tribunal, or

(b) rely on the Convention right or rights concerned in any legal proceedings,

but only if he is (or would be) a victim of the unlawful act.

(2)   In subsection (1)(a) 'appropriate court or tribunal' means such court or tribunal as may be determined in accordance with rules; and proceedings against an authority include a counterclaim or similar proceeding.

(3)   If the proceedings are brought on an application for judicial review, the applicant is to be taken to have a sufficient interest in relation to the unlawful act only if he is, or would be, a victim of that act.

(4)   If the proceedings are made by way of a petition for judicial review in Scotland, the applicant shall be taken to have title and interest to sue in relation to the unlawful act only if he is, or would be, a victim of that act.

(5)   Proceedings under subsection (1)(a) must be brought before the end of—
   (a) the period of one year beginning with the date on which the act complained of took place; or
   (b) such longer period as the court or tribunal considers equitable having regard to all the circumstances,

but that is subject to any rule imposing a stricter time limit in relation to the procedure in question.

(6)   In subsection (1)(b) 'legal proceedings' includes—
   (a) proceedings brought by or at the instigation of a public authority; and
   (b) an appeal against the decision of a court or tribunal.

(7)   For the purposes of this section, a person is a victim of an unlawful act only if he would be a victim for the purposes of Article 34 of the Convention if proceedings were brought in the European Court of Human Rights in respect of that act.

(8)   Nothing in this Act creates a criminal offence.

(9)   In this section 'rules' means—
   (a) in relation to proceedings before a court or tribunal outside Scotland, rules made by the Lord Chancellor or the Secretary of State for the purposes of this section or rules of court,
   (b) in relation to proceedings before a court or tribunal in Scotland, rules made by the Secretary of State for those purposes,
   (c) in relation to proceedings before a tribunal in Northern Ireland—
      (i)   which deals with transferred matters; and
      (ii) for which no rules made under paragraph (a) are in force,
      rules made by a Northern Ireland department for those purposes,

and includes provision made by order under section 1 of the Courts and Legal Services Act 1990.

(10)   In making rules, regard must be had to section 9.

(11)   The Minister who has power to make rules in relation to a particular tribunal may, to the extent he considers it necessary to ensure that the tribunal can provide

an appropriate remedy in relation to an act (or proposed act) of a public authority which is (or would be) unlawful as a result of section 6(1), by order add to—
(a) the relief or remedies which the tribunal may grant; or
(b) the grounds on which it may grant any of them.

(12) An order made under subsection (11) may contain such incidental, supplemental, consequential or transitional provision as the Minister making it considers appropriate.

(13) 'The Minister' includes the Northern Ireland department concerned.

8 Judicial remedies

(1) In relation to any act (or proposed act) of a public authority which the court finds is (or would be) unlawful, it may grant such relief or remedy, or make such order, within its powers as it considers just and appropriate.

(2) But damages may be awarded only by a court which has power to award damages, or to order the payment of compensation, in civil proceedings.

(3) No award of damages is to be made unless, taking account of all the circumstances of the case, including—
(a) any other relief or remedy granted, or order made, in relation to the act in question (by that or any other court), and
(b) the consequences of any decision (of that or any other court) in respect of that act,

the court is satisfied that the award is necessary to afford just satisfaction to the person in whose favour it is made.

(4) In determining—
(a) whether to award damages, or
(b) the amount of an award,

the court must take into account the principles applied by the European Court of Human Rights in relation to the award of compensation under Article 41 of the Convention.

(5) A public authority against which damages are awarded is to be treated—
(a) in Scotland, for the purposes of section 3 of the Law Reform (Miscellaneous Provisions) (Scotland) Act 1940 as if the award were made in an action of damages in which the authority has been found liable in respect of loss or damage to the person to whom the award is made;
(b) for the purposes of the Civil Liability (Contribution) Act 1978 as liable in respect of damage suffered by the person to whom the award is made.

(6) In this section—
'court' includes a tribunal;
'damages' means damages for an unlawful act of a public authority; and
'unlawful' means unlawful under section 6(1).

9   Judicial acts

(1)   Proceedings under section 7(1)(a) in respect of a judicial act may be brought only—
   (a)   by exercising a right of appeal;
   (b)   on an application (in Scotland a petition) for judicial review; or
   (c)   in such other forum as may be prescribed by rules.

(2)   That does not affect any rule of law which prevents a court from being the subject of judicial review.

(3)   In proceedings under this Act in respect of a judicial act done in good faith, damages may not be awarded otherwise than to compensate a person to the extent required by Article 5(5) of the Convention.

(4)   An award of damages permitted by subsection (3) is to be made against the Crown; but no award may be made unless the appropriate person, if not a party to the proceedings, is joined.

(5)   In this section—
   'appropriate person' means the Minister responsible for the court concerned, or a person or government department nominated by him;
   'court' includes a tribunal;
   'judge' includes a member of a tribunal, a justice of the peace and a clerk or other officer entitled to exercise the jurisdiction of a court;
   'judicial act' means a judicial act of a court and includes an act done on the instructions, or on behalf, of a judge; and
   'rules' has the same meaning as in section 7(9).

Remedial action

10   Power to take remedial action

(1)   This section applies if—
   (a)   a provision of legislation has been declared under section 4 to be incompatible with a Convention right and, if an appeal lies—
      (i)   all persons who may appeal have stated in writing that they do not intend to do so;
      (ii)   the time for bringing an appeal has expired and no appeal has been brought within that time; or
      (iii) an appeal brought within that time has been determined or abandoned; or
   (b)   it appears to a Minister of the Crown or Her Majesty in Council that, having regard to a finding of the European Court of Human Rights made after the coming into force of this section in proceedings against the United Kingdom, a provision of legislation is incompatible with an obligation of the United Kingdom arising from the Convention.

(2)   If a Minister of the Crown considers that there are compelling reasons for

proceeding under this section, he may by order make such amendments to the legislation as he considers necessary to remove the incompatibility.

(3)   If, in the case of subordinate legislation, a Minister of the Crown considers—
   (a) that it is necessary to amend the primary legislation under which the subordinate legislation in question was made, in order to enable the incompatibility to be removed, and
   (b) that there are compelling reasons for proceeding under this section,

he may by order make such amendments to the primary legislation as he considers necessary.

(4)   This section also applies where the provision in question is in subordinate legislation and has been quashed, or declared invalid, by reason of incompatibility with a Convention right and the Minister proposes to proceed under paragraph 2(b) of Schedule 2.

(5)   If the legislation is an Order in Council, the power conferred by subsection (2) or (3) is exercisable by Her Majesty in Council.

(6)   In this section 'legislation' does not include a Measure of the Church Assembly or of the General Synod of the Church of England.

(7)   Schedule 2 makes further provision about remedial orders.

Other rights and proceedings

11 Safeguard for existing human rights

A person's reliance on a Convention right does not restrict—
   (a) any other right or freedom conferred on him by or under any law having effect in any part of the United Kingdom; or
   (b) his right to make any claim or bring any proceedings which he could make or bring apart from sections 7 to 9.

12 Freedom of expression

(1)   This section applies if a court is considering whether to grant any relief which, if granted, might affect the exercise of the Convention right to freedom of expression.

(2)   If the person against whom the application for relief is made ('the respondent') is neither present nor represented, no such relief is to be granted unless the court is satisfied—
   (a) that the applicant has taken all practicable steps to notify the respondent; or
   (b) that there are compelling reasons why the respondent should not be notified.

(3)   No such relief is to be granted so as to restrain publication before trial unless the court is satisfied that the applicant is likely to establish that publication should not be allowed.

(4)   The court must have particular regard to the importance of the Convention right to freedom of expression and, where the proceedings relate to material which the respondent claims, or which appears to the court, to be journalistic, literary or artistic material (or to conduct connected with such material), to—

(a) the extent to which—
   (i)   the material has, or is about to, become available to the public; or
   (ii) it is, or would be, in the public interest for the material to be published;
(b) any relevant privacy code.

(5)   In this section—
'court' includes a tribunal; and
'relief' includes any remedy or order (other than in criminal proceedings).

13   Freedom of thought, conscience and religion

(1)   If a court's determination of any question arising under this Act might affect the exercise by a religious organisation (itself or its members collectively) of the Convention right to freedom of thought, conscience and religion, it must have particular regard to the importance of that right.

(2)   In this section 'court' includes a tribunal.

Derogations and reservations

14   Derogations

(1)   In this Act 'designated derogation' means—
(a) the United Kingdom's derogation from Article 5(3) of the Convention; and
(b) any derogation by the United Kingdom from an Article of the Convention, or of any protocol to the Convention, which is designated for the purposes of this Act in an order made by the Secretary of State.

(2)   The derogation referred to in subsection (1)(a) is set out in Part I of Schedule 3.

(3)   If a designated derogation is amended or replaced it ceases to be a designated derogation.

(4)   But subsection (3) does not prevent the Secretary of State from exercising his power under subsection (1)(b) to make a fresh designation order in respect of the Article concerned.

(5)   The Secretary of State must by order make such amendments to Schedule 3 as he considers appropriate to reflect—
(a) any designation order; or
(b) the effect of subsection (3).

(6)   A designation order may be made in anticipation of the making by the United Kingdom of a proposed derogation.

15   Reservations

(1)   In this Act 'designated reservation' means—
   (a)   the United Kingdom's reservation to Article 2 of the First Protocol to the Convention; and
   (b)   any other reservation by the United Kingdom to an Article of the Convention, or of any protocol to the Convention, which is designated for the purposes of this Act in an order made by the Secretary of State.

(2)   The text of the reservation referred to in subsection (1)(a) is set out in Part II of Schedule 3.

(3)   If a designated reservation is withdrawn wholly or in part it ceases to be a designated reservation.

(4)   But subsection (3) does not prevent the Secretary of State from exercising his power under subsection (1)(b) to make a fresh designation order in respect of the Article concerned.

(5)   The Secretary of State must by order make such amendments to this Act as he considers appropriate to reflect—
   (a)   any designation order; or
   (b)   the effect of subsection (3).

16   Period for which designated derogations have effect

(1)   If it has not already been withdrawn by the United Kingdom, a designated derogation ceases to have effect for the purposes of this Act—
   (a)   in the case of the derogation referred to in section 14(1)(a), at the end of the period of five years beginning with the date on which section 1(2) came into force;
   (b)   in the case of any other derogation, at the end of the period of five years beginning with the date on which the order designating it was made.

(2)   At any time before the period—
   (a)   fixed by subsection (1)(a) or (b), or
   (b)   extended by an order under this subsection,

comes to an end, the Secretary of State may by order extend it by a further period of five years.

(3)   An order under section 14(1)(b) ceases to have effect at the end of the period for consideration, unless a resolution has been passed by each House approving the order.

(4)   Subsection (3) does not affect—
   (a)   anything done in reliance on the order; or
   (b)   the power to make a fresh order under section 14(1)(b).

(5)   In subsection (3) 'period for consideration' means the period of forty days beginning with the day on which the order was made.

(6)   In calculating the period for consideration, no account is to be taken of any time during which—

(a) Parliament is dissolved or prorogued; or

(b) both Houses are adjourned for more than four days.

(7)   If a designated derogation is withdrawn by the United Kingdom, the Secretary of State must by order make such amendments to this Act as he considers are required to reflect that withdrawal.

17   Periodic review of designated reservations

(1)   The appropriate Minister must review the designated reservation referred to in section 15(1)(a)—
  (a) before the end of the period of five years beginning with the date on which section 1(2) came into force; and
  (b) if that designation is still in force, before the end of the period of five years beginning with the date on which the last report relating to it was laid under subsection (3).

(2)   The appropriate Minister must review each of the other designated reservations (if any)—
  (a) before the end of the period of five years beginning with the date on which the order designating the reservation first came into force; and
  (b) if the designation is still in force, before the end of the period of five years beginning with the date on which the last report relating to it was laid under subsection (3).

(3)   The Minister conducting a review under this section must prepare a report on the result of the review and lay a copy of it before each House of Parliament.

Judges of the European Court of Human Rights

18   Appointment to European Court of Human Rights

(1)   In this section 'judicial office' means the office of—
  (a) Lord Justice of Appeal, Justice of the High Court or Circuit judge, in England and Wales;
  (b) judge of the Court of Session or sheriff, in Scotland;
  (c) Lord Justice of Appeal, judge of the High Court or county court judge, in Northern Ireland.

(2)   The holder of a judicial office may become a judge of the European Court of Human Rights ('the Court') without being required to relinquish his office.

(3)   But he is not required to perform the duties of his judicial office while he is a judge of the Court.

(4)   In respect of any period during which he is a judge of the Court—
  (a) a Lord Justice of Appeal or Justice of the High Court is not to count as a judge of the relevant court for the purposes of section 2(1) or 4(1) of the

Supreme Court Act 1981 (maximum number of judges) nor as a judge of the Supreme Court for the purposes of section 12(1) to (6) of that Act (salaries etc);

(b) a judge of the Court of Session is not to count as a judge of that court for the purposes of section 1(1) of the Court of Session Act 1988 (maximum number of judges) or of section 9(1)(c) of the Administration of Justice Act 1973 ('the 1973 Act') (salaries etc);

(c) a Lord Justice of Appeal or judge of the High Court in Northern Ireland is not to count as a judge of the relevant court for the purposes of section 2(1) or 3(1) of the Judicature (Northern Ireland) Act 1978 (maximum number of judges) nor as a judge of the Supreme Court of Northern Ireland for the purposes of section 9(1)(d) of the 1973 Act (salaries etc);

(d) a Circuit judge is not to count as such for the purposes of section 18 of the Courts Act 1971 (salaries etc);

(e) a sheriff is not to count as such for the purposes of section 14 of the Sheriff Courts (Scotland) Act 1907 (salaries etc);

(f) a county court judge of Northern Ireland is not to count as such for the purposes of section 106 of the County Courts Act (Northern Ireland) 1959 (salaries etc).

(5)   If a sheriff principal is appointed a judge of the Court, section 11(1) of the Sheriff Courts (Scotland) Act 1971 (temporary appointment of sheriff principal) applies, while he holds that appointment, as if his office is vacant.

(6)   Schedule 4 makes provision about judicial pensions in relation to the holder of a judicial office who serves as a judge of the Court.

(7)   The Lord Chancellor or the Secretary of State may by order make such transitional provision (including, in particular, provision for a temporary increase in the maximum number of judges) as he considers appropriate in relation to any holder of a judicial office who has completed his service as a judge of the Court.

Parliamentary procedure

19   Statements of compatibility

(1)   A Minister of the Crown in charge of a Bill in either House of Parliament must, before Second Reading of the Bill—

(a) make a statement to the effect that in his view the provisions of the Bill are compatible with the Convention rights ('a statement of compatibility'); or

(b) make a statement to the effect that although he is unable to make a statement of compatibility the government nevertheless wishes the House to proceed with the Bill.

(2)   The statement must be in writing and be published in such manner as the Minister making it considers appropriate.

Supplemental

20 Orders etc under this Act

(1)   Any power of a Minister of the Crown to make an order under this Act is exercisable by statutory instrument.

(2)   The power of the Lord Chancellor or the Secretary of State to make rules (other than rules of court) under section 2(3) or 7(9) is exercisable by statutory instrument.

(3)   Any statutory instrument made under section 14, 15 or 16(7) must be laid before Parliament.

(4)   No order may be made by the Lord Chancellor or the Secretary of State under section 1(4), 7(11) or 16(2) unless a draft of the order has been laid before, and approved by, each House of Parliament.

(5)   Any statutory instrument made under section 18(7) or Schedule 4, or to which subsection (2) applies, shall be subject to annulment in pursuance of a resolution of either House of Parliament.

(6)   The power of a Northern Ireland department to make—
   (a)   rules under section 2(3)(c) or 7(9)(c), or
   (b)   an order under section 7(11),

is exercisable by statutory rule for the purposes of the Statutory Rules (Northern Ireland) Order 1979.

(7)   Any rules made under section 2(3)(c) or 7(9)(c) shall be subject to negative resolution; and section 41(6) of the Interpretation Act (Northern Ireland) 1954 (meaning of 'subject to negative resolution') shall apply as if the power to make the rules were conferred by an Act of the Northern Ireland Assembly.

(8)   No order may be made by a Northern Ireland department under section 7(11) unless a draft of the order has been laid before, and approved by, the Northern Ireland Assembly.

21 Interpretation, etc

(1)   In this Act—
   'amend' includes repeal and apply (with or without modifications);
   'the appropriate Minister' means the Minister of the Crown having charge of the appropriate authorised government department (within the meaning of the Crown Proceedings Act 1947);
   'the Commission' means the European Commission of Human Rights;
   'the Convention' means the Convention for the Protection of Human Rights and Fundamental Freedoms, agreed by the Council of Europe at Rome on 4th November 1950 as it has effect for the time being in relation to the United Kingdom;
   'declaration of incompatibility' means a declaration under section 4;

'Minister of the Crown' has the same meaning as in the Ministers of the Crown
Act 1975;

'Northern Ireland Minister' includes the First Minister and the deputy First Minister
in Northern Ireland;

'primary legislation' means any—

    (a) public general Act;

    (b) local and personal Act;

    (c) private Act;

    (d) Measure of the Church Assembly;

    (e) Measure of the General Synod of the Church of England;

    (f) Order in Council—

        (i)   made in exercise of Her Majesty's Royal Prerogative;

        (ii) made under section 38(1)(a) of the Northern Ireland Constitution
Act 1973 or the corresponding provision of the Northern Ireland
Act 1998; or

        (iii) amending an Act of a kind mentioned in paragraph (a), (b) or (c);

and includes an order or other instrument made under primary legislation
(otherwise than by the National Assembly for Wales, a member of the Scottish
Executive, a Northern Ireland Minister or a Northern Ireland department)
to the extent to which it operates to bring one or more provisions of that
legislation into force or amends any primary legislation;

'the First Protocol' means the protocol to the Convention agreed at Paris on
20th March 1952;

'the Sixth Protocol' means the protocol to the Convention agreed at Strasbourg
on 28th April 1983;

'the Eleventh Protocol' means the protocol to the Convention (restructuring the
control machinery established by the Convention) agreed at Strasbourg on
11th May 1994;

'remedial order' means an order under section 10;

'subordinate legislation' means any—

    (a) Order in Council other than one—

        (i)   made in exercise of Her Majesty's Royal Prerogative;

        (ii) made under section 38(1)(a) of the Northern Ireland Constitution
Act 1973 or the corresponding provision of the Northern Ireland
Act 1998; or

        (iii) amending an Act of a kind mentioned in the definition of primary
legislation;

    (b) Act of the Scottish Parliament;

    (c) Act of the Parliament of Northern Ireland;

    (d) Measure of the Assembly established under section 1 of the Northern
Ireland Assembly Act 1973;

    (e) Act of the Northern Ireland Assembly;

    (f) order, rules, regulations, scheme, warrant, byelaw or other instrument
made under primary legislation (except to the extent to which it operates
to bring one or more provisions of that legislation into force or amends
any primary legislation);

    (g) order, rules, regulations, scheme, warrant, byelaw or other instrument made under legislation mentioned in paragraph (b), (c), (d) or (e) or made under an Order in Council applying only to Northern Ireland;

(h) order, rules, regulations, scheme, warrant, byelaw or other instrument made by a member of the Scottish Executive, a Northern Ireland Minister or a Northern Ireland department in exercise of prerogative or other executive functions of Her Majesty which are exercisable by such a person on behalf of Her Majesty;

'transferred matters' has the same meaning as in the Northern Ireland Act 1998; and

'tribunal' means any tribunal in which legal proceedings may be brought.

(2) The references in paragraphs (b) and (c) of section 2(1) to Articles are to Articles of the Convention as they had effect immediately before the coming into force of the Eleventh Protocol.

(3) The reference in paragraph (d) of section 2(1) to Article 46 includes a reference to Articles 32 and 54 of the Convention as they had effect immediately before the coming into force of the Eleventh Protocol.

(4) The references in section 2(1) to a report or decision of the Commission or a decision of the Committee of Ministers include references to a report or decision made as provided by paragraphs 3, 4 and 6 of Article 5 of the Eleventh Protocol (transitional provisions).

(5) Any liability under the Army Act 1955, the Air Force Act 1955 or the Naval Discipline Act 1957 to suffer death for an offence is replaced by a liability to imprisonment for life or any less punishment authorised by those Acts; and those Acts shall accordingly have effect with the necessary modifications.

22 Short title, commencement, application and extent

(1) This Act may be cited as the Human Rights Act 1998.

(2) Sections 18, 20 and 21(5) and this section come into force on the passing of this Act.

(3) The other provisions of this Act come into force on such day as the Secretary of State may by order appoint; and different days may be appointed for different purposes.

(4) Paragraph (b) of subsection (1) of section 7 applies to proceedings brought by or at the instigation of a public authority whenever the act in question took place; but otherwise that subsection does not apply to an act taking place before the coming into force of that section.

(5) This Act binds the Crown.

(6) This Act extends to Northern Ireland.

(7) Section 21(5), so far as it relates to any provision contained in the Army Act 1955, the Air Force Act 1955 or the Naval Discipline Act 1957, extends to any place to which that provision extends.

SCHEDULE 1
THE ARTICLES

Section 1(3)

Part 1   The Convention

Rights and Freedoms

Article 2   Right to life

1   Everyone's right to life shall be protected by law. No one shall be deprived of his life intentionally save in the execution of a sentence of a court following his conviction of a crime for which this penalty is provided by law.

2   Deprivation of life shall not be regarded as inflicted in contravention of this Article when it results from the use of force which is no more than absolutely necessary:
   (a) in defence of any person from unlawful violence;
   (b) in order to effect a lawful arrest or to prevent the escape of a person lawfully detained;
   (c) in action lawfully taken for the purpose of quelling a riot or insurrection.

Article 3   Prohibition of torture

No one shall be subjected to torture or to inhuman or degrading treatment or punishment.

Article 4   Prohibition of slavery and forced labour

1   No one shall be held in slavery or servitude.

2   No one shall be required to perform forced or compulsory labour.

3   For the purpose of this Article the term 'forced or compulsory labour' shall not include:
   (a) any work required to be done in the ordinary course of detention imposed according to the provisions of Article 5 of this Convention or during conditional release from such detention;
   (b) any service of a military character or, in case of conscientious objectors in countries where they are recognised, service exacted instead of compulsory military service;
   (c) any service exacted in case of an emergency or calamity threatening the life or well-being of the community;
   (d) any work or service which forms part of normal civic obligations.

Article 5   Right to liberty and security

1   Everyone has the right to liberty and security of person. No one shall be deprived

of his liberty save in the following cases and in accordance with a procedure prescribed by law:

(a) the lawful detention of a person after conviction by a competent court;

(b) the lawful arrest or detention of a person for non-compliance with the lawful order of a court or in order to secure the fulfilment of any obligation prescribed by law;

(c) the lawful arrest or detention of a person effected for the purpose of bringing him before the competent legal authority on reasonable suspicion of having committed an offence or when it is reasonably considered necessary to prevent his committing an offence or fleeing after having done so;

(d) the detention of a minor by lawful order for the purpose of educational supervision or his lawful detention for the purpose of bringing him before the competent legal authority;

(e) the lawful detention of persons for the prevention of the spreading of infectious diseases, of persons of unsound mind, alcoholics or drug addicts or vagrants;

(f) the lawful arrest or detention of a person to prevent his effecting an unauthorised entry into the country or of a person against whom action is being taken with a view to deportation or extradition.

2   Everyone who is arrested shall be informed promptly, in a language which he understands, of the reasons for his arrest and of any charge against him.

3   Everyone arrested or detained in accordance with the provisions of paragraph 1(c) of this Article shall be brought promptly before a judge or other officer authorised by law to exercise judicial power and shall be entitled to trial within a reasonable time or to release pending trial. Release may be conditioned by guarantees to appear for trial.

4   Everyone who is deprived of his liberty by arrest or detention shall be entitled to take proceedings by which the lawfulness of his detention shall be decided speedily by a court and his release ordered if the detention is not lawful.

5   Everyone who has been the victim of arrest or detention in contravention of the provisions of this Article shall have an enforceable right to compensation.

Article 6   Right to a fair trial

1   In the determination of his civil rights and obligations or of any criminal charge against him, everyone is entitled to a fair and public hearing within a reasonable time by an independent and impartial tribunal established by law. Judgment shall be pronounced publicly but the press and public may be excluded from all or part of the trial in the interest of morals, public order or national security in a democratic society, where the interests of juveniles or the protection of the private life of the parties so require, or to the extent strictly necessary in the opinion of the court in special circumstances where publicity would prejudice the interests of justice.

2   Everyone charged with a criminal offence shall be presumed innocent until proved guilty according to law.

3   Everyone charged with a criminal offence has the following minimum rights:

(a) to be informed promptly, in a language which he understands and in detail, of the nature and cause of the accusation against him;

(b) to have adequate time and facilities for the preparation of his defence;

(c) to defend himself in person or through legal assistance of his own choosing or, if he has not sufficient means to pay for legal assistance, to be given it free when the interests of justice so require;

(d) to examine or have examined witnesses against him and to obtain the attendance and examination of witnesses on his behalf under the same conditions as witnesses against him;

(e) to have the free assistance of an interpreter if he cannot understand or speak the language used in court.

Article 7   No punishment without law

1   No one shall be held guilty of any criminal offence on account of any act or omission which did not constitute a criminal offence under national or international law at the time when it was committed. Nor shall a heavier penalty be imposed than the one that was applicable at the time the criminal offence was committed.

2   This Article shall not prejudice the trial and punishment of any person for any act or omission which, at the time when it was committed, was criminal according to the general principles of law recognised by civilised nations.

Article 8   Right to respect for private and family life

1   Everyone has the right to respect for his private and family life, his home and his correspondence.

2   There shall be no interference by a public authority with the exercise of this right except such as is in accordance with the law and is necessary in a democratic society in the interests of national security, public safety or the economic well-being of the country, for the prevention of disorder or crime, for the protection of health or morals, or for the protection of the rights and freedoms of others.

Article 9   Freedom of thought, conscience and religion

1   Everyone has the right to freedom of thought, conscience and religion; this right includes freedom to change his religion or belief and freedom, either alone or in community with others and in public or private, to manifest his religion or belief, in worship, teaching, practice and observance.

2   Freedom to manifest one's religion or beliefs shall be subject only to such limitations as are prescribed by law and are necessary in a democratic society in the interests of public safety, for the protection of public order, health or morals, or for the protection of the rights and freedoms of others.

Article 10   Freedom of expression

1   Everyone has the right to freedom of expression. This right shall include freedom to hold opinions and to receive and impart information and ideas without interference by public authority and regardless of frontiers. This Article shall not

prevent States from requiring the licensing of broadcasting, television or cinema enterprises.

2   The exercise of these freedoms, since it carries with it duties and responsibilities, may be subject to such formalities, conditions, restrictions or penalties as are prescribed by law and are necessary in a democratic society, in the interests of national security, territorial integrity or public safety, for the prevention of disorder or crime, for the protection of health or morals, for the protection of the reputation or rights of others, for preventing the disclosure of information received in confidence, or for maintaining the authority and impartiality of the judiciary.

Article 11   Freedom of assembly and association

1   Everyone has the right to freedom of peaceful assembly and to freedom of association with others, including the right to form and to join trade unions for the protection of his interests.

2   No restrictions shall be placed on the exercise of these rights other than such as are prescribed by law and are necessary in a democratic society in the interests of national security or public safety, for the prevention of disorder or crime, for the protection of health or morals or for the protection of the rights and freedoms of others. This Article shall not prevent the imposition of lawful restrictions on the exercise of these rights by members of the armed forces, of the police or of the administration of the State.

Article 12   Right to marry

Men and women of marriageable age have the right to marry and to found a family, according to the national laws governing the exercise of this right.

Article 14   Prohibition of discrimination

The enjoyment of the rights and freedoms set forth in this Convention shall be secured without discrimination on any ground such as sex, race, colour, language, religion, political or other opinion, national or social origin, association with a national minority, property, birth or other status.

Article 16   Restrictions on political activity of aliens

Nothing in Articles 10, 11 and 14 shall be regarded as preventing the High Contracting Parties from imposing restrictions on the political activity of aliens.

Article 17   Prohibition of abuse of rights

Nothing in this Convention may be interpreted as implying for any State, group or person any right to engage in any activity or perform any act aimed at the destruction of any of the rights and freedoms set forth herein or at their limitation to a greater extent than is provided for in the Convention.

Article 18   Limitation on use of restrictions on rights

The restrictions permitted under this Convention to the said rights and freedoms shall not be applied for any purpose other than those for which they have been prescribed.

Part II   The First Protocol

Article 1   Protection of property

Every natural or legal person is entitled to the peaceful enjoyment of his possessions. No one shall be deprived of his possessions except in the public interest and subject to the conditions provided for by law and by the general principles of international law.

The preceding provisions shall not, however, in any way impair the right of a State to enforce such laws as it deems necessary to control the use of property in accordance with the general interest or to secure the payment of taxes or other contributions or penalties.

Article 2   Right to education

No person shall be denied the right to education. In the exercise of any functions which it assumes in relation to education and to teaching, the State shall respect the right of parents to ensure such education and teaching in conformity with their own religious and philosophical convictions.

Article 3   Right to free elections

The High Contracting Parties undertake to hold free elections at reasonable intervals by secret ballot, under conditions which will ensure the free expression of the opinion of the people in the choice of the legislature.

Part III   The Sixth Protocol

Article 1   Abolition of the death penalty

The death penalty shall be abolished. No one shall be condemned to such penalty or executed.

Article 2   Death penalty in time of war

A State may make provision in its law for the death penalty in respect of acts committed in time of war or of imminent threat of war; such penalty shall be applied only in the instances laid down in the law and in accordance with its provisions. The State shall communicate to the Secretary General of the Council of Europe the relevant provisions of that law.

SCHEDULE 2
REMEDIAL ORDERS

Section 10

Orders

1   (1)   A remedial order may—
- (a) contain such incidental, supplemental, consequential or transitional provision as the person making it considers appropriate;
- (b) be made so as to have effect from a date earlier than that on which it is made;
- (c) make provision for the delegation of specific functions;
- (d) make different provision for different cases.

(2)   The power conferred by sub-paragraph (1)(a) includes—
- (a) power to amend primary legislation (including primary legislation other than that which contains the incompatible provision); and
- (b) power to amend or revoke subordinate legislation (including subordinate legislation other than that which contains the incompatible provision).

(3)   A remedial order may be made so as to have the same extent as the legislation which it affects.

(4)   No person is to be guilty of an offence solely as a result of the retrospective effect of a remedial order.

Procedure

2   No remedial order may be made unless—
- (a) a draft of the order has been approved by a resolution of each House of Parliament made after the end of the period of 60 days beginning with the day on which the draft was laid; or
- (b) it is declared in the order that it appears to the person making it that, because of the urgency of the matter, it is necessary to make the order without a draft being so approved.

Orders laid in draft

3   (1)   No draft may be laid under paragraph 2(a) unless—
- (a) the person proposing to make the order has laid before Parliament a document which contains a draft of the proposed order and the required information; and
- (b) the period of 60 days, beginning with the day on which the document required by this sub-paragraph was laid, has ended.

(2)   If representations have been made during that period, the draft laid under paragraph 2(a) must be accompanied by a statement containing—
- (a) a summary of the representations; and
- (b) if, as a result of the representations, the proposed order has been changed, details of the changes.

Urgent cases

4   (1)   If a remedial order ('the original order') is made without being approved in draft, the person making it must lay it before Parliament, accompanied by the required information, after it is made.

(2)   If representations have been made during the period of 60 days beginning with the day on which the original order was made, the person making it must (after the end of that period) lay before Parliament a statement containing—
   (a)   a summary of the representations; and
   (b)   if, as a result of the representations, he considers it appropriate to make changes to the original order, details of the changes.

(3)   If sub-paragraph (2)(b) applies, the person making the statement must—
   (a)   make a further remedial order replacing the original order; and
   (b)   lay the replacement order before Parliament.

(4)   If, at the end of the period of 120 days beginning with the day on which the original order was made, a resolution has not been passed by each House approving the original or replacement order, the order ceases to have effect (but without that affecting anything previously done under either order or the power to make a fresh remedial order).

Definitions

5   In this Schedule—
   'representations' means representations about a remedial order (or proposed remedial order) made to the person making (or proposing to make) it and includes any relevant Parliamentary report or resolution; and
   'required information' means—
   (a)   an explanation of the incompatibility which the order (or proposed order) seeks to remove, including particulars of the relevant declaration, finding or order; and
   (b)   a statement of the reasons for proceeding under section 10 and for making an order in those terms.

Calculating periods

6   In calculating any period for the purposes of this Schedule, no account is to be taken of any time during which—
   (a)   Parliament is dissolved or prorogued; or
   (b)   both Houses are adjourned for more than four days.

SCHEDULE 3
DEROGATION AND RESERVATION

Sections 14 and 15

Part I   Derogation

The 1988 notification

The United Kingdom Permanent Representative to the Council of Europe presents his compliments to the Secretary General of the Council, and has the honour to convey the following information in order to ensure compliance with the obligations of Her Majesty's Government in the United Kingdom under Article 15(3) of the Convention for the Protection of Human Rights and Fundamental Freedoms signed at Rome on 4 November 1950.

There have been in the United Kingdom in recent years campaigns of organised terrorism connected with the affairs of Northern Ireland which have manifested themselves in activities which have included repeated murder, attempted murder, maiming, intimidation and violent civil disturbance and in bombing and fire raising which have resulted in death, injury and widespread destruction of property. As a result, a public emergency within the meaning of Article 15(1) of the Convention exists in the United Kingdom.

The Government found it necessary in 1974 to introduce and since then, in cases concerning persons reasonably suspected of involvement in terrorism connected with the affairs of Northern Ireland, or of certain offences under the legislation, who have been detained for 48 hours, to exercise powers enabling further detention without charge, for periods of up to five days, on the authority of the Secretary of State. These powers are at present to be found in Section 12 of the Prevention of Terrorism (Temporary Provisions) Act 1984, Article 9 of the Prevention of Terrorism (Supplemental Temporary Provisions) Order 1984 and Article 10 of the Prevention of Terrorism (Supplemental Temporary Provisions) (Northern Ireland) Order 1984.

Section 12 of the Prevention of Terrorism (Temporary Provisions) Act 1984 provides for a person whom a constable has arrested on reasonable grounds of suspecting him to be guilty of an offence under Section 1, 9 or 10 of the Act, or to be or to have been involved in terrorism connected with the affairs of Northern Ireland, to be detained in right of the arrest for up to 48 hours and thereafter, where the Secretary of State extends the detention period, for up to a further five days. Section 12 substantially re-enacted Section 12 of the Prevention of Terrorism (Temporary Provisions) Act 1976 which, in turn, substantially re-enacted Section 7 of the Prevention of Terrorism (Temporary Provisions) Act 1974.

Article 10 of the Prevention of Terrorism (Supplemental Temporary Provisions) (Northern Ireland) Order 1984 (SI 1984/417) and Article 9 of the Prevention of Terrorism (Supplemental Temporary Provisions) Order 1984 (SI 1984/418) were both made under Sections 13 and 14 of and Schedule 3 to the 1984 Act and substantially re-enacted powers of detention in Orders made under the 1974 and 1976 Acts. A person who is being examined under Article 4 of either Order on his arrival in, or on seeking to leave, Northern Ireland or Great Britain for the purpose of determining whether he is or has been involved in terrorism connected with the affairs of Northern Ireland, or whether there are grounds for suspecting that he has committed an offence under Section 9 of the 1984 Act, may be detained under Article 9 or 10, as appropriate, pending the conclusion of his examination. The period of this examination may exceed 12 hours if an examining officer has reasonable grounds for suspecting him to be or to have been involved in acts of terrorism connected with the affairs of Northern Ireland.

Where such a person is detained under the said Article 9 or 10 he may be detained for up to 48 hours on the authority of an examining officer and thereafter, where the Secretary of State extends the detention period, for up to a further five days.

In its judgment of 29 November 1988 in the Case of *Brogan and Others*, the European Court of Human Rights held that there had been a violation of Article 5(3) in respect of each of the applicants, all of whom had been detained under Section 12 of the 1984 Act. The Court held that even the shortest of the four periods of detention concerned, namely four days and six hours, fell outside the constraints as to time permitted by the first part of Article 5(3). In addition, the Court held that there had been a violation of Article 5(5) in the case of each applicant.

Following this judgment, the Secretary of State for the Home Department informed Parliament on 6 December 1988 that, against the background of the terrorist campaign, and the over-riding need to bring terrorists to justice, the Government did not believe that the maximum period of detention should be reduced. He informed Parliament that the Government were examining the matter with a view to responding to the judgment. On 22 December 1988, the Secretary of State further informed Parliament that it remained the Government's wish, if it could be achieved, to find a judicial process under which extended detention might be reviewed and where appropriate authorised by a judge or other judicial officer. But a further period of reflection and consultation was necessary before the Government could bring forward a firm and final view.

Since the judgment of 29 November 1988 as well as previously, the Government have found it necessary to continue to exercise, in relation to terrorism connected with the affairs of Northern Ireland, the powers described above enabling further detention without charge for periods of up to 5 days, on the authority of the Secretary of State, to the extent strictly required by the exigencies of the situation to enable necessary enquiries and investigations properly to be completed in order to decide whether criminal proceedings should be instituted. To the extent that the exercise of these powers may be inconsistent with the obligations imposed by the Convention the Government has availed itself of the right of derogation conferred by Article 15(1) of the Convention and will continue to do so until further notice.

Dated 23 December 1988.

The 1989 notification

The United Kingdom Permanent Representative to the Council of Europe presents his compliments to the Secretary General of the Council, and has the honour to convey the following information.

In his communication to the Secretary General of 23 December 1988, reference was made to the introduction and exercise of certain powers under section 12 of the Prevention of Terrorism (Temporary Provisions) Act 1984, Article 9 of the Prevention of Terrorism (Supplemental Temporary Provisions) Order 1984 and Article 10 of the Prevention of Terrorism (Supplemental Temporary Provisions) (Northern Ireland) Order 1984.

These provisions have been replaced by section 14 of and paragraph 6 of Schedule 5 to the Prevention of Terrorism (Temporary Provisions) Act 1989, which make comparable provision. They came into force on 22 March 1989. A copy of these provisions is enclosed.

The United Kingdom Permanent Representative avails himself of this opportunity to renew to the Secretary General the assurance of his highest consideration.

23 March 1989.

Part II   Reservation

At the time of signing the present (First) Protocol, I declare that, in view of certain provisions of the Education Acts in the United Kingdom, the principle affirmed in the second sentence of Article 2 is accepted by the United Kingdom only so far as it is compatible with the provision of efficient instruction and training, and the avoidance of unreasonable public expenditure.

Dated 20 March 1952. Made by the United Kingdom Permanent Representative to the Council of Europe.

SCHEDULE 4
JUDICIAL PENSIONS

Section 18(6)

Duty to make orders about pensions

1   (1)   The appropriate Minister must by order make provision with respect to pensions payable to or in respect of any holder of a judicial office who serves as an ECHR judge.

(2)   A pensions order must include such provision as the Minister making it considers is necessary to secure that—
  (a)   an ECHR judge who was, immediately before his appointment as an ECHR judge, a member of a judicial pension scheme is entitled to remain as a member of that scheme;

(b)   the terms on which he remains a member of the scheme are those which would have been applicable had he not been appointed as an ECHR judge; and

(c)   entitlement to benefits payable in accordance with the scheme continues to be determined as if, while serving as an ECHR judge, his salary was that which would (but for section 18(4)) have been payable to him in respect of his continuing service as the holder of his judicial office.

Contributions

2   A pensions order may, in particular, make provision—

(a)   for any contributions which are payable by a person who remains a member of a scheme as a result of the order, and which would otherwise be payable by deduction from his salary, to be made otherwise than by deduction from his salary as an ECHR judge; and

(b)   for such contributions to be collected in such manner as may be determined by the administrators of the scheme.

Amendments of other enactments

3   A pensions order may amend any provision of, or made under, a pensions Act in such manner and to such extent as the Minister making the order considers necessary or expedient to ensure the proper administration of any scheme to which it relates.

Definitions

4   In this Schedule—

'appropriate Minister' means—

(a)   in relation to any judicial office whose jurisdiction is exercisable exclusively in relation to Scotland, the Secretary of State; and

(b)   otherwise, the Lord Chancellor;

'ECHR judge' means the holder of a judicial office who is serving as a judge of the Court;

'judicial pension scheme' means a scheme established by and in accordance with a pensions Act;

'pensions Act' means—

(a)   the County Courts Act (Northern Ireland) 1959;

(b)   the Sheriffs' Pensions (Scotland) Act 1961;

(c)   the Judicial Pensions Act 1981; or

(d)   the Judicial Pensions and Retirement Act 1993; and

'pensions order' means an order made under paragraph 1.

Appendix 2

European Convention for the Protection of Human Rights and Fundamental Freedoms (as amended by Protocol No 11)

Rome, 4.XI.1950

The text of the Convention had been amended according to the provisions of Protocol No 3 (ETS No 45), which entered into force on 21 September 1970, of Protocol No 5 (ETS No 55), which entered into force on 20 December 1971 and of Protocol No 8 (ETS No 118), which entered into force on 1 January 1990, and comprised also the text of Protocol No 2 (ETS No 44) which, in accordance with Article 5, paragraph 3 thereof, had been an integral part of the Convention since its entry into force on 21 September 1970. All provisions which had been amended or added by these Protocols are replaced by Protocol No 11 (ETS No 155), as from the date of its entry into force on 1 November 1998. As from that date, Protocol No 9 (ETS No 140), which entered into force on 1 October 1994, is repealed and Protocol No 10 (ETS No 146) has lost its purpose.

The governments signatory hereto, being members of the Council of Europe,

Considering the Universal Declaration of Human Rights proclaimed by the General Assembly of the United Nations on 10th December 1948;

Considering that this Declaration aims at securing the universal and effective recognition and observance of the Rights therein declared;

Considering that the aim of the Council of Europe is the achievement of greater unity between its members and that one of the methods by which that aim is to be pursued is the maintenance and further realisation of human rights and fundamental freedoms;

Reaffirming their profound belief in those fundamental freedoms which are the foundation of justice and peace in the world and are best maintained on the one hand by an effective political democracy and on the other by a common understanding and observance of the human rights upon which they depend;

Being resolved, as the governments of European countries which are like-minded and have a common heritage of political traditions, ideals, freedom and the rule of law, to take the first steps for the collective enforcement of certain of the rights stated in the Universal Declaration,

Have agreed as follows:

Article 1 – Obligation to respect human rights[1]

The High Contracting Parties shall secure to everyone within their jurisdiction the rights and freedoms defined in Section I of this Convention.

Section I – Rights and freedoms[1]

Article 2 – Right to life[1]

1. Everyone's right to life shall be protected by law. No one shall be deprived of his life intentionally save in the execution of a sentence of a court following his conviction of a crime for which this penalty is provided by law.

2. Deprivation of life shall not be regarded as inflicted in contravention of this article when it results from the use of force which is no more than absolutely necessary:

   a. in defence of any person from unlawful violence;

   b. in order to effect a lawful arrest or to prevent the escape of a person lawfully detained;

   c. in action lawfully taken for the purpose of quelling a riot or insurrection.

Article 3 – Prohibition of torture[1]

No one shall be subjected to torture or to inhuman or degrading treatment or punishment.

Article 4 – Prohibition of slavery and forced labour[1]

1. No one shall be held in slavery or servitude.

2. No one shall be required to perform forced or compulsory labour.

3. For the purpose of this article the term "forced or compulsory labour" shall not include:

   a. any work required to be done in the ordinary course of detention imposed according to the provisions of Article 5 of this Convention or during conditional release from such detention;

   b. any service of a military character or, in case of conscientious objectors in countries where they are recognised, service exacted instead of compulsory military service;

   c. any service exacted in case of an emergency or calamity threatening the life or well-being of the community;

   d. any work or service which forms part of normal civic obligations.

Article 5 – Right to liberty and security[1]

1. Everyone has the right to liberty and security of person. No one shall be deprived of his liberty save in the following cases and in accordance with a procedure prescribed by law:

   a. the lawful detention of a person after conviction by a competent court;

   b. the lawful arrest or detention of a person for non-compliance with the lawful order of a court or in order to secure the fulfilment of any obligation prescribed by law;

   c. the lawful arrest or detention of a person effected for the purpose of bringing him before the competent legal authority on reasonable suspicion of having committed an offence or when it is reasonably considered necessary to prevent his committing an offence or fleeing after having done so;

   d. the detention of a minor by lawful order for the purpose of educational supervision or his lawful detention for the purpose of bringing him before the competent legal authority;

   e. the lawful detention of persons for the prevention of the spreading of infectious diseases, of persons of unsound mind, alcoholics or drug addicts or vagrants;

   f. the lawful arrest or detention of a person to prevent his effecting an unauthorised entry into the country or of a person against whom action is being taken with a view to deportation or extradition.

2. Everyone who is arrested shall be informed promptly, in a language which he understands, of the reasons for his arrest and of any charge against him.

3. Everyone arrested or detained in accordance with the provisions of paragraph 1.c of this article shall be brought promptly before a judge or other officer authorised by law to exercise judicial power and shall be entitled to trial within a reasonable time or to release pending trial. Release may be conditioned by guarantees to appear for trial.

4. Everyone who is deprived of his liberty by arrest or detention shall be entitled to take proceedings by which the lawfulness of his detention shall be decided speedily by a court and his release ordered if the detention is not lawful.

5. Everyone who has been the victim of arrest or detention in contravention of the provisions of this article shall have an enforceable right to compensation.

Article 6 – Right to a fair trial[1]

1. In the determination of his civil rights and obligations or of any criminal charge against him, everyone is entitled to a fair and public hearing within a reasonable time by an independent and impartial tribunal established by law. Judgment shall be pronounced publicly but the press and public may be excluded from all or part of the trial in the interests of morals, public order or national security in a democratic society, where the interests of juveniles or the protection of the private life of the parties so require, or to the extent strictly necessary in the opinion of the court in special circumstances where publicity would prejudice the interests of justice.

for the Protection of Human Rights and Fundamental Freedoms

2. Everyone charged with a criminal offence shall be presumed innocent until proved guilty according to law.

3. Everyone charged with a criminal offence has the following minimum rights:

   a. to be informed promptly, in a language which he understands and in detail, of the nature and cause of the accusation against him;

   b. to have adequate time and facilities for the preparation of his defence;

   c. to defend himself in person or through legal assistance of his own choosing or, if he has not sufficient means to pay for legal assistance, to be given it free when the interests of justice so require;

   d. to examine or have examined witnesses against him and to obtain the attendance and examination of witnesses on his behalf under the same conditions as witnesses against him;

   e. to have the free assistance of an interpreter if he cannot understand or speak the language used in court.

Article 7 – No punishment without law[1]

1. No one shall be held guilty of any criminal offence on account of any act or omission which did not constitute a criminal offence under national or international law at the time when it was committed. Nor shall a heavier penalty be imposed than the one that was applicable at the time the criminal offence was committed.

2. This article shall not prejudice the trial and punishment of any person for any act or omission which, at the time when it was committed, was criminal according to the general principles of law recognised by civilised nations.

Article 8 – Right to respect for private and family life[1]

1. Everyone has the right to respect for his private and family life, his home and his correspondence.

2. There shall be no interference by a public authority with the exercise of this right except such as is in accordance with the law and is necessary in a democratic society in the interests of national security, public safety or the economic well-being of the country, for the prevention of disorder or crime, for the protection of health or morals, or for the protection of the rights and freedoms of others.

Article 9 – Freedom of thought, conscience and religion[1]

1. Everyone has the right to freedom of thought, conscience and religion; this right includes freedom to change his religion or belief and freedom, either alone or in community with others and in public or private, to manifest his religion or belief, in worship, teaching, practice and observance.

2. Freedom to manifest one's religion or beliefs shall be subject only to such limitations as are prescribed by law and are necessary in a democratic society in the interests of public safety, for the protection of public order, health or morals, or for the protection of the rights and freedoms of others.

Article 10 – Freedom of expression[1]

1. Everyone has the right to freedom of expression. This right shall include freedom to hold opinions and to receive and impart information and ideas without interference by public authority and regardless of frontiers. This article shall not prevent States from requiring the licensing of broadcasting, television or cinema enterprises.

2. The exercise of these freedoms, since it carries with it duties and responsibilities, may be subject to such formalities, conditions, restrictions or penalties as are prescribed by law and are necessary in a democratic society, in the interests of national security, territorial integrity or public safety, for the prevention of disorder or crime, for the protection of health or morals, for the protection of the reputation or rights of others, for preventing the disclosure of information received in confidence, or for maintaining the authority and impartiality of the judiciary.

Article 11 – Freedom of assembly and association[1]

1. Everyone has the right to freedom of peaceful assembly and to freedom of association with others, including the right to form and to join trade unions for the protection of his interests.

2. No restrictions shall be placed on the exercise of these rights other than such as are prescribed by law and are necessary in a democratic society in the interests of national security or public safety, for the prevention of disorder or crime, for the protection of health or morals or for the protection of the rights and freedoms of others. This article shall not prevent the imposition of lawful restrictions on the exercise of these rights by members of the armed forces, of the police or of the administration of the State.

Article 12 – Right to marry[1]

Men and women of marriageable age have the right to marry and to found a family, according to the national laws governing the exercise of this right.

Article 13 – Right to an effective remedy[1]

Everyone whose rights and freedoms as set forth in this Convention are violated shall have an effective remedy before a national authority notwithstanding that the violation has been committed by persons acting in an official capacity.

Article 14 – Prohibition of discrimination[1]

The enjoyment of the rights and freedoms set forth in this Convention shall be secured without discrimination on any ground such as sex, race, colour, language, religion, political or other opinion, national or social origin, association with a national minority, property, birth or other status.

Article 15 – Derogation in time of emergency[1]

1. In time of war or other public emergency threatening the life of the nation any

High Contracting Party may take measures derogating from its obligations under this Convention to the extent strictly required by the exigencies of the situation, provided that such measures are not inconsistent with its other obligations under international law.

2. No derogation from Article 2, except in respect of deaths resulting from lawful acts of war, or from Articles 3, 4 (paragraph 1) and 7 shall be made under this provision.

3. Any High Contracting Party availing itself of this right of derogation shall keep the Secretary General of the Council of Europe fully informed of the measures which it has taken and the reasons therefor. It shall also inform the Secretary General of the Council of Europe when such measures have ceased to operate and the provisions of the Convention are again being fully executed.

Article 16 – Restrictions on political activity of aliens[1]

Nothing in Articles 10, 11 and 14 shall be regarded as preventing the High Contracting Parties from imposing restrictions on the political activity of aliens.

Article 17 – Prohibition of abuse of rights[1]

Nothing in this Convention may be interpreted as implying for any State, group or person any right to engage in any activity or perform any act aimed at the destruction of any of the rights and freedoms set forth herein or at their limitation to a greater extent than is provided for in the Convention.

Article 18 – Limitation on use of restrictions on rights[1]

The restrictions permitted under this Convention to the said rights and freedoms shall not be applied for any purpose other than those for which they have been prescribed.

Section II – European Court of Human Rights[2]

Article 19 – Establishment of the Court

To ensure the observance of the engagements undertaken by the High Contracting Parties in the Convention and the Protocols thereto, there shall be set up a European Court of Human Rights, hereinafter referred to as "the Court". It shall function on a permanent basis.

Article 20 – Number of judges

The Court shall consist of a number of judges equal to that of the High Contracting Parties.

Article 21 – Criteria for office

1. The judges shall be of high moral character and must either possess the

qualifications required for appointment to high judicial office or be jurisconsults of recognised competence.

2. The judges shall sit on the Court in their individual capacity.

3. During their term of office the judges shall not engage in any activity which is incompatible with their independence, impartiality or with the demands of a full-time office; all questions arising from the application of this paragraph shall be decided by the Court.

Article 22 – Election of judges

1. The judges shall be elected by the Parliamentary Assembly with respect to each High Contracting Party by a majority of votes cast from a list of three candidates nominated by the High Contracting Party.

2. The same procedure shall be followed to complete the Court in the event of the accession of new High Contracting Parties and in filling casual vacancies.

Article 23 – Terms of office

1. The judges shall be elected for a period of six years. They may be re-elected. However, the terms of office of one-half of the judges elected at the first election shall expire at the end of three years.

2. The judges whose terms of office are to expire at the end of the initial period of three years shall be chosen by lot by the Secretary General of the Council of Europe immediately after their election.

3. In order to ensure that, as far as possible, the terms of office of one-half of the judges are renewed every three years, the Parliamentary Assembly may decide, before proceeding to any subsequent election, that the term or terms of office of one or more judges to be elected shall be for a period other than six years but not more than nine and not less than three years.

4. In cases where more than one term of office is involved and where the Parliamentary Assembly applies the preceding paragraph, the allocation of the terms of office shall be effected by a drawing of lots by the Secretary General of the Council of Europe immediately after the election.

5. A judge elected to replace a judge whose term of office has not expired shall hold office for the remainder of his predecessor's term.

6. The terms of office of judges shall expire when they reach the age of 70.

7. The judges shall hold office until replaced. They shall, however, continue to deal with such cases as they already have under consideration.

Article 24 – Dismissal

No judge may be dismissed from his office unless the other judges decide by a majority of two-thirds that he has ceased to fulfil the required conditions.

Article 25 – Registry and legal secretaries

The Court shall have a registry, the functions and organisation of which shall be laid down in the rules of the Court. The Court shall be assisted by legal secretaries.

Article 26 – Plenary Court

The plenary Court shall:

a. elect its President and one or two Vice-Presidents for a period of three years; they may be re-elected;

b. set up Chambers, constituted for a fixed period of time;

c. elect the Presidents of the Chambers of the Court; they may be re-elected;

d. adopt the rules of the Court, and

e. elect the Registrar and one or more Deputy Registrars.

Article 27 – Committees, Chambers and Grand Chamber

1. To consider cases brought before it, the Court shall sit in committees of three judges, in Chambers of seven judges and in a Grand Chamber of seventeen judges. The Court's Chambers shall set up committees for a fixed period of time.

2. There shall sit as an *ex officio* member of the Chamber and the Grand Chamber the judge elected in respect of the State Party concerned or, if there is none or if he is unable to sit, a person of its choice who shall sit in the capacity of judge.

3. The Grand Chamber shall also include the President of the Court, the Vice-Presidents, the Presidents of the Chambers and other judges chosen in accordance with the rules of the Court. When a case is referred to the Grand Chamber under Article 43, no judge from the Chamber which rendered the judgment shall sit in the Grand Chamber, with the exception of the President of the Chamber and the judge who sat in respect of the State Party concerned.

Article 28 – Declarations of inadmissibility by committees

A committee may, by a unanimous vote, declare inadmissible or strike out of its list of cases an application submitted under Article 34 where such a decision can be taken without further examination. The decision shall be final.

Article 29 – Decisions by Chambers on admissibility and merits

1. If no decision is taken under Article 28, a Chamber shall decide on the admissibility and merits of individual applications submitted under Article 34.

2. A Chamber shall decide on the admissibility and merits of inter-State applications submitted under Article 33.

3. The decision on admissibility shall be taken separately unless the Court, in exceptional cases, decides otherwise.

Article 30 – Relinquishment of jurisdiction to the Grand Chamber

Where a case pending before a Chamber raises a serious question affecting the interpretation of the Convention or the protocols thereto, or where the resolution of a question before the Chamber might have a result inconsistent with a judgment previously delivered by the Court, the Chamber may, at any time before it has rendered its judgment, relinquish jurisdiction in favour of the Grand Chamber, unless one of the parties to the case objects.

Article 31 – Powers of the Grand Chamber

The Grand Chamber shall:

a. determine applications submitted either under Article 33 or Article 34 when a Chamber has relinquished jurisdiction under Article 30 or when the case has been referred to it under Article 43; and

b. consider requests for advisory opinions submitted under Article 47.

Article 32 – Jurisdiction of the Court

1. The jurisdiction of the Court shall extend to all matters concerning the interpretation and application of the Convention and the protocols thereto which are referred to it as provided in Articles 33, 34 and 47.

2. In the event of dispute as to whether the Court has jurisdiction, the Court shall decide.

Article 33 – Inter-State cases

Any High Contracting Party may refer to the Court any alleged breach of the provisions of the Convention and the protocols thereto by another High Contracting Party.

Article 34 – Individual applications

The Court may receive applications from any person, non-governmental organisation or group of individuals claiming to be the victim of a violation by one of the High Contracting Parties of the rights set forth in the Convention or the protocols thereto. The High Contracting Parties undertake not to hinder in any way the effective exercise of this right.

Article 35 – Admissibility criteria

1. The Court may only deal with the matter after all domestic remedies have been exhausted, according to the generally recognised rules of international law, and within a period of six months from the date on which the final decision was taken.

2. The Court shall not deal with any application submitted under Article 34 that:

    a. is anonymous; or

    b. is substantially the same as a matter that has already been examined by the Court or has already been submitted to another procedure of international investigation or settlement and contains no relevant new information.

3. The Court shall declare inadmissible any individual application submitted under Article 34 which it considers incompatible with the provisions of the Convention

or the protocols thereto, manifestly ill-founded, or an abuse of the right of application.

4. The Court shall reject any application which it considers inadmissible under this Article. It may do so at any stage of the proceedings.

Article 36 – Third party intervention

1. In all cases before a Chamber or the Grand Chamber, a High Contracting Party one of whose nationals is an applicant shall have the right to submit written comments and to take part in hearings.

2. The President of the Court may, in the interest of the proper administration of justice, invite any High Contracting Party which is not a party to the proceedings or any person concerned who is not the applicant to submit written comments or take part in hearings.

Article 37 – Striking out applications

1. The Court may at any stage of the proceedings decide to strike an application out of its list of cases where the circumstances lead to the conclusion that:
   a. the applicant does not intend to pursue his application; or
   b. the matter has been resolved; or
   c. for any other reason established by the Court, it is no longer justified to continue the examination of the application.

   However, the Court shall continue the examination of the application if respect for human rights as defined in the Convention and the protocols thereto so requires.

2. The Court may decide to restore an application to its list of cases if it considers that the circumstances justify such a course.

Article 38 – Examination of the case and friendly settlement proceedings

1. If the Court declares the application admissible, it shall:
   a. pursue the examination of the case, together with the representatives of the parties, and if need be, undertake an investigation, for the effective conduct of which the States concerned shall furnish all necessary facilities;
   b. place itself at the disposal of the parties concerned with a view to securing a friendly settlement of the matter on the basis of respect for human rights as defined in the Convention and the protocols thereto.

2. Proceedings conducted under paragraph 1.b shall be confidential.

Article 39 – Finding of a friendly settlement

If a friendly settlement is effected, the Court shall strike the case out of its list by means of a decision which shall be confined to a brief statement of the facts and of the solution reached.

Article 40 – Public hearings and access to documents

1. Hearings shall be in public unless the Court in exceptional circumstances decides otherwise.

2. Documents deposited with the Registrar shall be accessible to the public unless the President of the Court decides otherwise.

Article 41 – Just satisfaction

If the Court finds that there has been a violation of the Convention or the protocols thereto, and if the internal law of the High Contracting Party concerned allows only partial reparation to be made, the Court shall, if necessary, afford just satisfaction to the injured party.

Article 42 – Judgments of Chambers

Judgments of Chambers shall become final in accordance with the provisions of Article 44, paragraph 2.

Article 43 – Referral to the Grand Chamber

1. Within a period of three months from the date of the judgment of the Chamber, any party to the case may, in exceptional cases, request that the case be referred to the Grand Chamber.

2. A panel of five judges of the Grand Chamber shall accept the request if the case raises a serious question affecting the interpretation or application of the Convention or the protocols thereto, or a serious issue of general importance.

3. If the panel accepts the request, the Grand Chamber shall decide the case by means of a judgment.

Article 44 – Final judgments

1. The judgment of the Grand Chamber shall be final.

2. The judgment of a Chamber shall become final:

   a. when the parties declare that they will not request that the case be referred to the Grand Chamber; or

   b. three months after the date of the judgment, if reference of the case to the Grand Chamber has not been requested; or

   c. when the panel of the Grand Chamber rejects the request to refer under Article 43.

3. The final judgment shall be published.

Article 45 – Reasons for judgments and decisions

1. Reasons shall be given for judgments as well as for decisions declaring applications admissible or inadmissible.

2. If a judgment does not represent, in whole or in part, the unanimous opinion of the judges, any judge shall be entitled to deliver a separate opinion.

Article 46 – Binding force and execution of judgments

1. The High Contracting Parties undertake to abide by the final judgment of the Court in any case to which they are parties.

2. The final judgment of the Court shall be transmitted to the Committee of Ministers, which shall supervise its execution.

Article 47 – Advisory opinions

1. The Court may, at the request of the Committee of Ministers, give advisory opinions on legal questions concerning the interpretation of the Convention and the protocols thereto.

2. Such opinions shall not deal with any question relating to the content or scope of the rights or freedoms defined in Section I of the Convention and the protocols thereto, or with any other question which the Court or the Committee of Ministers might have to consider in consequence of any such proceedings as could be instituted in accordance with the Convention.

3. Decisions of the Committee of Ministers to request an advisory opinion of the Court shall require a majority vote of the representatives entitled to sit on the Committee.

Article 48 – Advisory jurisdiction of the Court

The Court shall decide whether a request for an advisory opinion submitted by the Committee of Ministers is within its competence as defined in Article 47.

Article 49 – Reasons for advisory opinions

1. Reasons shall be given for advisory opinions of the Court.

2. If the advisory opinion does not represent, in whole or in part, the unanimous opinion of the judges, any judge shall be entitled to deliver a separate opinion.

3. Advisory opinions of the Court shall be communicated to the Committee of Ministers.

Article 50 – Expenditure on the Court

The expenditure on the Court shall be borne by the Council of Europe.

Article 51 – Privileges and immunities of judges

The judges shall be entitled, during the exercise of their functions, to the privileges and immunities provided for in Article 40 of the Statute of the Council of Europe and in the agreements made thereunder.

Section III – Miscellaneous provisions[1, 3]

Article 52 – Inquiries by the Secretary General[1]

On receipt of a request from the Secretary General of the Council of Europe any High Contracting Party shall furnish an explanation of the manner in which its internal law ensures the effective implementation of any of the provisions of the Convention.

Article 53 – Safeguard for existing human rights[1]

Nothing in this Convention shall be construed as limiting or derogating from any of the human rights and fundamental freedoms which may be ensured under the laws of any High Contracting Party or under any other agreement to which it is a Party.

Article 54 – Powers of the Committee of Ministers[1]

Nothing in this Convention shall prejudice the powers conferred on the Committee of Ministers by the Statute of the Council of Europe.

Article 55 – Exclusion of other means of dispute settlement[1]

The High Contracting Parties agree that, except by special agreement, they will not avail themselves of treaties, conventions or declarations in force between them for the purpose of submitting, by way of petition, a dispute arising out of the interpretation or application of this Convention to a means of settlement other than those provided for in this Convention.

Article 56 – Territorial application [1]

1.[4] Any State may at the time of its ratification or at any time thereafter declare by notification addressed to the Secretary General of the Council of Europe that the present Convention shall, subject to paragraph 4 of this Article, extend to all or any of the territories for whose international relations it is responsible.

2. The Convention shall extend to the territory or territories named in the notification as from the thirtieth day after the receipt of this notification by the Secretary General of the Council of Europe.

3. The provisions of this Convention shall be applied in such territories with due regard, however, to local requirements.

4.[4] Any State which has made a declaration in accordance with paragraph 1 of this article may at any time thereafter declare on behalf of one or more of the territories to which the declaration relates that it accepts the competence of the Court to receive applications from individuals, non-governmental organisations or groups of individuals as provided by Article 34 of the Convention.

Article 57 – Reservations[1]

1. Any State may, when signing this Convention or when depositing its instrument of ratification, make a reservation in respect of any particular provision of the Convention to the extent that any law then in force in its territory is not in conformity with the provision. Reservations of a general character shall not be permitted under this article.

2. Any reservation made under this article shall contain a brief statement of the law concerned.

Article 58 – Denunciation [1]

1. A High Contracting Party may denounce the present Convention only after the expiry of five years from the date on which it became a party to it and after six months' notice contained in a notification addressed to the Secretary General of the Council of Europe, who shall inform the other High Contracting Parties.

2. Such a denunciation shall not have the effect of releasing the High Contracting Party concerned from its obligations under this Convention in respect of any act which, being capable of constituting a violation of such obligations, may have been performed by it before the date at which the denunciation became effective.

3. Any High Contracting Party which shall cease to be a member of the Council of Europe shall cease to be a Party to this Convention under the same conditions.

4.[4] The Convention may be denounced in accordance with the provisions of the preceding paragraphs in respect of any territory to which it has been declared to extend under the terms of Article 56.

Article 59 – Signature and ratification[1]

1. This Convention shall be open to the signature of the members of the Council of Europe. It shall be ratified. Ratifications shall be deposited with the Secretary General of the Council of Europe.

2. The present Convention shall come into force after the deposit of ten instruments of ratification.

3. As regards any signatory ratifying subsequently, the Convention shall come into force at the date of the deposit of its instrument of ratification.

4. The Secretary General of the Council of Europe shall notify all the members of the Council of Europe of the entry into force of the Convention, the names of the High Contracting Parties who have ratified it, and the deposit of all instruments of ratification which may be effected subsequently. Done at Rome this 4th day of November 1950, in English and French, both texts being equally authentic, in a single copy which shall remain deposited in the archives of the Council of Europe. The Secretary General shall transmit certified copies to each of the signatories.

1.   Heading added according to the provisions of Protocol No 11 (ETS No 155).
2.   New Section II according to the provisions of Protocol No 11 (ETS No 155).
3.   The articles of this Section are renumbered according to the provisions of Protocol No 11 (ETS No 155).
4.   Text amended according to the provisions of Protocol No 11 (ETS No 155).

Index

Index

Index

Index